Fulfil Your Ministry

CONTENTS

I
INTRODUCTION

This book contains 22 articles, written in the magazines *Clarion, Shield & Sword, Lux Mundi,* and *In Holy Array.*

Most of the articles were written at the time I gave my lectures at the Theological College of the Canadian Reformed Churches, during the years 1984-1990, and several lectures form also the contents of this book. In chapter IV my inaugural speech is published and in chapter V my farewell speech.

In some cases something is omitted, while in other cases something is added, because the contents had to be updated.

At the end of the book a separate *Bibliography* for each chapter is inserted.

Leaving for the Netherlands, I look back with gratefulness to my Canadian years and I hope that this book may be profitable for God's people, especially in this country.

The title of the book is derived from Paul's second letter to Timothy, ch. 4:5. For *ministry* the word *"diakonia"*, service, is used there. So it is an admonition, not only for the ministers of the Church, but for all who have to fulfil their service before God, as office-bearers, but also as members of the Church. This service has to be fulfilled, that means: it must be done completely, in its magnitude, without any hesitation or interruption. Actually this is the final word which Paul has to say to his successors in God's service. It is a timely word, also with respect to our own ministry today, in God's service!

II
"... HE DESIRES A NOBLE TASK" (1 Timothy 3:1)

PROFILE OF A PASTOR

Gifts of Christ

Among the offices which function in the Church of Jesus Christ, the office of the minister of God's Word takes an important place. It is an excellent start of the *Form for the ordination (or installation) of ministers of the Word* when first of all the congregation is referred to Christ Himself. I quote, "the exalted Christ gathers His church through His Word and Spirit, and in His grace uses the ministry of man." Right from the beginning the office in the Church is placed in clear daylight. Christ did not *need* office-bearers as if He would be dependent on men. But in His grace He *gave* them to His Church. Hence the reference to Eph. 4:11,12, "And His gifts were that some should be apostles, some prophets, some evangelists, some pastors and teachers, to equip the saints for the work of ministry, for building up the body of Christ." It is Christ Himself who gave these gifts. First He humbled Himself, but after that He is exalted into the highest majesty. So we may say that the office-bearers are donations of victory, given by the highest Office-bearer Himself.

It is very important that this text from the letter to the Ephesians is placed in front. In the first place it is to be maintained that it is the exalted Christ Himself who gives these office-bearers to the Church. He who is only stressing that the offices rise from the congregation, is incorrect in this one-sidedness. At least it has to be added to this that the office-bearers are given by Christ Himself. Moreover, this text answers the question whether or not the present office-bearers might be placed on the same line with the apostles, as far as their origin and calling are concerned. Then one made the contrast: the apostles were appointed by God Himself, but ministers of the Church are chosen and appointed by men. It is true indeed, "they are not to be charged with an image of their task which is loaded in too sacred a way, set up in analogy to that of Paul" (Trimp, 1988: 39). But the apostle Paul places indeed "pastors and teachers" (mentioned as one group by the one article in Greek) on the same line with "apostles" and "prophets." That does not mean that thereby all the differences are wiped out. But it is remarkable that about both groups we read that they are gifts of victory from Christ. I agree with S. Greijdanus, "Dealing here with the congregation he is using the word *gifts* in order to show that these offices and office-bearers are a gift of His goodness for the congregation. (. . .) Now he is going to mention some offices, and he is going to set forth the variety of the gifts. He does not want to give a complete enumeration. Then he could have mentioned many more persons and gifts. (. . .) He only gives some examples" (Greijdanus, 1925: 89). So generally speaking we may say that the office-bearers in the Church are gifts of Christ, but it is explicitly said about the ministers of the Word. These matters are important in connection with the question how the congregation has to consider the pastor. The LORD did not need him. That keeps the office-bearers humble and restrains them from over-estimation. At the same time the congregation must be restrained from glorifying man and mistaken adoration. On the other hand, the Church is also restrained from under-estimation of the office. One cannot dispose of an office-bearer as if he was a 'quantité négligeable.' Hence at the end of the first part of the Form the congregation is admonished, "Obey your leaders and submit to them; for they are keeping watch over your souls, as men who will have to give account" (Heb. 13:17). The Church would have been spared many troubles, if the ministers would have been more faithful in their office. But also: if the congregation would have prayed more for the ministers instead of talking about them!

To minister and to proclaim

When first the idea is emphasized that the office-bearers, including the pastors and teachers, are gifts of the exalted Christ, the Form refers to Christ as the Chief Shepherd, who unceasingly cares for the flock and who appoints shepherds to take heed of the flock in His Name. With respect to this, 1 Pet. 5:4 is quoted. The shepherds are to take care of the sheep of Christ. I think it is nice that the new Dutch Form also points to some texts of the Old Testament with respect to this, namely Jer. 3:14 and 23:4. Also Ezek. 34 could have been quoted and I miss that in the Form.

In the old Form it is said: "The pasture with which His sheep are fed is nothing else but the proclamation of the divine Word, accompanied with the offering of prayer and the administration of the holy sacraments." To that is added then in the old Form, "The same Word of God is also the staff with which the flock is guided and governed." The new Form does not give an explicit explanation of the words "pasture" and "staff," but says indeed that the shepherds are to take care of the sheep of Christ "by means of the proclamation of the Word, by the administration of the sacraments, and by prayers and pastoral supervision. In this way the flock is tended and led in the right paths."

In my opinion this new formulation is an improvement, especially because here is given up that the Word of God is the "pasture" as well as the "staff." It is important that the care of the sheep is primarily connected with the proclamation of God's Word, especially over against all kinds of modern conceptions of "counseling." In these conceptions the office-bearer is sometimes thrown over in favour of the psychiatrist, while on the other hand the whole matter of counseling is overdone over against the preaching of God's Word.

It is the proclamation of God's Word through which the congregation is fed and led in the right path in the first place.

The Form continues, "In the early Christian Church this task was fulfilled by the apostles." When the 'twelve' (apostles) delegate a part of their task to the 'seven,' they say in Acts 6:4 to the congregation, "But we will devote ourselves to prayer and to the ministry of the Word." The apostles devoted themselves to the public prayers and to the 'deaconry' of the Word. It appears from Acts 6 that the early Church was not a free charismatic communion without ecclesiastical offices. From the very beginning the apostles took the lead. They devoted themselves to prayer. They proclaimed the Word of God, and under their guidance the 'seven' were appointed. In Acts 11:30 we read that there were also elders in the Church of Jerusalem. The apostles appointed elders in every Church under the guidance of the Holy Spirit, the Form says. "According to 1 Timothy 5:17 (the edition of 1984 says wrongly 1 Tim. 3:17) there were elders who ruled the congregation. Some of them were also called to labour in preaching and teaching. The latter are now called ministers of the Word." Be aware of this formulation. "There is not said, the latter *are* the ministers of the Word. But it is formulated more carefully and in a somewhat detached way: the latter are *now called* ministers of the Word" (Hendriks, 1981:6).

Then two literal quotations follow of two portions of the Scripture which deal with the proclamation and preaching of God's Word.

In the first place 2 Cor. 5:18-20, where Paul presents himself as the ambassador

9

of Christ, who has received from God the ministry of reconciliation, and who is now beseeching on behalf of Christ, be reconciled to God. Also in this case one said, that was a specific apostolic task, and it won't go to call the ministers of God's Word ambassadors, as if they should have received, like Paul, the ministry of reconciliation. But the Form says indeed, "They have received the ministry of reconciliation, of which Paul speaks." For how can men preach unless they are sent? So, unless they are ambassadors? The apostles have trusted to the congregations the apostolic word in a written way, and also orally. "That apostolic word asks for ministry and therefore for ministers of the Word. New revelations will not fall to the share of these ministers. But the given and entrusted word is there to be passed on to the congregation" (Trimp, 1988: 39).

It is, therefore, completely understandable that the Form mentions as the first task of the ministers of the Word that they must declare the whole counsel of God to His congregation. In connection with this, the other portion of the Scripture is quoted, namely, 2 Tim. 4:1 and 2, "I charge you in the presence of God and of Christ Jesus who is to judge the living and the dead, and by His appearing and His kingdom: preach the Word, be urgent in season and out of season, convince, rebuke and exhort, be unfailing in patience and in teaching." While the preaching and proclamation of God's Word belonged to the task of the apostle Paul himself, it is remarkable that Timothy receives exactly the same assignment. It is even a very penetrating exhortation, which comes with serious oaths. It is an established fact that the preaching of God's Word has to go on continuously, even if it will not suit the hearers.

For 'preaching' Paul uses a characteristic word that actually means 'to give the message as a herald.' The word deals with the exclamation of an event, so it is a *proclamation*. It is the dramatic call of the herald and it also brings about what is proclaimed. The herald announced in former days the arrival of the king. When he appeared, people knew that the king was coming and that the feast started. Actually the herald was in his appearance the first point of the feast program. So we may say, the preaching as proclamation brings about what the people are waiting for. By means of this proclamation the kingdom of God is coming. In this way Timothy and in him also the succeeding preachers of God's Word have to take care that they are *present*, and that the proclamation of the king is given indeed, welcome or not.

To bring the message as a herald is translated differently in the New Testament. Usually the translation is: *to preach*, but often the word is also translated by: *to proclaim*. Sometimes other words are used, for instance in 1 Cor. 2:4 the translation of the proclamation or the preaching is simply: the *message*.

The proclamation is in the first place the announcement of the *grace* of the great King. But when the coming of the great King is announced, it can also contain an element of *judgment*. His coming can be to advantage, but also to disadvantage. In this way it is said of Noah, for instance, that he was a preacher of justice. But emphasis is put in the New Testament on the proclamation of God's salvation. In this way the herald stands antithetically over against the Stoic philosopher who, in Greece, was also a herald. This hearld marched through the country with staff and knapsack and appeared as a preacher on the street. He showed himself moved by the wickedness of the people. But he was of the opinion that in each and every man a divine germ was hidden, which had to be developed. He is the example of the humanistic missionary who stimulates the good things in man. But the herald of the Scripture is different, as far as his *motive* for preaching is concerned, but also as far as the *contents* of his preaching is concerned. He brings the message to the people because God has sent him and because Jesus Christ wants to bring about His dominion. As far as the contents of his preaching is concerned, he does not proclaim new morals or a new law, but conversion to forgiveness of sins and the coming of God's kingdom. He does not preach the way of deification of man, but the fact of salvation of God's Son becoming flesh, and the way to become a new man in His image. He does not try to bring to life a divine germ, but he is preaching the new life of Christ's resurrection.

The New Testament is full of this herald with his message of the great King. More than 60 times the words which are connected with this are used in the gospels, the Acts of the apostles, the Letters, and the Revelation to John.

Beside this word the Scripture uses another word, which means literally *to evangelize* and which is used even twice as often in the New Testament. The word means: to bring the good tidings, glad tidings. It is more than only to speak. It is a proclamation with authority and with power. Songs and miracles accompany this proclamation. This message of good tidings has effect. Where this message is brought, there is gladness. It brings salvation, it is also the way to salvation, it brings about regeneration. It is not a mere word of man, but God's eternal, living Word. I give some examples. In Romans 10 first the word is used that is connected with the herald. We read in verse 14, "But how are men to hear without a preacher?" Literally it says, "How are men to hear without someone who brings the message as a herald?" And verse 15 continues then, "And how can men bring the message as a herald unless they are sent?" But then follows in the same verse a quotation from Isaiah 52:7, "How beautiful are the feet of those who preach good news." I quote now the whole verse of Isaiah: "How beautiful upon the mountains are the feet of him who brings good tidings, who publishes peace, who brings good tidings of good, who publishes salvation, who says to Zion, 'Your God reigns.' "

In the Greek translation of the Old Testament the word *to evangelize* is used twice: to bring good tidings. The situation in the time of Isaiah is that the prophet expects a great victory of the LORD, namely His ascension to the throne. His dominion as a King, the beginning of a new era. With respect to this the messenger of joy is very important. This man goes on ahead to the people that come back from Babylon to Jerusalem. Many people are waiting on mount Zion and expect the crowd of those who return. There one sees the messenger, the man who brings good tidings. He proclaims, "Peace, salvation, the LORD became King." The LORD Himself comes back to Jerusalem. The messenger proclaims that and at the same time the new era begins. He does not announce that it will happen once and that God's dominion is coming. No, he proclaims God's victory and with that this victory is reality. Salvation appears simultaneously with the proclaimed Word.

The Word is not mere wind and sound, but a power with effect. Those who are standing on the wall of the city hear that word, they pass it on with joy, it sounds through the city, the messengers carry it through the country, "The LORD is King." This idea of the proclamation of the gospel is also worked out and applied in the *Form for the ordination (or installation) of missionaries*. In that Form we are taught about the office of those ministers of the Word who are set apart for the preaching of the gospel to those who are outside. One of the texts which are quoted is John 10:16, where it says that the Good shepherd calls His sheep not only from Israel but also from all the nations and leads them to His fold. Also Acts 13:2 is quoted, from which text is concluded, "From the time of the apostles, the Holy Spirit has commanded the Church to set men apart for the work to which He has called them." Rightly we are pointed in this Form to Eph. 2:12 and 13 about those who were far off. But why not elaborate on the nature of preaching to those who were not God's people? That could have been done in connection with Rom. 9:24-26 and 1 Pet. 2:10 where Hos. 1:10 and

2:23 are quoted.

It is also important that in this Form reference is made to 2 Cor. 5:19 and 20, "God was in Christ reconciling the world to Himself." Then the Form continues, "He has entrusted the ministry of reconciliation to men whom He made ambassadors of Christ. Therefore the missionary shall beseech men in the Name of Christ, *be reconciled to God.*"

Completely in accordance to the data from the Holy Scripture the Reformed confessions speak about the first task of the ministers of God's Word. So we read in the Belgic Confession, art. 30, "There should be ministers or pastors to preach the Word of God. . . ." Lord's Day 31 of the Heidelberg Catechism gives the answer to the question (83), "What are the keys of the kingdom of heaven?": "The preaching of the holy gospel. . . ." So that is actually the main point of the keys of the kingdom and therefore it comes first. I quote also the Canons of Dort, ch. I, par. 3, "So that men may be brought to faith, God mercifully sends heralds of His most joyful message to whom He will and when He wills."

I like to mention also some other confessions of Reformed origin. In the *Larger Catechism* which belongs to the *Westminster Standards* it is asked in question 35, "How is the covenant of grace administered under the New Testament?" The answer is: "Under the New Testament, when Christ the substance was exhibited, the same covenant of grace was, and still is to be, administered in the preaching of the Word (. . .) in which grace and salvation are held forth in more fulness, evidence, and efficacy to all nations." In the *Westminster Confession of Faith* is spoken about "spiritual efficacy" and to "all nations" is added, "both Jews and Gentiles."

In ch. 18 of the *Second Helvetic Confession* is spoken in an extensive way about the ministers of the church, their institution and duties. This confession mentions first the Greek word for ministers (huperetas) "that means *rowers,* who have their eyes fixed on the coxswain, and so men who do not live for themselves or according to their own will, but for others — namely, their masters, upon whose command they altogether depend." Later on, this confession says, "The duties of ministers are various; yet for the most part they are restricted to two, in which all the rest are comprehended: to the teaching of the Gospel in Christ, and to the proper administration of the sacraments." Especially that first duty of the ministers is worked out: "For it is the duty of the ministers to gather together an assembly for worship in which to expound God's Word and to apply the whole doctrine to the care and use of the Church, so that what is taught may benefit the hearers and edify the faithful. It falls to ministers, I say, to teach the ignorant, and to exhort; and to urge the idlers and lingerers to make progress in the way of the Lord. Moreover, they are to comfort and to strengthen the faint-hearted, and to arm them against the manifold temptations of Satan; to rebuke offenders; to recall the erring into the way; to raise the fallen; to convince the gain-sayers to drive the wolf away from the sheepfold of the Lord; to rebuke wickedness and wicked men wisely and severely; not to wink at nor to pass over great wickedness." After that something is said about the second duty of the ministers, namely to administer the sacraments, and also something about to catechize the unlearned, to visit the sick and those afflicted with various temptations. Already earlier in the chapter is spoken about the combination of proclaiming the Word of God and administering the sacraments. Therefore reference is made to Eph. 3:3 and 9. I quote, "The apostle adds that ministers of the Church are administrators and stewards of the mysteries of God. Now in many passages, especially in Eph., ch. 3, Paul called the mysteries of God the Gospel of Christ. And the sacraments of Christ are also called mysteries by the ancient writers. Therefore for this purpose are the ministers of the Church called — namely, to preach the Gospel to the faithful, and to administer the sacraments."

It is remarkable that in more than one confession and also in the forms the administration of the sacraments is immediately mentioned as the task of the ministers of the Church, after first is mentioned their task to proclaim the Word of God.

Two things are important. In the first place, with respect to the preaching of God's Word no separation is made between the unique office of the apostles on the one hand and the permanent office of the pastors and teachers on the other hand. In the second place, time and again emphasis is put on the preaching, the proclamation, and not on the preacher, the minister. That has consequences to two sides. To the side of the pastor and teacher himself: he may never place himself on the foreground or presume on his knowledge and talents. But also to the side of the congregation. The hearers of this very joyful message have to accept the preaching as the Word of God, not as the word of man. No wonder that especially two texts are quoted in the part of the Form in which the congregation is addressed: 1 Thess. 2:13 and Heb. 13:17. Then is said, "Take heed to receive the Word of God, which you shall hear from him, and accept his words, spoken according to the Holy Scriptures, not as the word of man *but as what it really is, the Word of God."*

In one breath follows then, "Obey your leaders and submit to them; for they are keeping watch over your souls, as men who will have to give account. . . ."

Sacraments and prayers

We touched already on the administration of the sacraments, which is immediately connected in the Form with the proclamation of God's Word. "Second, he is called to administer the sacraments, because Christ has joined this administration to the preaching of the gospel."

In the text of the Form Matt. 28:19 and 1 Cor. 11:24 are quoted, in which texts the institution of baptism and the Lord's Supper are mentioned. The Form for the ordination of missionaries elaborates a little bit on the administration of the sacraments, not only about Matt. 28:19, but also about 1 Cor. 10 and 11, about the Lord's Supper.

The connection between the service of the Word and the service of the sacraments has to make the Church careful in giving a mandate to others than the ministers for administrating the sacraments. We also have to bear in mind that the Church Order says in art. 56, "The sacraments shall be administered . . . by a minister of the Word. . . ."

Then follows in the Form the service of *prayers.* "Third, it is his duty as pastor and teacher of the congregation to call upon the name of the Lord in public worship." With respect to this are mentioned four different public prayers according to 1 Tim. 2:1 and 2:

"a. Supplications: requests concerning specific needs;

b. Prayers: requests regarding needs that are always present;

c. Intercessions: the believers are always received by God, the heavenly King, in audience, in order that they may submit a petition in the interest of others; and

d. Thanksgiving: the expression of one's gratitude for blessings received.

This has to be done 'for all men,' and not only for our fellow Christians" (Van Rongen, 1984: 13).

Especially are mentioned in this text "for kings and all who are in high positions." For they bear great responsibility, not only for public order, but also for the "protection of the Church and its ministry," just as we confess in art. 36 of the Belgic Confession. That is also the purpose of this public intercession: "that we may lead a quiet and peaceable life, godly and respectful in every way." But in order to be a good interpreter of the congregation, the minister has to know exactly the needs of God's congregation. How can he interpret this need before God, when he is not well posted in the subject? But he must also know the need of the world, what is going on in the world, in the whole development of the nation, which powers are rising against God and which conspiracies are set up against God's holy Word.

From the side of the congregation it is also very important that the brothers and sisters are able to pray together with the minister, that they do not simply undergo the prayers, but that they know themselves completely involved in all the public petitions.

To tend and to feed

We discussed already the image of the shepherd with respect to the preaching of God's Word. The pastoral work of the minister of God's Word is expressed in the first place by leading God's sheep in the green pastures of God's Word. But that collective part of the motive of the shepherd does not exclude the individual care for the flock. Hence the Form deals not only with the duty of the minister "*in public*," but also "*from house to house*." With respect to this is pointed to the farewell of the apostle Paul on the sand of Miletus. There the apostle reminds the elders of Ephesus how he did not shrink from declaring to them anything that was profitable, and teaching them in public and from house to house (Acts 20:20).

Also in the houses the sheep must be fed and tended. In the description of the fourth task of the ministers is therefore to be read that it is their duty, "with the elders as stewards of the house of God, to see to it that in the congregation all things are done in peace and good order. Together they shall supervise the doctrine and life of the membership and tend the flock of God, not as domineering over those in their charge but being examples to the flock." That reminds us of the first letter of the apostle Peter when he admonishes the pastors to tend the flock "not by constraint but willingly, not for shameful gain but eagerly." At the end of this passage of the Form also verse 4 of that chapter 1 Pet. 5 is added, "When the Chief Shepherd is manifested they as faithful servants will obtain the unfading crown of glory."

The idea of *to feed* or *to tend* is an important datum of the Scripture with respect of the office of the shepherd. We meet it already in the Old Testament. When we think about the shepherd, we have in mind the image of a quiet and peaceful existence and we replace ourselves in our thoughts to a rural picture of the shepherd who is tending the flock and who has little more to do than to keep an eye on the flock. Yet the image of the Bible is quite different from such a rural picture. In the Bible the shepherd is rather the heroic figure. We meet him as a nomad who marched with his family through barren regions in order to discover somewhere any pasture for the flock. He lived in a tent, made from goat's hair. I remind you of the description of Jacob, given by himself to his uncle Laban: "These twenty years I have been with you; your ewes and your she-goats have not miscarried, and I have not eaten the rams of your flocks. That which was torn by wild beasts I did not bring to you; I bore the loss of it myself; of my hand you required it, whether stolen by day or stolen by night. Thus I was, by day the heat consumed me, and the cold by night, and my sleep fled from my eyes" (Gen. 31:38-40). All kinds of things could happen to the flock. Some sheep were torn up, other sheep strayed off and perished. In the one case theft was committed, but it happened also that the flock was struck by lightning. The latter disaster took for instance place in the case of Job, "the fire of God fell from heaven and burned up the sheep and the servants, and consumed them" (Job 1:16). In order to protect the sheep the shepherd bore rod and staff, which served for defense and sometimes for the attack against rapacious gangs and ferocious animals. Hence a sling was not a superfluous attribute in the hand of the shepherd. It served for bringing back a sheep that strayed away from the flock. It is well-known that in 1947 a shepherd boy used the sling and that the stone hit a bottle in a cave. That was the beginning of the "Dead-Sea Scrolls." The stone missed its proper goal, but the result was an enormous discovery.

Many times the motive of the shepherd is used in Scripture. It is important with respect to this what the prophet Ezekiel is writing, especially in chapter 34. The prophet receives the mandate to prophesy against the shepherds who have been feeding themselves. "Should not shepherds feed the sheep? You eat the fat, you clothe yourselves with the wool, you slaughter the fatlings, but you do not feed the sheep. The weak you have not strengthened, the sick you have not healed, the crippled you have not bound up, the strayed you have not brought back, the lost you have not sought, and with force and harshness you have ruled them. So they were scattered, because there was no shepherd; and they became food for all the wild beasts. My sheep were scattered, they wandered over all the mountains and on every high hill, My sheep were scattered over all the face of the earth, with none to search or seek for them" (vs. 3-6).

"Behold, I am against the shepherds," is said in the follow-up of this chapter. The LORD will set up over the sheep one shepherd, His servant David (vs. 23). The false shepherds will be punished, and there will come a true shepherd who will execute his office in the right way. So this chapter is also full of Messianic prophecy. It is also called the 'magna charta' about the care of the shepherds who are God's office-bearers. (Magna charta is actually the name of the letter of liberty, given in 1215 to the British people). It appears that Ezekiel 34 functions as the background of many texts in the New Testament which deal with the pastoral work. In Hebrews the word *bākār* is used in Ezekiel 34, which can have the meaning of 'to take care of', 'to look after', 'to feel sorry for.' In the Greek translation of the Old Testament the word is translated by *episkeptomai*, from which the English word *bishop* is derived. But this word has not the meaning of a ruler, a commander, but rather of someone who takes care of another one and who is moved by his situation.

In this way it is used in Luke 1:68 in the song of praise of Zechariah, "Blessed be the Lord God of Israel, for He has *visited* and redeemed His people." When later on in this gospel according to Luke the entry of Christ into Jerusalem is mentioned, this word comes back in the address to the city, ". . . the days shall come upon you, when your enemies will cast up a bank about you and surround you, and hem you in on every side, and dash you to the ground, you and your children within you, and they will not leave one stone upon another in you; because you did not know the time of your *visitation*" (19:43.44). That was the time that God looked after His people.

Usually the word *episkopos* (which is used many times in the New Testament) will be translated by *overseer*. But bear in mind that the meaning is rather: '*to take care of*', or '*to look after*'. An excellent combination of the idea of the shepherd and the care for the flock is delivered in 1 Pet. 2:25, "For you were straying like sheep, but have now returned to the Shepherd and Guardian of your souls." Here it could also be translated: "to Him who tends you and who takes care of you."

It is said in the first place of Christ that He is the Good Shepherd. I remind you of John 10. But in the same gospel Christ also says to the apostle Peter, "Feed my lambs," "Tend my sheep," and "Feed my sheep" (21:15-17). It means that the apostle Peter (and in him also the other apostles) have to take care for the flock. But this care is not limited to the apostles. The apostle Paul uses on the sand of Miletus the same word to the elders of the church of Ephesus, "Take heed to yourselves and to all the flock, in which the Holy Spirit has made you guardians, to feed the church of the Lord which He obtained with His own blood" (Acts 20:28). This task of to take care for the flock is not only said of the apostles, but is also for the ministers of God's Word and for the whole consistory. It is the task of the care for the flock. The well and woe of the flock has to touch their heart. It is not a kind of inspection or control, much less a kind of service of espionage which trace the walks of the members of the congregation in order to look if there is something wrong with them. No, it is a matter of real interest, to offer help if necessary in order to bring and to keep them on the right way, to support them in the right choice, if necessary also to warn against the dangers which they perhaps had overlooked. In Paul's farewell speech on the sand of Miletus the element of *to guard* of the shepherds is especially emphasized and worked out. They have to take heed to themselves (they have to take care that they themselves stay on the right way), and to all the flock.

Immediately the apostle adds to that the warning, "I know that after my departure fierce wolves will come in among you, not sparing the flock" (vs. 29). So there is a threat from outside through which the flock can be scattered. But there is also a threat from inside, which can also work in a destroying way: "From among your own selves will arise men speaking perverse things, to draw away the disciples after them" (vs. 30). There is not only the danger of fierce wolves from outside, but also the danger of false shepherds from inside. Especially to these two dangers the shepherds of the flock have to give attention. "Therefore be alert" is the apostolic command. The shepherd who takes heed of the flock in the right way may not sleep or slumber!

This does not mean for the sheep that they can doze off because the shepherd is on guard. Precisely the fact that the true shepherd takes care for the flock and looks after the sheep, must stimulate them to lay his admonition to heart and to be aware of the dangers. The warning of Paul to the elders of Ephesus in Acts 20 is continued by his admonition in the letter to the Ephesians to put on the whole armor of God, the spiritual armor, ". . . to keep alert with all perseverance, making supplication for all the saints" (Eph. 6:18).

To lead and to suffer

There is strong emphasis on the care of the shepherd for the flock. Is not the element of supervision involved in that?

Sure, but not in the sense of *to reign, to rule*. It is rather the element of *to lead, to go in front*. In the same verse in which the apostle Paul admonishes the consistory of Ephesus to be alert (Acts 20:31), he reminds them that for three years he himself did not cease night or day to admonish every one with tears. In that word *to admonish* is also the element of warning, especially in the sense of to bring someone back from wrong paths. The same word is used by the apostle in 1 Thess. 5:12, together with the word *to be over*: ". . . we beseech you, brethren, to respect those who *labor among you* and *are over you* in the Lord and *admonish you,* and to esteem them very highly in love because of their work." Those who are over the members of the congregation earn respect, not because of their formal authority, but because of the *work* that they do on behalf of the Lord. They are not leaders in the sense of rulers, who decide everything, so that everyone has to follow them without any further ado. No, they are the people who go in front, who show the way, who detain from wrong ways.

In this sense is also to be understood the prayer for the minister of the Word according to the Form: "Grant him wisdom and faithfulness to guide the flock in the right path and to keep them in Christian peace, that by his ministry and under his good leadership Thy Church may be preserved and increased." In this sense is also to be understood the prayer with regard to the congregation: "Grant that those entrusted to his pastoral care may acknowledge this servant as sent by Thee. Give that they may receive the instruction and admonition of Christ which this shepherd shall bring to them and that they may joyfully submit to his direction. Grant that through his ministry all may believe in Christ and thus inherit eternal life."

When a minister is leading the congregation in this way, it does not mean that he meets no hinder or troubles. Hence in the Form is also applied the text of 2 Tim. 2:3 to the minister of God's Word, "Share in suffering as a good soldier of Christ Jesus."

A pastor has to give guidance, in the sense of to lead the way, but at the same time he must also be able to *follow*. As a good soldier he has to follow his Principal, his Commander Jesus Christ. Paul had already said to his spiritual son Timothy that the fulfillment of his calling would cause suffering from the side of the world: ". . . take your share of suffering for the gospel in the power of God" (1:8). In the second chapter the apostle comes back to that. Timothy has to know that suffering is inevitable when he as a good soldier is fighting in the army of Jesus Christ. "To suffer as a good soldier" deals with the nature of the task, but also with the mentality of a soldier. Suffering can come from different sides. There are enemies who attack. That brings about suffering. Adversaries can cause suffering to God's servants.

There can be slander, also persecution and oppression. Violence and guile can also go together. Contradiction can also come from the side of enemies *in* the congregation. There can be jealousy, intrigues can be undertaken. Then God's servants have to bear in mind that they may never suffer as a wrongdoer, just as Peter writes in his first letter (1 Pet. 4:15, cf. also 3:17). He writes also, "Even if you do suffer for righteousness' sake, you will be blessed" (3:14). Then they may not have fear for the enemies, nor be troubled. Peter is writing that in general to those who are in the dispersion. It is the more in force for God's ministers who can be placed so easily in a suspicious corner. Precisely then the point is that they persevere in the struggle and that they do not give up the fight!

To expose and to rebuke

A special expression in the Form is the verb to *expose*: "He shall expose all errors and heresies as unfruitful works of darkness, and exhort the membership to walk as children of the light." These words are actually a kind of summary of what the apostle Paul wrote to the Ephesians in ch. 5:8-14. This is also in the first place an admonition to the *congregation* of Ephesus. But this does not mean that office-bearers and especially ministers of the Word are excluded. The word that is used for to *expose* means in the first place to *rebuke*. In this way it is used in the Greek translation of Lev. 19:17: ". . . you shall *reason* with your neighbor, lest you bear sin because of him." The word is used about fifteen times in the New Testament, also in the sense of to *rebuke*. So for instance in 1 Tim. 5:20, "As for those who persist in sin, rebuke them in the presence of all, so that the rest may stand in fear." In the second letter to Timothy, Paul places the word on one line with the preaching of God's Word: "Preach the word, be urgent in season and out of season, convince, rebuke, and exhort, be unfailing in patience and in teaching" (2 Tim. 4:2). It is not sufficient that the people hold aloof from the unfruitful works of darkness. No, they must be shown up. That is very clear from the passage of Eph. 5, just mentioned. The unfruitful works of darkness must be exposed. What is darkness must be exposed by the light, that is here: the light of God's Word. Hence the word comes back in verse 13: ". . . when anything is exposed by the light it becomes visible, for anything that becomes visible is light." In connection with this the apostle qoutes what was probably a Christian hymn from the early Church: "Awake, O sleeper, and arise from the dead, and Christ shall give you light" (vs. 14). The masks must be ripped off. Hypocrisy must be uncovered. The works of darkness must be exposed. That contains the element of *to rebuke* also.

These elements are missed in the *Form for the ordination (or installation) of missionaries*. I regret that this is not referred to in that Form. For if anywhere the unfruitful works of darkness have to be exposed and rebuked, it is on the mission field!

Do not serve reluctantly

There is still one special point I want to mention in connection with the service of the ministers of the Word, namely, that they do not have to serve reluctantly.

"Not reluctantly" — the apostle Paul is using this expression to the church at Corinth in the framework of his admonition to offer to the saints abundantly. "For God loves a cheerful giver" (2 Cor. 9:7).

"Not reluctantly" — that is also in force of the service of the ministers of the church. In the letter to the Hebrews the readers are admonished, "Obey your leaders and submit to them; for they are keeping watch over your souls, as men who will have to give account. Let them do this joyfully, and not sadly, for that would be of no advantage to you" (Heb. 13:17).

This text is also quoted in the Form. It is an admonition to the congregation. The members of the congregation have to obey the ministers and to submit to them. What does that mean? Is it a kind of slavish obedience, so that criticism, in whatever form, is contraband? In no way. Also the minister of God's Word is fallible and it is merciful to point out his faults to him.

But that may not be destructive but constructive criticism. The minister may not become the defenceless object of a merciless judgment of man. He himself has to know: he who judges me is God, but at the same time he has to give account of his work as an office-bearer. And especially that work as an office-bearer is important. The Form placed the admonition of the Letter to the Hebrews completely in the framework of the necessity that the congregation has to honour the minister because of his *work*.

Instead of needless criticism on his *person* the prayer must be made that he could fulfil his *task* as he ought to do. Not the person, but the office is important. If the person would be in force, the one could be praised abundantly while the other one could be despised completely. Deification of men and abuse of men are sometimes not far apart. It happened to Paul and Barnabas in Lystra. The one moment they were esteemed as gods, but the other moment the people stoned Paul and dragged him out of the city (Acts 14:11,12,19). But the people did not understand anything about the office and the message of Paul and Barnabas.

Obedience and submission in the sense of Heb. 13 are to be seen as obedience and submission to the Word of truth. On the one hand that forces the ministers to bind to nothing but the Word of God, which they may proclaim. On the other hand it compels the hearers to submit themselves completely to the Word that is preached. If the pastors understand their office in this way, and if the congregation is also living in this way, the ministers do not need to be bowed down by a heavy burden which they cannot lift up, but they can do their work with joy.

In this way we also have to understand the prayer that follows in the Form, "Grant that those entrusted to this pastoral care may acknowledge this servant as sent by Thee. Give that they may receive the instruction and admonition of Christ which this Shepherd shall bring to them and that they may joyfully submit to his direction."

18

If the congregation receives God's servant in this way, the end of the Form says according to Matt. 10:12 and 13, "the peace of God will come upon you, and you will inherit eternal life through Christ."

Conclusion

I come to a conclusion. I have four final remarks.

1. First of all: generally speaking the *Form for the ordination (or installation) of ministers of the Word*, and also the *Form for the ordination (or installation) of missionaries* (cf. p. 619-628 of the *Book of Praise*, ed. 1984) give an adequate description of the office of ministers of the Word and missionaries, and deliver a good profile of the pastor according to the Scriptures.

2. It is remarkable that — although many texts of the New testament are quoted or referred to — almost no texts of the Old Testament are mentioned in both Forms. In the new Dutch version of the Form reference is made, for instance, to Jeremiah 3:15 and Jeremiah 23:4, and I would have mentioned also the important chapter of Ezek. 34.

3. It is regrettable that in the *Form for the ordination (or installation) of the missionaries* no reference is made to Ephesians 5:8-14 in which passage also the important task of the missionaries is to be described as to expose all errors and heresies as unfruitful works of darkness."

4. Finally, the *Form for the ordination (or installation) of the missionaries* does not elaborate on the nature and character of preaching to those who were not God's people before. That could have been done in connection with Rom. 9:24-26 and 1 Pet. 2:10 in which texts Hos. 1:10 and 2:23 are quoted.

ARE ELDERS AND DEACONS OFFICE-BEARERS?

Importance

When we discuss the office of elders and deacons, we deal with a very *important topic*. Paul writes to his spiritual son, Timothy, about elders and deacons and he gives instructions which are apparently so important that they could not be *delayed*, not even for a short time. The apostle says, "I hope to come to you soon, but I am writing these instructions to you so that, if I am delayed, you may know how one ought to behave in the household of God, which is the church of the living God, the pillar and bulwark of the truth" (1 Timothy 3:14, 15). Especially by pointing to the LORD of the house, the Apostle Paul emphasizes his command.

Therefore, the topic of elders and deacons is not a *temporary* matter, and also today we have to execute the rules of the household of God's Church, faithfully and precisely, being obedient to the assignment given by the LORD Himself. "For if we want to maintain the church," Calvin once said, "we must have that regiment which the LORD has established as an inviolate regiment" (compare 1 Timothy).

Confession and Church Order

In Article 31 of our *Belgic Confession* we profess this Scriptural importance of the offices of elders and deacons in the church. "We believe that . . . elders and deacons ought to be chosen to their offices by lawful elections of the church, with prayer and in good order as stipulated by the Word of God." In accordance with this confession, the *Church Order* starts, after the introductory Article 1, in the second Article as follows: "The offices are those of the Minister of the Word, of the Elder and of the Deacon." Do we indeed profess and accept that?

Time and again we hear that these offices are not prescribed in the New Testament, and that it belongs to the freedom of every congregation, to extend or to minimize these offices. Are these offices indeed instituted? Were some of these offices only temporary, or were they all permanent? In other words are elders and deacons indeed officer-bearers, or not? Are they all at the same level or is there a kind of gradation between them? And what about women in the congregation? May they serve in a special office? We will try to answer these questions, especially in connection with contemporary publications in this respect.

Presbyters

It is a remarkable fact that the origin of the office of the elders is not mentioned in the Bible. The elders of the Church at Jerusalem suddenly appear on the scene. We read in Acts 11:29 and 30, "The disciples determined, every one according to his ability, to send relief to the brethren who lived in Judea; and they did so, sending it to the elders by the hand of Barnabas and Saul." J. van Bruggen is of the opinion that these elders are not the elders in our sense of consistory members. He says it is remarkable that their election is not mentioned by Luke. And it is also remarkable that they appear in the picture so late. His conclusion is that these elders only had a temporary task and they were the same as the "disciples" from the gospel (van Bruggen, 1984: 78ff.).

But is it so strange that their election is not mentioned? Just three chapters after this story in Acts 11 we read, "When they [Paul and Barnabas, K.D.] had appointed elders for them *in every church,* with prayer and fasting, they committed them to the Lord in whom they believed" (Acts 14:23). J. van Bruggen argues that these elders were at another level than the elders of Chapter 11. But I do not believe that. We must not conclude too much from the fact that no election is mentioned for the first elders in Chapter 11. And besides that, already before Pentecost there were hundreds and hundreds of believers. Paul writes to the Corinthians that "Christ appeared to more than five hundred brethren at one time, most of whom are still alive, though some have fallen asleep" (1 Corinthians 15:6). They were disciples, all of them. But it is quite impossible that all these disciples were involved with the relief mentioned in Acts 11. It is more reasonable that the office of the elders mentioned in Acts 11 and the office of the elders mentioned in Acts 14 are the same. And it is also very likely that there were elders in the New Testament church just as there were leaders in the synagogue. There were many house congregations, and probably elders played a role in them from the very beginning.

In any case, in the rest of the book of Acts we hear about elders time and again. They were involved in the decision of the meeting with the apostles according to Acts 15. They were present at the visit of Paul to James according to Acts 21. These elders are called by two names: presbyters and overseers.

Overseers

Is there any difference between presbyters and overseers? When we translate the Greek words literally, we get the words presbyters and bishops, or, priests and bishops. All of you know that these words have been claimed by the Roman Catholics, and also that these words do not have exactly the same meaning. But I am of the opinion that these words point to the same office-bearers. I ask you to compare, for instance, Acts

20:17 with 20:28. Paul called the elders of Ephesus, and he said to these same elders, "Take heed to yourselves and to all the flock, in which the Holy Spirit has made you overseers." Compare also the first letter of Peter, Chapter 5:1 with verse 2. Peter calls himself a fellow elder, and he exhorts the elders, "Tend the flock of God that is your charge, not by constraint but willingly." Compare also Titus 1:5 with verse 7. Paul writes to Titus, "This is why I left you in Crete, that you might amend what was defective, and appoint elders in every town as I directed you." And then, in verse 7, writing about the same office-bearers, he says, "For a bishop, as God's steward must be blameless . . . ."

Why, then, are two words used, pointing to the same persons? The name presbyter has been copied from the Jews, and usually this word was used by the Jewish Christian congregations. Also the synagogues had their "elders," their presbyters — as I mentioned already — and these presbyters made decisions in all kinds of matters, also concerning church discipline. But the name overseer is especially used by the Christian churches of Gentile origin. Probably under the influence of the Septuagint, the Greek translation of the Old Testament, where this word is used for instance in 2 Kings 11:19, 2 Chronicles 34:12, Isaiah 60:17 and Nehemiah 11:9.

We can conclude that many names are used to designate the special office-bearers of the New Testament, whom we call elders or overseers.

Disappearance

In the beginning of the apostolic church, the elders played an important role. But in the course of time, the episkopoi (also called "bishops") became increasingly dominant, and slowly but surely the elders disappeared. There were still "priests" as a general name, but they did not form a board or consistory. The bishop was the regional ruler and the other priests had to listen to and obey him. So we may say that the rank of elder sank away below that of the bishops, who ruled the church.

It took a long time before the office of elder was rediscovered: It was during the Reformation and it was especially Calvin who put the elder on the stage again. It has once been said, "Calvin checkmated the Pope of Rome with the pawn of the Reformed elder." Everywhere in the Reformed churches the elders were recognized and honoured again. Unfortunately, after the Reformation the elder disappeared again in several regions.

In September 1979, Prof. D. Deddens presented his inaugural address on the topic: *"The disappearing elder," about the omission of the office of elders in the congregational churches in Massachusetts*. This omission occurred already in the seventeenth century! How did that come about? The main reason was that especially the ministers of the church let the elders disappear. Dominocracy went hand in hand with independentism, and the result was that there was no work anymore for the Reformed elder.

Rehabilitation

It is very important to keep the elders in honour. For also today there is a danger that we underestimate the elders over against the ministers of the church. If the position of ministers were to become central, and if one would consider the elders only as the assistants of the minister, then there would be something wrong. It happened in the past, and it happens today, especially in the U.S.A., that one sees the elder as the *ruler*, but the minister as *ruler* and *counsellor*. If there are problems and difficulties, people pass by the elders and go directly to the pastor.

Maybe the old *"Form for the ordination of elders and deacons"* gave some rise to that. In that old form the government of the elders is stressed, while in the "Form for the ordination (or installation) of Ministers of God's Word" the task of the shepherd is extensively mentioned. But let us bear in mind that the elders are also pastors. Paul said to the elders of Ephesus, "Take heed to yourselves and to all the flock, in which the Holy Spirit has made you overseers, to care for the church of God which He obtained with the blood of His own Son."

I think the new forms are better. Both of them point to the important pastoral task of the elders and ministers. I remind you for instance of these two passages concerning the elders: "Together they tend the flock of God which is in their charge" (in the margin reference is made to 1 Peter 5:1-4) and also: "To do their work well as shepherds of God's flock, the overseers should train themselves in godliness. . ." (with reference to 2 Timothy 3:14-17).

So let us not underestimate the important office of the elders. Let us bear in mind what the letter to the Hebrews prescribes: "Obey your leaders and submit to them; for they are keeping watch over your souls, as men who will give account. Let them do this joyfully, and not sadly, for that would be of no advantage to you."

Deacons

More than the office of elders, the office of *deacons* is in danger today. That is not only the case in our days for we can say that none of the special offices in the church experienced so much alteration of assignment and change of duty as the office of deacons. One said, "Just as Laban dealt with Jacob's wages, so they dealt with the office of the deacon: they changed it ten times!"

Already in the second half of the second century the deformation began; deacons slowly but surely became no more than helpers, the *adjutants* of the bishop. They could not do anything without his order or permission. Besides that, one placed between the bishops and the deacons the presbyters, and this hierarchical order was maintained very strictly. Also archdeacons and subdeacons appeared, and it looked like the order in the Old Testament — the bishops being compared to the high priest, the presbyters to the priests and the deacons to the Levites. As a rule the deacons had to stand, while the higher clergy might sit.

In the Middle Ages the image is even more sombre. There is nothing left of the care of the deaconry for the poor. There is begging everywhere, and that is not discouraged by the clergy, but rather promoted. The poor complain that nobody takes care of them. Meanwhile there is great luxury and wealth in the monasteries, as well as the costly splendour and lustre of the higher clergy, especially at the papal court, attained by exploitation of the people. But from the beginning it was not so.

Therefore, the Reformers had the enormous task, of looking back to the beginning and restoring the office of deacons completely. Luther discovered from Scripture what the office of deacons actually was, but time and again he let himself be ruled by the spirit of his time. So in the Lutheran church the deacon received the function of assistant preacher. Zwingli recommended the care of the poor to the government, so he did not restore the office of deacons. But Bucer first, and after him Calvin, rediscovered the beauty of the office of deacons, and they read again the Scriptures in order to reform this office.

Diakonein

It is also our task, to read the Scriptures again in order to understand what the task of the deacon is. In the New Testament the verb *diakonein* (and also the noun *diakonos*) has a general and a special meaning. According to its proper significance, *diakonein* means "to serve at the table" (namely, for food and drink), according to Luke 17:8 and John 12:2). Hence the word is used for all "provision" (see Luke 8:3, Matthew 27:6, Mark 15:41), while the personal provision with love is stressed (see Matthew 25:42-44, Acts 2:19 and 1 Corinthians 16:15).

The *diakonos* is he who practices *diakonein*, and our Lord Jesus Christ continues to practice it as no one else. He experienced in this world the call from His Father as a service, endlessly great, immeasurably deep, totally unique in its appearance. Although He is the Son of God Himself, He did not come into this world in order to be served, but to serve. He completely breaks the idea of the old world that to serve is something less worthy. He turns around all human ideas of greatness and rank. He tells His disciples, "You know that the rulers of the Gentiles lord it over them, and their great men exercise authority over them. It shall not be so among you; but whoever would be great among you must be your servant, and whoever would be first among you must be your slave" (Matthew 20:25-28, see also Mark 10:42-45). So Jesus Christ did Himself. He did not seek a *crown*, but the *cross*.

When Jesus Christ, the great diakonos, ascended into heaven, He continued this office in the first place by His apostles. They have the task, to glorify God's Name on earth, to proclaim His great deeds. They have to serve God by serving their brethren, also with material goods. That was an enormous task! No wonder that when the number of believers increased that much, this enormous task excelled the powers of the twelve. After a short time, there were problems with the care of the poor. The apostles had received and taken charge of the money given by the people of the church. The whole task had become a large one, and the care for the poor did not function as it ought to have. We read in Acts 6 that the Hellenists murmured against the Hebrews because their widows were neglected in the daily distribution.

Widows neglected

What does that mean, that the Hellenists' widows were neglected in the daily distribution? J. van Bruggen is of the opinion that this means that those widows were neglected, not as *objects*, but as *subjects*. In other words: they were not neglected in *receiving* support, but in *giving* support (van Bruggen, 1984: 65ff.). He appeals to Acts 9, where we read that Dorcas was also one of the women who was full of good works and acts of charity. And Dorcas was one of the leaders of the widows, who made clothes for the poor. But I do not think that van Bruggen is right. In the first place, we do not read that Dorcas was a leader of a group, but we only read that the people very much regretted that with her death the charity of making clothes had stopped. In the second place, turning back to Acts 6, if the negligence had been in the fact that no women were involved in the distribution of the goods and money, then we might expect that this would be rectified by appointing *women* now. But that did not happen. Neither did the seven brothers receive the assignment to *enlist women* in the future as a kind of help to the sisters. No, seven brothers were installed. They were appointed to that duty (verse 3), namely, to serve tables (verse 2).

The seven

Time and again, the objection has been made that the word "deacons" is not mentioned in Acts 6. But I am of the opinion that this does not at all prove that this chapter does not deal with deacons. I think we have here the *prototype* of the later deacons,

23

in the special sense of those who have to *diakonein*.

Repeatedly people have tried to deny and to dispute the ecclesiastical office of the deacons. For instance, one pointed to the fact that in the rest of the book of Acts no deacons are mentioned. In Acts 14:23 we read about election of presbyters, but not of election of deacons. In Chapter 11:27-30 we read that the relief to the brethren of Judea was sent to the elders, so not to the deacons. But we cannot see that this poses a great difficulty. For in Acts 8:1 we read that a great persecution arose against the Church at Jerusalem. So it already happened very soon that the office of deacons could not function any more in the Church at Jerusalem. And also later on, when the persecution grew less, it appeared that the office of deacon was not necessary in Jerusalem, for we read in Acts 21:8 that Philip, one of the seven, lived in Caesarea.

Another objection was that what is said about the seven does not have anything to do with the care of the poor. Philip goes to work as an evangelist, Stephen delivers sermons and does great wonders and signs among the people. Also this objection does not hold water. It is explicable that the work of the deacons is not mentioned in Acts 6, because the reason for the trouble had been solved. The measure was undoubtedly effective. In addition, the "seven" could have received the charisma of *didaskalia*, the special gift of teaching, just as it happened often in the beginning of the New Testament church. Neither is it excluded that, for instance, Philip started preaching when it was impossible to function as deacon.

There are also the objections that the "seven" had no office at all, that they had the same office as the presbyters, that they had a special status between presbyters and deacons, or that they had a temporary task in order to solve specific problems. These are all arguments against the permanent office of deacons. But I am of the opinion that Acts 6 deals with the service of deacons as a *permanent, special, independent* and *proper* office.

Office

It is an *office*. The seven were not appointed by the apostles or by the presbyters as "helpers." The whole, broad, solemn course of facts shows us that this is more than a kind of subordinate, less important function; the calling together of the congregation, the exposition of the necessity and the requirements of the service of mercy by the apostles, the election by the congregation, the approval of the apostles, their prayer and laying on of hands — all that is an indication of the institution of a certain office.

It is also a *permanent* office and not a temporary service. Of course there were in that time temporary services. We should not consider the organization of the Christian church in the very beginning as if everything concerning the offices was finalized. But we may say: the more the extraordinary offices disappeared, the more the normal offices came to the foreground. The distinction in Acts 6 between *diakonia tou logou* (preaching the Word of God) and *diakonein trapedzais* (to serve tables) is rather sharp. What was united for the apostles in their service, is now split into two services: the preaching of the Word of God, and the service of mercy.

It is also a *special* office, distinguished from the extraordinary office of the apostles and the prophets of the New Testament. It is a special service in the local church. We do not read that the seven executed their office outside Jerusalem.

It is also an *independent* office. That independence is strongly expressed by the apostles when they say "whom we may appoint to this duty." The word that is used here points to the ordination to an office. The apostles leave the whole matter of the care for the widows to the deacons because this whole care became too heavy for them. It appeared that the preaching of the Word required all their energy. They had to hand over the care of the poor to others in an independent office. Therefore the seven were given the responsibility for caring for the needy.

Finally, it is also a *proper* office. In former Latin publications we can read the term *proprius,* from which the English word "proper" is derived. That means: this is an office with its own task, not to be shared with others. That also means that the deacons may not claim what belongs to the duties of other office-bearers. Neither is the office of the deacons to be equalled with the function of government officers. What the deacons exercise is Christian mercy, according to Christ's mandate, to the honour of the Name of the LORD and to the well-being of the poor and lonely members of Christ's body.

This permanent, special, independent proper office is not less holy or worthy than the office of minister of God's Word or the office of elder.

No female deacons

It is clear that the office of Acts 6 was instituted as an office of *men,* so there were no *female deacons.* I agree with J. van Bruggen that according to the New Testament the sisters of the congregation cannot become office-bearers. I also agree with him that there are many tasks for the sisters. We can read in the New Testament that women played an important role, and so, also today women may help in all kinds of ways.

But the thesis of van Bruggen is now, over against all kinds of emancipation theories, that the deacons have no special office in the church either. He says, "the deacon, as we know him, is a kind of colleague-office-bearer of the elder and he has his own place. But the Biblical deacon is not an office-bearer, and he is only a help for the overseers." His conclusion is that it would be better if the deacon left his place in the pew of deacons beside the pulpit and that he went to the pew beside his wife. So he could, together with the female deacons, execute help-services in the church. He also concludes that it would be better not to install the deacons, because they have no special office. The best would be that they were appointed by the elders (van Bruggen, 1984: 117ff.).

I am of the opinion that van Bruggen is wrong here. Of course the deacon has a general title, deacon, that means, servant. But I am convinced, just as I said before, that the deacon has a permanent, special, independent and proper office in the church. I think there are more texts in the New Testament besides Acts 6, pointing to that.

Philippians

Van Bruggen says that the deacons are not mentioned very often, because they stand beyond the elders and overseers and they do not fulfill an independent service besides them. In this respect I want to point to the letter of the Apostle Paul to the Philippians. Paul and Timothy directed their letter to "all the saints in Christ Jesus who are at Phillippi, with the bishops and deacons." But S. Greijdanus argued that we have to consider the words "overseer" and "deacon" in their official, technical sense. And he adds to that, "There is nothing that points to the idea that the deacons would be helpers of the overseers in the material, financial things" (Greijdanus, 1937: 55ff.).

Timothy

In the second place, I would like to point to the first letter of Paul to Timothy, Chapter 3, the verses 1-13. There we read about the requirements of overseers, deacons and women. It may not escape our attention that many conditions are required of the elders, more than of the deacons, and also more than of the women. We may also note that the female helpers are here clearly distinguished from the overseers and the deacons. And the female deacons are absolutely not the same as the deacons, who apparently have their own, special, official task in the congregation.

I am of the opinion that the development is very clear. In Acts 6 we have what we called the prototype of the deacons, but in the letter to the Philippians and in the first letter to Timothy, the offices are already more established and Paul then writes down the requirements for the office-bearers.

Clemens

We also want to point to a writing that does not belong to the Bible, but that gives us insight into the situation of the church right after the time of the apostles. It is the first letter of *Clemens,* on behalf of the Church at Rome, directed to the Church at Corinth, and presumably originating in the year 96 A.D., that is only a few years after the death of the Apostle John. We read in that letter: "So preaching everywhere in country and town, they [the apostles, K.D.], appointed their first-fruits, when they had proved them by the Spirit, to be overseers and deacons unto them that should believe. And this they did in no new fashion; for indeed it had been written concerning overseers and deacons from very ancient times; for thus said the Scripture in a certain place: 'I will appoint their overseers in righteousness and their deacons in faith.' "(42,1; cf. Kirch, 1947: 11 ff.; cf. also Lightfoot, 1976: 31.) Clemens quotes here the prophecies of *Isaiah,* Chapter 60:17, and he tries to prove that the Old Testament already delivered a basis for the New Testament offices. In this respect I think Clemens was not right. Isaiah 60:17 (second part) says: "I will make your overseers peace and your taskmasters righteous." I am of the opinion that this prophecy points to the future luxury and riches of Jerusalem.

Nevertheless, it is very clear that at the end of the first century the Church at Rome had elders and deacons, and it is also clear that one was convinced at the time that these two offices were instituted by the apostles as independent offices.

Pastor Hermae

There is a second source, originating from the early part of the second century, called *Pastor Hermae.* Hermas was not an office-bearer, but a businessman in Rome. His book is written in the form of visions. He shows in these visions how an angel lays bare the sins and deviations of the church and summons to do penance and to convert. He writes that there are, besides the former apostles, overseers, teachers and deacons as office-bearers in the church. I quote now the passage of the vision concerning deacons who did not execute their office as they ought to have: "And from the ninth mountain, which was desert, which had reptiles and wild beasts in it which destroy mankind, they that believed are such as these; they that have the spots are deacons that exercised their office ill and plundered the livelihood of widows and orphans, and made gain for themselves from the ministrations which they had received to perform. If then they abide in the same evil desire, they are dead and there is no hope of life for them; but if they turn again and fulfill their ministrations in purity, it shall be possible for them to live."

There are also faithful office-bearers. "The stones that are squared and white, and that fit together in their joints, these are the apostles and overseers and teachers and deacons, who walked after the holiness of God, and exercised their office of overseers and teacher and deacon in purity and sanctity for the elect of God, some of them already fallen in sleep, and others still living." (Vision III, 5, cf. Lightfoot, 1976:173.)

This book, just as *Clemens* had great authority in the church of the second century. Of course they did not have the authority of the Bible books but the church regarded them very highly. It appears from the *Pastor Hermae* that the office of the deacons was to take care of the poor. It also appears that they distributed the goods reather independently.

Didachè

The third and last witness of that time (also in the first part of the second century) is the so-called *Didachè*, or *Teaching of the Apostles to the Gentiles.* It was of course not written by the apostles themselves, but it is based on the doctrine of the apostles and it also had great authority. It originated in Palestine and Syria, and it delivers clear insight into the preaching and life of the old church.

Also in this book we read about the deacons as office-bearers. We read: "Appoint for yourselves therefore overseers and deacons worthy of the Lord, men who are meek and not lovers of money, and true and approved; for unto you they also perform the service of the prophets and teachers. Therefore despise them not: for they are your honourable men along with the prophets and teachers." (XV, 1,2; cf. Kirch, 1947: 6; cf. also Lightfoot, 1976: 128.) The *Didachè* says: "They perform the service." The word used for service is one which always refers to an *ecclesiastical service.* So also the *Didachè* recignizes the deacons as office-bearers in the church.

Reformation

It would be possible to quote more writings from this time, but I think these quotations are sufficient. They show us very clearly that in the time just after the apostles the deacons were honoured as office-bearers, just as in the time of the apostles themselves, as Paul wrote in Philippians and Timothy.

I already said that *deformation* came very soon, and it would take a long time before *Reformation* came. It was Bucer who restored the office of the deacons, and he said they had special tasks, for instance at the Lord's Supper. To Bucer the deacons have a permanent office and within the consortium of servants of the church they have their own place, characterized by the original meaning of New Testament *Diakonia.* Calvin took that over and he said in his *Institutes* that the deacon's office was not only to take care of the poor, but also to look after the sick people.

I do not want to follow the whole history. I only want to stress that the Reformers went back to the early church, just as Calvin always said that he aimed to do.

Disappearing?

We saw that after the Reformation the elder disappeared in some regions quite quickly. What about the deacon? Time and again attempts were made to change this office or make it disappear altogether. On the one side there was the effort to separate it from the local congregation, by saying we have to look for a *world-deaconry,* thereby charging the deacons with the task of looking after the needs of the whole world rather than leaving it to the initiative of all individual believers. On the other hand there is the opinion of van Bruggen (and he is not the first one in history) that the deacon could better leave the chair of the office-bearers and take his place in the pew.

Over against both efforts I want to stress the *importance* of the office of the deacon in the church, but then connected with the local church and taking care of the needy, the poor, the sick, and the old people in that local congregation. Let the deacons keep their own office! Let the deacons keep that beautiful office! Let the deacons maintain that office in the church and persevere in it! There are many tasks for everybody in the church, for men and women, for old and young people. But let us continue to preserve the offices in the church for the ministers, the elders and the deacons.

High office

It is very good that the "Forms for the ordination of elders and deacons" (especially the new form) shows that the offices, including the office of deacons must be held in high regard. After having quoted several texts from the Old and New Testament, we read in the form: "Also today the Lord calls us to show hospitality, generosity, and mercy, so that the weak and needy may share abundantly in the joy of God's people. No one in the congregation of Christ may live uncomforted under the pressure of sickness, loneliness, and poverty. For the sake of this service of love Christ has given deacons to His Church. When the apostles realized that they would have to give up preaching the Word of God if they had to devote their full attention to the daily support of the needy, they assigned this duty to seven brothers chosen by the congregation. It is therefore the responsibility of the deacons to see to the good progress of this service of charity in the church."

We may conclude that it is an office, and even a high office, that the deacons received. I want to stress that offices in the church are *Gifts* of the exalted Christ Himself, just as we for instance can read in Paul's letter to the Ephesians. And we may not neglect this element! No doubt it is good to say, what for instance C. Trimp says, that the office-bearers are to be discovered and recognized by the congregation in respect of their *charismata* (Trimp, 1978: 50ff.). So we may say indeed that the special office in the church is not to be separated from the service of the believers.

But there is more. This is only one element. The other one is that office-bearers are gifts from heaven. The "highness" of the offices in the church is that there is a divine assignment, and connected with that assignment there is also a divine qualification. Each and every office-bearer will ask time and again, "Who is *sufficient* for these things?" (cf. 2 Corinthians 2:16). So also the Apostle Paul himself asked that question. But he knew the answer: "He who *calls* you is *faithful*, and He will do it" (1 Thessalonians 5:24). Therefore, I emphasize that he who is an office-bearer in the church does not receive only a *calling,* but also *capability* for it. I miss that often in publications concerning the offices in the church.

Conclusion

In conclusion, I come back to the question I posed at the beginning: "Are elders and deacons really office-bearers?" My answer is: Yes, without any doubt. Their offices are different from one another, but both offices are true offices. Both of them are also "high" offices, not to be separated from the congregation by whom they are elected, neither to be separated from the exalted Lord Jesus Christ who granted them as gifts from heaven. So let us honour the office-bearers in the church. Let us pray for them, in order that they may exercise their office joyfully, and not sadly, for that would be of no advantage to the congregation. In this way we may be sure that God will grant the office-bearers the gifts they need: wisdom, courage, discretion and mercy, so that each of them may fulfill his office as it is pleasing to our heavenly Father.

III
"IF YOU CONFESS . . ." (Romans 10:9)

THE STRENGTH OF THE CATHOLIC CHURCH

Introduction

Let me begin on a personal note. In the seventies, I found myself in Jerusalem in a library which held valuable treasures related to the situation of the golden city in the fourth century. This was the very thing I wanted, because with a view to my intended thesis, I was searching for data concerning this period, especially in Jerusalem. A kind Roman priest pointed me to various sources and was helpful in my investigation of this era. At one point in the course of conversation, my identity was revealed. I can still see the astonished look in the priest's eyes, and I can still hear his not-less-astonished voice when he said, "A Reformed minister who is interested in the fourth century! The fourth century belongs to us — Catholics!"

You can understand that this was an opportunity for me to assert that the ideas of "Catholic" and "Reformed" are not opposites or mutually exclusive and to deny Rome the privilege of being truly "Catholic" and on the contrary to make this claim for the church which remained in the truth. In this lies the clear starting point I would use as introduction. We speak of the Catholic church as the Apostles' Creed speaks of the "Catholic church" and in the sense of Lord's Day 21 of the Heidelberg Catechism when it states that the Son of God gathers this church out of the whole human race from the beginning to the end of the world.

Catholic

It is interesting to study how people in the fourth century, for example, looked at the words "catholic" or "universal" in relation to the church. In an explanation of the twelve articles given by way of a catechism lesson in 348 A.D., one reads: "The church is called 'catholic' because she is spread out over the whole earth from one end to another, and because she teaches universally and completely all which men ought to know concerning things visible and invisible, heavenly and earthly; further because she directs the whole human family, rulers and subjects, educated and uneducated, to God; also because she heals and treats every sort of sin committed in body or soul and finally, because she possesses in herself every form of virtue which is revealed as much in deeds as in words and every sort of spiritual gift" (Schaff/Wace, 1952: 139ff.). It is as if this catechism teacher (who was then bishop of Jerusalem) exerted himself to discover every possible meaning of "catholic." Such a broad definition of the word is not common with writers of that time.

But it is striking that in situations where the church is attacked and slandered, where heretics appear with their own notions, and where many have already turned away from the church, there the word "catholic" appears in one confession after another.

The word is not, however, found only in the Apostles' Creed (which in its earliest form dates from the second century); it also returns in the Confession of Nicea; "I believe one, holy catholic and apostolic church." That is the text as it was ultimately established at the Council of Constantinople in 381. But the first and foundational text of the first ecumenical Council of 325 also refers to the "catholic church" in its conclusion when it speaks of the true deity of the Saviour. In that connection, those who deny the deity of the Saviour are laid under the "anathema" of the "catholic church."

J. Kamphuis has pointed out that this is, in fact, the concluding point of this confession established by this first ecumenical council. "Let everyone note that it is the catholic church which speaks here. She confesses and she gainsays. She draws the boundaries wide; moved by the mercy of the Son of God, she takes within her boundaries all who await their salvation from Him. But in the midst of all sorts of sects and errors, she draws a clear and sharp line. Also in this she is the catholic church" (Kamphuis, 1980: 785).

High claims

L. Doekes has demonstrated that over against Rome and other religious bodies, the Reformation maintained the high claim that she was the one catholic church. Three examples will suffice. The Augsburg Confession (a Lutheran Confession, 1530) teaches that the one holy church will always remain. This church is the gathering of all believers, a gathering in which the pure Gospel is preached and the true administration of the sacraments maintained (Doekes, 1975: 298).

In the Genevan Catechism, Calvin asks why the church is called catholic. The answer reads: "Because she is one body under one head, so that there is not more than one, but only one church, spread out through the whole world" (Doekes, 1975: 300).

Equally clear is Art. 27 of the Belgic Confession:

We believe and profess one catholic or universal Church, which is a holy congregation and assembly of the true Christian believers who expect their entire salvation in Jesus Christ, are washed by His blood, and are sanctified and sealed by the Holy Spirit. This church has existed from the beginning of the world and will be to the end for Christ is an eternal King who cannot be without subjects. This holy church is preserved by God against the fury of the whole world, although for a while it may look very small and as extinct in the eyes of man. Thus during the perilous reign of Ahab, the Lord kept for Himself seven thousand persons who had not bowed their knees to Baal. Moreover, this holy church is not confined or limited to one particular place or to certain persons, but is spread and dispersed throughout the entire world. However, it is joined and united with heart and will, in one and the same Spirit, by the power of faith.

It is precisely this high claim which the Reformation upheld over against Rome.

Ursinus and Olevianus

The Heidelberg Catechism, then, speaks a very clear language in answer to the question, "What do you believe concerning the holy, catholic, Christian church?" We cite only the first part of the answer:

I believe that the Son of God, out of the whole human race, from the beginning of the world to its end, gathers, defends, and preserves for Himself, by His Spirit and Word, in the unity of the true faith, a church chosen to everlasting life.

It is instructive to note the explanation which Ursinus (one of the authors of the Catechism) gave of the word "catholic." He says first of all, that the word "church" here was to be taken in the sense of the whole or catholic multitude of righteous and true believers - from all times, lands and nations, of whom some are now in triumph in heaven, and some still "in warfare" on earth. He then continues: "the word 'catholic', by which the church is named, points mainly to the recognition of all times, nations, lands and places, on which, from which and in which the congregation is gathered" (Ursinus, 1956: 289 ff.).

Another of the writers of the Catechism, Olevianus, wrote an explanation of the 12 Articles of the faith. He also asks, "Why do you call the church catholic?" The answer reads:

There is only one head of the church, namely Christ. So all believers from Adam to the end of the world are his members and are one body through the Holy Spirit. Through belief in Him, all are saved through one head; they are incorporated into one head, and preserved through one head. So from the beginning, now and always, the Church has had only one way to eternal life; her one head Christ, the only Mediator, who has crushed the head of the Serpent. Through the grace of our Lord Jesus, we believe that we will be saved in the same way as they. Now each believer needs to know for himself all the promises given by God to the whole church and people of God (Olevianus, 1778: 149).

Still a reality

The high claim taken by the Reformation against Rome concerning the one catholic Christian church is still a reality.

In a course, called *The Catholic Religion*, it says that "Rome" is the only church, all other denominations are at a great disadvantage.

"In contrast with these divided groups is the great Christian Church of the world, united about the Pope and the Catholic bishops" (Taylor, 1964: 66).

And if anyone thinks that this claim of Rome has been greatly toned down since the Second Vatican Council (1962), then I point to the "dogmatic constitution" of this Council. Without mincing words, this explanation is given:

This is the one church of Christ which we confess in the Creed to be one, holy, catholic and apostolic. After His resurrection, our Saviour entrusted the church to Peter as shepherd. This church, established and built up in this world as a society, one finds in the catholic church governed by the successor of Peter and whose bishops assembled with him, although one can find outside her bosom true and holy members who as the personal gifts of the church of Christ are propelled toward the Catholic unity."

Now it is true that there are nuances here and there, especially with respect to the "members outside her bosom." Yet Rome frankly maintains the old claim. Even with all the talk of a new course, it is her concern to hold fast her teaching. The recognition of true and holy member is taken up in one clause. The main sense and intent remains: one finds this church in the catholic church which is governed by the successor of Peter and those bishops assembled with him. This has been clearly pointed out by J. Faber (Faber, 1969: 127).

Catholic belief

The Belgic Confession sets itself very clearly against this when it states that the Catholic Church is not bound to special persons. No, the church characterizes herself as catholic because there is one catholic belief. For example, in the third ecumenical creed, the Athanasian Creed, belief is more than once characterized as "catholic." I think here especially of the beginning and the end of this confession. The beginning is as follows: "Whosoever will be saved, before all things it is necessary that he hold the catholic faith; which faith except every one do keep whole and undefiled, without doubt he shall perish everlastingly." And at the end of this confession there is another reminder: "This is the catholic faith which except a man believe faithfully, he cannot be saved."

J. Kamphuis, whom we cite with agreement, writes that in the vocabulary of the ancient church, the word "catholic" was given the striking meaning of the catholic church WITH her catholic belief; the church exists through the strength of her catholic belief. Through the centuries, this word has come down to us. In our Christian vocabulary, the word has the same place as with the Christians of the first century. Indeed, we have the same confession as OUR confession. This is expressly stated in the Reformed confession which originated in the 16th century. For instance, Article 9 of the Belgic Confession reads that, "we willingly receive the three creeds, of the Apostles, of Nicea and of Athanasius." Therefore, the Heidelberg Catechism in Lord's Day 7 refers to the Apostles' Creed as a summary of "all that is promised to us in the Gospel" and which is necessary for a Christian to believe.

Isn't it striking that in this Lord's Day we come upon the same two intimately connected uses we discovered in the ancient church? The church is called "catholic" here (Q.A. 23) when the apostolic word is recited (Lord's Day 21 further explains and repeats the doctrine of the holy catholic church). But BELIEF also receives the same description of catholicity when the Apostles' Creed is spoken of as "the Articles of our catholic and undoubted Christian faith." This is language to make us rejoice. It is fortunate that Q.A. 22 does not speak of "the twelve articles," since that number is ultimately arbitrary and of no great significance for our faith. We may rejoice with the apostles' faith not with the twelve articles of apostolic belief. A three-fold division is much more accurate (compare Lord's Day 8). In our catholic faith, we confess belief in the Triune God. The creed breaks into three parts: "The first is about God the Father and our creation; the second about God the Son and our redemption; the third about God the Holy Spirit and our sanctification." As the Christian church and by the power of the character and content of our Christian belief, we retain this valuable word from the old Christian church (Kamphuis, 1980: 786).

Transmitted belief

And the old church certainly did not invent that belief! No, she knew that the apostles themselves had taught and transmitted it. The apostle Peter had testified before the Supreme Court that there is only one name by which man can be saved. The apostle Paul pointed out to the Ephesian church that there is only one belief, and one God and Father of all. But this does not only indicate that gifts have been given to the church. It is at the same time an indication of the TASK of the church. For that one catholic belief must be transmitted and passed on. It must be preserved and protected. In the same sense, we read in the letter of our Lord's brother, Jude, when he makes an appeal to "contend for the faith," that the faith was "once for all delivered to the saints." For that faith - for the content and worth of that faith, the church must always contend to the utmost, with every exertion of her powers. It is a valuable possession. It has been delivered. Through the inspiration of the Holy Spirit, the holy men of God under the old covenant spoke the word of truth. Christ repeated and elaborated on that word. He spoke the Word of God to the apostles and they in turn passed it on to the inhabitants of Asia Minor, Greece and Italy. The Word was passed on from generation to generation and through ways prepared by God spread through the whole world.

But this is not to say that the church has arrived or has reached a restingplace, as if to say that since the church has the faith, nothing can happen to her now - she has a monopoly on wisdom. No, instead it is a motive and a mandate which must spur her to the greatest activity and to an intense extreme struggle to preserve this faith and its content and to pass it on.

Pillar and foundation

The apostle writes of these same things in one of his pastoral epistles, in 1 Tim. 3:15. The apostle there characterizes the church as the household of God, the congregation of the living God and as a pillar and bulwark of the truth. A pillar is a column which supports, for example, the roof of a building, and a bulwark (or 'foundation') is something which lies under a building and as a foundation supports a whole building. The last term is, thus, more comprehensive than the first; the church is a column, but even more, it is a foundation. That which is supported is the TRUTH - the gospel of grace.

Roman Catholics have derived the doctrine of the infallibility of the church from this text, but one can find nothing of this idea here. In fact, this text teaches that the truth exists independently from the church. "Bearing of the truth," writes C. Bouma in his explanation of this text, "does not end in an infallible ability to teach truth and error, but it provides a place for the truth in the midst of the world. The words of God are entrusted to the congregation. The congregation must preach that Word and preserve it in purity through confession and life. This is here said by means of the image of the pillar and foundation. This image expresses not a description of the church, but points to her CALLING - in order that she might always fulfill this calling faithfully" (Bouma, 1942: 145).

Calvin also clearly rejects the Roman appeal to this text; "So the papists trifle shamelessly when they conclude from this word of Paul that all their madness must be recognized as the Word of God and that they cannot err because they are the pillar and bulwark of the truth." And then the Reformer continues positively by stating that the church is called a pillar of the truth because the office of the ministry of the word which God has established in her is the only way that truth might be preserved so that it is not lost from the thoughts of the people. The congregation must maintain the truth so that it is preached, preserved pure and uncorrupted and passed on to the next generation.

So far Calvin's "Commentaries." In his "Institutes" he writes; "It is of no small significance that the church is called the pillar and bulwark of the truth and the house of God. With these words, Paul teaches that the church is the trusted custodian of God's truth so that it is not lost in the world; for God has desired to preserve the pure preaching of His Word through the ministry and vigilance of the church, and show himself to us a house-father because He feeds us with spiritual food and cares for everything that is necessary to our salvation" (Calvin, 1960: 1024).

We should note that Calvin speaks here of THE truth; from the context it is clear that he means the full truth of the now sovereign Christ which the church confesses.

Power against might

This preservation of the full truth is the power of the church. But here power stands against might. Where the truth of the Word of God is not preserved and maintained, man may well form a large power-structure, but the church has there lost her power and in fact does not anymore deserve the name CHURCH. This happened to the Roman church; she became a colossal conglomerate. In a similar way, the Reformed Church (Hervormde Kerk, the Dutch State church) became what the missionary H. Kraemer once called a "hotel-church": "birds of a different feather all under one roof as in a large hotel where everyone has his own room and does his own thing." In that situation the only common feature is that people live under the same roof. But this has nothing to do with UNITY OF BELIEF, in which the congregation is called the house of God, and comes together as a household, nourished through one Word of truth, sitting at one table and standing at one baptismal font" (Deddens/Drost, 1989: 10).

So the false unity movement of today is not grounded in the unity of belief; rather, with a MINIMUM foundation, people seek to manifest MAXIMUM might and external togetherness. Sooner or later, however, such a building must fall. Whoever wants to erect an enormous skyscraper but gives hardly a thought to the foundation, should not be surprised if after a short while it appears that such a building cannot possibly stand.

False ecumenism

This power of the catholic church needs to be maintained in the face of today's false ecumenism which does not sufficiently stress the unity of true belief.

In itself, "ecumenical" is a good, Biblical word. It appears approximately 15 times in the New Testament in the sense of the "whole world." In the Greek word, one also finds root "house"; this implies the reference is to the INHABITED world. Thus, the words catholic and ecumenical have similar meanings. Under the old dispensation, the church was temporarily restricted to one people, Israel. But since Pentecost, Christ again gathers His church from all peoples over the whole world. The exalted Redeemer gathers His catholic or ecumenical church as a church from all times and places.

But the ecumenical spirit, especially as it is embodied in the "Word Council of Churches" (W.C.C.), gives short shrift to the unity of true belief.

I confine myself now to the Assembly of the W.C.C. held at Nairobi in 1975 under the theme "Jesus Christ Liberates and Unites." One can uncover four basic themes in the thinking of this Assembly.

1. Man can determine out of his own experience who Jesus Christ is, without letting the Scripture have the last word.
2. All men are reconciled to God. In fact, personal belief and conversion are not necessary for salvation.
3. "Liberation" does not, in the first place, refer to sin and guilt, but to oppressive structures.
4. A strong unity of all people is necessary to solve world problems.

This assembly has made it perfectly clear that this world-wide organization is not in the first place concerned with the honour of God, who saves sinners from ruin, nor with preserving the truth of God's Word, but much more with the well-being of man - man who by means of grandiose projects and through a massive movement of unity is thought capable of providing a better world.

The thinking of the last Assembly of the W.C.C. held in 1983 at Vancouver under the theme "Jesus Christ, the Life of the World" moves in the same direction. Some have thought the W.C.C. is moving in an orthodox direction, but this is to have sand in one's eyes. It is a modern humanism which continues to set the tone.

Surface unity

In the way the W.C.C. goes further in the direction of horizontality and political power struggles. That which K. Schilder already prophesied in 1948 when the W.C.C. was established now comes to the fore. At that time Schilder stated that this movement would later serve anti-Christian powers. Revelation 17:3 speaks of the false church as an unfaithful woman, a whore sitting on a scarlet beast. That beast means the political world-power which is hostile to God and His service. John sees the beast ridden by the wicked woman; her sitting on the beast means that the unfaithful communion will also strive for the power of this world. The whore who sits on the beast is called, "Babylon the great, mother of harlots and of earth's abominations." With this, Scripture wants to make clear the horrible reality that this false communion is apparently ITSELF a part of the godless Babylon of the God-hating world. This is an account of spiritual prostitution and therefore, of unfaithfulness to the Bridegroom of the church. Bablyon displays the style of the surface unity which is based on false prophecy and which is dedicated to the glory and the rights of man.

This false prophecy also reveals itself in misuse of God's Word. For example, in the circles of the W.C.C., people often bring up the words from the Saviour's high-priestly prayer of John 17, namely the words "that they may all be one." Some think this unity refers to ALL church communions and even to ALL men. But John 17 actually refers to the unity IN THE TRUTH: "Thy Word is truth." That is a unity of faith and of the contents of faith. A unity above the truth is a human fantasy and only a surface unity.

In the circles of the W.C.C. one also hears the slogan, "Division is sin." But the Saviour said that He came to bring a sword and discord (Mt. 10:34,35), to cast fire on the earth and to bring division (Lk. 12:49,51). This means that the Saviour maintains and sharpens the antithesis - after the pattern of the mother promise of paradise (Gen. 3:15).

The W.C.C. does not want to recognize texts as Is. 52:11, 2 Cor. 6:17 and Rev. 18:4 where the instruction "separate yourself" is given to believers who are in danger of being encircled by a false communion. This command stands in the framework of the antithesis between Christ and Belial, between Jerusalem and Bablyon.

It is striking that those associated with the W.C.C. are very tolerant and do not wish to speak of church discipline but at the same time they are very INTOLERANT to those who do not recognize THEIR surface unity. A. Kuyper's words, spoken in 1892 apply here: "He who defends the boundaries of the doctrine is set outside the boundaries of the communion." Man will permit no opposition and no breach of unity. As Rev. 13:15 reveals, man wants standardized thinking; towards those who break this myth of unity, the world is full of hate, just as the Saviour prophesied.

Catholic versus sectarian

The power of the catholic church must also be emphasized with respect to the work of the sects. The word "sect" is derived from the Latin word "sequi" which means "follow." Sectarians follow a limited number of doctrines and tirelessly maintain them whatever the consequences might be. But they do so at the cost of the TOTALITY of the truth and thus they work against the catholic character of the church.

The typical trait of the sects is that their adherents do not see the catholicity of the church and indeed, even reject the undoubted CATHOLIC faith of the church. Because of this, sectarians come to a special exclusivistic knowledge or they speak continually of private views concerning, for example, the 1000-year reign (Millennialism), or of rejection of infant baptism, or of speaking in tongues and miraculous healing (Pentecostalism) or of rejection of the deity of Christ or of the Holy Spirit (Jehovah's Witnesses). But this is of course, inconsistent with the Saviour's injunction to maintain ALL that He had commanded (Matt. 28:19) and a denial of the Apostle Paul's word that doctrine saves (1 Tim. 4:16).

The question may be asked how these one-sided views arise. The answer must be that the sects are characterized by belief in TEXTS rather than belief in SCRIPTURE. People see a particular text and suddenly have no eye for the whole Bible. Often they fail to consider the context and to compare Scripture with Scripture. In a word, they see neither the power of the catholic church nor that of the catholic, universal faith.

The result of this is that people easily fall into BIBLICISM. They swear by a single text and drag out of it what the context shows is not there.

Some have wittily called the sects the "unpaid bills" of the church. Sects often lay their finger on forgotten chapters, and one often finds in them the warmth which is so often missing in the cold, stony orthodoxy of the mainline church.

But be careful with such conclusions! It is the power of the church that she may maintain not one truth, but the WHOLE truth. The whole truth — this cannot be equated with dead orthodoxy or cold inactivity. In response to the charge of dead orthodoxy one can only answer that the truth must not only be CONFESSED but also LIVED.

Evangelical or Reformed

Today, in close connection with the existence of the sects, one often finds the "evangelical" attitude coming to the fore. The word "evangelical" — like so many words in the history of the church — is heavily burdened, because it was and is used in more than one sense. But we deal now especially with the movement which began in the previous century and which wanted to uphold the evangel (gospel) and the Bible, especially in the face of the then rising Bible criticism, but which unfortunately often worked in the manner of Biblicism — stressing certain texts without maintaining the whole Scripture. Because of this, people within the movement often see neither the catholic character of the church nor the catholic character of the church's doctrine. And this means that people do not see the power of the confession of the doctrine of the church.

C. Trimp has shown that the word "evangelicalism" has a strong American flavour. "It seems," he writes, "that when the European immigrants set foot in America and began to build up the new American world, the history of the church had a completely new beginning. That new beginning is contemporary with the revivals. So people shorten the historical horizon within which we stand as churches and within THOSE horizons people get to work with great commitment. As a result, the history of God's covenant through the ages and the history of Christ's continuing church-gathering work (Lord's Day 21) does not come into consideration with respect to the beginning of the ambitious undertaking in which the evangelicals are united."

"We think," continues Trimp, "that at the moment a strong American influence is at work in the Netherlands. Outside the (reformation of the) church, and her confessional witness, people establish 'free organizations' for special purposes like evangelism (Youth for Christ), Christian learning (Evangelical Outreach) and political action. The short-term benefits are obvious. People break through or ignore the difficult and often fossilized church situation in this country and get to work in a quickly secularizing society. One quickly brings together many Christians whose devotion and piety cannot be doubted and so one enjoys harmony outside the walls (of the church). But these 'free organizations' only work on the short term. Ignoring history is not only a rejection of the burden of human weakness, it is also a denial of Christ who makes and leads history. The history of the Netherlands is not only a series of human errors. Through the Spirit of Christ, there have also been clear victories of the faith in our societal life. The one who respects this will perhaps work slower and with less man power but will have more endurance at his disposal. Respect for the ways of the Lord is an important part of the fear of the Lord who is the beginning of wisdom" (Trimp, 1977: 36ff.). We also see the influence of American ideas in Canada.

J. Kamphuis has taken up this thread from C. Trimp and has developed a few thoughts with respect to the term "reformatory" while in a later series of articles entitled "Evangelical or Reformed" he further dealt with several other questions. At the end he comes to this conclusion: "The more radically one falls into the grip of the Reformation, the more strange it will seem to him that the evangelical movement has traded the church for the denomination, Christian confession for special testimony and the Scriptures which testify of Christ for special Biblical themes — strange, not because he personally feels awkward in this climate, but 'strange' because he sees the radicalism of the Gospel disappearing. This is nowhere clearer in my opinion than with respect to the two points which receive new attention in every reformation of the church, namely, the church and the covenant. It is a matter of honour to the God of the Word, who wishes to be the God of our lives, not that we glorify our position, but that we believe that God maintains His norm and continues to ask us whether we have made the most of our talents when He pointed us to a place in the way of the reformation in the CATHOLIC church and also made that known to us. It is the Lord of our life, and also of our study who impresses on us the rule: 'Everyone to whom much is given, of him will much be required; and of him to whom men commit much they will demand the more' " (Kamphuis, 1977: 52ff.).

Bible belief vs Bible criticism

Whenever one speaks of the catholic church, he speaks also of the catholic faith. And whoever speaks of the catholic faith, speaks of the whole of Holy Scripture. How the Scripture is and has been attacked! Here looms before us the monster of Bible criticism in its many forms. Bible criticism is a sort of approximation of the Scripture in which it is not received in its ENTIRETY as the infallible and trustworthy Word of God, but in which only certain limited parts are recognized as trustworthy.

One thinks here not only of the freethinkers who have always made attempts to strengthen their position by means of supposed contradictions or so-called "doublets" in the Bible and who in the free-thinking way have retained practically nothing of the Holy Scripture. Nor does one think only of the "ethical" school of thought which instead of saying, "God's Word is the Bible" came with the view "God's Word is in the Bible." (This latter view, in a particular form, was later adopted and developed by Karl Barth.) One also thinks here of a whole list of theologians, or, better, philosophers, who brought salvation-facts from the Bible into doubt, who explained historical passages as myth and who stressed the "time-bound" character of the books of the Bible. One could hear the explanation that a distinction must be made between the "packaging" and the "message" — and the latter was that which is of significance to us, it was said. The THEOLOGIAN would then make clear where the "packaging" ended and the kernel began. H.M. Kuitert once said of this distinction between "packaging" and message: "Whoever does not distinguish between these two, moves away from the intent of the Scriptures and compels the congregation to understand being a Christian as accepting a number of outdated propositions" (Kuitert, 1970: 44).

There also arose the concept of "relational truth"; the truth of God exists "in relation." By this is not meant the great wonder that God through revelation and proclamation of His truth linked Himself to man. "No," as M.K. Drost writes, "one is concerned here with the origin, the source and the character of God's truth. It emanates from

"God and Co." as someone has pithily expressed it in a critical analysis of the Report (the Report of the Synodical church concerning the nature of Biblical authority, K.D.). The truth of God never exists apart from us" (Drost, 1982: 18).

It is needless to say that the strength of the catholic church is systematically attacked through the many forms of Bible criticism which have existed and do exist. Yet, to stand for the infallible and trustworthy Word of God — that remains the strength of the catholic church.

"Now we must live" — so K. Schilder in the thirties ended his reigning summons in "Ons Aller Moeder" — out of the revealed Word. Well then, as the revealed Word says: Repent! and do so immediately and in covenant obedience" (Schilder, 1935: 97).

Is it not basically a matter of obedience to the indivisible Word of God as the truth which leaves not a single doubt and which is the rich possession of faith in God's catholic church?

Confessed and Experienced

A while ago we said that the catholic faith needs not only to be confessed but also to be experienced. Now that we come to the end of our discussion, we would like to once again clearly underline this point. It is by the unspeakable grace of God that He still goes on gathering His church in this land — a church chosen to everlasting life. This candle could have been taken away a long time ago.

We do not know how long the candle will remain in Canada. We shall not speculate on the church's chance of survival. But thankfulness that the Lord Jesus still goes on gathering His congregation must never allow us to forget the call to confess and to live the truth of God's Word.

A dreadful secularism grows all around us. Sects rise as mushrooms from the ground. All sorts of movements overwhelm thousands. Has the church had her day? Must we take refuge in a weakened confession and add water to the wine?

There is only one answer. We must show our gratitude for the strength of the catholic church by not being indifferent or introverted ourselves. Not, indifferent, as if we more or less stand outside the church. Do we not personally confess that we are and forever shall remain a living member of this church? And not indifferent, inward-directed, as if the power was not a dynamic reality. We have a message for the world! Not a partial Gospel, not a weakened confession but a word from the catholic church, a word charged with power and radiating strongly to the outside — because it is the catholic belief which touches ALL:

We have a word for the world.
We have a word for the modern man.
We have a word for the wandering.
We have a word for the young person, also in the church.
For we have the Word of truth, which is the gospel of our salvation!
(Ephesians 1:13)

FUNCTION OF THE BELGIC CONFESSION

Adopted by the Church

In 1561 Guido de Brès had completed a booklet in which he had shown as clearly as possible that the Calvinists had nothing to do with the Baptists (Wederdopers) and in which he had made manifest their desire to go the legal way. This was the booklet that later would enter into history as the Belgic Confession. De Brès had given it to the theologian Savaria, later Professor at Leiden when the latter stayed in the Netherlands for a few months.

It also had obtained a certain approval from the Church because the congregation of Antwerp had shown its unconditional agreement with it (De Pater, 1950: 9).

But not as many as fifty years later the **Remonstrants** would rear their heads.

One of their spokesmen, Wtenboogaert writes: At first the Reformed did not even have their own creed but they simply lined up behind the Augsburg creed, the confession of the Lutherans, because this was the most simple thing for them to do. But at that time, so he tells, a booklet was published in the Netherlands, entitled "Confession of faith of all believers, scattered across the Netherlands, who wish to live in accordance with the purity of the Gospel, containing thirty-seven articles." This creed, he says, did not only disagree with the Romans and Baptists, but also with the Lutherans. Actually it is only a translation of the French Confession. And if this creed has obtained a certain place in the churches it is in no way legally entitled to that place. "I do not find," he writes literally, "that any synodical or other general assembly of all churches in the Netherlands previously has been held to that end or that a general order thereto has been given by them all and even less so that it originally would have been tested and thoroughly examined by them all and that it, according to the Word of God and with full knowledge of the facts, would have been adopted by them all."

How much is true of this story of Wtenboogaert? Is it true that the confession never had been tested and adopted by a general synod? We wish to say at once: NOT A WORD of Wtenboogaert's stories is reliable! It is out of the question that the Belgic Confession only is a translation of the French one. The Belgic Confession deals briefly with some points, the French one extensively, with other matters it is just the reverse. The numbering is not the same. Moreover the French confession has 40 articles, the Belgic has 37. Already we mentioned the fact that the Congregation of Antwerp, in the year 1561, the year the Belgic Confession was written, had adopted it. It was spoken about at that time, probably for that reason, as the "Confession d'Anvers," i.e., the Confession of Antwerp. Besides, de Brès had written in the letter that accompanied the Confession when he delivered it to the Commissioners in the night of November 2nd, that he spoke "on behalf of the citizenry of the city" (the city of Doornik), that he presented to them the confession as made "with general accord" of more than half of the citizens, and even that he knew to speak on behalf of over 100,000 believers in the country. It is clear from it all that Guido de Brès most certainly had consulted with others, and that right from the start, the confession had been adopted by the church.

The remarkable point is exactly that in that time of persecution, when it was extremely difficult to hold an ecclesiastical meeting, the Belgic Confession nevertheless has been brought into discussion right from the beginning, as soon as a possiblity to meet arose. In 1563, therefore even during Guido de Brès' life a provincial synod was held at Armentieres in French Flanders. In this meeting already the regulation was made that the confession which has been adopted among us, should be subscribed by elders and deacons. This course of action has also been followed by other provincial synods in the Southern Netherlands. On the Synod held in June of the year 1565, called the Pentecostal Synod, the confession was spoken of as "the creed of the Churches in this country." On this synod it was namely agreed that at the beginning of every synod reading of the confession of the churches in this country should take place (Bakhuizen van den Brink, 1976: 17; cf. Vonk, 1955: 106 ff.).

Testify agreement

In 1568 a convent was held in Wesel, where it was decided that ministers of the Word before being installed in their service, should testify their agreement with the doctrine which was contained in the Belgic Confession and the Heidelberg Catechism. In 1571 a synod of deputies from the Dutch churches was held in Emden where the following decision was made: "In order to prove the concord among the Dutch Churches concerning the confession, the brethren though it proper to subscribe to the confession of faith of the Dutch Churches." Noteworthy is also the decision of the Classis Walcheren in 1574: "We believe and acknowledge hereby that every portion of the aforementioned confession of faith of the Christian congregation of the Netherlands is in accordance with the Word of God and we therefore promise to conform our doctrine and church service to it."

Therefore there is not a word true of Wtenboogaert's pretention that no ecclesiastical assembly had adopted the confession. The very facts contradict this pretention. It is exactly from the side of the Remonstrants, that RESISTANCE against the confession arose. Wtenboogaert thought it a form of inquisition when one had to subscribe to the confession again. The Remonstrant minister Duifhuis spoke mockingly of the Belgic Confession as the "measuring cord" (het meetkoordeken). "It was not right," as it was said by the Remonstrant-inclined classis of Nijmegen, "to burden brethren with repetition of the confession." Professor Polman remarks in this connection: Where the tie to the confession loosens and secretly all sorts of deviations are nurtured, such sort of legalistic reasoning arises, and this is very instructive, because the accusation of legalism and sticking to the letter of the law is usually started vice versa. Then the subscription to the confession does not become a repitition of the confession of the heart, but the humiliating creeping through a narrow gate in order to get access, an act, when once inside, one wishes to forget as soon as possible and not to repeat.

In those days, full of tension when the Remonstrant errors took shape, the church in our native country became mobile everywhere. Her precious heritage was threatened. She did not wish to admit preaching on her pulpits that would disturb the concord in the pure sound doctrine, as laid down in her Confession and Catechism. She would not suffer the seed of the church to be instructed by false teachers. She asked guarantees out of necessity imposed upon her.

Therefore clearly edited subscription forms came into use. Formerly one simply set his signature under the confession, but that would not suffice for the church any longer. The sense of the subscription was to be described extensively. Rev. Arnold Cornelii of Delft held secret meetings in 1605 with other ministers in order to get major assemblies to decide for the banning of all corruption of the doctrine, that "those who are freshly accepted in the service, not simply subscribe to the Catechism and 37 articles, but besides, that they by setting their own signature declare that, if they get to dispute any point of the doctrine contained in them, they will be deposed of their service and promise to renounce it." He got his wish.

Subscription form

Numerous regional synods drew up a subscription form for their district. At last in the National Synod of Dort 1619 the well-known subscription form is made up, which contains the following elements:
1. A clear declaration that the doctrine of the Free Forms of Unity in every respect is conform to the Word of God;

2. The solemn promise to teach this doctrine and to faithfully promote it and reject, refute, and resist all errors in contradiction with it, without teaching or writing openly or secretly, directly or indirectly anything against it;
3. The clear promise that if one would conceive any thought or feeling against the aforesaid doctrine or any point of it, this never will be openly or secretly presented, promoted or written, but first it will be submitted to the classis or synod, for examination;
4. At last the promise, if consistory, classis or synod by important reasons of thought would deem it proper to demand more explicit feeling and explanation, to be willing to give it, on penalty of immediate suspension from the service.

This form speaks for itself. Here the binding to the confession is effected as strongly as possible. In the high consciousness of her calling the church, guarding the doctrine and along with it the words of God, entrusted to her, imposes this great obligation and her office-bearers accept it and willingly make this vow, because they wholeheartedly feel and believe that this doctrine in everything is in conformity with the Word of God. The concord in the doctrine, the well-being of the church, the seriousness of every heresy, the right to submit objections, fully justify for them the demand of subscription to the confession.

"Dordrecht chains"

The church would have stayed out of much trouble if every office-bearer would have stuck to these sound rules for the churches' federate life contained in the subscription form of Dort, and the churches themselves would not have put up their own regulations for bargaining. Formally this sound rule remained in existence until 1816. Practically it had become a dead rule for many already in the 18th century. It is one of the first acts of the state created by King William I, when by the synodical Board of the Reformed Denomination the old subscription form is so modified that one "in good faith accepts and heartily believes the doctrine, which according to the Holy Word of God, is contained in the adopted Forms of Unity of the 'Nederlands Hervormde Kerk'. "

Scorn was heaped upon Rev. Molenaar and Rev. Schotsman when they called this new form a trap, and against Bilderdijk who took sides with them; a storm of indignation broke loose.

Donker Curtius later unscrupulously declared that by "according to" was meant: "as far as." Everybody could therefore make out for himself in how far this accordance was under discussion, people dared to speak of "most miserable forms" and "Dordrecht chains."

In 1854 the subscription form was modified again and one could suffice by declaring "that we wish and want to faithfully maintain the spirit and essence of the doctrine which is contained in the adopted forms of unity of the 'Nederlands Hervormde Kerk'. "

Things become more stretchable yet in 1888: "We promise in deep awareness of our calling and in confidence in God, that we diligently and faithfully will be working in it and, according to the principles and the character of the 'Nederlands Hervormde Kerk' in this country, will preach the gospel of Jesus Christ, and promote to the best of our ability the interests of the Divine Empire and accordingly those of the 'Nederlands Hervormde Kerk,' in obedience to her regulations."

Here the Forms of Unity are not mentioned at all any more. The lawlessness in the doctrine has made a perfect triumph. The confession had been pushed aside. The tie to the confession has been cut. The un-Christian tolerance has triumphed. It is true that Article 11 still speaks of maintaining the doctrine, but numerous synodical verdicts shed a sharp light on what was understood by it.

To give a single example, the classes Alkmaar and Deventer pleaded in addresses to the synod of 1874 for deletion of this article, because maintaining it in the present situation was impossible, and meant untruth and mystification, since general deviation from the old doctrine had taken place.

The reporting committee fully agreed with this.

"The disputed words (maintaining the doctrine) tempt to self-deceit, to shameful injustice, to widening of the split between the various religious currents in our church; they can chase from heads and hearts the interest in the development of God-devoted feeling and willing of the mind according to the Word and the Spirit of Christ." Discipline of doctrine would mean: "the inevitable shattering and doom of our church. All those who do not really and unconditionally agree with the doctrine contained in the Belgic Confession, the Heidelberg Catechism and the Canons of the Dort Synod, the modern, the evangelicals and also the majority of the orthodox are then banned from the 'Hervormde Kerk' by those who in their conscience can find the liberty of maintaining the doctrine."

Every shadow of discipline of the doctrine was to be avoided and therefore the committee proposed to establish: "Since the doctrine contained in the Belgic Confession, the Heidelberg Catechism and the Canons of the Synod of Dort, these historic foundations of the 'Nederlands Hervormde Kerk' is no longer confessed by the congregation with sufficient accord as being the expression of her Christian belief, the duty of maintaining this doctrine cannot be imposed upon the governors of the church any longer, as it was done formerly. While the congregation developing itself on the principles of the 'Hervormde Kerk' as the latter appear to be in their origin and development, goes on shaping a way of expression for her Christian belief which once may again give rise to a confession of the 'Nederlands Hervormde Kerk,' pronounced with sufficient accord, nobody may in the meantime be banned from the church as a member or a teacher, who complying with the remaining compulsory requirements, is convinced in his conscience that he, according to the principles of the 'Nederlands Hervormde Kerk,' may belong to her."

The synod adopted this proposal, but for secondary reasons the said article was not deleted. The synod in 1978 did state: "Further, as far as the word 'maintain' is concerned, this can impossibly mean: take care, if need be, by means of canon law enforcement, that nothing be changed in it, because growth of religious knowledge follows immediately, which presumes development as mentioned and therefore tolerates different appreciation of the Gospel truth."

The lesson for today

In the meantime in the nineteenth century — this is the crying misery and the terrible consequence of this attitude of the church, which is supposed to be the pillar and foundation of the truth — people are surrendered to rationalists, freemasons, liberals, socialists and numerous other evil currents. In her midst acted office-bearers who unpunishedly denied the basic truths, rejected God's Word, definitely denied the Divine Sonship of Christ, mocked the blood theory (as some still do today), replaced baptizing in the name of the Triune God with baptizing in liberty, equality and fraternity. The congregation suffered under this "dominocracy" (ministers' rule) and the ministers without a backbone became slaves of the cherished images of leading groups.

This lesson of the nineteenth century has stronger than ever convinced the Reformed people of the correctness of the point of view of the Dort Fathers wherever it concerned maintaining the confession. It is noteworthy therefore that already on the first synod of the Christian Seceded Church in Amsterdam the old subscription form of Dort was introduced again and the same thing is true of the "Dolerende Kerken." Both returned to the sound church order and followed the good track of the Dort Fathers in the matter of the binding to the confession, a track that had been left at an ill hour.

This lesson may never be forgotten!

CONFESSION AND SCHOOL

Some theses

In what follows these eight theses are worked out:

1. The confession does not deal only with ecclesiastical life, but has to function in the whole life of Christians.

2. The consequence of this function of the confession is that the schools to which we send our children, must have their own Reformed character.

3. To provide for Reformed schools means much more than to respect the tradition of ancestors: we must have the same faith and the same consciousness of a calling.

4. To maintain the confession with respect to the school means to maintain that we confess our faith in our triune God, as stated at the baptism of our children.

5. According to Lord's Day 8 of the Heidelberg Catechism we have to confess God the Father and our creation, God the Son and our redemption, and God the Holy Spirit and our sanctification.

6. This confession means in the first place that our children have to learn to live to the honour and praise of the Name of God the Father.

7. Furthermore, this confession means that our children are set apart as children of God's covenant, being bought by the Mediator of God's covenant, our Lord Jesus Christ.

8. Finally, this confession means that our children are governed by the Holy Spirit, that they may be nurtured in the Christian faith and in godliness.

Function

To say that our confessions only deal with ecclesiastical life shows a lamentable misunderstanding. Some people have the opinion: in the *church* we are bound to the confession, but in our common daily life we are free from it. When we think in this manner, we create a contrast. However, we are bound to our confessions not only on Sunday, but on Monday as well. We are bound not only in ecclesiastical life as members of the church, but also in daily life as members of society.

It does not need proof that we are bound to the law of our heavenly Father every day and every hour of our life. We also know that the obedience to this law is the true freedom for God's children. God's law is *universal* and deals with our whole life. In the same way we can say: what we confess as Christians is universal and has to do with our whole life. There is not a so-called *neutral* territory, in which we are allowed to follow our own desires and to feel free from God's law.

Consequence

When we say that there is no neutral zone it becomes obvious that this has also consequences with respect to school life. Such a consequence of this universal function of our confession is that — to the utmost of our power — the schools to which we send our children must have their own Reformed character. We are not able yet to establish a Canadian Reformed College or University. However, we have the calling to establish schools for our children with their own Reformed character, on the basis of our confessions as much as we can. That is not a matter of a kind of *hobby* of some enthusiastic people, but that is the precious calling of Reformed believers, who profess their faith by words and deeds.

Respect

It remains necessary to emphasize this our duty and calling with respect to establishing schools for our children. For it is possible that we still have a certain feeling of *alliance* with that which has grown in the course of history and which has been given to us by a previous generation. There can be a kind of respect for tradition, and a kind of piety. This has, of course, a certain value. However, when this piety is not motivated by an awareness of calling, it becomes a worldly matter. This danger can threaten us also with regard to our Reformed schools. We know that a previous generation struggled hard for these schools; so we can feel obliged to maintain them and to give our money for them, while we do so out of *tradition*. This would not be good. We should maintain our oneness in faith with the previous generation. We should retain the same awareness of calling as our fathers had. If that faith is not there anymore, then we can inherit the books with the minutes and the buildings, we can preserve them respectfully and carefully, but we would have lost that inheritance as a work of faith. So it remains very important to see the school in the first place as a matter of faith. This implies that we must act on the basis of the same confession.

No confessionalism

If we stress that the confessions really are to function in our schools and that we must have the same contents of faith as our ancestors had, that does not mean that we want to *overestimate* the confession. This would be a kind of *confessionalism*. In such a case we would not do justice to the unique dominion of God's Word. A confession can only have a derived certainty, derived from the original certainty of Holy Scripture.

But we must say at the same time: if there is room and a calling for having a scriptural confession, then this confession may not be made suspect.

No biblicism

When we say: we should not go in the direction of confessionalism, we must add: neither in the direction of *biblicism*. It was a slogan of the Arminians: only the Bible! If the Arminians were correct then it would be possible to attach a function to the Bible which the Bible does not have. It would place the Word of God outside the reality of life, namely, outside the reality of church-life in her age-long struggle to guard and to keep what had been entrusted to her.

Exactly because of the character of the confession as *confession*, which is based on the Word of God, we may not abandon it, as long as the confession is not disproved

44

with clear and firm arguments from God's Word. Even in that case we may not say farewell to the confession, but we have to go the eclesiastical way. Therefore on the one hand there should be no overestimation of the confession, but on the other hand no *underestimation* either.

No dead formula

The confession may never function like a dead formula. That is what *Calvin* said when he stressed that the confession always has to function as a spiritual guide. He writes: "We have to esteem the confession highly. Indeed, the confession is a human writing. But the contents and the ornament of it are derived from the prophets and the apostles."

Calvin put emphasis on that fact that the confession may never become a dead formula. Just three hundred years after Calvin's death *Groen van Prinsterer* said the same in connection with the State Church in the Netherlands: "The confession of the Church has to be respected above every form of the Church and every regulation, and no stipulation may be considered as binding which could be an obstacle on the way of maintaining the confession of the Church."

No limitation

However, there was the tendency to place *limitations* on the confession, especially in the sense that people would not be bound by the whole confession in each and every activity or situation. One would like to have a special confession for mission, for politics and also for education.

J. Faber pointed to the fact that there is a tendency in the U.S.A. and in Canada to exchange the Reformed Creeds and confessions in the constitution of the school societies for an educational creed.

He gave an example of a so-called educational creed formulated in Toronto, which speaks about life, Scripture, Christ, reality, knowledge, scholarship, and academic freedom. He said: what is good in this statement is found in broader and better form in the Reformed confessions, and he concludes: "Whoever studies the samples of educational summaries of principles offered during the last decades and compares them with the contents of the creeds and confessions must conclude that, if in school communities they are to replace the historic confessional documents of the Reformed churches, they will impoverish Christian life and action" (Faber, 1982: 5). In fact, what J. Faber warns against is a limitation of the confessions. We must be aware of the danger of going in that direction!

Relevant

The background of such a desire for educational confessions or creeds can be that one has the idea that the confessions are not *relevant* to school life, or that one is not able to apply the Reformed creeds and confessions to the education of the children. However, consider this: what did the parents promise at the baptismal font with respect to the education of their children? It is very clear. The third and last question directed to the parents of the children of God's covenant is: "Do you promise as father and mother to instruct your child in this doctrine (that is the doctrine of the Old and New Testament, summarized in the confessions, as the true and complete doctrine of salvation), and to have him (or her) instructed therein to the utmost of your power?" When the parents answer in the affirmative, the children are baptized into the Name of God the Father, God the Son and God the Holy Spirit. From this baptism formula we can see right away what the *content* of our confession is. It is clearly stated in Lord's Day 8 of the Heidelberg Catechism. The articles of our catholic and undoubted Christian faith profess God the Father, God the Son and God the Holy Spirit, into whose name the children are baptized. So the three parts of our confession are about God the Father and our creation, about God the Son and our redemption, and about God the Holy Spirit and our sanctification. Are these three parts not relevant to our schools and to the education of our children?

Very important and still relevant is what the late B. Holwerda said about the matter of school education in a speech held in 1941 and printed in one of the books, published after his death. I will give extensive quotations.

God the Father and our creation

God the Father and our creation: that is the first article of our confession that is also the beginning of our school. We are saying here: "The earth is the LORD's and the fulness thereof." If we do not see this, we do not understand anything of the school with the Bible. . . . The school with the Bible is something other than a school plus a Bible. It is something other than a school with some education in religion. The school is not a school with the Bible if just a psalm is to be learned, or the history of the Bible is told to the chidlren; but a school is truly a school with the Bible, when all of the education is ruled by the Scriptures; when each and every subject is ruled by the confession of God the Father and our creation (Holwerda, 1958: 91ff.).

Holwerda continued to say (in 1941):

It is still quite strongly so that for many among us the characteristic distinction between the Christian and the public schools is seen in a Bible story, in a stanza of a psalm and in prayer, while the other subjects are considered as being neutral. We have so little defense against the well-known remarks from public school supporters, that our speaking of counting and writing in a Christian way is actually nonsense. Outsiders say: "Also for your children two times two is four, precisely as at the public school. They get the same results as others in adding and subtracting, in multiplying and dividing. Of course, if two times two for Christian children would be five, then we could see a good reason for a Christian school; but not now." Outsiders say: "When your children learn to write, they do this in the beginning in just as clumsy a fashion. Whey they start reading, they stutter in the beginning, and drone with the same tone as at the public schools. In history they learn the same dates; in geography they study the same map. Are not all these subjects neutral?" Do we have only little defense over against such reasoning? Are we aware that in this way the Christian character of the entire education is actually attacked, and that by such contemplations the whole Christian life is fundamentally undermined?

Holwerda writes, in the war situation:

Many parents are happy when their children are able to learn well: such children have later, when they have finished school, a good possibility to make a decent living; then they can nicely find their way through life; add to this some knowledge of the Bible and all will be fine for eternity as well. However, in this way life as a whole is secularized. For such Christian parents consider a good school a vehicle for a good position.

Should we not agree that these words of Holwerda are still relevant? He refers to *Psalm 8*, calling this the psalm which Jesus Christ had in mind, as often as He thought about little children.

This poet says: "O LORD, our Lord, how majestic is Thy name in all the earth!" Why is that name majestic here on earth? It is because among other things, "by the mouth of babes and infants, Thou hast founded a bulwark because of Thy foes, to still the enemy and the avenger." He considers the mouth of a child, the chatter even of babes, a tremendous instrument, by which God breaks here on earth the dominion of the evil one, by which He builds His kingdom, and reconquers the world for Himself. We are inclined to say: that is somewhat overdone. The dominion of Satan stands firmly and it is surely not blown down by mouths of children. But that poet is confident and he knows what he says. He enjoys the crying of a baby who is born. He does not do that because that mouth will sing pslams later on, and will say prayers. Of course, that is also important. He is doing this because this child is also chosen by God to royal dominion. Also to this child God paid attention as a son of man, and also this child is crowned with glory and honour in order to have dominion presently over the works of God's hands. He knows very well that not each and every boy is a born minister. Most of them will be busy in the country or in the city in other jobs. But these sons of man will have their occupation as servants of God and in their business the name of the LORD will be glorious over all the earth. That is the expectation of this poet: not that these children will have a good *job*, but that they will become *God-fearing* farmers and labourers; that they will keep in their business and in their job the commandments of the LORD; that they in their own place will repel the enemy and the avenger, and that they will conquer the rebellion against God (Holwerda, 1958: 93ff.).

The majesty of God's name

Do we see the significance of our Reformed schools? Holwerda says further:

Of course, two times two is four, also in our schools. But our children have to know that, not because they must presently be able businessmen, but in order to sanctify their business "for the LORD."

Covenant children learn the same letters as other children, and when they begin to use a pen and ink, they make the same stains as the others do. But by the young brains, by the mouths, by the little fists of our children, God has founded a *bulwark* because of His foes, in order that His name will be glorious on earth. If that were not the case, then do not teach them at all. If your boys only have to count in order to advance in life and surpass father and mother, then do not teach them and do not let them be taught. Then life will be profaned and desecrated, and this child will become a tool of the enemy and the avenger.

Instead they learn to count ant they learn to read because of God's foes. The LORD, whose glory is above the heavens, is on the way to His glorious kingdom on earth also in the scratching pens of our children.

Holwerda goes on:

A recruit does not learn to handle weapons without purpose. He is learning this in order to be able to fight on behalf of his king, and his fatherland. If he isolates it from that purpose, he is engaging in crime.

So it is with our schools. Our children do not learn to read and to count as if education were an end in itself. Geography and history are not subjects which are to be considered apart from God. Children can only work with them either for or against God. There is not a third way. For the earth is the LORD's and the fulness thereof. The children will serve God in the world and will give thanks to Him. If they are not doing that, and if they do not learn to do that, then God will give them over to a wrong mind, because they have not honoured or thanked Him; then in their thoughts and deliberations they will come to vanity and their unwise heart will have become darkened.

Holwerda says to the parents:

This is your calling regarding the school with the Bible: that you see and confess things in this way: that you say: my children shall be educated in the service of God for their whole life; and in no other way; that you maintain it and stand for it, whatever the consequences are: my children are for the honour and the Name of the LORD. For nothing else. You do not send them to the school because they have to know how they have to go through their life and how they can go to heaven, but in order that God's name will be glorified in all the earth. If the sole purpose of education would be to make them skilled for life and nothing more, then it would be alright to let them go to a public school. If it is desirable that they know something about religion, well, then the church and the catechism class are there. But if you say: the earth is the LORD's then you say: now never any other school, but only the school with the Bible. For us, that is the school which maintains the Reformed confession. Not all of them will become ministers of the church — a good thing too! — but presently they have to know on the farm, in the shop, in the factory, in the kitchen and in the garage how to serve the LORD.

B. Holwerda added:

I wish that this motive of the great enmity would dominate us again; that we would see it again that in our whole life here on earth, in all its aspects, the name of the LORD must be hallowed; then we would know again what Christian education actually is, and we would again stand behind it. Then we would again be immovable as our fathers were: here we stand, we cannot do otherwise. For the name of the LORD on the earth! For anything else we never will give our children! (Holwerda, 1958: 95 ff.).

God the Son and our redemption

We listened to B. Holwerda telling us that as we educate our children there can be no question as to how we have to consider the work of God our Father. There may be no uncertainty with respect to the goal of the education of our children: that the name of the Father may be glorious in all the earth.

Holwerda goes on to speak about the relevance of the confession about God the Son and our redemption in the education of our children. There should not be any uncertainty with respect to the position of our children in this world, thanks to the work of *God the Son.*

For there is the reality of God's covenant. There is the immovable firmness of God's *promise,* that our chidlren are washed in the blood of Jesus Christ.

I quote in this respect the Form for the Baptism of Infants: "When we are baptized into the Name of the Son, God the Son promises us that He washes us in His blood from all our sins and unites us with Him in His death and resurrection."

Holwerda goes on to say:

If we lose sight of this even for one moment, then our children have become baptized heathens, maybe with a somewhat greater chance for salvation because they are more in contact with God's grace. However, then our schools with the Bible have lost their significance because we would have erased the radical difference between our children and the children of unbelievers. . . ." (Holwerda, 1958: 97).

Holwerda stressed that not we, as Christian parents, ourselves, but that the LORD makes the distinction. If we had our Reformed schools only with the intention to create a distinction on our own authority, we would not have a leg to stand on. Saying, the schools are good for bringing the children to Jesus Christ, then we do not see things right. Then the unbelievers are right, saying that Reformed education is a disrupting influence. You know the reproaches of unbelievers, stating that we sow divisions in the nation: we break the national unity. But we reply: the LORD Himself made the distinction, already in the baptism of our children. The fellowship of blood and place and time is broken by God Himself where He established the antithesis of His covenant.

In line with B. Holwerda we say: This we have to maintain over against everyone who wants to say it differently. If we tried to dissolve the antithesis by a so-called unity, we would commit a crime over against outsiders. But now we have Reformed schools which maintain the confession because God Himself made the distinction in His covenant. "This is the second pillar upon which the Reformed schools stand: the covenant of the LORD as a great and deep reality."

Therefore, in the first place, we see the connection between God's Word with the confession based on it and the school because "the *cosmos* cannot be broken: the earth is the LORD's and the fulness thereof." But, secondly, we also want the connection between Bible with confession and the school because there is *indeed* a split in mankind. This God, to whom the whole world belongs, makes a distinction, an antithesis, in Christ Jesus. Our children are set apart by Him as children of God's covenant, being bought by the Mediator of God's covenant, our Lord Jesus Christ.

Of course, also with respect to our children we confess that they are conceived and born in sin, and therefore subject to all sorts of misery, even to condemnation. But in the same breath we also confess that our children are sanctified in Christ and thus as members of His church ought to be baptized. With that we confess that God Himself in Christ Jesus made the distinction with His covenant.

God the Holy Spirit and our sanctification

Holwerda then writes about the third part of our confession: God the *Holy Spirit* and our sanctification. Let me first quote again from our beautiful Form for the Baptism of Infants. "When we are baptized into the Name of the Holy Spirit, God the Holy Spirit assures us by this sacrament that He will dwell in us and make us living members of Christ, imparting to us what we have in Christ, namely, the cleansing from our sins and the daily renewal of our lives, till we shall finally be presented without blemish among the assembly of God's elect in life eternal." Holwerda points to the prayer of thanksgiving after baptism where the church prays to God: "We pray Thee through Thy beloved Son that Thou wilt always govern this child by Thy Holy Spirit, that he (or she) may be nurtured in the Christian faith and in godliness, and may grow and increase in the Lord Jesus Christ." Holwerda adds:

The church professed the Holy Spirit as the sovereign Worker [of grace], as the great Governor of her children: God the *Holy Spirit* is working, not men. But the church also professed the Holy Spirit as her God who in His good pleasure, chooses His instruments, and who wants to govern the children of the covenant by the means, provided by Himself: the educational office of the parents. He also grants the freedom to make use of others in the education of the children, but He never allows them to pass that office to others or to have others take away that office from them.

The Holy Spirit has said to the parents [in the baptism of the children of God's covenant]: it is I who govern your children, but it pleased Me to do that via your education. He has bound them to this, to His sovereign decree.

Therefore, as Reformed people we are called to establish Reformed schools, being parents of God's covenant children. This is not a *right* of ours, but it is the consequence of the *rightful claim of God the Holy Spirit* on the children of the covenant. Therefore this confession means that we believe that the Holy Spirit promised: "I am the One to rule over your children, but it pleased Me to do that through your education." Therefore, the Holy Spirit wants the children of the covenant to be nurtured in the Christian faith and in godliness (Holwerda, 1958: 101).

Called by God Himself

Holwerda concludes with this summary:
I believe in God the Father, the Creator; this means: I believe that if I am faithful and acknowledge His claim on my whole life, He Himself will take care that the whole earth will be filled with His glory. Maybe I do not see the results, but I trust in Him: He will do it.

I believe in God the Son, the Redeemer; this means: I believe that if I accept obediently the antithesis also with respect to the education [of the children], He Himself will realize and maintain this antithesis; . . . that He Himself casts fire upon the earth and is bringing the discord among men [namely, between faith and unbelief] . . . .

I believe in God the Holy Spirit who sanctifies; this means: I believe that, certainly, the rights of the parents in the school can be denied [e.g., by a government], but that never the calling by the Holy Spirit can become undone. When I remain faithful on the post where He put me, the situation can become frightening for me [1941: Hitler's occupation] and I can be attacked from several sides, but the Spirit will maintain His calling [for me] also over against those who attack it. Perhaps I cannot do this, but *He* will.

Therefore, we go on working, offering, praying for schools with the Bible [i.e., Reformed schools where the Bible rules over, and the confession is maintained in the entire education of our chidlren, K.D.]. Perhaps, the time is coming when we are only able to pray. But even then we are not beaten. For God, who, in the end, will let the world perish upon the prayer of His church, will, upon the prayer for the hallowing of His Name, create the new world also in and through the [faithful Christian] school. It may not look that way at all at the present moment, but that new world will come, also via our faithfulness to the school with the Bible [and the Reformed Confession, K.D.]: O LORD, our Lord, how majestic is thy Name in all the earth (Holwerda, 1958: 102).
Let us not forget this urgent appeal of Holwerda.

Halloween

"Hallowing" — brings me to the name *Halloween,* the feast that is celebrated on October 31. This feast goes back to a practice of the ancient Druids in Britain and France, the Celtic tribes who lived hundreds of years before Christ was born. This celebration honoured one of their gods, namely, the *Lord of the Dead.* The date for the celebration was the last day of October, the eve of the Celtic new year. At that occasion the people needed much food, because the souls of the dead returned to their former homes. It was a big feast.

The church of the early Middle Ages wanted to *accommodate* the conquered people in these Celtic areas and replaced therefore All Saints Day (originally celebrated in May) to the 1st of November. On the evening before All Saints Day, the churches held a vigil for the saints called *All Hallows' Eve* (Eve of the Holy Ones) or All Hallows'

E'en, thus Halloween. So actually Halloween is a combination of the heathen feast of the Dead and the Roman Catholic feast of "all saints." A bad combination!

Luther Day

We celebrate a different fact on that day. For a long time, the last day of October was regarded the day of the *Reformation*. That had also to do with All Saints Day, because Luther wanted to dispute his 95 theses on the first day of Novermber 1517, when many theologians were together in Wittenberg on the occasion of the All Saints Day. In connection with the Reformation Day, I ask attention for Luther's words about *ongoing* reformation in a letter written seven years later. It was sent to the princes of the German states. Luther stated in it that Christian *schools* needed to be established and maintained. He wrote: "It is perfectly true that if universities and monasteries were to continue as they have been in the past, and there were no other place available where youth could study and live, then I could wish that no boy would ever study at all, but just remain dumb. For it is my earnest purpose, prayer, and desire that these asses' stalls and devil's training centers should either sink into the abyss or be converted into Christian schools. Now that God has so richly blessed us, however, and provided us with so many men able to instruct and train our youth aright, it is surely imperative that we not throw his blessing to the winds and let him knock in vain. He is standing at the door; happy are we who open to him! He is calling us; blessed is he who answers him! If we turn a deaf ear and he should pass us by, who will bring him back again?

Let us remember our former misery, and the darkness in which we dwelt. Germany, I am sure, has never before heard so much of God's word as it is hearing today; certainly we read nothing of it in history. If we let it just slip by without thanks and honor, I fear we shall suffer a still more dreadful darkness and plague. O my beloved Germans, buy while the market is at your door; gather in the harvest while there is sunshine and fair weather; make use of God's grace and word while it is there! For you should know that God's word and grace is like a passing shower of rain which does not return where it has once been. It has been with the Jews, but when it's gone it's gone, and now they have nothing. Paul brought it to the Greeks; but again when it's gone it's gone, and now they have the Turk. Rome and the Latins also had it; but when it's gone it's gone, and now they have the pope. And you Germans need not think that you will have it forever, for ingratitude and contempt will not make it stay. Therefore, seize it and hold it fast, whoever can; for lazy hands are bound to have a lean year" (Luther, 1962: 352ff.).

OUR PARENTAL PASTORATE

A quarter of a century ago someone in the Netherlands decided to publish a book of interviews. Fourteen people, formerly members of the Reformed church, had abandoned their Reformed faith. As a matter of course, such a book often contains quite an inventory of complaints, of many frustrations, and disappointments. In conclusion, however, the interviews were summarized, and then we also read the remarkable news that a professor of the synodical churches indicated feelings of sympathy with the remarks, and exclamations made by those ecclessiastical renegades, who had withdrawn themselves from the communion of the church.

It is even more remarkable to read that this professor agrees that "Calvinism does injury to children." He adds that, "It is well-known that Calvin used to stumble over the children" (Rothuisen, 1965: 214ff.).

Indeed, they dare to maintain the notion that Calvinism harms children. Their approach to the child was totally mistaken. Children missed proper guidance, and therefore the arrival of emancipation was an understandable phenomenon.

Over against this accusation, we want to show that our fathers did *not harm children at all. On the contrary, they understood their parental task. They also understood that parents have a pastoral* task over against their children. In this presentation we want to briefly discuss the parental pastorate as our fathers considered it. And then we will also see that in their care and concern for this pastorate they even promulgated synodical decrees during the reformation.

Guido de Brès

For just a moment, let us let our imagination take us back to the southern part of the Netherlands more than 400 years ago. The Reformed people were in the thick of many activities in that region. Some years before, Guido de Brès, minister of the church of Doornik (Tournay), had drafted a document to prove as clearly as possible to its readers, that the Calvinists had absolutely nothing to do with the rebellious Anabaptists. Over against this false allegation of rebellious collusion with the Anabaptists, he clearly expressed the desire of the Reformed church to conduct their relationship with the government along legal and legitimate channels.

This document was the booklet which would later be known in history as the Belgic Confession. In the summer of 1561, Guido de Brès probably had this booklet read by the University of Leyden professor, Saravia. Moreover, this booklet also received a form of ecclesiastical approbation and approval when the church of Antwerp officially expressed its agreement with it.

At this point, Rev. G. de Brès also wanted to send this booklet to the authorities, to make an urgent appeal to the rulers not to tar the Reformed people with the same brush used for the Anabaptists, as they had in the past.

Since the official channels had been closed to Guido de Brès, he had someone throw the booklet over the wall of the castle of Doornik, in the night of November 2, 1561. With the booklet de Brès also sent two letters directed to the attention of the king, Philip II, and another to the subordinate court officials. In addition, he also addressed a letter addressed to the commissaries of the king, or in their absence, the civil magistrates of the government of Doornik.

Neither de Brès' letter, nor the booklet ever reached its desired object. On November 4, 1561, already, Margaretha of Parma, the governor enacted a sharp edict against the propagation of the Confession which she had scarcely read! (De Pater, 1950:11).

As a direct consequence of this edict, Guido de Brès had to become a wanderer, always on the alert for enemies of the church. Initially he became a pastor of several churches in France, and then received a call from the church in Antwerp in 1566. The congregation in Valenciennes called him the year afterwards. In the latter place the enemies of the church caught up with him and persecuted him with imprisonment and then with death on the gallows in the same year, 1567, when he received the martyr's crown (Braekman, 1960: 264 ff.).

Antwerp

Antwerp has been mentioned several times already. In this city the Reformed church had immediately received the Belgic Confession as their own. Small wonder then, that this confession was initially called the "Confession d'Anvers" (confession of Antwerp).

I already mentioned earlier that Guido de Brès had been a minister of the church in Antwerp in the year before his death. Antwerp had become an important centre for the Reformed churches, for several synods had been held there and a number of important decisions had been made pertinent to the acceptance of the confession. This city had also become a very important international commercial centre by this time in history. And therefore very important to her Spanish overlords. This city would also become a focal point in the struggle for God and His Word in the Netherlands. Among the believers, the pen name of this city was "Capernaum." The church itself in this city was called "La Vigne" (the Vine).

You will notice that the churches in the southern Netherlands had such pen names more often. Armentieres was called "Flower bud" and Ghent was called "Lily" and the church in Valenciennes was called "the Eagle."

The Reformed people in Antwerp not only had a fierce struggle against the Romish, but they also had to fight the Anabaptists. This city had become an important Anabaptist centre. By 1565 they had no less than 25 to 30 places of public worship. No wonder that the church of Antwerp had asked for the help of Guido de Brès who had shown himself to be an indefatigable and well equipped opponent of the anabaptists.

The year before de Brès had come to Antwerp, Fabricius, their minister had suffered martyrdom. After the execution of their minister, the Reformed people of Antwerp made a united appeal to the governor, Margaretha. Is it not remarkable that they again submitted — together with their request — the Belgic Confession? Of course, it had become their confession of faith. But they too waited in vain for a response from the authorities.

Synod in "the Vine"

In the same year, 1565, a synod was held in Antwerp, the so-called Pentecost synod, held in "the Vine." This synod again dealt with the Belgic Confession. In Article 1 of the Acts of this synod, the Belgic Confession is called "the confession of faith of the churches in this country," as we saw already in the paragraph about the *Function of the Belgic Confession*.

"Pastors of their Families"

Perhaps you will ask: but what does this all have to do with our special topic. We also read at the very beginning (Article 3) of the Acts of the synod of Antwerp, 1565 — that is after having just established the place of the confession — the following statement: "The parents, as pastors in their families, must educate their children in the fear of God. Therefore they shall *not* send their children to schools or to other houses, where these children could be spoiled or attacked by an evil lifestyle and false doctrines." It is very remarkable that in the official decision of synod, the Reformed parents are called *"pastors of their families."* The parents, said this "Pentecost Synod in the Vine," have a pastoral task with regard to their children. What the minister is for his congregation, the parents must be for their children. There must be a pastorate in the families, which functions in such a way, that parents educate their children in the *fear of God*. In order to be able to execute this task in a positive way the parents must take care that their children are not drawn away from the fear of God at schools or other houses where they could be infected by evil lifestyles or false doctrine.

At that time there were indeed many houses where evil lifestyles and false doctrines were taught. Many people lived licentiously. And one should not forget the evil behaviour of so many clergymen in the Roman Catholic church. There was also false doctrine: in the false church, but also in the schools evil thoughts were rampant.

Confession and Pastorate

I am of the opinion that there is a stronger connection between the first and third articles of the Acts of the Synod of Antwerp than we would initially suppose. In the beginning, the synod again established the confession as the common accord among the churches. An emphatic statement of confessional commonality had to be established to show the unity of doctrine. But what sense would it have if a doctrine is officially established, but it does not function in the practice of daily church life?

In other words, the pastorate of the pastor and teacher can be based on the pure doctrine, which has been officially accepted in the church, but the primary task now lies in the hands of the parents in their "small pastorate," so that they instruct their children and have them instructed in the Reformed doctrine.

No Silted Reformation

More than four centuries ago, our fathers understood very well that a reformation may never be allowed to become silted up, and may never be placed on a dead track. But then, to prevent such calamities, it will be necessary that this reformation should receive a wide response in the families where the next generation must be educated in the fear of God. Then it will also be necessary that this reformation be continued in the *schools*, where the children must be instructed in the *"pura doctrina,"* the doctrine according to the confession, based on the infallible Word of God. This *"pura doctrina"* had been clearly defined over against Roman Catholics and Anabaptists, the double fronts in the time of the Reformation. Our fathers had high regard for that confession, for which its author and many believers had given their lives. They recognized the great importance of the unity of faith. Not everybody had to suffer the extreme experiences with respect to the confession, but together they did have to defend their common faith. And therefore it was of paramount importance to maintain this particular confession.

When pastors and teachers defended this doctrine, they had to lay a bridge with the families, where parents in their turn instructed their children in the doctrine. This pastoral task of the parents did not only become evident in their instruction, but also in the choice of places to which their children were sent: the houses and the schools.

These parents had the responsibility to examine whether good behaviour and the pure doctrine were promoted in these places. If the aforegoing was not evident, then it was part of their pastoral task to remove their children from these places, and then to look for houses and schools where doctrine and lifestyle in accordance with the Scriptures were defended and upheld.

Calvin's Inheritance

Do not think that these ideas, as stated in official decisions of a synod four centuries ago, were brand new. Our fathers at the "Pentecost Synod in the Vine" were good disciples of *Calvin*, who had died just a year earlier.

From the beginning, Calvin emphatically stressed the pre-eminent importance of the instruction of the *youth of the church*. It is important to take note of this fact. Generally speaking it is well-known that Calvin paid much attention to ecclesiastical discipline. But it is remarkable that many people often overlook the fact that Calvin considered the instruction of the young people in the church of equal importance with the ecclesiastical discipline.

No, Calvin did not harm the children. On the contrary, he paid great attention to the children of the church, by binding them to the doctrine which the parents had accepted as the pure doctrine according to the Word of God. Calvin said, "If the youth of the church is not instructed in the pure doctrine, in the houses, in the schools and in the church, then that would be at least as shameful and harmful as if the discipline were not maintained and the Holy Supper were defiled."

Calvin's first deed in the organization of ecclesiastical life in Geneva was the drafting of a regulation in which, in addition to discipline, also the instruction of the youth was established. Calvin said, "The instruction and education of the seed of the covenant is so important that the church cannot exist without it. Together with the discipline of the church, it is the important mean to further the perseverance and to promote the success of the reformation of the church. If this instruction of the youth fails, then all other labour is fruitless and useless, and there is no hope for the church anymore."

In Calvin's regulations we also read: "It is of great importance and very necessary — in order to keep the people in the pure doctrine — that the children of the church be instructed already, from their youngest age, that they are able to make profession of their faith, so that the doctrine of the gospel will not be destroyed, and that its significance will be remembered diligently, and be passed on from hand to hand and from father to son" (Van't Veer, 1942: 61 ff.).

Divine Command

Calvin understood very clearly that the foundation of this instruction of the youth of the church was not to be an idle wish, let alone a certain hobby, but rather, a *divine command*. He said: "If this command was ever fitting and suitable, now it is the more necessary, when we discover the disregard of the Word of God which we observe with most of the people, and also the neglect of the parents to instruct their children in the way of God. In this regard, an astonishing ignorance is noted, which is in no way acceptable in the church."

Time and again Calvin pointed to the parental task, which is, in this respect, a *pastoral task*. He says: "The parents are primarily responsible for the baptismal instruction. They have the duty to instruct their children, that a new generation may arise, equipped to the service of God. The LORD entrusted us with the doctrine of salvation, so that we would pass on that doctrine to our offspring. We must be diligent that God's government will be continued, that His service will not be interrupted, but will always flourish. We are entrusted with the responsibility that the true service of the LORD will be maintained and continued, also after our death. The existence of the church itself is at stake. That means: the progression of the service of the LORD in the generations after us. The seed of religion must remain after our death. And we as parents must take care that in the upcoming army of Jesus Christ, our children will receive their place."

The Priority of this Task

In Geneva, Calvin taught the elders of the church that this task with respect to their children, must have the highest priority. He obliged the parents not only to teach their children in the Scriptures of the Old and New Covenant, but also in the doctrine of the church. The ministers of the church had to supervise the progress of the instruction given by the parents. But also the church when it instructed the children every week, the parents were still obliged to instruct their children in the doctrine of the church. Their were given the responsibility that the pertinent part of the doctrine was really known by the children. The ministers asked questions, to evaluate the knowledge of the children, but also in to check the diligence of the parents.

As far as the schools were concerned: the teachers had the task to instruct the children in the Scriptures, but also in the *doctrine of the church*. This instruction was not considered to be a branch or a subject beside many others. In the first school order of 1538, the relationship of this instruction is described in this respect: that the Word of God and the doctrine of the church is the *foundation of the whole education.* The other branches of learning were to be considered as valuable aids, to promote true and full knowledge.

In this way, parents in Calvin's time, had to be pastors in their families, who instructed their children themselves, and had them instructed in the doctrine according to the Word of God. Completely in accordance with this practice, the synod of Antwerp decided one year after Calvin's death, that the parents had to educate their children in the Fear of God, as pastors of their families. And because of this pastorate in the family, they could not send their children to schools or other houses in which these children would be infected by wrong ideas, contrary to the pure doctrine.

Our fathers thoroughly understood: if there is to be a future for the church of the LORD, if the church is not to perish in this world, then new generations must arise time and again, which in the homes, in the schools and in the church, will be instructed in the doctrine of the Word of God.

This is a *primary* pastorate, this pastoral task in the families, that the parents pay close attention to these matters!

I am of the opinion that the church would have been spared much grief if this primary pastorate of the parents had been honoured continuously. If *father and mother* no longer understand their pastoral task with respect to their children; if parents do not give *priority* to this task, then without any doubt, *deformation* in the church will raise its ugly head!

Therefore this matter is also a primary concern: what is the state of the instruction of the seed of the covenant? Our concern is not only directed to the instruction in the church, the catechism instruction, but also the instruction done through the pastoral offices of the parents.

And no less, the instruction given in the schools.

Parents must also concern themselves with the question: to which school must we send our children? Do we keep a close eye on these schools in which our children receive instruction, that these schools do not spoil our children so that they become infected by bad behaviour and bad doctrines?

Are the schools connected to the instruction in the homes and in the church?

Do we really fight, and sacrifice for such schools which have this relationship, that they are properly maintained? Are we on our guard, that these schools, which began as Reformed schools, really *remain* Reformed schools?

Are the parents diligent, to the utmost of their power as pastors of their families to educate their children in the fear of God?

In one word, that is the calling of parents who fulfill their promises given at the baptism of their children, and who also understand their task.

Automatically?

Will everything then automatically go all right with respect to our children?

Of course not!

We cannot keep our children.

We can only *guard* them. That watchful service is a difficult but beautiful office. It is a pastoral office.

And if later these children turn away from the church, then it may never be said to have been caused by their parents who neglected their pastoral office.

Then never may we hear the reproach that "Calvinism does harm to the children" and that Calvin used children as a stumbling block.

Parents do not stumble over children, but children stumble over parents. They stumble over the office and the doctrine of the parents, which the parents wanted to entrust to them.

In this time of indoctrination of *false* doctrines, especially by means of the modern media, we have to dare to stand for the oath sworn at the baptismal font. We have to dare to say "no!" to the spirit of our days, which reproaches us of narrow-mindedness.

We will have to bear the accusation that we are extremist and conservative. Throughout the ages similar accusations have been heard. Such accusations are not the worst things to bear. What is much worse, is that we would neglect our primary pastoral task, that we refused to equip our children against the dangers of our time, and that we were passive over against the danger of the infections of evil behaviour and bad doctrines.

May the LORD grant us parents who want to be pastors in their families, who will teach their children to use the weapons with which they have to contend — not against flesh and blood — but against the principalities, against the powers, against the world rulers of this present darkness, against the spiritual hosts of wickedness in the heavenly places.

Therefore, may the LORD grant us parents and children who take the whole armour of God, that they may be able to withstand in the evil day, and having done all, to stand!

IV
". . . I WILL WORSHIP" (Psalm 5:7)

ESPECIALLY ON THE DAY OF REST

Lord's Day

We all know the expression taken from Lord's Day 38 of the Heidelberg Catechism, in answer to the question "What does God require in the fourth commandment?": "first . . . that, *especially on the day of rest,* I diligently attend the church of God to hear God's Word, to use the sacraments, to call publicly upon the LORD, and to give Christian offerings for the poor."

There are four elements mentioned in this answer concerning public worship. I am of the opinion that there is a special *order* in it: Word — sacraments — prayer — collection. I think it is wrong to throw these elements around, as if the order is arbitrary. But we will let that matter rest for now. Let us pay attention to the expression "that, especially on the day of rest, I diligently attend the church of God." That means that I have to attend the church of God, in the first place, on Sunday. Especially the day of rest is the day of public worship. But, apparently, there are more worship services than only on that day.

The question is now: Are there many other days of worship? If so, how many? Is it desirable to observe a number of those days? What about the Christian festivals? It is remarkable about 30% of the "Hymns and Paraphrases" of the *Book of Praise* are connected with Christian Feast days. That is quite a lot! But it is also remarkable that Article 52 of the Church Order says: "The consistory shall ensure that; as a rule, once every Sunday the doctrine of God's Word as summarized in the Heidelberg Catechism is proclaimed."

Other days?

There is, therefore, an obligation for public worship on Sunday, even twice. But what about the other days of public worship? In Article 53 of the Church Order we read about "Days of Commemoration," and there it says: "Each year the Churches shall, in the manner decided upon by the consistory, commemorate the birth, death, resurrection, and ascension of the Lord Jesus Christ, as well as His outpouring of the Holy Spirit." But we do not read there that these facts of salvation must be celebrated on special days *besides* the Lord's Day. No, there must be a commemoration of these facts, but "in the manner decided upon by the consistory." We see the same in Article 54 about "Days of Prayer": "In time of war, general calamities, and other great afflictions the presence of which is felt throughout the churches, a day of prayer may be proclaimed by the churches appointed for that purpose by general synod." (It is of interest to know that the Church of Burlington-West is one of these churches, appointed for this purpose, the other the Providence Church of Edmonton). Again, one cannot read in this article that a special day must be chosen for this purpose *besides* the Lord's Day.

In Article 65 we read that funerals are not ecclesiastical but family affairs, and should be conducted accordingly. That means, without a special public worship service on a workday. And what about marriages? According to Article 63, there may be a *choice:* "The solemnization of a marriage may take place either in a private

58

ceremony or in a public worship service." The conclusion is that neither confession (e.g., Heidelberg Catechism) nor Church Order point to many services on workdays, but that on the contrary, both of them stress the celebration of the Lord's Day as the day of rest, the day of public worship.

Scriptures about festivals

But I can imagine that one says: It may be true that confession and Church Order do not point to many services on workdays, but ultimately they are *based* on *Scripture*. So the question really is: what does Scripture say about this?

The Bible does not tell us very much concerning special days and special services. There *were* in the Old Dispensation special days and times. But that is not decisive for our days, because we confess in Article 25 of the Belgic Confession that Christ is the fulfillment of the law: "All shadows have been fulfilled, so that the use of them ought to be abolished among Christians."

In the New Testament, the dispensation of the Holy Spirit, we read about *Passover* (Acts 12:4) not in the context of the celebration of that day as a special day for the Christian church, but only as a reference to the time mentioned ("intending after the passover to bring him out to the people").

We read also about the day of *Pentecost* (Acts 20:16, 1 Cor. 16:8), "Paul had decided to sail past Ephesus, so that he might not have to spend time in Asia; for he was hastening to be at Jerusalem, if possible, on the day of Pentecost." I agree with *Calvin* in his commentary on this text: "There is no doubt that Paul had strong and important reasons for hurrying to Jerusalem, not because the sacredness of the day meant so much to him, but because strangers were in the habit of flocking to Jerusalem from all directions for the feastdays." So it concerned *Jewish* feast days!

And as for the second text: "But I will stay in Ephesus until Pentecost, for a wide door for effective work has opened to me, and there are many adversaries" — it is remarkable that Paul only mentions *Pentecost* in connection with a time-schedule, but that he writes in the same chapter about the *first day* of the week as a special day concerning worship. He points to one of the elements of public worship, namely, the *collection* (verse 2): "On the first day of every week, each of you is to put something aside and store it up."

Indeed the first day of the week was a special day. We read in the last book of the Bible that this day even received a special name. John writes (Rev. 1:10): "I was in the Spirit on the Lord's Day." *The Lord's Day*, that means without any doubt the first day of the week, the day of the resurrection of the Lord Jesus Christ. What about other special days?

We only read in the New Testament a reproach of Paul to the Galatians (4:10): "You observe days, and months, and seasons, and years!" Paul lists there what is involved in living by the Mosaic law: *days* (sabbaths, fast days, feast days, new moons), *months* (particularly observd during the Babylonic exile, Isa. 66:23), *times or seasons* (Passover, Pentecost, Tabernacle feast, Dedication days), and finally, *years* (the sabbatical year every seventh year and the year of Jubilee). Calvin asks in his commentary on this text: "What sort of observance did Paul reprove?" and he answers: "It was that which would bind the conscience by religion, as something that was necessary to the worship of God, and which, as he says in Romans 14:5ff., "would make a distinction between one day and another." So also should we understand the admonition of Paul to the Colossians: "Therefore let no one pass judgment on you in questions of food and drink or with regard to a festival or a new moon or a sabbath. These are only a shadow of what is to come; but the substance belongs to Christ." So, for instance, festivals had been prescribed in the Old Testament, but now, in the New Testament, after Christ's coming in the flesh one cannot be obliged to observe them.

I quote Calvin again: "Those who make a distinction of days, separate, as it were, one from another. Such a partition was suitable for the Jews, that they might celebrate religiously the days appointed, by separating them from others. Among Christians such a division has ceased. But someone will say, 'We still keep some observance of days.' " "I answer," Calvin says, "that we do not by any means observe days, as though there were any sacredness in holy days, or as though it were not lawful to work on them, but this is done for government and order, not for the days." Calvin respected the decisions of the government, and I shall come back to that point. It is quite understandable, therefore, that the early church celebrated only one Christian feast day, namely, the Lord's Day.

Abolishment of festivals

In the beginning of the Christian church there were no special public worship services besides the services on the Lord's Day. The congregation held her meetings, often early in the morning and in the evening. There was a festal celebration of the Lord's Supper as well. But there were no other festivals.

When later on the Reformers of the 16th century fell back on the early church, they would have liked to abolish the many festivals beyond the Lord's Day. In 1520 Luther sighs that the Lord's Day might be the only feast day. When Calvin arrived in Geneva in 1536 he stressed from the very beginning of the Reformation the Lord's Day as the only feast day. Farel and Vinet were not inclined to acknowledge any human institution, but to respect only the Lord's Day.

Even the matter of the celebration of festivals was one of the reasons for Calvin's and Farel's banishment. After their return the council of Geneva instituted four feast days: Christmas Day, Circumcision Day, Mary-Annunciation Day and Ascension Day. To work on these days was forbidden.

As for the Reformation in the Netherlands, the Synod of Dort 1574 decided that one had to be satisfied with only the Lord's Day. Synod approved of preaching on the Lord's Day before Christmas concerning Christ's birth, of giving attention in the sermon on Easter to Christ's resurrection and on Pentecost to the pouring out of the Holy Spirit. But these days must not be considered as festivals above the Lord's Day.

This synodical decision was not appreciated by the civil government, who wanted to maintain some festivals, although not the same in all the provinces. So the next Synod of Dort 1578 decided that preaching should take place on those feast days which had been maintained by the government "in order that people should not loaf." This included both Christmas days, which had been established again (although reluctantly), the days of Easter and Pentecost, in some regions New Year's Day and Ascension Day, and sometimes some other festivals, not mentioned. But it is very clear that there was much ecclesiastical resistance against special Christian festivals besides the Lord's Day (Koopmans, 1941:22 ff,).

Oldest festival: Easter

In the beginning of the Christian Church one celebrated only the Lord's Day. One considered the Lord's Day as the *weekly* commemoration of Christ's resurrection. Christ rose from the dead on the first day of the week. So that was *the* festival, which was celebrated in the meeting of the congregation. Very early data are available to confirm that. Although the Jewish Sabbath had not been abolished right away in the beginning of the new dispensation of Pentecost, it was gradually abolished and substituted by the Lord's Day (cf. Francke, 1973:194; Koole, 1974:13). *Ignatius* writes for example, in the beginning of the 2nd century that the Sabbath must not be observed any more by the Christians. He also uses, in Rome, the term "Lord's Day" as a day of public worship. But besides the *weekly* celebration of Christ's resurrection, there was the beginning of the *yearly* commemoration (Rozdorf, 1972: 134ff.).

There are data which go back to the middle of the 2nd century and that are within one century after the apostles' death. In the time of *Tertullian,* the old-Christian author from the end of the 2nd and the beginning of the 3rd century, the celebration of Easter already extended for more than one day. In the term *"Pascha"* he summarizes a period of fasting, and administering baptism (Dekkers, 1947:147ff.). Also an Easter sermon by *Melito* of Sardes, which was held very early in the day, has been preserved. He lived in the latter part of the 2nd century. We learn from it that at that time there was a kind of "comprehensive" celebration of Easter. The suffering, the death and the resurrection of Jesus Christ were not separated, but considered as a whole. So there was not a special "Good Friday," to commemorate Christ's death and a separate Easter day to remember Christ's resurrection, but it was considered in its entirety: the comprehensive, all-inclusive work of salvation of the Redeemer, summarized in "Pascha" (Vander-Waal, 1979:161).

It would take too much time to explain how it was possible that besides the weekly Lord's Day there was also a yearly celebration of Christ's resurrection. It must be sufficient to know that this was connected with the Jewish calendar year. The Passover date was the 14th of Nisan to the Jews, but the Council of Nicea 325 left that date over against the Jews as a fixed date for the celebration of Easter. It was decided then to celebrate Easter depending on when there was a new moon. Until now that decision is still executed, namely, to celebrate Easter on the first Lord's Day after the first full moon of Spring.

Jerusalem in the 4th century

Starting with the rule of Constantine the Great, important changes occurred in the Christian Church. Simplicity was then replaced by abundance. The antithetical attitude of the church changed into one of accommodation. The doctrine of salvation acquired, from pagan mystery religions, a mystical notion. Important ecclesiastical centres arose and also with respect to liturgical matters considerable changes came to pass. After the Council of Nicea 325, Constantine visited Jerusalem and the church buildings which he and his mother Helena had built. This contributed greatly to the development of the liturgy of the Jerusalem Church in the 4th century. The pilgrimage of Helena to the holy city was taken as an example by many others.

There was, for instance, a nun of Northern Spain, called *Egeria,* who visited Jerusalem in 381-384 A.D. She wrote a travel story about that journey and gave many details of the Jerusalem liturgy of bishop *Cyril.* Time and again she writes that in the services in Jerusalem hymns, antiphons and Scripture-readings were "according to the day and the place." Special attention is paid to Palm Sunday, the Sunday before Easter, when the bishop enters Jerusalem like Christ did before, surrounded by the people, saying "Hosanna!" Special attention is also paid to the many, many services in the so-called "Great Week," the week before Easter, and in the Easter week itself. The bishop again took Christ's place, He performed as a holy person, who impersonated Christ. All the services were conditioned by *topographical* factors. The places at which the bishop performed were carefully chosen, according to the requirements of the situation and the time. A *dramatic repetition* was staged of the things which happened when salvation was accompanied by Christ Himself (Wilkinson, 1971:131ff.).

But the frequent services were very tiring, so that by the end of the week the people that followed the bishop from the one holy place to the other and from the one service to the other, were extremely tired. Egeria writes concerning the early morning of Good Friday: "The bishop addresses the people, comforting them, because they have laboured the whole night long and they are to work this whole day, encouraging them not to weaken, but to have hope in God, who will for this labour bestow on them an even greater reward. So comforting them as he is able, he adresses them, 'Now go again, each one of you to your homes, sit there for a while, and be ready to be back here about eight o'clock, so that from that hour until about noon you may be able to see the holy wood of the cross, which we believe to be profitable to the salvation of each of us. And from noon on we must again assemble here, that is, before the cross, that we may devote ourselves to readings and prayers until the night.' "

Actually there was a whole Easter cycle with many special days and special services. Rome itself adopted from Jerusalem the Palm Sunday procession and the adoration of the cross. It was told that Helena found the wood of the cross in the neighborhood of Jerusalem, more than four centuries after Christ's death! Egeria is convinced, too, that it was the wood of Christ's cross. So on Good Friday she writes, "the bishop's chair is set up on Golgotha behind the cross, which now stands there; the bishop is seated on the chair, and before him is placed a table covered with a linen cloth. The deacons stand in a circle around the table and the silver casket decorated with gold is brought in, in which is the holy wood of the cross. It is opened and taken out, and both the wood of the cross and the title are placed on the table. While it is on the table, the bishop sits and grasps the ends of the holy wood with his hands, and the deacons, who are standing around him, keep watch. Here is why they guard it so. It is the custom that all of the people here come one by one, the faithful and the catechumens, bowing before the table, kissing the holy cross and moving on. I was told that this was because someone (I do not know who) bit off and stole some of the holy cross. Now it is guarded by the deacons so that it dare not be done by someone again. So all of the people pass through one by one, bowing, first with their foreheads and then with their eyes touching the cross and the title and so kissing the cross they pass through, but no one is permitted to put a hand on the cross. But when they have kissed the cross, they go on. . . ."

The whole Easter cycle is marked by a development according to this description of Egeria of the Jerusalem model.

After the 4th century the church calendar is gradually filled up with festivals, feastdays, and saints days. In the 8th century 106 dates are occupied in the calendar year as special days and festivals. In the 16th century, at the end of the Middle Ages, only four dates are still vacant. . . .

The whole Christian year becomes a sacramental preaching of special services with a sacrosanct meaning.

Christmas

So there is a development from Jerusalem to Rome, and there is a development from one day, the Lord's Day, as a festival, to many days, almost all the days of the year, with special services. There are three main cycles: before Easter (the fasting time), then the time between Easter and Pentecost, and at last the Christmas cycle.

As for *Christmas Day,* it is remarkable that the Eastern Church celebrated Christ's birth on the 6th of January, the so-called *Epiphany,* while the Western Church since about 336 said, "No, it must be December 25th." But both dates originated in heathenism. In the East the Epiphany, the appearance of the godhead on earth, played a big role in religion. It was a matter of showing the power of the godhead. Epiphany became more and more the day of the appearance of Christ, a combination of His birth and His baptism.

In the Western world one celebrated the 25th of December as the day of Christ's birth. But this day originated also in heathenism as a festival. All kinds of calculations had been made in order to "find" that date. The 25th of March was the Roman start of Spring, also the date of the creation of the world. So it was argued that that *must* have been the date of annunciation of the angel Gabriel to Mary. The next conclusion was that the resurrection should have taken place on the same date, namely March 25th. That must have been exactly on the 30th birthday of Christ, because actually the new beginning, the start, was His conception on the annunciation day. The final conclusion was that Mary was of course pregnant for nine months, so she gave birth to Jesus on December 25th. . . . But this calculation is as fantastic as it is incredible!

How did one come to December 25th? The answer is not difficult, if we keep in mind that to the world of Rome in the 3rd and 4th century the 25th of December was called "the day of the invincible Sun." This Sun service originated in the East as well, but it was extended to the whole Roman empire. In the background we must also see the influence of the mystery religions, with which the Roman soldiers were involved, as for example in Persia. A kind of Sun religion came about. The Sun, in its mild warmth and big scorching power, high above the earth, but powerful on earth, became a symbol of the godhead, who sees everything, but is not ruled by anything. This Sun is called the conqueror of darkness. The victory of the Sun was especially celebrated on the day of the change of winter season as the day of turning. The Sun, which in the preceding weeks always seemed to diminish, then resumed glorifying its power.

But how is it that about the year 336 in Rome the date came up as a Christian festival? About this question a late Syrian text from the 13th century sheds some light. We read in it: "The reason, why the fathers changed the feast of 6th of January and shifted it to December the 25th, was this. The heathen were used to celebrating, on December the 25th, the feast of the birthday of the Sun and to light lamps on that day. They also let Christians participate in that feast of joy and spectacle. Because the teachers of the church perceived that the Christians were attracted by it, they made precautions and celebrated on that day — December 25th — henceforth the feast of the true birth, the birth of Jesus Christ, but on January 6th the feast of His appearance."

Here is said clearly that the necessity of *competition* with a heathen festival caused the celebration of Christ's birth on December 25th. But the truth is that nobody knows on what date Christ was born, and the Holy Spirit, who wrote the Scriptures, did not deem it of that importance, that it should be mentioned in the Bible. In any case, it could not have taken place on December 25th. When I was in Bethlehem 12 years ago I was told that at that time of the year it never happened that sheep were in the field. From at least the month of December until the end of February the sheep were always kept inside the stables.

After the year 325, when freedom had been given to the church, Christendom became the main religion. The world joined the church, but then the great danger appeared that the church would become worldly. Many people took their heathen pattern of life with them and all kinds of customs survived under the cloak of Christianity. In this way all kinds of adoration of many female godheads were delegated to "Mother Mary."

In the same light we have to consider the maintaining of December 25th as the birthday of Christ. One was accustomed to celebrating that day as the festival of the invincible Sun. The Christian leaders now maintained this day as the birthday of the "Sun of justice," and applied that to Christ.

So Christmas on December 25th became a Christian festival. We can speak here of a *concession* to heathenism, at least of an accommodation to heathen data. We have to keep that in mind when people sometimes consider December 25th as "the day of days" and Christmas as the most holy feast! (Van Unnik, 1951:9; cf. also Zwart, 1947:57ff.).

Abolition?

We do not plead for *abolition* of all Christian festivals. It is not possible to turn back the clock. Especially when there is a *social* motive, in which the historical element also plays a role. But we plead for *soberness*. There is no reason for many festivals besides the Lord's Day. There is also the right soberness in the new version of the Church Order. Let us be sober in all kinds of weekday services. Then we have to do our daily work. Maybe it will be good to mention that the weekly services, for instance, in the refugee congregation of London, had the character of *prophecy*. It was more a matter of teaching and discussing a special passage of Scripture. But, we now have our Christian societies for Bible studies, and I like to emphasize the importance of them!

The conclusion, therefore, is, come and let us worship on the Lord's Day, the real and true Christian festival. Keep in mind that there are people, who easily neglect public worship on Sunday, but who do not want to miss one service on the "Christian festivals," and who would rather enlarge the number of them! There is an abundant celebration of these special days, with all kinds of connotations, in which soberness is totally missed. There is much reason, to consider the Lord's Supper as a festive celebration, in which the *whole* work of Christ's salvation is comprehensively surveyed: the purpose of His coming into the world, His suffering and crucifixion, His resurrection and ascension, His sitting on the right hand of the Father, His return on the clouds of heaven. There is no clear order to celebrate all kinds of special days: New Year's Eve, New Year's morning, Good Friday, Ascension Day, Easter, Pentecost, Christmas even on second days, and so on. So let us be sober in it. But there is a clear order of a regular and joyful celebration of the Lord's Supper by the words of Christ Himself: "Do this in remembrance of Me." And we shall do that, until He comes!

LITURGY AS COVENANT SERVICE

Covenant service

Those who say *worship* also say *covenant service*. Not that these two are completely similar to each other, but in the worship service the covenant of God with His people is always present. When the LORD establishes a covenant with His people, He wants to *live* with that people. He proclaims His word to that people. He elicits a response from His people. For that reason a house was built for Him in the wilderness and therefore the tabernacle was called the "tent of meeting." Because Israel may share in the merciful communion with the Lord, the poet sings in Psalm 84 that he longs for God's courts.

In addition to the place of meeting, God also established fixed *times* of meeting. On the seventh day there was a holy convocation. This gathering was convened by the priests blowing upon silver trumpets and was considered a festive gathering, as often is emphasized in the Psalms.

The sacrifice of the atonement is central in Old Testament temple worship. On the day which the LORD had determined for this holy gathering, the offering was *doubled*. The assembled congregation was clearly shown that the communion with the LORD was based on the atoning blood. Without the pouring of the blood there is no forgiveness (Hebrews 9:22). The worship service of the Old Testament shows: the two parties in the covenant *meet* each other. On the foundation of the blood of the atonement they exercise *communion*. On the day hallowed for that purpose, the day of meeting, God calls His people *together*.

In the Old Testament, God approached His people with the *glad tidings* of the atonement. He put His Name upon Israel and blessed the people. In the temple God's grace was shown to the people by means of the ministry of the priests. The people also heard about God by means of the *instruction* by the priests.

But also the *second party* in the covenant was active. They approached God with the *incense* of their prayers and came to Him with their *exultant hymns*.

Liturgy

In the New Testament, the word *leitourgia* makes its appearance. This is a Greek word, which actually means: a service for the *well-being* of the people. This service does not concern *private* or *individual* occasions, but refers to the *community*. It concerns the people as a whole, in their totality. We must see the people as a community, organized in the form of a "polis," a city-state.

Our word "liturgy" has been derived from this word; it is the word we also use for our worship services.

But in the first place, this word typifies the *official position and work of Christ, wherein and through which He has completed the Old Testamentic cult, in that He brought the real sacrifice and now completes His work as high priest in the real heavenly sanctuary*.

After Christ had founded the new covenant, the word (liturgy) becomes an indication of the worship service, such as this takes place in the assemblies of the congregation. The *altar* and the *sacrifice have disappeared*. The atonement has been accomplished. The shadows have been fulfilled. Now it is called a gathering, an assembly of the church, a gathering of the congregation.

The central idea of the New Testamentic worship service is that God and His people meet each other in the assembly of the exalted Christ-with-His-own people, on the day of Christ's exaltation, the first day of the week. Now, whenever two or three — the smallest possible plurality — are gathered in His Name, there He will be in their midst. In the worship service, the two parties of the covenant are together. God is the First. The initiative comes from Him. He calls the gathering together. But the two parties meet each other in the mutual exchange of love. Therefore the congregation is also active: she may pray and sing. But it is response-motivated, as instigated by God, who, as the First One, comes to meet His people.

Not prescribed

"All right," one will say, "but is there anywhere a certain liturgy *prescribed?"* Is it not true that the whole matter of liturgy is actually a matter of *tradition*? That tradition plays such a big role in liturgical matters is shown by the fact that each and every *change* often is considered by many as an *attack* on their spiritual life.

According to our Belgic Confession, Article 7, we confess that "we may not consider any writings of men, however *holy* these men may have been, of equal value with the divine Scriptures; nor ought we to consider *custom*, or the great *multitude*, or antiquity, or *succession* of times and persons, or councils, decrees or statutes, as of *equal value* with the truth of God." Over against the Roman Catholics with their tradition, our *fathers* stated this very clearly and maintained it consistently. Tradition does not have the *same value*, nor stands on the same level as the Word of God, let alone that tradition would have the final word. Time and again we have to *test* church matters, also liturgical matters by the Word of God itself. It is also wise that Article 50 of the Church Order says, in the last sentence: "On minor points of Church Order and ecclesiastical practice Churches abroad shall not be rejected." In former days, especially *liturgical matters* were meant in this respect.

I think one is right in saying that *nowhere* in the Bible a complete liturgy is prescribed and that much is based on custom. However, we have to add two things. In the first place: although not *everything* is prescribed in the Bible concerning the liturgy of the church, there is given us a certain basic pattern, from which all liturgy is to be derived. In the second place: not all customs are wrong. There is also a *good tradition,* which is not to be abandoned without good reason.

Basic pattern

The *basic pattern* of "liturgy" for the church of the New Dispensation is given in the same chapter in which is mentioned the pouring out of the Holy Spirit, namely, Acts 2. After Luke mentions immense growth of the church at Pentecost, he adds in verse 42: "And they devoted themselves to the apostles' teaching and fellowship, to the breaking of bread and the prayers." As a matter of fact that are four elements, which can be called decisive for the dispensation of the New Testament church. The teaching of the apostles means: the doctrine, taught by the apostles. We could interpret this as: *the reading and preaching of the Word of God.* In the RSV it is not fully clear that "fellowship" is a new element. The Greek word speaks of the communion of saints in a concrete manner, namely, in what later on was called the "offering," or the "collection" in the worship service. In the beginning the believers brought their offerings in natural gifts. In that way the poor were provided for by the rich. The third element is the *breaking of bread,* which is the celebration of the *Lord's Supper.* In the church of Corinth it was preceded by the so-called "agapai," the meals of love. Finally Luke mentions in Acts 2 the *prayers.* It appears that the prayers formed an essential part of the worship service already in the beginning of the New Testament church.

When we oversee these *four elements,* we can say that there is a remarkable *order* in them: *doctrine — communion — sacrament — prayer.* It is the order of Word and answer in God's covenant. First comes the doctrine, the reading and explanation of God's Word, in which the LORD Himself speaks. Then follows the answer of the congregation in the communion of saints: the care for one another. Again the LORD comes with His *promises* in the sacrament, the breaking of bread, and the *answer* follows, in the prayers of God's people, prayers which are at the same time offerings of thanksgiving, and also sometimes in the singing of the congregation.

When we place these elements of the worship service after Pentecost beside the *explanation of the Fourth Commandment* of God's covenant law in the Heidelberg Catechism, we see a remarkable agreement. Lord's Day 38, referring to Acts 2:42, mentions that the ministry of the gospel must be maintained, and continues to say that, especially on the day of rest, I have to diligently attend the church of God, in order to do especially four things:

1. to hear God's Word;
2. to use the sacraments;
3. to call publicly upon the LORD;
4. to give Christian offerings to the poor.

The reading and the preaching of the Word of God is the most important part and, therefore, comes first. Then the sacraments follow, as an underlining and affirmation of the Word of God. Moreover the prayers, inclusive the intercessions are mentioned, and finally the response of the congregation receives its place in the Christian charity. There is a clear *parallel* here with what is mentioned in Acts 2, whereby the two parts and the two parties of God's covenant are shown very clearly.

Arbitrary elaboration?

When we now pay attention to the other elements which have received a place in the worship service, it will be clear that they are *grouped* around the four main elements mentioned in Acts 2, and in Lord's Day 38. Of course, a certain *tradition* has been formed here, but that does not mean that an arbitrary extension has taken place. We take our starting point in the second order of worship as recommended by the Synod of Cloverdale 1983 (Orders of Worship B, *Book of Praise*, p. 582 ff.), because these orders go back to Calvin who himself always pointed to the early church. We follow hereby the *16* elements for the *morning service*.

1. *Votum.* We have here a quotation of the last verse of Psalm 124, one of the songs of Ascents (Psalms 120-134). These Psalms were sung in processions when the Israelite pilgrims were ascending Mount Zion at the occasion of the three great temple festivals of the Jewish year. Then the people of Israel came to present themselves before the LORD, the God of the covenant, in order to worship Him, to call upon His Name, since their only help was in the Name of the LORD, the Almighty God, who created heaven and earth. Israel was dependent on the active presence of the LORD. The same can be said of God's people today, who are starting each and every public worship service in dependence on the God of the covenant, who created all things.

2. *Salutation.* When, in the beginning of his letters, the apostle Paul gives his apostolic *greetings* to the congregation he points to the rich promise of God's covenant in which the LORD meets His people with His grace and peace. The apostle John does the same in the last book of the Bible. In the very same way the *salutation* in God's Name to the congregation follows the votum. It is the mouth of the minister speaking words like 1 Corinthians 1:3, 1 Timothy 1;2 or Revelation 1:4 and 5a, but, actually, it is the very Word of God Himself; it is the LORD God Himself greeting His covenant people with His covenant promises.

3. Congregational Singing. Upon that Word of promise expressed in the salutation there follows then an answer-Psalm from the side of the people of God's covenant. It is clear that this singing has this character of being a response. It is not just an arbitrary song, but an answer to God's Word of promise. I would like to make the remark here that each Psalm in the Bible is to be taken in its entirety. Therefore, it is advisable, if possible, not to sing just one or two stanzas, but the whole Psalm, just as Israel did. Of course, many Psalms are too long, and would take too much time to sing them as a whole, but it is important to stress that the ideal is not only a single stanza but the entire Psalm.

4. *The Ten Words of the Covenant.* They can be taken from Exodus 20:2-17 or Deuteronomy 5:6-21. Already in the Old Testament the reading of the *law* of the LORD was an important element of the worship service, and the same can be said

of the synagogue. Also before the Reformation of the 16th Century, here and there the law of the LORD was read in the worship service, but Calvin brought the law back into the worship service as a regular part of it. Actually, the name *law* is not completely correct, for in Exodus 20 (and also Deuteronomy 5) there is a clear coherence between the promise and the obligation of God's covenant.

First there are the opening *words* of the law, in which the LORD God *announces* Himself. I refer to that one sentence, written in the beginning of Exodus 20 (we hear that *every* Sunday morning in public worship): "I am the LORD your God, who brought you out of the land of Egypt, out of the house of bondage." We have to *bear in mind* what this sentence *means*. It is *not* a mere *introduction*, which has little or nothing to do with the *contents* of God's law, but these opening words are the PROMISE of God, which accompanies *all* Ten Commandments. In this promise, the LORD God *announces* Himself as the God of His *covenant,* who is very *high* and *exalted,* but who, at the same time, bows Himself down in deep *mercy* to His people, and who wants to *show* Himself as the Father of His children.

Therefore, in these opening words we have, right from the beginning, the *twofold* idea, which must be remembered with all God's commandments, namely, that in this promise the LORD announces Himself as the *Almighty,* who is exalted *far above* all creatures, while, at the same time, He announces Himself as the *God of His covenant,* who *magnifies* Himself by His great *deeds* in history, the God of the *communion,* the fellowship in His covenant.

Then the Ten Words follow, expressing the covenant obligations. These Ten Words must always be read in the light of the opening words, God's promise. Therefore, I prefer to speak about the *constitution of God's covenant,* consisting of two parts: the promise and the obligation of the covenant of the LORD.

Already for this reason we should not replace this *constitution* of God's covenant by some admonishing parts of letters from the *New Testament.* There are some who prefer this and say: let us read a few parts of the New Testament letters instead of the law from Exodus 20 or Deuteronomy 5. However, the whole of God's covenant with its two parts is involved! I also do not like to read after the constitution of Exodus 20 or Deuteronomy 5 the *summary* as found in the New Testament, in the words of Christ found in Matthew 22. In the first place, Christ gave that summary in a very special context, in an argument with the *Pharisees.* In the second place, Moses had summarized God's Ten Words in the same way. However, my main reason is that in this summary the *first constituting element* of God's covenant, namely His promise, is not mentioned.

5. *Congregational Singing.* After this Word of God's covenant the answer of God's people follows again in the singing of a *Psalm.* This Psalm must have something to do with that constituting idea of God's covenant. It can be a Psalm in which we confess our sins, because we did not keep God's commandments as we ought to do. It can also be a *Psalm of praise,* because of God's faithfulness in His covenant. If possible, it is to be preferred that a Psalm is chosen in line with the first Psalm, or — when not the whole Psalm was sung — another part of that Psalm.

6. *Prayer.* (In this order of worship it is the prayer that contains, among others, a public confession of sins, as well as a prayer for forgiveness, for spiritual renewal, and for illumination by the Holy Spirit.) We have to be *aware of this nice order.* First of all, the law of the LORD is read to the people, together with the promise of God's covenant. The life of God's children does not respond to the obligation of God's covenant. But God's people may pray for forgiveness, renewal of heart

and *illumination* by the Holy Spirit, who promises to work with the Word of God. Hence this prayer is also an introduction to the reading and the preaching of God's Word.

7. Now follows the *reading of the Bible*. It has been said that one or more passages may be read, related to the sermon, and that this can be followed by *singing*. However, according to the custom of the early church the reading of the Bible and the preaching of God's Word belong together. Our Lord Jesus Himself followed this custom, by reading a passage of Isaiah, and preaching on that Word of God, right away (cf. Luke 4).

8. After one or more passages of the Holy Scriptures are read, there follows the *reading of the text,* and then comes the:

9. *Ministry of the Word.* This ministry of the Word of God is the proclamation of God's Word which is, at the same time, the explanation of the Holy Scriptures, the *administration of reconciliation,* appropriated and applied to God's people today, in their special circumstances. This teaching and preaching is the first element mentioned in Acts 2 and Lord's Day 38. It also received its position of honour in the whole of the (reformed) *liturgy of God's covenant.* It is and has to remain the main part of public worship service, and it may not be replaced by a short meditation or by a short timely word, the "topic of the day." No, it is to be the living proclamation of God's Word itself. With it the Holy Spirit will work in the hearts of God's people. Therefore we may not reduce this preaching, but we have to give it its rightful place. After the preaching of the Word of God follows:

10. *The Responsive Song* of the congregation: the Word of God is responded to by the people of God's covenant. Also this song may not be an *arbitrary* Psalm or Hymn, but should be such a song which expresses the idea that the Word of God that was heard is to be affirmed by a life which is fitting to God's covenant.

11. It is at this point that the *administration of the Holy Baptism* can take place. In this way we have a more correct order: the first means of grace with which the LORD comes to His people in His Word, in the administration of this Word. It is followed by the second means, the sacrament.

12. Hereafter will take place *prayer,* that is, the thanksgiving for the Word of God, as well as the prayer for all the needs of Christendom, the intercessions, also in response to the Word of God and its preaching.

13. Now the congregation brings her *offerings,* according to what is said in Lord's day 38, "to give Christian offerings to the poor," and Acts 2:42. Therefore, the collection has a proper, Scriptural place in the public worship service. To offer something for the poor is an integral part of worshiping God.

14. After the sermon also the *administration of the Lord's Supper* can follow, again as the second means of God's grace in His covenant. It is not correct to speak about a service of the Lord's Supper. The *Form for the Lord's Supper* is not a sermon. It is only an explanation for the people of God's covenant. Also when we celebrate the Lord's Supper, we should first listen to the preaching of the Word of God, the first means of God's grace in His covenant.

15. In the *closing song* God's people may again give their response to God's grace and praise the LORD with their singing.

16. Then follows the *benediction.* Just as the people of the Old Dispensation received the Aaronitic blessing according to Numbers 6, and as the apostle wrote his farewell to the church of the New Testament, e.g., as in 2 Corinthians 13, so the congregation receives, and takes home in faith, God's blessing.

In the afternoon service, the *Apostles' Creed* has not the same place as the *Constitu-*

tion of God's Covenant in the morning service. We refer again to the order B, as advised by the Synod of Cloverdale 1983. Also the confession of faith fits within the framework of the covenant communion: God speaks and God's people respond. First, in the morning service, there is the Law, or rather, the constitution of God's covenant. It is God speaking His Word. Then, in the afternoon service, in the confession of faith, we have the response of faith of God's people. It is, therefore, a good thing that the congregation herself is actively participating in this act of confessing, for instance by *singing* the Apostles' Creed.

Variety

In the beginning of this article we said that there is such a beautiful order in our public worship service, especially as presented sub number B (p. 582ff. of the *Book of Praise*), and that this order is derived from the order of *John Calvin*. We know that Calvin was in favour of going back to the early church and that he stressed that the church of the Reformation should honour the good customs of the early New Testament church in the times of the apostles and shortly thereafter. In this order, the Word and the response of God's people alternate constantly.

Besides order B, we have order of worship A variety in this sense that in A (p. 581ff. of the *Book of Praise*). This is the so-called "old order." In fact, this order is not so very old; it goes back to the Dutch synod of Middelburg, 1933. I do not want to say that this order A misses the Biblical, covenantal characteristic of expressing the meeting of God and His people in which God speaks His Word and God's people respond in faith, but I want to stress that the best Reformed tradition is given in order B.

"Out of custom or superstition"

Our conclusion is in the first place that we may not do anything in the whole matter of liturgy out of custom or superstition. We all know these words. They are derived from the beginning of the questions asked at the baptismal font. Over against the danger of an act "out of custom or superstition" it is stated that we have to use the sacrament of baptism for the purpose that to us and our children God's *covenant* is sealed.

"Out of custom" is wrong also with respect to the liturgy of God's covenant but *according to a custom* is not wrong! In the passage of the Scriptures in which Jesus' preaching in the synagogue in Nazareth is mentioned, we read that the Lord "went to the synagogue, as His custom was, on the Sabbath day" (Luke 4:16). That was a good custom! Let us, therefore, continue this good custom, as a Scriptural tradition: to "diligently attend the church of God," "especially on the day of rest." In this respect we can even speak of an "apostolic tradition." This has nothing to do with the Roman equalization of Scripture and tradition, nor with the Roman "apostolic succession," but it is a matter of continuing what, already in the apostolic era, was seen as *liturgy of God's covenant.*

This does not mean that in the liturgy of God's covenant nothing could be improved any more. On the contrary, discussions on the worship service and the customs and traditions in it, are always necessary. We do not need to aim for a *multitude* of liturgical forms, but we ought to have as goal that in our liturgy we remain *true* to God's covenant. Let our liturgy not become a dead service. Not the extent, but the intensity must be our goal. We can also say, let us aim for depth rather than for breadth in our liturgy. K. Schilder said once: "No liturgical forms, just because of tradition." And also: "The Word of life demands living words" (Schilder, 1952:76). Dead forms can lead to the situation in which a congregation is preached to death or, at least, gets tired. But the LORD wants to have a living congregation, living people of His covenant, which is taught by the living proclamation of His Word!

A MISSING LINK IN REFORMED LITURGY

Cradle

Four and a half centuries ago John Calvin had to leave Geneva and go to Strasbourg.

What Calvin did in that European city with respect to liturgy is very important. No doubt T. Brienen was right when he recently said that Calvin already in the first edition of his *Institutes* had drafted a certain order for public worship, especially for the service of Word and sacrament (Brienen, 1987:82ff.). No doubt it is also true that Calvin remained faithful to this first draft throughout his whole life. Nevertheless I would like to maintain that the cradle of Reformed liturgy is neither Basle (where Calvin wrote his *Institutes*), nor Geneva (where the Reformer lived for a long time), but Strasbourg, where he was in exile for three years. There Calvin, to a large extent, crystallized a detailed order which had been used already for several years, with special attention to what precedes the reading and preaching of the Word of God. There Calvin was also in a position to start the Psalter in a rhymed version, which was finished later on in Geneva. This appeared to be of great importance for Reformed worship.

Preaching

As far as preaching is concerned, Calvin followed the custom which originated in the beginning of the 16th century. In 1503, Johann Ulrich Surgant of Basle wrote a handbook for preaching in which he pleaded that worship services be improved. This improvement had to start with the preaching. He directed himself especially to the young preachers, the "freshmen." He also described the preaching as it existed in his days in some parish churches at Basle and in some villages in Alsace. This preaching was done completely in the German language, in contrast with the Latin part of worship in the mass.

It is also important that the Ten Commandments had a place in this worship service. Not that Surgant ushered in reformation, for theologically he did not deviate from the Romish doctrine of the church. But Surgant's book certainly proved to be useful to the reformation when it first attempted to create a renewed worship service (cf. Dankbaar, 1978:201ff.). Leo Judae and Huldrich Zwingli, for instance, used Surgant's book in Zurich. The same can be said of Strasbourg and the changes made by Martin Bucer with respect to liturgy. But pre-eminent is the name of Theobald Schwartz, who in February 16, 1524 — even before Martin Luther! — read the mass in Strasbourg in the German language. Some consider this to be the date of the first Protestant worship. Not only did church Latin have to make place for the language of the people, but also the "communion" was to be distributed to the believers in both elements, bread *and* wine.

Martin Bucer

In the same year a book written by Martin Bucer was published in which he gave an account of the liturgical changes (he himself called them "renovations") which had taken place in Strasbourg.

In the second chapter Bucer gave a description of public worship as it took place in Strasbourg:

When the congregation comes together on Sunday, the minister exhorts the people to confess their sins and to pray for pardon; and on behalf of the whole congregation he makes confession to God, prays for pardon, and pronounces absolution to the believers. Thereupon, the whole congregation sings a few short psalms or hymns. Then the minister says a short prayer, reads to the congregation a passage from the writings of the apostles, and, as briefly as possible, expounds the same. Then the congregation sings again, this time the Ten Commandments, or something else. After that, the minister reads the gospel, and preaches the sermon proper. The sermon ended, the congregation sings the Articles of our Belief (i.e. the Apostles' Creed in metre]; and the minister says a prayer for the Magistrates and for all men, and specially for the congregation there present, beseeching an increase of faith, love, and grace to hold in reverence the memory of Christ's death. Then he admonishes those who wish to observe the Lord's Supper with him that they are to do so in memory of Christ, to die to their sins, and bear their cross willingly, and be strengthened in faith for what must come to pass when we contemplate with believing hearts what measureless grace and goodness Christ has shown to us, in that for us He offered up to His Father His life and blood upon the cross. After this exhortation, he reads the gospel concerning the Lord's Supper, as the three Evangelists and Paul in 1 Corinthians 11 have described it. Then the minister distributes the Bread and the Cup of the Lord among them, having partaken of it also himself. The congregation then sings again a hymn of praise; and afterwards the minister closes the Supper with a short prayer, blesses the people, and lets them go in the peace of the Lord. This is the manner and custom with which we now celebrate the Lord's Supper on Sundays only (cf. Maxwell, 1982:100ff.).

Opening of the service

Now I address especially the opening of the public worship service on Sunday morning, as Calvin experienced it in Strasbourg in 1538. We have the following description of it.

When the congregation is assembled, the Pastor (Pfarrer) enters, and goes to the Holy Table (altartisch) taking up such a position that he faces the people, and in order that every one may hear every word he stands upright, and begins the Common Worship, using approximately the following words; for he is able to lengthen or shorten them as opportunity or time affords:

1. The Confiteor

Make confession to God the Lord, and let each one acknowledge with me his sins and iniquity:

Almighty God, eternal Father, we acknowledge and confess unto Thee that we were conceived in unrighteousness, and in all our life are full of sin and transgression, in that we have not gladly believed Thy Word nor followed Thy holy commandments. For Thy goodness' sake and for Thy Name's sake, be gracious unto us, we beseech Thee, and forgive us our iniquity, which is very great.

2. An absolution or comforting word: 1 Timothy 1.

This is a faithful saying, and worthy of all acceptation, that Christ Jesus is come into the world to save sinners.

Let each make confession in his heart with St. Paul in truth and believe in

Christ. So in His Name do I pronounce forgiveness unto you of all your sins, and I declare you to be loosed of them in earth so that ye may be loosed of them also in heaven and in all eternity. *Amen.*

Sometimes he takes other Words which comfort us in the forgiveness of sins and in the ransom of Christ for our sins, such as St. John 3:16, or 3:35-6, or Acts 10:43, or 1 John 2:1-2.

3. Thereafter, the Church begins to sing a Psalm or hymn instead of the Introit; and sometimes the Kyrie eleison and the Gloria in excelsis follow.

4. When this has been done, the Minister (Diener) says a short prayer for grace and for a right spirit, in order that the Word of God and the Sermon which are to follow may be heard with fruitful effect. The content of this prayer is based upon those desires which a Christian ought to have, and is usually drawn from the Sermon which follows it. I will now take one of the sort to which I refer, which I have formerly allowed to be issued.

The Lord be with you.

Let us pray.

Almighty, ever gracious Father, forasmuch as all our salvation depends upon our having truly understood Thy holy Word: therefore grant us that our hearts be set free from wordly things, so that we may with all diligence and faith hear and apprehend Thy holy Word, that thereby we may rightly understand Thy gracious will, and in all sincerity live according to the same, to Thy praise and glory; through our Lord Jesus Christ. *Amen.*

5. Then the Church sings a Psalm or some verse, and the Minister (Diener) goes to the front of the chancel, and reads from one of the gospels (Evangelisten), reading it in order, and selecting as much as he is minded to expound in a Sermon (cf. Maxwell, 1982:102ff.).

Calvin in the French congregation

In the French refugee congregation at Strasbourg Calvin followed this order which Bucer employed in the German congregation of Strasbourg. But it must be said that he did not slavishly imitate that which had been accepted as a custom in Strasbourg.

The order of the opening of the public worship service of Calvin's congregation at Strasbourg can be summarized in the following manner:

1. Scripture sentence with the words of Psalm 121:2.
2. Confession of sins.
3. Scriptural words of pardon to comfort the consciences, with the "absolution," the words of acquittal and forgiveness.
4. Singing by the congregation of the Constitution of God's covenant (the address of God and the first table of God's law in a rhyming version of Exodus 20, sung with *Kyrie eleison* after each commandment).
5. Short prayer.
6. Singing by the congregation of the second table of God's law in the same way as mentioned sub 4.
7. Prayer of the minister (now from the pulpit), ending with the Lord's Prayer, as a prayer for the opening of God's Word.

After this prayer for the illumination of the Holy Spirit, there follows the reading of the Scriptures and the preaching of the Word of God.

It is remarkable that the confession of sins (and the subsequent absolution) takes place at the very beginning of the worship service. Calvin used the following words:

Almighty, eternal God and Father, we confess and acknowledge that we, alas, were conceived and born in sin, and are therefore inclined to all evil and slow to all good; that we transgress Thy holy commandments without ceasing, and ever more corrupt ourselves. But we are sorry for the same, and beseech Thy grace and help. Wherefore have mercy upon us, most gracious and merciful God and Father, through Thy Son our Lord Jesus Christ. Grant to us and increase in us Thy Holy Spirit, that we may recognize our sin and unrighteousness from the bottom of our hearts, attain true repentance and sorrow for them, die to them wholly, and please thee entirely by a new godly life. *Amen.*

The words of absolution which follow the Scriptural words of pardon are as follows: "Let each of you confess that he is really a sinner who has to humble himself before God. He must believe that the heavenly Father will be gracious to him in Jesus Christ. To all who have repentance and who seek Jesus Christ for their salvation, I pronounce forgiveness in the name of the Father, the Son, and the Holy Spirit, Amen."

Actually there are only a few differences between Martin Bucer's order of liturgy in the German congregation at Strasbourg and the one which Calvin employed in the French congregation of the same city.

The main difference is at the beginning of the service.

Bucer started right away with a confession of sins, while Calvin preceded it with the words of Psalm 124 (some say it was Psalm 121:2). Another difference concerns the Constitution of God's covenant, which Calvin had the congregation sing in place of a Psalm or a Hymn sometimes connected by Bucer with *Kyrie eleison,* and always used by Calvin after each commandment).

Common

Calvin was of the opinion that this order of the public worship service was very important. In his *Institutes* (III,4,11) he shows the reason for this very common confession of sins at the beginning of the service:

Seeing that in every sacred assembly we stand in the view of God and angels, in what way should our service begin but in acknowledging our own unworthiness? But this you will say is done in every prayer; for as often as we pray for pardon, we confess our sins. I admit it. But if you consider how great is our carelessness, or drowsiness, or sloth, you will grant me that it would be a salutary ordinance if the Christian people were exercised in humiliation by some formal method of confession. For though the ceremony which the Lord enjoined on the Israelites belonged to the tutelage of the Law, yet the thing itself belongs in some respect to us also. And, indeed, in all well-ordered churches, in observance of an useful custom, the minister, each Lord's day, frames a formula of confession in his own name and that of the people, in which he makes a common confession of iniquity, and supplicates pardon from the Lord. In short, by this key a door of prayer is opened privately for each, and publicly for all.

In this respect, Calvin points also to the example of Holy Scripture. Not only personally but also together, in common, confession of guilt and sin has to be made:

On this latter description we have an example in the solemn confession which the whole people made under the authority and guidance of Ezra and Nehemiah (Neh. 1:6,7). For their long captivity, the destruction of the temple, and suppression of their religion, having been the common punishment of their defection, they could not make meet acknowledgment of the blessing of deliverance without previous confession of their guilt. And it matters not though in one assembly it may sometimes happen that a few are innocent, seeing that the members of a languid and sickly body cannot boast of soundness. Nay, it is scarcely possible that these few have not contracted some taint, and so bear part of the blame.

Calvin considered himself in this respect to be in the line of the church fathers. For instance, Chrysostom had stated in a sermon on the gospel of Matthew in the year 390 A.D. that the first prayers in public worship must always request the forgiveness of sins and appeal to God's mercy.

Calvin's opinion was that also the common forgiveness of sins was very important (*Institutes*, IV, 1, 20ff.):

Our first entrance into the Church and the kingdom of God is by forgiveness of sins, without which we have no covenant nor union with God. For thus he speaks by the Prophet, "In that day will I make a covenant for them with the beasts of the field, and with the fowls of heaven, and with the creeping things of the ground: and I will break the bow, and the sword, and the battle, out of the earth, and will make them to lie down safely. And I will betroth thee unto me for ever; yea, I will betroth thee unto me in righteousness, and in judgment, and in loving-kindness, and in mercies" (Hos. 2:18, 19). We see in what way the Lord reconciles us to himself by his mercy. So in another passage, where he foretells that the people whom he had scattered in anger will again be gathered together, I will cleanse them from all their iniquity, whereby they have sinned against me (Jer. 33:8). Wherefore, our initiation into the fellowship of the church is by the symbol of absolution, to teach us that we have no admission into the family of God, unless by his goodness our impurities are previously washed away.

Nor by remission of sins does the Lord only once for all elect and admit us into the Church, but by the same means he preserves and defends us in it. For what would it avail us to receive a pardon of which we were afterwards to have no use? That the mercy of the Lord would be vain and delusive if only granted once, all the godly can bear witness; for there is none who is not conscious, during his whole life, of many infirmities which stand in need of divine mercy. And truly it is not without cause that the Lord promises this gift specially to his own household, nor in vain that he orders the same message of reconciliation to be daily delivered to them. Wherefore, as during our whole lives we carry about with us the remains of sin, we could not continue in the Church one single moment were we not sustained by the uninterrupted grace of God in forgiving our sins."

Back to the early church!

Did Calvin link up with liturgical customs of the late Middle Ages and with the situation in Strasbourg for the sake of convenience or because he himself was not very inventive?

Neither is the case! We already saw that Calvin consciously wanted to base himself on Holy Scripture. Besides, he also very much stressed the connection with the early church (*L'église ancienne*). Especially when liturgical matters were involved he pointed to the customs of the New Testament church and the first period after Pentecost. Frequently he quoted apostolic fathers and church fathers in order to emphasize his argument.

It must also be said that Calvin was absolutely not aiming for a multitude of forms in worship. But that which had shown itself to be significant in former ages, especially in the early church, had to be taken over.

As for the first part of the worship service, which we are now discussing, I want to investigate why Calvin stressed the importance of:

1. Confession of sins.
2. Forgiveness of sins.

3. God's words of His covenant.
4. The *Kyrie-eleison.*

Confession of sins

We have already discovered that Calvin stressed the importance of common guilt, an emphasis which he based on the Bible.

Evidently also personal guilt had to be confessed, but that is not a matter of a sacramental auricular confession before the priest. Calvin here quoted James 5:16, from which text we learn that we have to confess our sins before each other and that we have to pray for forgiveness of sins.

In the New Testament we more than once find indications that there is the necessity of the confession of sins and the petition for forgiveness. But it is also clear that the Christian church realized this from the very beginning.

In the first letter of Clement to the church at Corinth (dated before the end of the first century) we find this prayer: "O merciful and compassionate, forgive us our iniquities, and unrigheousness, and transgressions, and shortcomings.

Reckon not every sin of Thy servants and handmaids, but cleanse us with the cleansing of Thy truth, and guide our steps. . . ." We agree with the comments of A.B. Macdonald, who notes that the reference to men and women ("servants and handmaids") is one of the clearer indications that Clement's prayer had its origins in the public worship of the community (Macdonald, 1935:100).

I draw a second example from the *Didachè* ("Teaching of the twelve apostles"), probably also written at the end of the first century, or else not long after.

We read in that book two statements which are important. "In church, confess your transgressions, and do not go to prayer with an evil conscience. This is the way of Life" (IV, 14), and: "When you gather together each Lord's Day, break bread and give thanks. But first confess your transgressions so that your sacrifice may be pure" (XIV,1).

Later on, this confession of sins was limited to the priest personally in the *Confiteor:* "We beseech Thee, Lord, take away from us our sins, that we may be worthy to enter the holy of holies with a pure conscience."

That concerned the personal preparations of the priest before he celebrated the mass. The priest was not to start his work before he had personally confessed his unworthiness and sinfulness. But that had to be done just before the mass.

Bucer said in Strasbourg: No, before anything else there must be confession of sins; and Calvin agreed with that. Moreover, both of them were of the opinion that this was a matter concerning the whole congregation. Before the Word of God was administered, and before the minister went to the pulpit, sins were confessed on behalf of the whole congregation.

Forgiveness of sins

Confession of sins and forgiveness of sins are closely connected. Therefore the forgiveness of sins is an element in the liturgy which Calvin placed immediately after the confession of sins. He preceded the words of absolution with a word of comfort from Holy Scripture. He also came into contact with this in Strasbourg, for in Bucer's congregation the worship service started with confession of sins, after which was quoted the word of acquittal from 1 Timothy 1:15, that Christ Jesus came into the world to save sinners.

Another word of comfort from the New Testament could also be quoted, e.g., John

3:16, John 3:35 and 36, Acts 10:43, or 1 John 2:1 and 2.

Evidently the absolution had nothing to do with the sacramental absolution of Rome, let alone the mediation of the saints or any form of indulgence. It was a word of comfort that God is a good and forgiving God, who after confession of sins does not mark transgression.

God's words of His covenant

After the word of comfort from Holy Scripture and the forgiveness of sins, Calvin followed with the singing of the Decalogue by the congregation. This singing of God's law was done "in order to bring the congregation to the awareness that it was the duty of the congregation to walk in holiness before God, thankful for the forgiveness of sins" (Kruijf, 1901:76ff.).

This rhymed version of the Decalogue came from Calvin himself. The opening words of the Decalogue were, in Calvin's opinion, not just a kind of introduction, but the promise of the LORD God in the covenant with His people: "I am the LORD your God, who brought you out of the land of Egypt, out of the house of bondage."

H. Hasper correctly writes: "Ex. 20:2 is not an 'introduction' in the sense of the introductory stanzas of rhymed versions. Ex. 20:2 is the *main point: God's* deed of love, God's action. After that must follow *man's* deed of love, his reaction" (Hasper, 1955:592).

In the light of the forgiveness and acquittal of sins and also in the light of God's promise that He brings His people in Christ out of the house of bondage of sins, His people have to live according to the obligation of God's covenant. In connection with this what is also remarkable is Calvin's last stanza, which is not directly derived from Exodus 20:

> Dieu, qui de toute saincteté,
> contiens seul la vertu en toy,
> à la Justice de ta Loy,
> veuilles noz meurs conformer.

> (O God, in whom alone is
> the power of all holiness,
> let our behaviour be according
> to the justice of Thy law.)

Calvin here followed Luther's version of "Dies sind die heilgen zehn Gebot."

However, Luther added to his rhymed version a New Testament stanza, in which the help of the Mediator Jesus Christ was invoked.

Did the Reformers invent the practice of reciting the words of God's covenant? No, actually this custom is much older.

Think of the priests serving in the temple, who had to impress God's law upon the people of God's covenant.

Think about the reading of the whole Torah in the synagogue. There are indications that the law played a role in the liturgy of the early church. With respect to this I quote E.F. Kruijf: ". . . when the gnostics had appeared, who spoke more about trust in God than fear before God, some had the opinion that the Law should be placed more in the foreground; and even before traces are found of the reading of the Law in the worship services, it appears that some had sown it into the hearts of young and old" (Kruijf, 1901: 761). Kruijf refers then to the Apostolic Constitutions of the fourth century, which partially go back to the second century.

Also later on, at the end of the Middle Ages, the reading of the Law, or the singing of it, was used in some churches.

In Calvin's case the reading of the Law replaced more or less the *Great Gloria,* which was used for many centuries after the *Introitus* and which was derived from the song of the angels in Luke 2: "Glory to God . . . ." That Gloria had the tone of thanks to God, who had sent His Son into the world. Hence it is noteworthy that in Calvin's case the singing of the Decalogue was placed in the framework of thankfulness, *after* the forgiveness of sins.

Later on the Law was emphasized much more as the source of the knowledge of misery, but for Calvin its function in worship service was different. Something of this is retained in the last part of stanza 9 of Hymn 7 in the *Book of Praise:*

> That we, delivered from all evil,
> May live in thankfulness to Thee.

The *Kyrie-eleison*

As we have seen, Calvin had the *Kyrie-eleison* sung after each stanza of the Decalogue. He prayed a short prayer after the singing of the first table of the Law and twelve times the people sang "Lord, have mercy."

We see that Calvin is again in harmony with Luther, who also connected the *Kyrie* with the singing of the Law.

The *Kyrie-eleison* was well-known as the refrain of an old Christmas song, also dating from the century of the reformation. This hymn goes back to an old German song from the 11th century: "Nu sis uns willekomen, herro Christ, du unser aller herro bist."

In popular language the *Kyrie-eleison* was well-known in the times of Luther and Calvin. But its history is much older.

In the years 381-384 the nun Egeria came from northern Spain or southern France and stayed in Jerusalem. There she attended many worship services when Cyril was bishop of Jerusalem. In the account of her travels she speaks about these services. In the daily service at four P.M. the bishop rose and one of the deacons prayed. Then, "many little children standing around always responded: *Kyrie eleison,* which means: 'Have mercy'. " Egeria relates that this singing happened often in Jerusalem's liturgy.

From the East this *Kyrie-eleison* was brought to the West, and the Greek words were maintained for a long time.

Often the *Kyrie-eleis* took turns with *Christe-eleis.*

It is not impossible that stadtholder Plinius in his well-known letter to the emperor Trajan in the beginning of the second century alluded to this *Christe-eleis* and *Kyrie-eleis* when he wrote that the Christians in prayer called upon Christ as a God. Definitely this same *Kyrie-eleison* was found in Egypt coinciding with the morning prayer, while the faces of the people were turned to the East, to the rising sun.

We also have to bear in mind that the *Kyrie-eleison* is used more than once in the New Testament (cf. e.g., Matt. 15:22 and 25; 20:30 and 31), but also in the Greek translation of the Old Testament, the Septuagint (cf. e.g., Psalm 6:3; 9:14; 31:10; 41:5 and 11; 56:2; 86:3, and Isa. 33:2). In the *Apostolic Constitutions* it is said that this *Kyrie* had to be the response in the prayer of the deacons. Already in early times *Kyrie* as well as *Gloria* were hymns which received their place at the beginning of the worship service. It is typical of Calvin that he did not abolish these hymns but placed them in his liturgy. The singing of God's Law as a rule of thankfulness took the place of the *Gloria,* while the refrain to it became the *Kyrie.* It should also be mentioned that this *Kyrie* did not have the character of a confession of sins (that had already been done), but the character of a petition for help, in order to live according to the obligations of God's covenant.

Continuation of the service

The first part of the Sunday morning service in Strasbourg was closed with the final *Kyrie-eleison* after the last stanza of Calvin's rhymed version of God's law. Until this point in the service, Calvin stood the whole time at the table in front of the pulpit. This first part of the service was placed in the framework of humility and thankfulness. Now, after the conclusion of this first part, the opening of God's Word followed. For that purpose the minister ascended the pulpit. Before the reading (or readings) from Holy Scripture took place, there was first the prayer for the opening of God's Word and also the prayer for the illumination of the Holy Spirit. Right after the reading, the preaching followed. The other elements of the service (also the service of the sacraments) had their place *after* the sermon.

To these other elements belonged the singing of Psalms, the intercessions, the collection and finally the benediction. In the eventuality that there was the administration of the Holy Baptism and/or the celebration of the Lord's Supper, these also were placed after the sermon.

Obviously, respecting the traditions of the church, without becoming formalistic, Calvin had a carefully considered order for the first part of the service.

Calvin declared he was not against forms, but emphasized that it was necessary to get the essence of forms. One must be conscious of what is going on in the worship service!

Back to Geneva

Calvin was called to return to Geneva and finally he complied with the urgent request. But he could never completely accomplish in Geneva what he had been aiming for and appeared to have been accomplishing in Strasbourg.

When Calvin came back in Geneva in the year 1541, he was confronted with Farel's liturgy, which was already in use when he had left the city three years earlier.

That was a liturgy without congregational singing and with an infrequent celebration of the Lord's Supper. There were similarities between this liturgy and that of Zwingli, but not so much that of Bucer and Calvin at Strasbourg. Calvin did his best to change this liturgy and he partially succeeded. A very important point to him was the singing by the congregation. Indeed, the whole Psalter was finished in 1562, two years before Calvin's death. But he did not succeed in bringing about more frequent celebrations of the Lord's Supper, which caused grief to Calvin. The Reformer was troubled by the fact that even a monthly celebration did not appear to be possible. Once he wrote about that fact: "I mentioned in the public announcements that our custom is abnormal in order that our offspring would feel freer to improve upon it." But that offspring did not change it very much!

In the year after Calvin's return to Geneva, an important book by Calvin about liturgy was published; in it he made mention in the title already that he would like to go back to the custom of the early church. He was aiming to continue what he had written already before in his *Institutes,* and what he had worked out in Strasbourg. But in certain points he had to give in, also concerning the first part of the worship service on Sunday morning. (Calvin did not give a specific order for the Sunday afternoon service.) Accordingly there were five ways in which it was different from the order of Strasbourg:
1. The omission of the words of comfort from Holy Scripture after the confession of sins.
2. The omission of the words of "absolution."

3. The change from the rhymed version of the law to the reading of it.
4. The omission of the singing of the *Kyrie-eleison* after the individual stanzas of the rhymed version of the law.
5. The change from standing behind the table in the first part of the service: from the very beginning the service was now conducted from the pulpit.

Some considered these things as "novelties." Not each and every point weighed equally heavily with Calvin. For instance, the omission of the words of comfort from Scripture after the confession of sins, and also the "absolution" he really wanted to introduce in Geneva, and, indeed, later on he advised its introduction elsewhere. At a later time Calvin answered a question concerning liturgy in the following manner: "To add to the public confession of sins a promise, which exhorts the sinners to the hope of forgiveness and reconciliation — there will be no one who does not acknowledge that this would be very useful. I wanted to introduce this use from the very beginning; but because some feared the novelty of it, I was willing to abolish this use. Therefore this matter is omitted. It would not be opportune to change things now.

For many are busy standing up (from kneeling prayer, K.D.) before others have reached the end of the confession of sins. But more so it is our wish to get people used to both of these things, because they are not bound to anything yet."

So the confession of sins was maintained, but not the words of comfort afterwards. Calvin introduced the confession of sins in Geneva with these words: "Brothers, let everyone of us place himself before the LORD with confession of his sins and debts and let him say with me these words in his heart."

Refugee congregations

Was this the end of the elements which had been omitted from the beginning of the Sunday morning worship? Let us turn for a moment to London, England, where Martin Micron had fled in 1549, seven years after the publication of Calvin's liturgical book in Geneva. In 1554, just a year after he had to leave London again, he wrote his *Christlicke Ordinancien,* from which we learn the order of worship of the refugee congregation in London. The first part of this service was only an exhortation to prayer which ended with the Lord's Prayer and the singing of a Psalm.

After the sermon followed the reading of the law, exhortation to confession of sins, a prayer in which this confession was expressed, and the proclamation of the "loosing and binding of sins."

Several things are noteworthy. In the first place almost the entire first part of the service was placed in a later phase of the service, namely, after the sermon. Moreover, the confession of sins was placed after the reading of the law, and the law was apparently considered as the source of knowledge of misery. The exhortation to confession of sins was worded in this way: "We see in this divine law as in a mirror how much and in how many ways we have incensed God with our transgressions; so let us now wholeheartedly desire that He will forgive them, saying, . . ." (there follows a prayer with confession of sins).

What is new is the "binding of sins," the so-called formula of retention, directed to those who do not repent from their sins: ". . . I proclaim to them from the Word of God that all their sins are bound in heaven and are not loosed until they will repent."

So the forgiveness of sins came back, but in a totally different place than in Calvin's Strasbourg liturgy. Here should also be mentioned the name of Vallérand Poullain, who served the French refugee congregation at Strasbourg after Calvin and who departed to England in 1547, where he in 1551 received the function of superintendent of the French-speaking refugee congregation at Galstonbury.

In that year his *Liturgia Sacra* was published. In this book we find the *Liturgia diei dominici* (the order of Sunday), which contains (as far as the first part of it is concerned):

1. Singing: first part of the song of the Ten Commandments.
2. Confessio peccatorum (confession of sins).
3. Absolutio (formula of forgiveness).
4. Singing: second part of the song of the Ten Commandments.
5. Short prayer.
6. Singing: last stanza of the song of the Ten Commandments.

Then followed the reading of Scripture and the preaching. When "Bloody Mary" started her reign, Poullain, Micron and many others had to flee to the continent. Poullain continued his work in Frankfurt and established church life in the same way as in England.

Other countries

At the same time John Knox was a minister of the English refugee congregation at Frankfurt. A year later he became a minister of the English refugee congregation at Geneva and met Calvin. The year thereafter he published in Geneva his liturgical book *the Forme of Prayers and Administration of the Sacraments, etc., used in the Englishe Congregation at Geneva; and approved by the famous and godly learned man, John Calvin.*

Knox started the service as follows:

1. Confession of sins.
2. Prayer for forgiveness.
3. Singing of a rhymed Psalm.

Then followed the prayer for illumination, the reading of Scripture and the preaching. Again Calvin's influence is to be seen: the service started with humiliation, followed by prayer for forgiveness and the singing of a psalm that has to do with forgiveness. Only after the sermon there followed intercessions, the Apostles' Creed, and the celebration of the Lord's Supper.

This liturgy was maintained in Scotland.

As far as the Hungarian Reformed churches were concerned, we would like to point to the fact that the custom was maintained that during the singing of Psalms of humiliation, confession of sins, and forgiveness of sins (with the Genevan melodies!), the minister was seated below the pulpit. After that first part of the service he ascended the pulpit, just as Calvin also did in his French congregation at Strasbourg.

It was not always the same elements and the same order that entered the Reformed liturgies of several countries, but it is clear that Calvin's liturgy had a great influence. It is also clear that not only in Strasbourg but also in several other places that which Calvin was not able to realize in Geneva was indeed achieved.

Datheen in Frankenthal and in the Netherlands

A clear link to Calvin was found in Frankenthal in the Dutch refugee congregation of the Palatinate.

In 1562 Petrus Dathenus became the minister of this congregation. He had been in London, but in 1553 he, too, had fled. In 1555 he had become a minister of the Flemish congregation at Frankfurt, where he had met Calvin.

In Frankenthal, he first made a translation of the Heidelberg Catechism, and after that a version of the rhymed Psalms of Marot and Beza. In 1566 Datheen's *Book of Praise* was published. Datheen was in his last year a minister of the refugee congregation at Frankenthal. The opening of Datheen's worship service can be reconstructed as follows: Datheen started with prayer, and after the singing (or reading) of the law there was an exhortation to penitence and to faith in God's promises. Then followed words of admonition and comfort, retention, and declaration of grace. After the sermon followed confession of sins and intercessions. It is noteworthy that several elements of Calvin's beginning of the service are found here. But the element of *Gloria* (the law as a rule of thankfulness) diasappeared, and there was added a confession of sins after the sermon.

The first synod in the Netherlands, Dordrecht 1574, dropped the matter of confession of sins, words of comfort from Scripture, absolution, and retention-formula.

Gaspar van der Heyden was the chariman and he received the assignment to draft a shorter prayer for after the sermon. Van der Heyden also drafted a new liturgy in 1580, in which retention and declaration of grace were missing completely.

At the Synod of Dordrecht 1578 Peter Datheen presided, but his colleague Gaspar van der Heyden was in the chair again at the Synod of Middelburg 1581.

This synod made an important decision concerning retention and declaration of grace. The delegates from Gelderland had placed on the table the question whether or not it would be good after the sermon to proclaim to the converted forgiveness of sins and to the unbelievers the binding of sins.

But the synod was of the opinion that because the binding and loosing of sins was proclaimed sufficiently in the preaching of God's Word, it was not necessary to introduce a separate form. Indeed, the first part of the service would now be: Reading of Scripture, Singing of a Psalm, Votum and Prayer before the sermon.

Some have said that the Synod of 1574, and especially the Synod of 1581 (both of them chaired by Gaspar van der Heyden) spoiled the beautiful start of Calvin's liturgy (cf. Hendriks, 1970:223 ff.).

Not after the sermon

Apparently some were impressed by the argument of the Synod of Middelburg 1581 that the binding and loosing of sins is done sufficiently in the preaching of God's Word. This was supported by Lord's Day 31 of the Heidelberg Catechism, which confesses that the key of preaching God's Word opens and closes God's Kingdom. A special formula after the preaching of God's Word appeared superfluous: a kind of sermonette after the sermon.

No doubt there is an element of truth in this. But one must be aware of the question placed upon the table of the Synod of 1581. The delegates of Gelderland asked about a formula *after* the sermon. That would be a kind of appendix which never had a function before in the worship service. What Calvin did in Strasbourg was different. He maintained Confiteor, Absolution, Gloria, and *Kyrie,* but in the Scriptural sense, and as a beautiful whole: the humble beginning of the service with confession of sins, comfort from Scripture, acquittal from God, His words of the covenant in promise and obligation, and the petition to live according to God's will.

Thereafter there was a prayer for the opening of God's Word and then followed reading of the Scriptures and preaching. Much later there was again an attempt to insert the "absolution" in the first part of the worship service on Sunday morning.

Deputies, appointed by the Synod of Leeuwarden 1920 to study the Order of Liturgy, placed on the table of the Synod of 1923 a report in which they pleaded for the re-introduction of the declaration of forgiveness of sins. This would then commence with the words: "The minister speaks to all who sincerely regret their sins and take refuge in the only Saviour Jesus Christ, I declare the forgiveness of sins in the

Name of the Father, the Son, and the Holy Spirit. Amen." But this proposal was not adopted by the Synod of Utrecht.

Ten years later when the Synod of Middelburg (!) again dealt with the whole matter of liturgy, the status quo was maintained as it had developed over the course of time in the churches.

After the liberation in 1944 in the Netherlands, the Synod of Kampen 1975 again dealt with the order of worship.

The synod took over a large part of Calvin's order of liturgy for the Sunday morning. Unfortunately his complete Strasbourg liturgy was not taken over.

The Synod of the Canadian Reformed Churches at Cloverdale 1983 followed the sister churches in the Netherlands by recommending to the churches this second order of liturgy. But together with A. Kuyper, G. van Dooren, G. van Rongen and others I would like to plead for the re-introduction of the beautiful beginning of Calvin's liturgy at Strasbourg, which is now a missing link in Reformed liturgy. I agree with the recent remark of C. Trimp that there is room for a third order of liturgy. It could be done in the way of the congregation at Blue Bell, where especially the confession of sins and the absolution is maintained.

Repetition?

Is it true that a word of comfort from Scripture after confession of sins, together with a word of acquittal and forgiveness would be an unnecessary repetition because it is already done in the sermon? The answer is no. In the first place there are other elements in the liturgy which take place more than once. I point to the service of praise. The singing of the congregation is not limited to one selection, but it comes back (fortunately!) several times in the liturgy.

Also praying is not limited to one prayer only.

In the second place: in the *Form for the celebration of the Lord's Supper* we have the traditional invitation and the retention. This is also true in the *Abbreviated Form for the celebration of the Lord's Supper*. There the invitation-formula is: "All who by the grace of God repent of their sins, desiring to fight against their unbelief and live according to God's commandments, will certainly be received by God at the table of His Son Jesus Christ. They may be fully assured that no sin or weakness which still remains in them against their will shall keep God from accepting them in grace and granting them this heavenly food and drink."

Then follows the retention-formula (in the Form called "the admonition"): "But to all who do not truly grieve over their sins and do not repent from them, we declare that they have no part in the kingdom of God. We admonish them to abstain from the holy supper; otherwise their judgment will be the heavier."

Calvin esteemed this retention-formula very highly and placed it at the beginning of the service.

The argument is used that invitation and retention are found here in the context of self-examination with a view to the celebration of or abstinence from the Lord's Supper. But I ask: is the whole matter of self-examination limited to that? Is this not something which we have to execute continually, even daily?

With respect to this I would like to point to the fact that it is not right that in some churches the Form for the celebration of the Lord's Supper is cut into two parts. One reads the first part on the so-called Sunday of preparation, namely, the part concerning self-examination, while the rest of the Form is read on the Sunday of the celebration itself. But apart from the question whether or not it is desirable to have a separate Sunday of preparation, liturgically it is not right to spread a Form over two Sundays.

When the words of comfort concerning forgiveness of sins and the retention come back in the Sunday morning service, the matter of that continual obligation of self-examination will prove to be a real blessing.

Conclusions

In summary, I come to the following conclusions:
1. It was an important and laudable principle of Calvin that liturgically he sought connection with:
   a. what he found in Holy Scripture;
   b. the custom of the early church;
   c. good customs which had developed in the course of history.
2. The first part of Calvin's order of liturgy (the part before the prayer for the opening of God's Word) forms an organic whole according to the triad: misery, deliverance, and thankfulness.
3. Calvin rightly emphasized very strongly the element of humility at the very beginning of the worship service.
4. This humility is expressed in the confession of sins, which is to be followed directly by a word of comfort from Scripture and the declaration of forgiveness of sins for believers.
5. The argument that absolution is given already in the preaching and that it is therefore superfluous to do it in another way is an insufficient argument:
   a. there would be an element of truth to this if absolution were placed *after* the sermon;
   b. there are more elements in liturgy which take place more than once, e.g., singing and prayers;
   c. similarly, aside from the preaching of God's Word, a kind of absolution (and retention) takes place in the Forms for the celebration of the Lord's Supper.
6. When reintroducing the word of comfort from Holy Scripture and the formula of absolution, one must be on guard not to be uniform: Holy Scripture offers abundant material for this.
7. It is seldom realized that the (singing of the) law by Calvin was designed to be an expression of thankfulness and a replacement of the "great Gloria."
8. It is to be emphasized that the beginning of the law contains God's promise, which forms a complete unit with the Ten Words; this is to be called the Constitution of God's Covenant.
9. .Because of this unity of promise and obligation of God's covenant, a repetition of the law in the "summary" is superfluous:
   a. actually this summary had already been given by Moses in Deut. 6:5 and Lev. 19:18;
   b. when Christ gives this "summary" it is done in a different context;
   c. a repetition of the law in a summary weakens the character of the promise of God's covenant within the framework of the worship service.
10. Calvin had a special reason for having the *Kyrie-eleison* sung by the congregation, namely, the repeated petition for help from the Lord in order that the congregation would practice the service of love in thankfulness.
11. Calvin had a special reason for reserving the pulpit for the reading and preaching of the Word of God, while the beginning of the worship service and the administration of the sacraments took place in front of the pulpit.
12. With a view to the special character of the second worship service, namely, the emphasis on the confession of the congregation and the instruction in that

respect, Calvin's first part of the Sunday morning service was restricted to the morning service only and not interchanged with the afternoon service.

THE FUNCTION OF THE READER

Public reading

If things are normal, not one day passes by without the *reading of the Holy Scriptures*. We will do that in connection with the family and we will do that alone as well. It is a basic requirement of Christian life. The Holy Scriptures are the self-revelation of God, and Jesus Christ comes to us in the words of the Bible. He appears to us in the *garment* of the Holy Scripture, as Calvin expressed it (Inst. III,2,6). Not one Sunday passes by without the reading of the Bible in the church service. That starts in the morning service, when the Ten Commandments of the LORD are read. That is to be continued by the Scripture reading in the same morning service and also in the afternoon or evening service. From the very beginning of the Christian church, Scripture reading was a constituent part of public worship (Moule, 1961:94). It was a special honour as well, to be privileged to read the Holy Scriptures in the service of the church. Therefore, in the Apocalypse, the Revelation to John, it is written: "Blessed is he who reads aloud the words of the prophecy." This public reader is to be deemed happy. This is the first beatification of the book of Revelation to John. So the reading of the Holy Scriptures in public worship is very important.

The apostle Paul exhorts his spiritual son Timothy: "Till I come, attend to the *public reading* of Scripture, to preaching, to teaching." This is not an advice but an *order* of the apostle. Before "preaching" and "teaching," the public reading of the Holy Scripture has been prescribed with apostolic authority.

Old Testament

There is a long tradition of Scripture reading in the services of the church. Already Moses in his valedictory sermon of the book of Deuteronomy commanded the priests and the elders of the people of Israel: "You shall read this law before all Israel in their hearing. Assemble the people, men, women, and little ones, and the sojourner within your town, that they may hear and learn to fear the LORD your God, and be careful to do all the words of this law, and that their children, who have not known it, may hear and learn to fear the LORD your God, as long as you live in the land which you are going over the Jordan to possess" (Deut. 31:11 ff.).

After the time of exile we hear that Ezra the priest brought the Law of Moses which the LORD had given to Israel. "And he read from it facing the square before the Water Gate from early morning until midday, in the presence of the men and the women and those who could understand; and the ears of all the people were attentive to the book of the law. And Ezra the scribe stood on a wooden pulpit which they had made for the purpose. . . . And Ezra opened the book in the sight of all the people; and when he opened it all the people stood. And Ezra blessed the LORD, the great God; and all the people answered, "Amen, Amen," lifting up their hands, and they bowed their heads and worshipped the LORD with their faces to the ground. Later, the law of Moses and especially the Decalogue, was in use in the Palestinian synagogue. (Dugmore, 1964:21). Probably the reading of the law of Ezra was the model to the reading of the Torah in the synagogue, especially on feast days (Boon, 1973:128).

Little by little the reading of the law grew in regular services. At last, the Torah was divided into 54 parts, which had to be read in the course of a year in a so-called "lectio continua," a continuing reading. So there was reading of the law on all Sabbath days. For the convenience of the rural residents the Torah was later read on the market days as well. At last, there was no divine service in the synagogue without Scripture reading.

We know little about the origin of the prophetical lesson in the synagogue, the so-called "Haftarah." It may either have been an independent item, or it may have been chosen to complement the lesson of the Torah. At any rate, the lesson of the Torah was more important than the lesson of the prophets and the same can be said to the lecturer of both. If the lecturer was a very young man — and that could be in that time — then he could only read the *Haftarah*, not the *Torah*.

It is evident that such a lesson of the prophets formed part of the public worship on the Sabbath in the time of Jesus. Luke mentions that Jesus went to the Synagogue of Nazareth, as His custom was, on the Sabbath day. And He stood up to read; and there was given to Him the book of the Prophet Isaiah. He opened the book and found the place where it was written, "The Spirit of the Lord is upon me. . . ."

Personally I am of the opinion that the term: "He *found* the place . . ." means that Jesus was looking for a special and free pericope and not that this part had to be read at that time.

As a rule, the reader and the preacher were two different persons. However, in the case of Jesus in the Synagogue of Nazareth, the reader was the Man who preached as well.

Christian church

The history of Scripture reading in the Christian church is rather complicated. We only mention the main facts. In the beginning, the apostles visited the synagogues and listened to the reading of the law and the prophets, apparently in that time established parts, as we read in the book of the Acts of the apostles, concerning the Synagogue of Antioch. So there were links with the synagogue. What about the Scripture reading in the Christian church itself? The first announcement after the mentioned texts of the New Testament we find in the Apology of Justin Martyr in the second century. He writes: "On the day of the Sun all who live in towns or in the country gather together to one place, and the memoirs of the apostles or the writings of the prophets are read as long as time permits. Then when the reader has finished, the president verbally instructs and exhorts to the imitation of the good examples cited" (Apologia I, 67, cf. McDonald, 1935:3ff.). We read here that Justin knows only one Scripture reading, namely from the books of the apostles *or* the prophets. Later, the reading of the Scripture and the preaching were connected to each other. The sermon joined the reading. Justin wrote his Apology about 160 years after Christ.

In the books of Hippolytus of Rome (about half a century after Justin), we get the impression that there were already more Scripture readings in the service of the Christian church. In any event, there is an expansion in the readings, for in the *Constitutiones apostolorum*, a book dated from the fourth century, four readings are mentioned, namely, two of the Old Testament and two of the New Testament: "When both readings of the Old Testament are finished, another has to sing the Psalms of David and the congregation must repeat the last verses. After that the Acts and the letters of Paul must be read, and at last the deacon or the priest has to read the gospels (II, 57). In the same time, we hear about the services in Jerusalem. The nun Egeria, coming from Spain, describes in the account of her travels the Jerusalem liturgy of Bishop Cyril of Jerusalem in the second part of the fourth century. In the daily services, there was an absence of Scripture reading, but in the first service on Sunday the bishop himself read the gospel. "Then the bishop, standing inside the screen ("intro cancellos"), takes the gospel and goes to the door, where he himself reads the account of the Lord's resurrection. At the beginning of the reading the whole assembly groans and laments at all that the Lord underwent for us, and the way they weep would move even the hardest heart to tears. When the gospel is finished, the bishop comes out, and is taken with singing to the Cross, and they all go with him. They have one psalm there and a prayer, then he blesses the people, and that is the dismissal ("fit missa"). As the bishop goes out, everyone comes to kiss his hand" (XXIV).

At daybreak the people assemble in the Great Church built by Constantine on Golgotha behind the Cross. There are lectures of the Old and New Testament. Presbyters are preaching and when they have finished there is a sermon from the bishop. The object of having this preaching every Sunday is to make sure that the people "will continually be learning about the Bible and the love of God." Because of all the preaching, Egeria writes, it is a long time before the dismissal, which takes place not before ten or even eleven o'clock.

With respect to the services in the Church of Jerusalem in the fourth century the frequent use of the phrase "apte et diei et loco" (according to the day and the place) is to be noted. This phrase was used in relation to the several parts of the service, Scripture readings included. We also receive some information about the Jerusalem liturgy of the fourth century by the *Catecheses* of Cyril of Jerusalem. In his *Catecheses* on baptism, dating from the beginning of his episcopate (about 348 A.D.), the liturgical character of his teaching is already revealed in his explanation of the Jerusalem formula of baptism, but in his mystagogic *Catecheses* (dated from the end of his episcopate, about 380) this is much more so. Again we see that the Jerusalem liturgy of that time was "topographical," according to the day and the place, the Scripture readings as well (Cross, 1966: passim). The gaps in the information, left by the travel story of Egeria and the *Catecheses* of Cyril of Jerusalem, are mostly filled by the information furnished by the *Armenian lectionary*. The list of Scripture readings in Jerusalem, gleaned from this source, renders a significant addition (Renoux, 1969:161ff.). In this time the Christian Calendar had been built up, and the Scripture readings had been divided according to the feast, and even the day and the place where in Jesus' time the facts of salvation have occurred.

Slowly but surely Western Europe came under the influence of the East. In the days of Augustine there was still a certain liberty in the choice of the readings, but for the feasts the readings were fully prescripted. The readings took a long time, Augustine says. They were interrupted by the singing of psalms and hymns. For instance in the night before Easter, the Scripture reading was very long: it began with the first part of Genesis, the story of the passage through the Red Sea from Exodus, the first Passover, the song of Miriam, the sister of Moses, the history of Jonas, the hymn of the three men in the fire, and so on. Augustine complains of the long duration of the Scripture readings. He says: "The readings of the Bible are so long that we cannot complete with an interpretation. And even if we should be able to interprete, you would lose the thread and your attention" (van der Meer 1947:319).

Not only in Northern Africa was there the interruption of the Scripture readings by the song of psalms and hymns: we see the same thing in Rome, namely, in the Roman Mass Rite in the fifth century. There psalmody came between the readings as well. The usual number of three readings before the gospel reading was first reduced to two in the Church of Constantinople in the fifth century, and Rome followed this example in the late fifth or sixth century.

In other Eastern and Western rites the first of the usual readings was discarded later than the above dates, but not everywhere. There were several songs between the readings. The first chant was called "gradual," because it was sung on the steps (that is "gradus") of the ambo, the pulpit. The pulpit was the place where the sermon was delivered. But in the third and the fourth century the term "rostrum" is used to indicate the place from where the lections were read. The rostrum was situated where the readers could be easily heard. The name "rostrum" means a beak, a platform for public speaking, with reference to the speaker's platform in the Roman forum, which was decorated with the beaks of captured war galleys. Usually the sermon was preached from another place in the building, the pulpit, or the sanctuary steps. After the "gradual" came the "Alleluia" chant: a signal for the refrain, chanted by the people. And then, a chant of several verses of psalms was sung before the epistle.

In Milan, the "Ambrosian" rite closely resembled that of Rome. On many days of the year there were two lessons before the gospel. The first was usually taken from the prophets or other parts of the Old Testament, but on Sundays in Eastertide from the Acts of the apostles, and on some saints' feasts from the life of the concerning saint. That is remarkable, because the last reading was not a Scripture reading, and not the Word of God, but a story of men. Little by little saint worship was growing in this time. Each lesson was preceded by a special blessing given by the celebrant at the request of the reader. After the first lesson a little psalm was sung, called "psalmellus" (usually consisting of one or two verses from the psalms). The epistle was followed by Hallelujah with a verse, again usually taken from the psalms. On some solemn feasts a chant, called "Antiphon before the Gospel" was sung after the Hallelujah. After the gospel the celebrant chanted.

So there was a continual alternation of reading and singing, but in the time of Pope Gregory, in the beginning of the seventh century, the gospel and the epistle were not read, but sung. Thus the difference between Scripture reading and chants was not so sharp anymore. At the same time there appeared books, called *Comes,* guides for the reading and the preaching in the services. These books contained the titles of the pericopes, which had to be read according to the liturgical year. By degrees there came in the West many local and regional systems of pericopes. So there came a prescribed reading and preaching, especially in the time of Charlemagne in the beginning of the ninth century. This compulsory system of pericopes is still in effect in the Roman Catholic Church.

Reformation

Luther preserved the pericope system, but his ideal was the "lectio continua," the continued reading of the Scriptures. However, his argument for preserving the system of pericopes was for instance that in Wittenberg there were many students who would later be obliged to preach in congregations, where the pericopes were still in vogue. (Koopmans, 1941:41). In Lutheran churches it became and remained a custom to preach in the main service on Sunday the gospel of that Sunday and in the second service the prescribed epistle, or Luther's Catechism. Calvin rejected the system of pericopes. He wrote: in the early Christian church the ministers did not preach according to "sectiones" (divided parts), but according to "lectio continua" (continuing reading). There was a moment that certain parts joined certain times of the year. In that time, Calvin said, they made a pericopic system. But the whole system is established injudiciously. Calvin promoted the "lectio continua" and the "praedicatio continua" as well. There is a close connection between both and Calvin always preached just after the Scripture reading.

As for Zwingli, he promoted the "lectio continua" too and preached whole Bible books, especially of the New Testament, from the beginning to the end, sometimes during several months (Old, 1975:195ff.). In the refugee congregation of London, "lectio continua" and "praedicatio continua" had been given by the ministers, for instance of the whole letter of Paul to the Romans, and in the beginning of the Reformed churches in The Netherlands, more than one national synod promoted continuous preaching of a whole book of the Bible. More and more the Reformed churches opposed not only the pericope system, but the "lectio continua" as well. They feared the compulsion of the pericope system and the danger of neglecting many parts of the Bible, especially of the Old Testament. But they also objected that sometimes in "lectio continua" there was no connection between reading and preaching. Preaching whole Bible books in a great number of sermons leads to one-sidedness. Then it seems that one is eating for month after month for dinner only bread, after that for years only vegetables and at last for a long time only meat. That would be tiring and unhealthy (Kuyper, 1911:295). Therefore, it is advisable, to read the Bible, Old Testament, namely the law of the LORD, psalms and prophets as well, and the New Testament, gospel and epistles. But the Scripture readings must cohere with the text of the sermon.

In liturgical and historical sense it is not advisable to have a gap between reading and preaching. When the choice of a text is free, the reading is free too, in the same sense. On the other hand, it is neither advisable to jump from one thing to another. Therefore, a *compromise* is to be made between "lectio continua" and the free choice of a text. There is, for instance, the possibility of continuity in preaching and reading for a shorter series than a whole book of the Bible, or to preach and read a special theme for a number of sermons. But it is always preferable to select the readings in connection with the preaching. Scripture reading is a constituent part of the service. It has a special meaning, just as the reading of the Ten Commandments of the LORD, as the Constitution of God's Covenant.

It has a special meaning in connection with the text of the sermon as well, to open the context, to show the relations, to build up the knowledge of the Lord Jesus Christ as the central contents of the whole Word of God. Therefore, the reading of the Holy Scripture is the foundation and one of the pillars of Christian public worship (Wegman, 1976:98). The function of it is essential for the service, in which the two parties of God's covenant meet one another. The whole Bible is the infallible Word of God and the inscripturation of the covenant of the LORD. Therefore, the covenant document for today, the Bible, consisting of the Old and New Testament is to be read in every service. God wants His relationship with us to be known to us.

Reader

So the reading of the Holy Scriptures is necessary and indispensable to public worship in the Christian church. But what about the *reader?* Who must read the Scriptures? Does the reader have a *special and separate task* in the service?

In the Reformed churches it was the custom until this century that the service started with the appearance of the reader. Many times the reader came in action even before the service started. For instance in Scotland the reader started with a form like this: "Let us dispose our hearts to the service of God by singing the following psalm. . . ." In The Netherlands too, the reader entered before the service and asked the congregation to sing the first psalm. And after that, the service started.

But this custom was neither new nor a peculiar mark of Reformed churches. No, this custom already existed in the fourth century in Jerusalem. In the time of Bishop

Cyril in the second part of the fourth century, people came very early to the church. They "sit waiting there singing hymns and antiphons, and they have prayers between, since there are always presbyters and deacons there ready for the vigil, because so many people collect there, and it is not usual to open the holy places before cock-crow. Soon the first cock crows, and at that time the bishop enters and goes into the cave in the Resurrection church. The doors are all opened, and all the people come into the church, which is already ablaze with lamps. When they are inside, a psalm is said by one of the presbyters, with everyone responding." (Egeria, XXIV, 8,9). So not the bishop, but one of the presbyters started in that time the service. However, not only in the fourth century, but even in the very beginning of the Christian church this situation existed. It seems that presbyters and deacons read the Scriptures and led the song, and that the pastor delivered the sermon (Dix, 1954:39ff.).

In the second century we hear about a fixed office in the church under the name *lector*. Even laymen, although educated laymen, could fulfil this task.

In the third century this task became an official ecclesiastical degree. Already in the beginning of the third century the reader had achieved the status of an official in the congregations of Northern Africa.

Cyprian describes the reading desk as "the tribunal of the church." It was situated there in the centre of the church, like the reading desk in the synagogue.

From a letter of Cornelius, who was elected bishop of Rome in the year 251, to Fabius, bishop of Antioch, we learn that the Roman clergy in his day numbered forty-six presbyters, seven deacons, seven subdeacons, forty-two acolytes, fifty-two exorcists, fifty-two readers and janitors (that means doorkeepers). The readers were held in great esteem. Commodian addresses them in his "Instructions" as follows: "Vos flores in plebe, vos estis Christi lucernae" ("You are the flowers under the people, the lights of Christ"). Eusebius mentions that during the persecution under the emperor Diocletian in the beginning of the fourth century the prisons everywhere were filled with bishops, presbyters, deacons, *readers* and exorcists, so that room was no longer left in them for those condemned for crimes. Before that time Tertullian writes about the readers in the church: "Hodie diaconus, qui cras lector" ("Who is deacon today will be reader tomorrow"). And also: "The leaders of the congregation are "probati seniores" (experienced elders) or "praesidentes," and their assistants are deacons and readers" (Dekkers, 1947:38,72ff.).

In the fourth century we find in several places young men, who were not old enough to be ordained to other offices, proceeding as readers. So the later Pope Damasus was already lector at the age of thirteen. To become a lector, there was at first an "adlectio" (an examination) and after that came the "ordinatio." So it is understandable that in several churches, like Rome, Lyons and Reims, there were "scholae lectorum" (schools for readers), who became in the seventh century "scholae cantorum (schools for singers). In that time the readings of the Bible were given in charge with the deacons and the subdeacons. Remarkable is the decision of the council of Toledo (398): a penitent can be a lector again, but then he may not read the gospel and the epistles!

Further development

Several times the church father Augustine spoke and wrote about the "lectores." They must read the Scripture from the "rostrum" and sometimes from the steps of the "absis" (the higher part of the church building). Augustine called the readers "young men, who did not yet change their voices" (Van der Meer, 1947:31). In another place Augustine called the lectores even "infantuli" (little boys). The point was that the boys should have a clear, plain, unbroken voice. But they were in the time of Augustine always "pueri," boys, who were very young, and who even had little knowledge. Always after the greeting in the beginning of the service, done by the bishop himself, the congregation answered. But immediately the young lector then started to declaim the Scripture reading with a clear voice. No wonder that in later times decisions were made that the lector might not be too young. For instance, Justinian, a Byzantine emperor of the sixth century decided that no one could be lector before the age of eighteen. But the independent liturgical function of the lector was maintained through the ages. Still the pulpit was forbidden for him and reserved for the ordained priest.

Not only the lector, but also a deacon could read the Scripture. In any case, according to the decision of the Council of Trent in the sixteenth century, at least two readings were to be held in the service. The term "lector" is still in vogue and Rome still uses the word in the sense of an ecclesiastical task.

The Reformation of the sixteenth century knew the office of the reader as well. Calvin for instance maintained in the beginning two servants in the services. He called them according to the old names: deacons and subdeacons. Especially in the daily services there was a lectio continua. The task of the lector in the time of the Reformation was often: to read the Holy Scripture before the beginning of the service. So we can read in the articles of Wesel (1568) that it is useful, to prevent idle talk, that one of the elders or deacons should read a chapter of the Scriptures. But the readers must be mindful that it is not their office to explain the Scriptures. Therefore they have to stay away from any explanation. They may not strike their sickles in the harvest of another one, and in the second place they may not disturb the common understanding of the church by untimely explanations (Biesterveld & Kuyper, 1905:13ff.).

In the same way we read about readers in the Acts of Synod Dordrecht 1574. The reading must not be done from the pulpit and most of the time the readers should be teachers of the school. We also read about the readers in the *Acts* of particular and provincial synods in the end of the sixteenth and the beginning of the seventeenth century. The provincial synod of Haarlem 1606, in answering a question of the Church of Alkmaar, decided that the lector must be a member of the church.

In the same year the provincial synod of Nijmegen said: the readers may not interfere "in partes ministerii," the office of the ministers of the church (Reitsma/Van Veen, 1985: IV, 146). Apparently it was necessary to forbid that again and again. It is also to be noted that at the time of the synod of Dordt 1618/'19 a reader in Kampen did not only read the Holy Scripture, but he read a long letter defending the Remonstrant ideas and heresies as well. The provincial synod of Overijsel then decided that this reader should be suspended. (Reitsma/Van Veen, 1896:V, 340). At the same time there was the case of a reader at the provincial synod of Utrecht. He not only read the gospel, but gave explanations too and baptized as well. It was decided that he had to abstain from all ecclesiastical ministry because he had no licence for it. Moreover he was condemned to be unworthy to read the Holy Scriptures in the services (Reitsma/Van Veen, 1897:VI, 433).

In the meantime synod decided that the readers had to be examined. If it was clear that they could read well in public worship, they were allowed to do it. If not, they could not be a Scripture reader of the church. (Reitsma/Van Veen, 1897:VI, 323).

Amsterdam

It is most interesting to hear how the reader functioned in the capital city of Amsterdam in the beginning of the Reformation. Exactly half an hour before the service started, the organ stopped and the reader stepped behind his desk. In the beginning he did not read the announcements of the consistory. The ministers did that on the pulpit. But the Reverend Plancius proposed to change this and his proposal was adopted. So the lector read the announcements before the service. He filled the remaining time with reading the Bible. He started with Genesis 1 and proceeded to Revelation 22.

So it was a real "lectio continua," of course divided over many Sundays. Later the ministers made a list, more or less adapted to the liturgical year. Scripture reading was interrupted by singing psalms. This custom was maintained in Amsterdam until the twentieth century (Evenhuis, 1967:57ff.).

Dordrecht

In 1578 the Scripture reading before the preaching had been introduced in Dordrecht. The consistory decided to ask elders for that task, but also decided to wait until the new elders had been installed in their office.

In the beginning the elders only read in the services of the Lord's Supper, but after seven years, the consistory decided to do that every Sunday. The elder who was a reader in the cathedral of Dordrecht received a free habitation in the Guest House. In the year 1619 the municipality appointed the readers. The consistory examined them and presented them to the burgomasters, who elected them. Their function also included the visiting of the sick and hearing the children recite their Catechism lessons. For the last task they received twenty-five guilders yearly (Schotel n.d.:313ff.). This office of the reader was a very serious matter.

In Zeeland a synod decided that the calling of readers and singers should be done by the consistory. The argument was: their service is fully ecclesiastical. Another decision of the same synod was: "When both offices of reading and singing in public worship have been done by one and the same person, such a call must be extended in the same way as the call of the ministers of the church."

Other countries

How was the situation in other countries? In many churches there were readers. In the "Holy Liturgy" of the Byzantine rite of the "orthodox churches" in the East the reading belongs to the "cheirothesia," one of the lower ordinations.

As for England, we read in the "Form of Prayers" of 1556, used by the Puritans: "Upon the days appointed for the preaching of the Word, when a convenient number of the congregation are come together, that they make fruit of their presence till the assembly be full, one appointed by the eldership shall read some chapters of the canonical books of Scripture singing psalms between at his discretion: and this reading to be in order as the books and chapters follow, that so from time to time the holy Scriptures may be read throughout. But upon special occasion, special chapters may be appointed." (Maxwell, 1931:177).

In Scotland, a similar practice soon appeared. Readers were appointed from 1560 onwards to "read the Commoune Prayeris and the Scripturis," and this practice of reading was to be carried on daily in the town churches.

There is a description of the year 1635 of an English Puritan visiting Edinburgh. He writes: "Upon the Lord's Day they do assemble betwixt eight and nine in the morning, and spend the time in singing psalms and reading chapters in the Old Testament until about ten. . . . The afternoon's exercise, which begins soon after one, is performed in the same manner . . . save the chapters then read out of the New Testament."

Remarkable is the fact that sometimes women read the Scriptures. In the *Manual* of the French Carmelites, 1680, there is a full description of the solemn reading of the gospel at the washing of the feet on Maundy Thursday. A nun takes the gospel book from the altar and goes to the desk, preceded by lights and incense; she censes the book and reads the gospel exactly as the deacon does at High Mass.

But this replacement of deacons by women, as in this case in the Roman Catholic Church, is an exception. Almost always *men* fulfil the task of reading the Scripture, and this task had been maintained as a *constituent part* of public worship.

Often they were "lay readers." In Lutheran Germany the schoolmaster carried this burden more often than the pastor.

In Scotland in the majority of sixteenth-century parishes the Lord's Day services were also conducted by the readers, following the *Book of Common Order*. In those parishes the ordained minister (with some of the congregation) entered only just before the sermon. The minister also felt free to substitute prayers of his own in the stated liturgy. A similar institution developed in continental Reformed churches, the French with their "lectures," and the Dutch with "voorlezers" (Nichols, 1968:70).

As for the Presbyterians, they were uneasy about the rapid expansion of unlicensed preachers and laymen, which the Independents encouraged in congregational "prophesying." They also wished to set limits on "lecturing." "Lecturing" was a running exposition of Scripture and was especially popular through the system of Puritan "lectureships," of endowed preaching posts outside the regular benefices. The Directory permitted lecturing, but specified that if the Scripture was to be expounded, it should wait till the end of the chapter. What was merely permissive here soon became general practice. The minister added an expository "lecture" to his reading of Scripture in addition to the sermon. The Scotch assembly had to set the hour for morning worship half an hour earlier to accommodate the additional time added by the "lecturing." And the old "reader's service" disappeared altogether. The question was now, how to reunite the separate services of the reader and the preacher.

Special readers or not?

Are the readers (elders, deacons or laymen) able to read the Holy Scriptures in public worship? More than once the answer given is: No!

There are many stories about reading elders, who made mistakes, who could not read strange terms and strange names very well.

It is known that a reader in the morning service and in the afternoon service on account of two different ministers had to read the same chapter of the Epistles with many names for greetings. In the first service he stumbled over his words when he read all the names. In the second service he took it easier, saying in short: "Furthermore you may have the greetings of the same people as this morning!"

And well-known is the story of the reader who was the chanter as well. He had to sing an unknown song, but he could not read it very well. So he apologized for that, saying on a half melodious tune:

"My eyes are dim, I cannot see" —

The congregation, however, thought this sentence was the first of the song, and sang after him:

"I speak of my infirmity"
"I did not mean to sing a hymn"
"I only said: My eyes are dim!"

But good *preparation* is the way out here. And what about that minister who is sometimes unintelligible on the pulpit? That happens more than once!

Almost a century ago the advice had been given to each Scripture reader: "Do not read the Scripture like a notary but like an heir reads the last will!"

It is a challenge to those who read the Scriptures to do it well. The reader should never give the impression that he is reading just because the order of service calls for a reading from the Scripture at that time. He should convey to the congregation that what he is reading is of very great importance (Rayburn, 1980:208).

But to read well is a rare accomplishment. It is much more common to excel in singing or in public speaking.

It is very important that the reader prepares always the Scripture reading before the service. Already in the first century the synagogue reading was prepared very well. The reader knew at least the day before the service was held what part of the Scripture he had to read, and he was supposed to read in the service very well and "with melodious voice."

But the congregation must attend to the reading too. We agree with the wish of a contemporary liturgical scholar: "It is of great importance that members of the congregation should follow the reading of the Scriptures in their own Bibles or in Bibles provided for them in the pews." (Rayburn, 1980:209). We must not leave the Bible on the *pulpit* alone. That is the reason too why we would strongly defend to have a special reader of the Holy Scriptures in public worship, and to look for men who are able and capable to read the Bible in the services of the church. For the question is: is the Bible property of the minister of the church, so that only *he* is able to read it? The answer is: no, our LORD gave the Bible in the hands of all His people. The reading of the Bible, therefore, is not a privilege of a pastor, neither especially something of an office-bearer!

The institute of the "lector" as reader of the Holy Scripture has been defended strongly by A. Kuyper. He writes that the minister is already the Jack-of-all-trades and that is not good in the church. Moreover, from the beginning of the Christian church, the acts of the official services were divided among two or three persons. Kuyper pleads in favour of the reader apart from the preacher. He writes: public service means a meeting. It is not only a meeting between God and His people, but a meeting of the people together as well. And therefore it is not good to think that everything is to be done by one person and that everybody only comes to hear that one person (Kuyper, 1911:171ff., 262ff.).

Connection between reading and preaching

When should the Scriptures be read? We said already it would be good to have no gap between reading and preaching, except singing psalms or hymns between both. But should that close association of the Scripture reading with the preaching be an argument against the restoration of the institute of the lector, as has been said?

I do not believe that. It is a fine variation in the service, especially when things have been prepared very well. No doubt it would promote the beauty of the Reformed worship if the special task of the reader were to be restored. With A. Kuyper I say: think if over, consider it and discuss it! And we can use the pulpit and the reading desk as well, from which places even in large buildings, one can be quite understandable, with today's modern technology!

But let the minister announce all elements of the service previously. All elements. For the caretaker, for the organist, for the Scripture reader too, for the whole congregation, so that everybody can come to worship well-prepared!

And let us give content to the task of the public reader in the church. It was not good that the lector read the announcements of the consistory quite sometime before the service started. But why should it be impossible that the reader of the Scriptures reads the announcements at another time, when the whole congregation assembles? And would it be impossible that the reader announced the psalm which is to be sung after the reading of God's Law? And if there is no minister preaching in the service, is there any objection that in that case two brothers appear, namely as reader of the Scriptures and as reader of the sermon?

A sensitivity for these liturgical matters would be very desirable.

We have to see the exalted place of the Word of the covenant of the LORD in public worship, where He and His people meet one another.

We have to see the exalted place of the preaching of the Word of God by the ministers of the church in public worship.

We have also to see the exalted place of the Kingdom of priests, as all the members of the church are, especially when they meet together in the service. Let us all see our place and task, worshipping the LORD, praising our God in all the parts of the beautiful public worship! So we are now going to finish our address with the following:

Conclusions

1. The reading of the Holy Scripture was already known in the time of the Old Testament and in the synagogue; it was one of the constituent elements of the Christian public worship.

2. It is necessary that this principle of Scripture reading be maintained in public worship; for the Bible is the covenant document for today as well.

3. The Law of God in the Ten Commandments is to be read as the constitution of the covenant of the LORD; besides the reading of the Law of God, at least one other part of the Holy Scriptures is to be read in every service.

4. Scripture reading, preaching and teaching belong together; it would be better, not to interrupt these elements, except for instance by singing between the readings or between reading and preaching.

5. Reading of an arbitrary part of the Bible, without any relationship to the text of the sermon, is not good; it is preferable to select the readings carefully in connection with the preaching.

6. The Holy Scripture is not the property of the minister of the church, but the whole congregation possesses the Bible; it is therefore desirable that the reading of the Bible takes place by another reader.

7. It is not necessary that the Scripture reading be done by an office-bearer; the main thing is that the Bible will be read clearly in public worship.

8. It will be good that the function of Scripture reader is not limited to only one person; variety and interchange are here desirable.

9. Just as for all elements of public worship a good and timely preparation is indispensable, the best way is that the minister makes all the elements of the service known ahead of time.

10. It is desirable to give content to the task of the public reader; he can take care of the reading of the confession and the announcements of the consistory as well.

THE OFFICE AND DUTY OF THE ORGANIST

POETRY AND PROSE

The Organist

Up the stairs without a runner
Climbs he to the gallery.
Then begins, once he is seated,
Softly his soliloquy.
'Take a look at the first prelude,
Seven triplets in a row;
Here I'll use the sesquialtra,
There a flute should nicely go.'

So he tries to solve his problems.
'Tis already time to start . . .;
Softly he begins his prelude,
Left hand has the solo part;
In a pair of worn-out sneakers,
On the pedal, feet are on the go;
Now and then he plays a few notes
On the manual below.

To the brothers and the sisters
His endeavours are not known.
'Let him have his fun,' they're saying,
And they add, 'To each his own.'
If you judge by what you're hearing,
He's not very good, you know.
It's too loud, too soft he's playing,
Much too fast or much too slow.

With the psalm, in proper rhythm,
Utter chaos reigns below.
It's too fast that way already,
Yet much faster it must go.
And his offertory playing
Could have been much better, too.
Through that tootling one hears barely
That the neighbour says, 'Thank you.'

If per chance he plays a wrong note
('As the hart . . .' a child can play),
Heads are shaken in feigned pity:
'T was a proper mess today.
A hundred times it may be perfect;
If it's hundred-'n-one, watch out.
That the plaints are then forthcoming
Oh so quickly, there's no doubt.

Down the stairs without a runner
Wearily he makes his way.
Even though he sometimes grumbles,
There's no doubt he loves to play.
If it's Bach he plays or, worse still,
Feike Asma or Jan Zwart,
Once he's seated at the organ
He plays it with all his heart.
(Jaap Mijderwijk, transl. from Dutch by S. VanderPloeg)

Those who meditate about the organist and his task are involuntarily tempted to quote from the copious poetry written about the office and duty of the organist. It is difficult not to do this for the nature of the man's profession is such that one is almost automatically inclined to speak and write about him in verse.

The title of this essay, however, is taken from a very prosaic book which was published in 1694 by Reynier van Doesburg, bookseller on the Fish Market at Rotterdam. I mean that beautiful book *The Office and Duties of Elders and Deacons,* written by Jacobus Koelman, minister of the gospel.

Let it be said beforehand that when we speak about the "office" of the organist we do not give it the pregnant meaning which Koelman gives this word. We are not dealing with a special office in Christ's church, even though others in certain liturgical circles think differently. We are speaking about the organist's office as being synonymous with his duty.

The organist and his faith

The first point to be considered, in our opinion, is the organist and his faith. Kuyper was fond of quoting the 50th Psalm, wich speaks of Zion as "the perfection of beauty." "So high stood the Temple for beauty in Israel," writes Kuyper, "that when Solomon had to build the temple and was unable to find an architect in all Israel who could give form to this beauty, he did not say: 'Then we must sacrifice this beauty, for it must be a Jew who is going to do the work.' No, he went to the heathens and found in Hiram a man who could build it to the aesthetic and artistic requirements. It was this heathen builder who created the temple. That Solomon, in so doing, did not kick over the traces, but stayed in line with God's ordinances becomes clear from the lay-out and furniture of the Tabernacle. Then it is the Spirit of God Himself who gives Bezaleel and Aholiab artistic integrity and an eye for beauty and who to the smallest detail had the parts and the tools of the tabernacle constructed according to the law of aesthetics" (Kuyper, 1911:75).

Kuyper's conclusion is that there can be no objection against engaging an architect from outside our circle, if no suitable church architect can be found among the brethren.

Now one could perhaps think that Kuyper is of the same opinion with regard to organists. One could reason: the task of the organist is an artistic one; if we cannot find one among the brethren who meets our standards, we hire one from outside our circle.

Under no circumstances does Kuyper wish to go in that direction. He selects organists from among the brethren for in the worship service not only beauty, but above all holiness plays an important role (Kuyper, 1911:158).

This holiness comes first. The worship service is a matter of the communion of saints. "It would be improper, to give this direction in the hands of an unbeliever who only works in the field of art and who could not lead the singers entrusted to him in the area of faith. The choir-master would be a stumbling block to his chorister and could conceivabley keep them from the holy encounter" (Milo, 1946:216).

A few more quotations from Milo, for in our opinion he makes meritorious remarks on the subject. "Even when the organist is a confessing member of his church, he can only do his work properly if he has a rich life in faith. Isolation behind curtains for many years can lead to an 'ivory-tower culture.' When the organist literally as well as figuratively looks down on the congregation - *they* sang fairly well today; *they* do not know this tune; *they* like this minister - he has removed himself from the congregation and has become a wandering sheep. It is precisely the artistic type - also through lack of understanding on the part of the congregation - who runs the risk of losing himself in subjectivism. It is therefore dangerous to put an organist behind curtains. It harms his experiencing of the communion of saints. It is beneficial for an organist to sit from time to time among the brethren so that he can sing along. It is, however, not enough to see to it that the spiritual growth of the organist does not lag behind. The organist above all needs to have a rich life of faith and be an active churchmember. His playing 'according to the Word' is prophesying. Not only should he know the metrical psalter for the most part by heart and possess a great knowledge of Scripture, but also have a feeling for the content and spiritual value of churchsong and make this feeling correctly known to others. His playing is not sufficient if it merely avoids all giving of offence. It must edify positively and contribute to God's honour and the congregation's salvation. Now without promoting the organist to special officebearer we should insist that he be spiritually healthy and capable of growth in that respect. Organists with a derelict life of faith, indifference towards the sacraments, or chronic irresolution, cannot be chief-musicians."

Prophesying from the organ bench

That organ playing is related to prophecy, Jan Zwart already told the Reformed people in 1934. He spoke of "prophesying during the worship service, before and after the sermon, in a language the people understand." At Zwart's death Schilder wrote, "What our forefathers in not even circuitous ways concluded from 1 Cor. 12 (namely that also from the organ bench the neighbour has to be edified), that Jan Zwart felt burning within him and how he was consumed by that fire!" (Schilder, 1937:341).

A year later, during the unveiling of Zwart's tombstone, Prof. Schilder said: "His life's work was to prophesy from the organ bench, and when we say that we give true expression to what motivated this man."

In a commemoration address K.S. called Jan Zwart a confessor who did not wish to push prophecy aside. He ended with: "To those people for whom the language of art was foreign, and who had their own Christian faith content, he spoke in his own language; art's norms were obeyed and the church's 'credo' was honoured. He who is able to do that has done a great thing" (Schilder, 1947:349).

There is thus a clear connection between organ playing and prophecy. The organist who understands his task well will confess his faith in his organ playing and so contributes to the edification, that is, to the building up, of the congregation.

The organist and his art

First we saw that an organist has to be a believer, if he is to do his task in the worship service properly.

Although his spiritual disposition comes first, it can never replace the artistic knowhow. Faith, indispensable as it may be, does not make a person a capable organist;

talents for and skills in organ playing must go with it. When the tabernacle was built, God Himself filled men with His Spirit so that they could think of designs (Ex. 31:3,4). There follows for added emphasis: "and I have given to able men ability" (31:6). Chronicles, in dealing with the singers, speaks about people "who were *trained* in singing to the Lord" (1 Chr. 25:7). The word "skilful" is even used in this context.

From this it becomes clear that we should not be satisfied with a minimum, but should strive for the maximum (the optimum). Our rule should be: our best is not really good enough, for Christ holds the demand of perfection before us.

For that reason the organist has to be an artist. "The church selects that brother," according to Milo, "who perceives the churchsong correctly and who has developed his skills in order to lead the singing in the best possible manner. No one is born with this ability. Only his talents did the artist receive from His Creator; for the development and use of his gifts he himself is responsible . . . Some of us are born with a fine sense of justice, a warm love for humanity, with leadership qualities, or with an acute religious consciousness. Can these people by virtue of their inborn abilities present themselves as lawyers, ministers of social welfare, officers, or preachers? Neither does an organist become a skilled professional by the bare fact of his musical talents alone. The most musically gifted person would not be accepted by an orchestra, unless he has received a sound training. Even less should such an untrained person be allowed to play during the worship service (Milo, 1946:218).

The organist and his training

This brings us to the next point: the training of the organist. Regretfully, only a few of our churches have a proper tracker organ. Often we have to be satisfied with a harmonium, sometimes with a piano, or (the less said about them the better) electronics.

Among us professional organists are even rarer than proper church organs. If we have such persons let us treasure them! In the course of time many organists became estranged from the church. Of course, they have themselves to blame, too. Where was their faith when they had to make the choice between a lessor organ within the Reformed church or a better organ without? Such a choice must be made in faith. It remains a sad thing that a man like Jan Zwart became organist of a Lutheran church in Amsterdam. How many of the professional organists, in accepting a position, gave up their church membership or even their faith? At the same time, however, I ask: did the churches always understand the needs or problems of the organist? (I am not talking about money in the first place). Has there often not been misunderstanding or lack of appreciation that made these persons feel isolated from the congregation?

Training then is needed and that training we must appreciate. The organist should not play all kinds of bravura to show off his virtuosity and the congregation should not react too quickly to an effort by the organist to remain "fresh": "All modern stuff, you can keep it!"

Our requirements should not be put on the low side. One does not become an organist in a few years, if previous training is lacking. Where studies have to be undertaken in spare time, one can count on at least five years. Even then it still depends greatly on the talents of the teacher whether or not one will pass a comparative examination.

Do stimulate this study! We live in a time in which the modern media offer us everything in the easiest possible manner. Seated in a comfortable chair all things are within easy reach. You don't have to do anything for it. Our youth has to be stimulated to activity and creativity, especially now that leisure time increases. Let it not happen again that a minister, when he was unable to find an organist in the congregation, was forced to ask an accordionist to take place on the organ bench. The next Sunday the good man had to play with hands and feet already.

Comparative examinations are necessary. The organ committee should not select the least poor from among all the poor candidates. They must have the courage to state that no choice could be made and to advise the candidates to study some more. At best only a temporary appointment can be made under such circumstances.

Apart from competent playing of independent organ music, the organist must, above all, be capable of accompanying the congregation. That means: that he must make the psalm tunes his own and know the church modes. "Accompanying," writes H. Hasper, "means to go along with someone. It neither means to run ahead or drag along, nor to follow or to lag behind, but to be where the other is, not to lose him, if necessary to help him along, to escort him and so create a sense of security and peace." Hasper adds that an organist neglects his duty if he, during the singing of the congregation, does something other than accompanying and supporting (Hasper, 1941:140ff.).

The organist and his honorarium

If the church has capable organists in its employ, they must be esteemed, too. That, in the first place, means honouring him. Also the organist is worthy of honour if he does his work well. Does this have to be expressed in money? Here I touch a hot issue. On purpose I left out one of the stanzas of Van Mijderwijk's poem and quote it now in this context.

Renumerations for his service
Are generally quite small
(Or as frequently the case is
Th' organist gets none at all).
For 'it broadens his horizon.'
'Tis a labour-o'love you know.'
But the worn seat of trousers
Is but all he's got to show.

Nota bene: this stanza dates from a few decades ago. Since then the standard of living has risen considerably. Salaries of church functionaries have risen. Those of the organist, too?

"It has to be a labour of love," is often the reaction. Sometimes one adds naughtily: "He misses the collection already, too!"

I am afraid that in most cases his honorarium is no more than a sort of indemnification for services rendered during the week and then almost exclusively for marriage ceremonies. Sometimes forced, I am told because no organist would show up otherwise. They simply couldn't always quit early to take half a day off.

One is quick to draw a comparison with the special office-bearer, not with the minister but with the elder and deacon. It is said: how much free time do not these men often give to the church and that also is a labour of love. In the first place I wish to point out that everything in the church is a labour of love, in the sense that it must come from and be done in love. It is not possible to pay for all the hours given. Nobody would want that either. But if an elder, in the course of his duties, regularly has taken time off, e.g. as a delegate to all sorts of meetings, it shouldn't happen that he should have to give up all his holidays for that. It must be possible to indemnify him or at least offer to do that.

Furthermore I wish to speak in favour of making it possible for elders and deacons to keep up with the literature pertaining to their office. If they are to prove the spirits, if they are to remain fresh on home visits, in short, if they are to discharge their offices faithfully, they must study. That costs money. This they should not have to pay out of their own pockets.

Let me extend this parallel. We should at least, I believe, enable the organists to keep up with the developments in his field. They should not have to ask for that; it should be offered to them. They want to put their talents at the disposal of the church community. With love. That comes first. But more is needed than time. They must study if they do not want to play the same old tune over and over. For that books are needed, books about music, books about the worship service, also books with music for before, during, and after the service.

It becomes more difficult when we are dealing with professional organists. I would not like to make a rule, but would like to plead for proper renumeration, which does not turn it into just another job, but which shows appreciation for the work done. Will that kill the love? I am not afraid of that. Milo writes in this connection: "Where the organists form the musical conscience of the church, there is no place for wage-slaves or misers, but for church-members who vigorously stimulate the church's sacred song. And that not only by virtue of inborn talents, but also by virtue of sound training and costly sacrifices . . . Truly, even if they were paid, the character of the labour of love would not be lost" (Milo, 1946:218). In a footnote he adds: "Even though the comparison with the Levitical singers and instrumentalists is faulty (for theirs was a spiritual office), it is not superfluous to show how the Levite was honoured according to God's law; the tithes were their rewards for services rendered (Num. 18:31); they were free from other service, for they were on duty day and night (1 Chron. 9:33); the people were not to forsake the Levite (Deut. 12:19), and when they did that Nehemiah remonstrated with the officials (Neh. 13:10,11), for the singers, who did work, had fled each to his field and the house of God was forsaken. Yet . . . no one can deny that they performed a labour of love: the Dutch metrical psalter even speaks of a "burning with zeal for the service of the Lord." (Ps. 134) (Milo, 1946:231).

THE ORIGIN OF OUR PSALM MELODIES

John Calvin

During a long time in the middle ages, the people of the Church did not sing in the public worship services. It was John Calvin who rediscovered the book of Psalms for the people of the Church and who transferred the singing in the Church from the clergy to the Church as a whole. The Reformer of Geneva taught the Church again to sing her Psalms.

In the year 1537, still during Calvin's first stay in Geneva, the Reformer proposed to the Council of the city the introduction of the singing of Psalms by the whole congregation, "in order to lift up our hearts unto God and to exalt His Name by songs of praise." But the Council of Geneva rejected Calvin's proposal. They did not consider the time to be ripe for such a radical change.

But in Strasbourg the victory began! In 1538 Calvin was banished from Geneva to this city, and already in the following year he had a small book of Psalms printed; it contained 19 Psalms in a rhymed version, together with the Song of Simeon, the Ten Commandments, and the Apostles' Creed. The rhymed versions of 13 of these 19 Psalms were made by Clement Marot, servant and court poet of King Francis I of

France, a man who had great talents. The other six rhymed versions were made by Calvin himself. The melodies to which these 19 Psalms and 3 Hymns were sung originated mostly from Matthias Greiter at Strasbourg. These melodies disappeared later on from the *Book of Praise*; the well-known melody of Psalm 68 (the same as of Psalm 36) is the only melody from Greiter's hand, which is maintained in the *Book of Praise*. He was also the composer of the melody of the Apostles' Creed, the unrhymed version of the Twelve Articles. In the Dutch *Book of Praise* it is now Hymn 4.

In Strasbourg the basis of our singing of Psalms was actually laid.

From Strasbourg to Geneva

In 1542 Marot published another 30 Psalms. The rhymed versions of John Calvin were revised. When Calvin was back in Geneva, 49 Psalms could soon be published. Unfortunately, the cooperation between Calvin and Marot did not last very long. In the same year Clement Marot left Geneva, and he died in Turin in the year 1544. He did not feel at ease with Calvinism.

At that time only a third part of the book of Psalms was finished in a rhymed version. In Geneva many were strongly convinced that this work had to be continued, but the difficulty was: who was willing and able to finish this work? Calvin did not consider his own poetical talents to be very great. In later editions, Calvin's own rhymings are missing. The Reformer started this work and promoted and stimulated it, but he was too modest to promote his own work in this respect.

In 1548 he once visited Theodorus Beza. This young man (29) had been converted to the Reformation in that same year and had come to Geneva. Calvin did not find Beza at home, but on his desk he discovered a draft of a rhymed version of Psalm 16. It appeared that Beza had started on his own to rhyme Psalms. Historians mention the fact that Beza, after he for the first time attended the public worship service in Geneva, was so impressed with the singing of Psalms that very soon he started to rhyme Psalms himself.

Calvin took the paper with him and showed it to the other ministers, who immediately became enthusiastic. Therefore Beza received the request to finish the work of Marot. That did indeed happen: in 1551 "Thirty-four Psalms of David by Theodorus Beza" were published, and in the following year they were published together with the 49 Psalms mentioned earlier.

Behind the edition of 1551 there was not only the pressure of the congregation of Geneva to finish the Reformed Psalter. In Lausanne, where Beza had become a professor, lived Guillaume Franc, who was very much interested in the rhymed psalter and who had urged Beza more than once to give priority to the work of rhyming the Psalms. But after 1551 the work stopped more or less. In the following four years only six Psalms were done, while in the years which then followed only one Psalm was added.

When in 1559 in Geneva the academy was established and Beza had moved in because he received an appointment as professor there, 60 Psalms were still to be rhymed. He was urged from all sides to finish the work, and he did indeed complete it in a short time. He did not do it as a kind of hobby or by poetic impulse. He considered the work that Marot had started to be a *duty*. He felt himself compelled to do it and accepted responsibility for the task that was given to him. In 1561 he finished the whole project. The day after Christmas 1561 permission to print the complete Psalter was received from Paris. On the same day the Paris priests rang the bells of the Church of Saint Merardus in order to disturb the public worship of the Reformed people who were gathered together in the neighbourhood. That cause a struggle. The parliament seized the occasion to hang three Reformed men. Even the guard officers who had protected the Reformed men against the attackers were sentenced to death.

It was a difficult time, filled with enmity against the Reformed people. But Beza nevertheless received the printer's privilege or permission to publish the complete Psalter. He was not dependent on the Paris parliament. With the support of the French court, the young king, his mother, and many others, he was able, in the spring of 1562, to introduce the complete Psalter also among the people of France.

The development and the growth of the Psalter took altogether a period of more than twenty years. The many editions of fragmentary Psalters point to the fact that the singing of Psalms started already very early in the Reformed public worship services. It was not delayed until the Psalter was completed.

Melodies

Already the first edition of Strasbourg, 1539, was supplied with melodies. We have already mentioned the name of Matthias Greiter, who composed several melodies, e.g., the melody of Psalm 119, which was used by Calvin for his rhymed version of Psalm 36, while Beza later on used this melody also for his rhymed version of Psalm 68.

Almost all other melodies orginated in France. The composer of most of them was Louis Bourgeois, a cantor at the Church of Saint Pierre in Geneva; he had been attracted by John Calvin himself to work on the Psalms. Louis Bourgeois composed melodies on the so-called church modes.

The melodies are of an extremely high quality. As for the church modes, already in that time they had a very long history. Thus it is absolutely not true that the Psalm melodies were based on street songs of that time or on airs and tunes which were popular then. For many decades this theory has been repeated, but it is totally wrong. In a next article we hope to work this out.

Louis Bourgeois

In my former article I mentioned the name of Louis Bourgeois, a musician who was attracted by Calvin himself in order to compose melodies for the rhymed Psalms. He came to Geneva in 1541 and already in 1542 he published some melodies, and they were followed by many more in the years which followed. Besides him also a certain Guillaume Franc worked in Lausanne until 1552. Bourgeois refashioned old melodies which belonged to the rhymed Psalms of Marot and arranged new ones for Beza. But in Lausanne the old Marot melodies were preserved and for the Beza Psalms the melodies of Franc were chosen. In the end the Psalter of Geneva was preferred to the melodies of Lausanne. It is not sure whether Louis Bourgeois was also the composer of the 34 Psalms which Beza has rhymed and which were published in 1551. In this respect also the name of Francois Gindron is mentioned, who also composed melodies to spiritual songs written by Beza. In that time Beza lived in Lausanne, where Gindron was a cantor.

It is remarkable that there were already at that time Reformed hymns. They had of course nothing to do with the so-called evangelical hymns which played a role in the 18th and 19th centuries. These Reformed hymns (also called Cantica) were directly derived from the Scriptures and were set to music on beautiful melodies in the church modes. It is certain that Louis Bourgeois composed many melodies which are of a very high quality.

But these things did not happen without any troubles. Besides financial difficulties there was discord more than once. It is said that Bourgeois had left Geneva in 1557 because Calvin had forbidden him to introduce four-part singing in the public worship services. But there is no proof for this. Although Calvin was not in favour of four-part singing in public worship, it is certain that he helped Bourgeois in the publication of four-part compositions.

At any rate, Louis Bourgeois did not finish the melodies of the Psalter. At the time of his departure, 81 Psalms had received a melody. Somewhere he himself writes that one must not conclude that all the Psalm melodies were composed by himself.

After his departure a certain "*Maître Pierre*" delivered 40 melodies. Until now it is not clear who this cantor actually was. Neither is it cleared up until now whether this man was a composer or whether he just copied melodies from other sources.

Doubles

But apart from this work of Maître Pierre, each Psalm had not yet received its own melody. The rest of the Psalms were sung to the existing melodies of other Psalms. The reason was the desire to finish the whole Psalter in a hurry: the work had already extended over several decades and not enough time had been allowed for the composition of new melodies. That is the reason why up to now 15 Psalm melodies occur twice (5 + 64, 14 + 53, 18 + 144, 28 + 109, 31 + 71, 33 + 67, 36 + 68, 46 + 82, 51 + 69, 60 + 108, 65 + 72, 74 + 116, 77 + 86, 78 + 90, and 117 + 127).

But there are also four Psalm melodies which occur three times (17 + 63 + 70, 30 + 76 + 139, 66 + 98 + 118 and 100 + 131 + 142).

One melody even occurs four times (24 + 62 + 95 + 111).

The melody of Psalm 140 is also used for the Decalogue (Hymn 7 in the Canadian Reformed *Book of Praise*). Other Genevan melodies are those of Hymn 13 (the Song of Mary) and Hymn 18 (the Song of Simeon), while the Song of Zechariah (Hymn 14) orginates from Strasbourg (1525).

Several other Hymns in the *Book of Praise* have also a Genevan Psalm melody: Hymn 2 + 27 (= Psalm 89), Hymn 6 (= Psalm 134), Hymn 11 (= Psalm 42), Hymn 21 (= Psalm 22), Hymn 22 (= Psalm 54 + one line added), Hymn 44 (= Psalm 85), Hymn 49 (= Psalm 56), Hymn 53 (= Psalm 66, 98, 118), and Hymn 58 (= Psalm 124).

It is regrettable that several beautiful melodies of Beza's Hymns have been relegated to oblivion. (I mentioned that in Thesis XII, in my dissertation) (Deddens, 1975).

Already in 1968 (*Lucerna*, VII, 3) I wrote, "It is very desirable that Calvin's heritage in the Genevan Psalter be preserved; in case of a new rhymed version, let the rediscovered but not yet used existing melodies be introduced for the doubles of rhymed Psalms, and if possible let such melodies also be used in case of a revision of the book of Hymns." It has not been done, but I myself used the beaufitul melody of one of Beza's Hymns in my book of songs, *Kom, zing en speel* (Groningen, 1979).

No popular songs and street songs!

The Psalm melodies have a very long history. But it is strange that repeatedly a connection has been sought between Psalm melodies and street songs.

In his extensive work *Kerkelyke Historie van het Psalm-Gezang der Christenen* (Amsterdam, I, 1777; II, 1778), the minister of the church at Veere, Josua van Iperen, stated that the Psalms of Marot and Beza were originally sung to popular tunes and street songs, but that not until the year 1556 Louis Bourgeois was asked to compose other melodies. But in the light of the facts which I mentioned already, this statement appears to be absolutely wrong.

But here for the first time terms like "popular tunes" and "street songs" were used. Just a century later, the Frenchman Orentin Douen likewise used these terms in another two-volume work, *Clément Marot et le Psautier Huguenot, étude historique, musicale et bibliographique, contenant les mélodies primitives des Psaumes, et des spécimens d'harmonie* (Paris, I, 1878; II, 1879). This work is even more extensive than the work of van Iperen; van Iperen's work counts 1015 pages, but Douen's work no fewer than 1461 pages!

Douen stated that many melodies of the Genevan Psalter had been borrowed from folk tunes and "top-hits" of that time. This statement was pronounced with great authority, but if one examines the "proof" which Douen tried to give, it must be said that he presents something which only resembles it. Nevertheless, Douen's statement has been repeated and accepted by many writers for a long time. I do not want to list all the names of even famous authors who repeated O. Douen's words, but it is remarkable that even a great liturgist such as G. van der Leeuw could write, "The Psalm melodies, just as we know them now, are popular tunes and dance-songs. The main part of it consists of contra-facts. But from the light tunes which were as such very often not that nice, were made beautiful melodies for the church" (Van der Leeuw, 1939:168ff.).

But at least for two reasons it would be impossible that John Calvin worked in that way. In the first place, Calvin always stressed that there must be a close connection between the words and the melodies in singing. Therefore he said time and again that our singing in church was not to be "light and frivolous," but "worthy and majestic." Calvin had a great aversion to all kinds of street ballads, which made the people only licentious, as he said.

In the second place, Calvin always went back to the church of former ages, especially to the early church. He never wanted to break with the church of the ages. On the contrary, he wanted to preserve the continuity of the church. Thus also for this reason it is very unlikely that he consented to the use of contemporary "top-hits" as Psalm melodies.

Simple, not artificial

But Calvin's aim was to give the singing in the church back to the *congregation*. How would that be possible? In Reformation times the singing in the church was limited to the priests, with their Gregorian chants. But these church songs were too difficult for the common people of the church. They were too artificial for untrained singers. Calvin considered that the common people would never be able to sing in the church all the notes of the Gregorian chants, which were often quite aristocratic and luxurious, although very different from the "top-hits" of the day.

But in Strasbourg Calvin heard rhymed hymns in the German language, and they fascinated him. Then he rediscovered, as it were, the book of Psalms, and he wanted to make it accessible to the common people of the church. He sought a style that was proper to the church, but not artificial. Therefore, Calvin often used in this respect the word "*moderate*." In his writings about church music actually this word has a threefold meaning. This "moderation" stands in the first place over against the abundance of the Gregorian chants, but Calvin used this word also over against a very frequent use of music in the church. The singing of the congregation was to have a place in public worship, but not the first and the main place. But, thirdly, Calvin used this word also over against a kind of agitation and excitement in singing. Hence the expression "worthy and majestic."

Calvin promoted simple singing in the church, not in the sense of vulgar singing, but as a kind of singing which could be done by the whole congregation.

In the meantime, he also sought to continue the tradition of the church, as far as possible.

Did he succeed? Indeed, the Psalm melodies, which nowadays are esteemed very highly everywhere, meet these requirements, and the whole so-called contrafact-theory is proved to be a fantasy.

Emmanuel Haein

Almost half a century after the publication of O. Douen's work, another Frenchman delivered an important thesis, *Le Problème du Chant Choral dans les Eglises Réformées et le Trésor liturgique de la Cantilène huguenote*. This thesis was submitted in 1926 to the Faculté de Théologie Protestante of Montpellier. Haein discovered that there is a close connection between the Genevan Psalm melodies and what he called several "timbres" and "nomes" of Gregorian chants and medieval church hymns.

That was a very remarkable discovery. It dismantled the theory of O. Douen and led the investigation further back to the history of the church.

Further inquiries

Emmanuel Haein in his thesis dated 1926 showed that there was a connection between the melodies of the Genevan Psalter and the Gregorian chants and medieval church hymns. Of course they were not the same, and the Gregorian chants were also deprived of their exuberance that had been developed in course of time. But special motives, called by Haein "timbres" and "nomes" come back in the Psalm melodies, just as they were used in medieval singing.

In this respect the development agrees with Calvin's principle that he did not want to break with the church of the ages.

But there is more. In 1929 a study was published by *Abraham Zebi Idelsohn*, titled *Jewish Music in its Historical Development*.

Idelsohn studied the Jewish way of singing in the synagogue, especially the way of singing Psalms. He discovered that there was throughout the ages a remarkable consistence in the way of singing, in spite of the isolation and separation of synagogues outside the Palestine land. He discovered also that there is a remarkable connection between the singing of Psalms in the synagogues and in the Christian churches.

Furthermore, *Peter Gradenwitz* delivered another study, called *The Music of Israel: Its Rise and Growth through 5000 Years*. He furnished sufficient material to continue the investigations of Haein going back to the synagogical songs, but also to the temple chants.

The remarkable conclusion is then that, as far as the origin of the Genevan Psalm melodies is concerned, these tunes can be traced back even to the period of revelation.

In his very extensive work of almost 2000 pages, the late *H. Hasper* worked that out in his two volumes *Calvijns beginsel voor de zang in de eredienst*, I, ('s Gravenhage, 1955) and II ('s Gravenhage/Groningen, 1976).

Hasper brought many arguments together and on the basis of the explorations by Haein, Idelsohn and Gradenwitz and by combining the data brought to light by them, he came to totally different conclusions from those of Douen. There must have been a very long tradition in the way of singing Psalms, especially via the church modes.

Pierre Pidoux

Between the publication of the two volumes of Hasper, another important study was published, namely that of Pierre Pidoux, *Le Psautier Huguenot*, I *Les Melodies*, II *Documents et Bibliographie* (Basel, 1962).

Pidoux looked for the sources of the Psalm melodies of the Genevan Psalter and published many documents which are important in discovering the origin of the Psalm melodies. Time and again his conclusions go in the same direction as those of other contemporary investigations. He proved that in many cases the Psalm melodies were derived from hymns of the *Antiphonarium* and the *Gradual*, two books consisting of Gregorian chants. Remarkable is his discovery that not only the melodies of Geneva, but also those of Strasbourg go back to those sources.

S.J. Lenselink

A couple of years before Pidoux' study, S.J. Lenselink wrote a dissertation, called *De Nederlandse Psalmberijmingen van de Souterliedekens tot Datheen, met hun voorgangers in Duitsland en Frankrijk* (Assen, 1959), and some years after Pidoux's study but in connection with this, he wrote his book *Les Psaumes de Clément Marot* (Assen/Kassel, 1969).

He writes that although there is not always a sharp distinction to be made between worldly and church music in that time, it is certain that there is a very close connection between many Psalm melodies of the Genevan Psalter and the Gregorian chants. But characteristic of the Genevan melodies, more or less over against the popular songs, is their absolute syllabical structure.

So also Lenselink pointed out that the origin of the Psalm melodies is to be found in the medieval hymns and especially in the Gregorian way of singing.

Church modes

That brings us to the matter of the so-called *church modes*, which are characteristic of the Gregorian chants and which are also used for the Genevan tunes. What are these church modes? In the "Notes on the Genevan tunes" (cf. the *Book of Praise* of the Canadian Reformed Churches, p.VII ff.) it is mentioned that in the Genevan Psalter nine different modes are represented: Dorian, Hypodorian, Phrygian, Mixolydian, Hypomixolydian, Aeolian, Hypoaeolian, Ionian and Hypoionian.

These names come from Greece. The Greeks first used tone series of four tones (tetrachords) and called them *modes*. Each area, people or city (Phrygia, Lydia, Ionia) used its own specific order of tones or steps. These developed into tone systems of seven steps or intervals to fill a so-called *octave*. An octave is the distance between a male voice and a female voice singing the same note. The natural difference in tone is called the eight-step or rather the octave interval. This distance is usually filled with seven whole and half steps to fill the space of twelve semitones. The arrangement of whole and half steps can differ in many ways. Each particular order of small and big steps is called a mode, or a key. Most of the hymns of the *Book of Praise* are composed in the so-called *major* or *minor* key. But in the Gregorian chants the Greek names are used (although their names become somewhat confused in translation). But there is much more variety in these so-called church modes than in the major and minor system. The Dorian church mode is used most frequently in the Genevan Psalter: 45 Psalm melodies are based on this mode. To explain this mode briefly: the scale of the Dorian mode has no sharps or flats in the range d to d (while the major key has two sharps from d to d, namely f sharp and c sharp). The scale of the Phrygian mode has no sharps or flats in the range e to e. The scale of the Mixolydian mode has no sharps or flats in the range g to g. The scale of the Aeolian mode is more or less comparable with the minor key: it has no sharps or flats in the range a to a (although in the minor key actually the g sharp is used). The scale of the Ionian mode is comparable with the major key, because it has no sharps or flats in the range c to c.

When modulating or transposing, the space of the semitones has to be the same. To give an example: when the major key runs from c to c (the c being the so-called *finalis*), it does not have either sharps or flats. But when the same key has been modulated to d, it has two sharps, namely f sharp and c sharp.

So when the Dorian mode runs from d to d, it does not have any sharp or flat. But when it is transposed to e, it has two sharps, namely f sharp and c sharp.

As far as the term *hypo-* is concerned, this has to do with the same mode, so that e.g., the *finalis* of Dorian scale (without sharps or flats) is also d. But the meaning of *Hypo* is: below, or beneath. That means: this scale runs not from d to d (although the finalis is indeed d), but it runs from a to a.

It would go beyond the purpose of my articles if I worked out all the details in this respect. I just give these examples in order to show the great variety and the many possibilities in the church modes.

For more details I should like to refer the readers to the interesting study of Dennis Teitsma, *Tunes of the Anglo-Genevan Psalter,* 327 Pandora Avenue East, Winnipeg, MB, R2C 0A3, 1980 (80 stencilled pages).

The so-called Gregorian phrase is composed of a flexible undulating line, a kind of sonorous thread which is sensitive to the smallest music waves. The Gregorian phrase is not static, not stiff, not sharply delineated. But the hymn, of course, has a different structure. In the hymn the architecture dominates, because of the stanzas which are composed in a strophical construction.

Background of Gregorian chants

So we see that the background of the church modes of the Psalm melodies in our *Book of Praise* is found in the Gregorian chants, and just as Em. Haein already proved more than sixty years ago, Bourgeois and "Maître Pierre" used all kinds of motives, firm melodic formulas and many other elements from the treasure of church music before Reformation times.

But it is interesting to know also what the background is of the Gregorian chants. From more than one side it has been proved that they go back via Greece to the synagogue and even to the temple.

In an also extensive study, the famous Dutch musicologist Hélène Nolthenius who was a professor at the University of Utrecht from 1958 to 1976, pointed to the rich history of the Gregorian chants. Her book was called *De oorsprong van het Gregoriaans* and was published by Querido in 1981. She discovered in Italy that relief pictures on *sarcophagus* (stone tombs) had a close connection with melodical motives of Gregorian antiphones (responsorial chants).

She also found out that the final form of Gregorian chants was actually Frankish. About the year 900, Metz in France was the centre of it.

But the origin of the Gregorian chants are to be sought in the beginning of our era, about two thousand years ago, in the Jewish synagogues.

There were Jews from Yemen and also from other Asiatic countries who immigrated about sixty years ago to Israel. Their synagogical songs appeared to have exactly the same kind of Psalmody, the same music curves in their rises and falls as the Gregorian chants.

Temple and synagogue

As I already said before, there is also a connection between the way of singing in the synagogues and the way of singing before that, namely, in the temple.

The question is: do we know anything of that way of singing, especially in the temple?

In this respect there is another very important study, namely of *Suzanna Haik Vantoura,* concerning *"La Musique de la Bible révélée"* (Paris, 1976).

Of course, it was not easy to find out in which way the people of Israel have sung their Psalms. But in our next and final article we will see that Suzanna Haik Vantoura developed a very interesting theory, which in a certain sense offers us the missing link in the long chain of church singing throughout the ages.

Biblical signs

Sylviane Falcinelli tells us that Vantoura especailly scrutizined the relevant Biblical signs. "After trying out many hypotheses, deductions, and experiments, she discovered the key to that ancient notation, she revealed the significance of the musical signs and finally revived and transcribed in modern notation the music which was revealed to her following methodical deciphering and irrefutable verification, whereas the cantillation of the synagogue, varying (for the same text) from one country to another, could not claim any logical justification." Vantoura worked on it for a long time. The result of these years of labour is an historical work which has convinced musicologists as well as Hebrew scholars, and the revelation of musical treasures which have already seduced the greatest composers. "Listening to this music," Falcinelli says, "everyone will be made conscious once again that the history of the people of Israel is the cradle of our Western history . . . and of its musical language. Those musicians of long ago, travelling through various lands, absorbed their modes. These songs issuing from the foundation of the ages seem to be very contemporary. Astonishingly modern, too, is the answer found by Biblical musicians regarding the relationship between text and music. We notice first the expressive correlation between the texts and their melodic line, and then the economy of means used in this expression. This way of underlining the intentions of the text reconfirms the affiliation of Western music, for in some chants we recognize the poetic nuances (madrigalisms) of the composers of the 16th century. But between Biblical musicians and madrigalists there are numerous levels, notably Gregorian chant, of which we are in the process of discovering the middle eastern sources" (Cover of the record Harmonia Mundi 989).

Synagogue and temple

So there is not only a close connection between the church modes of the Genevan Psalter and the Gregorian chant, but there is also the background of this chant, found in the synagogue singing. And in turn, this synagogue singing is not to be separated from the singing in the temple. Listening to a record like HMU 989, especially in respect of Psalm singing, makes this connection clear. There are also indications that the singing in the temple of David's times was based on the so-called Egyptian pentatonic scale, on which Moses is said to have composed and sung his old 90th Psalm.

Is it not remarkable that with regard to Psalm singing one can point to a long line extending throughout the history of the church?

Psalms and Hymns

No wonder that not only musicians who are church members promoted the singing of the Psalms and praised the Genevan Psalter in respect of the melodies, but that also outsiders admired the great value of these melodies.

It is very important to know that there is a continuing line in Psalm singing in the church from days of old until today.

Therefore let us be careful not to abandon this heritage!

Sometimes there is a tendency to prefer the tunes of all kinds of hymns to the Psalm melodies. Then it is said: the tunes of the hymns are easier, they are played by ear, and especially the young people like that.

At the same time it is also said: the Psalm melodies are sometimes difficult to learn, you do not so soon get used to them, etc.

But I think that also has something to do with the relation between word and tone. In former days, when the Psalms were sung in a unitone way (although against the original tonality!) and when the rhymed version was not correct, there could indeed be a problem. But all that is improved now. It is therefore to be applauded that the Genevan melodies are more promoted than before. For instance in South Africa, there is the beautiful rhymed version of the poet Totius. Unfortunately, some Psalms are rhymed in a way in which the existing church modes cannot be sung. So the Psalter is more or less mixed up with church modes and other melodies. But now there is the attempt to make it possible that all Psalms are to be sung on church modes.

Let us sing Psalms!

To prevent misunderstandings: I do not want to say a bad word concerning hymns, especially not concerning the 65 Hymns of the *Book of Praise* of the Canadian Reformed Churches. I only stress that the singing of Hymns should not be promoted at the cost of singing Psalms.

A couple of years ago I was in South Korea, and the people of the church were used to singing all kinds of Hymns. When I delivered some guest lectures at the Theological Seminary at Pusan, I pointed also to the Psalm melodies. Then several students asked me, "Why do we not sing Psalms on these beautiful melodies?" And right away some students tried to make a start of it.

Sometimes it is asked just the other way around in the mission fields, especially by missionaries, "Why do we have to sing the Psalms to the Genevan tunes? Let the people sing in the church in the way they like and which they are used to, for instance using the tunes of popular songs." And one of the arguments is then: actually also the Psalms were sung in Reformation times to popular tunes!

But since it is clear that this appeared to be wrong, let us not argue any more in this way.

I think the people in the mission fields must have their own rhymed version, in their own language. But let us be careful not to abandon the beautiful melodies of our Psalms too soon!

I want to stress also: let us sing *Psalms* and not only one or two stanzas of a Psalm. Of course, some Psalms are too long to sing as a whole. One always points to, e.g., Psalm 119 with the many stanzas. But in that case there were also already from of old indications to sing a part of the Psalm, and many times that is forgotten. But if a Psalm is not that long, let the people sing the whole Psalm. Then they will also understand the better the contents of what they are singing.

I want to point also to the possibility of *antiphonal* singing, in which two parts of the people sing on turn. That was also done from of old! A clear example of that way of singing is Psalm 136: the burden or the chorus was sung by a part of the people, while the rest was sung by another part.

Do not say too soon: then you make a part of the congregation passive and silent. To *hear* is also a matter of being active and in your mind you are then still singing with the other part, just as you are praying with the minister, when he prays on behalf of the whole congregation.

Conclusion

We may conclude at the end of these articles that the Psalm melodies of the Genevan Psalter were of undoubtedly high quality for congregational singing. The link of the Genevan melodies with the ancient church and via the synagogue with the Old Testament church has been established as proven fact, over against the so-called "contrafact theory" as if the Psalm melodies were only derived from street songs and "top-hits" of that time.

Thankful use of the Psalm melodies of the Genevan Psalter will mean a really ecumenical labour of love: we will be singing in communion with the saints of bygone ages.

In this respect it is now up to us to show our gratitude to the Lord of the church of all ages.

I will end with Calvin's words about congregational singing in his *Institutes* (vol. III, 20): "Certainly if singing is tempered to a gravity befitting the presence of God and angels, it both gives dignity and grace to sacred actions, and has a very powerful tendency to stir up the mind to true zeal and ardent prayer. We must, however, carefully beware, lest our ears be more intent on the music than our minds on the spiritual meaning of the words." And in the same context (32) he says: "If this moderation is used, there cannot be a doubt that this practice is most sacred and salutary."

MAY CHILDREN PARTAKE OF THE LORD'S SUPPER?

A timely topic

Since the beginning of the seventies many publications have appeared concerning the question whether children may partake of the Lord's Supper or not. In the Netherlands, the general synod of the "synodical churches" decided to allow children at the Lord's Supper, "since God's Word neither commands nor forbids it." Also the Church at Rijsbergen (buiten verband [outside the federation]) decided to allow children at the Lord's Supper. In the circles of these churches the question has been under discussion for many years. K.C. Smouter and M.R. van den Berg wrote about this topic in *Opbouw,* and G. Visee wrote no fewer than eight articles concerning this matter in 1965 (reprinted in the book *Onderwezen in het Koninkrijk der hemelen,* Kampen, 1979). Translated into English, they were published in *Christian Renewal.* Especially the last fact is noteworthy in connection with the 1986 synod of the Christian Reformed Church. This synod dealt with a majority and a minority report (even two kinds of minority recommendations) of the "Committee to study the issue of covenant children partaking of the Lord's Supper." In *Outlook* of June 1986, J. Tuininga also wrote an article about "Children at the Lord's Supper." So we see that the topic is under discussion also in the Western hemisphere.

In the U.S.A. several "denominations" decided to allow the children of the church to partake of the Lord's Supper, and on the mission fields also it was the experience of Reformed missionaries that in the circles of more than one "denomination" the so-called "paedocommunion" had been accepted. Therefore, it was among the topics discussed at the Fifth Conference of Reformed Mission Workers in Latin America in April, 1985. It is also worth noting that the practice of "paedocommunion" is promoted in the liberal World Council of Churches.

So everywhere the topic is under discussion and quite often it has been concluded: we may not deny children the Lord's Supper. The Rev. G. Visee even wrote: "Today there is a wholesale suspension from the Lord's Supper, as far as the children of the covenant are concerned!" That is actually a bitter reproach and if this were true, we would have to be converted in this respect as soon as possible. But the question is: Is it indeed true? Do we deny the children of the church something they have a right to, so that we actually wrong the children of God's covenant?

God's covenant

Not infrequently the discussions about this topic start with God's covenant of grace. They point, for example, to what is said in Lord's Day 27 of the Heidelberg Catechism, Answer 74: "Infants as well as adults belong to God's covenant and congregation," and also to what follows: "Through Christ's blood the redemption from sin and the Holy Spirit, who works faith, are promised to them no less than to adults." I am of the opinion that this starting point as such is a good one. Over against all kinds of Anabaptist ideas, the Reformers stressed that the children of the believers belong also to the covenant of the LORD and to Christ's Church.

But I think it is wrong to step over right away from Q.74 to Q.75 of the Heidelberg Catechism, namely, from Holy Baptism, to the Lord's Supper, and to quote then the commandment and the promises concerning the Lord's Supper in this respect. We have to bear in mind that God's covenant is unilateral in its origin but bilateral in its existence, as our Reformed fathers used to say. This is also reflected in the way they viewed the two sacraments, according to the Scriptures.

The one pointed more to the unilateral origin of the covenant, namely, baptism, whereas the other pointed more to the bilateral existence of the covenant, namely, the Lord's Supper. In the former the child is passive, in the latter the believer is active. That is also the difference in formulation between Q.69 and Q.75 of the Heidelberg Catechism. In Q.69 it is asked: "How does holy baptism signify and seal to you that the one sacrifice of Christ on the cross *benefits* you?" (i.e., the children are the object of this benefit), but Q.75 asks: "How does the Lord's supper signify and seal to you that you *share* in Christ's one sacrifice on the cross and in all His gifts?" (i.e., it is the deed of the believers). I quoted now the revised edition of the *Book of Praise* (1984), but I am of the opinion that the difference is to be seen more clearly in the first complete edition of the *Book of Praise* (1972). In that edition the formulation of Q.69 is: "How is it signified and sealed unto you in holy baptism that you *have part* in the one sacrifice of Christ on the cross?", while Q.75 in this edition asks: "How is it signified and sealed unto you in the holy supper that you *partake* of the one sacrifice of Christ, accomplished on the cross, and of all His benefits?" The difference is clear: in the case of Holy Baptism we *have part* in the one sacrifice of Christ, and in the case of the Holy Supper we *partake* of the one sacrifice, namely, as believers. Of course, one can say: Q.69 does not yet speak about the children (that will be done especially in Q.74) but presents only a general view on baptism. But we have to bear in mind that in by far the most cases baptism of infants takes place in the church; that is the common and normal way.

Are benefits denied?

If we bear in mind the difference between Holy Baptism and the Lord's Supper, we cannot maintain that some benefits of the covenant of grace are denied to the children of the believers when they are not yet allowed to partake of the Lord's Supper. H. Bavinck showed that very clearly:

"To deny the Lord's Supper to the children does not let them miss any benefit of the covenant of grace. That would indeed be the case if Holy Baptism was denied to the children. For that is only to be done by those who are of the opinion that the children stand outside of the covenant of grace. But as far as the Lord's Supper is concerned it is different. He who administers to the children baptism, but not the Lord's Supper, admits that they belong to God's covenant and that they may share all the benefits of it. He only denies to them a particular *manner* in which the same benefits are signed and sealed, because this does not fit their age. The Lord's Supper does not give any benefit which was not granted before already in God's Word and in Baptism" (Bavinck, 1930:561).

And in *Our Reasonable Faith* Bavinck writes:

"Although Baptism and the Holy Supper have the same covenant of grace as their content, and although both give assurance of the benefit of the forgiveness of sins, the Holy Supper differs from Baptism in this regard that it is a sign and seal not of incorporation into but of the maturation and strengthening in the fellowship of Christ and all His members" (Bavinck, 1956:542).

Hasty transition

So the transition may not be made too hastily from Baptism to the Lord's Supper. And that is what for instance G. Visee did. I quote:

"We teach our children *after* they have received the sign and seal of the covenant: 'How does Baptism remind you and assure you that Christ's one sacrifice on the cross is for you personally? . . . .' In my catechism class I taught Lord's Day 28 as follows:

Answer: To eat the broken bread and to drink the cup.

Question: To whom did Christ give that command?

Answer: To the believers.

Question: Will you read out loud exactly what the catechism says?

Answer: 'Me and all believers.'

Question: What is meant by 'me'?

Answer: I.

Question: So. Christ commanded you and all other believes to eat the broken bread and to drink the cup. Why don't you do it then?

Answer: I'm not allowed yet" (Visee, 1986, IV, 16, p.11).

So far the quotation from Rev. Visee's article. His conclusion is clear: the church denies to the children something which they have a right to. But there is a mistake here. Although both sacraments deal with the covenant of grace, there is a clear difference. And it is wrong to make a very hasty transition from the one sacrament to the other one. But there is more. There is also a hasty transition from the Old Testament sacrament of Passover to the New Testament sacrament of the Lord's Supper.

Passover and the Lord's Supper

One of the arguments that children must be allowed to participate in the Lord's

Supper is derived from the Old Testament sacrament of Passover. One argues then simply in this way: just as baptism came in the place of circumcision, the Lord's supper is a New Testament adaptation of Israel's Passover. The Rev. G. Visee wrote in this respect:

"There is only this difference: Christ is not merely Israel's Passover Lamb, but the Lamb of God that bears the sins of the world, and, secondly, since His blood was shed, we now have the bloodless feast of the Lord instead of the bloody sacrament of the Passover. And the children partook of that Passover. They were not passive observers, but ate of the meal. The Passover was celebrated by the household, parents and children together. It was not simply a family affair, however, for if the household was too small to eat the whole lamb other Israelites were invited to share. That is also borne out by the fact that Christ celebrated the Passover with His disciples. He and His disciples did not constitute a family; that, however, did not detract from the validity of the meal. There simply were no children in this group, nor were there any women. Nevertheless, they did and do participate in this meal."

His conclusion is clear: we may not deny the Lord's Supper to the children of God's covenant, because they participated also already in the Old Testament sacrament of Passover (Visee, 1986, IV, 14, p.11).

Relation, but not mere transition

What are we to say about this? Of course, there is a certain relation between Passover and the Lord's Supper.

But at the same time we have to be aware of the fact that the Passover did not proceed simply to the Lord's Supper. When the Rev. G. Visee says that the words of the Apostle Paul in 1 Corinthians 5:7, "For Christ, our Passover Lamb, has been sacrified," "draws an unmistakably direct connection between the Passover and the Lord's Supper," he says too much. This text deals with the fact that the Passover Lamb was a *prefiguration* of Christ's sacrifice. Furthermore, we have to bear in mind in this respect at least two things.

In the first place: there was a considerable time lapse between the breaking of the bread and the giving of the (third) cup, namely, the whole period of the eating of the Passover. In the second place: Jesus Christ did not join all the moments of the Passover, only two moments of it, but especially not the moment of the eating of the Passover.

Therefore, the Lord's Supper is not to be considered a mere Christian form of the Passover. The Passover did not proceed simply in the Lord's Supper. We may say it in this way: the Lord's Supper is the fulfillment of the Passover. The line of the Passover is not extended in the Lord's Supper, but it is picked up in it.

History of redemption

This has also to do with the history of redemption. The Lord's Supper is a sacrament of another, a new covenant. He who appeals to the Passover, in which children participated, may not simply conclude: here we have the clear proof that children may participate in the Lord's Supper. Then he has to bear in mind that there is a new element in the Lord's Supper over against the Passover. That new element, in which the Lord's Supper does not result automatically from the Passover, is related to the different way of salvation. That does not deal with the *nature* of salvation, but with the manner of salvation. The self-evidence with which the people of Israel celebrated the

Lord's Supper, old and young people together, was connected with the degree of God's revelation. The celebration of the Passover was an obligation to the people of Israel under penalty of excommunication. The new element of the covenant of Christ's blood finds its kernel in the work of God the Holy Spirit, which is a personal matter and which is not simply founded on the tie of blood.

The Old and the New Covenant stand beside each other and one cannot simply draw a parallel between both in every respect. There are some diffrences.

Responsibility

One of those differences has to do with the emphasis on responsibility in the New Covenant. In the Old Dispensation there was of course responsibility, but that is different from the responsibility of the New Dispensation. We read about that difference in Hebrews 10: "A man who has violated the law of Moses dies without mercy at the testimony of two or three witnesses. How much worse punishment do you think will be deserved by the man who has spurned the Son of God, and profaned the blood of the covenant by which he was sanctified, and outraged the Spirit of grace?" (vs. 28 and 29). That has also to do with the responsibility in connection with the Lord's Supper.

In the same chapter of the letter to the Hebrews we read a quotation from the prophecies of Jeremiah concerning the new covenant: "This is the covenant that I will make with them after those days, says the Lord: I will put My laws on their hearts, and write them on their minds" (vs. 16). Also this text shows that increased grace brings along increased personal responsibility in the New Dispensation.

It is, therefore, totally wrong when for instance James B. Jordan states: " 'Unconverted' slaves ate the Passover in the Old Covenant — inward circumcision is not the ecclesiastical criterion for participation in the Lord's Supper" (Jordan, 1982, th. 15).

Here again a mere parallel is drawn between the Passover and the Lord's Supper. This takes into account neither the increased responsibility in the New Covenant nor the progress in the history of redemption.

Besides, there are the important words of 1 Corinthians 11:26-29 in connection with the responsibility of the celebration of the Lord's Supper (hope to come back to that passage).

The "inward circumcision" is justly stressed in the church as a condition for celebrating the Lord's Supper. I am reminded of the conclusion of article 35 of the Belgic Confession:

"Finally, we receive this holy sacrament in the congregation of the people of God with humility and reverence as we together commemorate the death of Christ our Saviour with thanksgiving and we confess our faith and Christian religion. Therefore no one should come to this table without careful self-examination, lest by eating this bread and drinking from this cup, he eat and drink judgment upon himself. In short, we are moved by the use of this holy sacrament to a fervent love of God and our neighbours. Therefore we reject as desecrations all additions and damnable inventions which men have mixed with the sacraments. We declare that we should be content with the ordinance taught by Christ and His apostles and should speak about it as they have spoken."

Especially the *confession of faith,* mentioned in this article, is very important. And he who confesses his faith declares in this confession that he is a true believer, a living member of the church of Jesus Christ. He has accepted his responsibility in God's new covenant.

115

Without commitment?

In the meantime, the responsibility of the new covenant does not mean that we are without obligation in respect of the Lord's Supper. There is an obligation to accept the promises of God's covenant. So there is also an obligation to partake of the sacrament of the Holy Supper. The church may not leave that to the good pleasure of the people themselves. So if it would be so that the children are allowed to partake of the Lord's Supper, they also had to do it.

It is therefore also wrong when James B. Jordan defends the following idea: "If a child or infant will not eat the food given him, he is not to be 'force-fed.' If a child won't eat, then he won't eat. There is nothing superstitious about it" (Jordan, 1982: th. 24). Of course, we reject the Roman Catholic idea of *ex opere operato*, as if the sacrament works automatically, exclusively by the act itself. But, precisely over against this idea, we point to the responsibility involved, and we say to the people: you are not free to partake of the Lord's Supper, but it is a matter of obligation in God's covenant.

It is only one of the two: the children are not allowed to partake of the Lord's Supper, unless they have made profession of faith, or the children are indeed allowed to partake of the Lord's Supper, but then that is not without consequences. Then they are *obliged* to partake of it. If they *may* go this means at the same time that they *must* go.

Proclamation

Especially 1 Cor. 11:26-29 is important in connection with the question whether children are allowed to partake of the Lord's Supper. This passage is placed in the framework of the whole pericope of the verses 17-34, in which the Apostle Paul points to the misuses in the Church at Corinth with respect to the Lord's Supper. Over against these misuses Paul shows the great importance of the Lord's Supper. What is actually the celebration of the Lord's Supper?

In verse 26 Paul says that it is a *proclamation*: "For as often as you eat this bread and drink the cup, you proclaim the Lord's death until He comes." The apostle does not use in this sentence an imperative, in the sense of "you *have* to proclaim the Lord's death," but he gives a description of the celebration of the Lord's Supper: "You *are* proclaiming the Lord's death." But that means also that one must be aware of what he is actually doing when he celebrates the Lord's Supper.

Then, *faith* is supposed in the one sacrifice of the Lord Jesus Christ! I quote here the majority report of the Christian Reformed Church (Agenda for Synod 1986, p. 355)' ". . . that sacramental eating and drinking will be a proclamation of the Lord's death until He comes (1 Cor. 11:26) . . . without such proclamation no true celebration of the sacrament can take place at all. That is what made the Corinthian celebration so horrifying. In Corinth what should have been a holy meal had turned into a common (literally, a profane) meal. The solution of that horror in Corinth lay in restoring the essence of the meal, a proclamation of the Lord of the covenant and his glory. The covenant is fulfilled in Christ not only by His death and resurrection but also by his 'proclaiming light to His own people and to the Gentiles' (Acts 26:23). The Lord's Supper continues that covenant celebration and declaration of Christ's light and so makes any meaningful partaking in itself a public declaration of faith in Jesus Christ."

That proclamation of the Lord's death has to do with the public profession of faith, which is not yet made by the children of God's covenant!

116

Examination

There is another important word in 1 Cor. 11:26-29, namely, what is said in verse 28: "Let a man *examine* himself, and so eat of the bread and drink of the cup." That self-examination means actually that the people ("a man" — but that means here: everyone who wants to partake of the Lord's Supper) have to *test* themselves. A similar expression is already used by the Apostle Paul in the same chapter, namely, in verse 19: "in order that those who are *genuine* among you may be recognized." But also this term has to do with *faith*. I quote Calvin's commentary on this text. Calvin rejects the Roman Catholic idea that this self-examination has to do with auricular confession. He explains the word as follows:

But now it is asked, what sort of *examination* that ought to be to which Paul exhorts us. It is an *examination* of such a kind as may accord with the legitimate use of the sacred Supper.

You see here a method that is most easily apprehended. If you would wish to use aright the benefit afforded by Christ, bring faith and repentance. As to these two things, therefore, the trial must be made, if you would come duly prepared. Under repentance I include love, for the man who has learned to renounce himself, that he may give himself up wholly to Christ and His service, will also, without doubt, carefully maintain that unity which Christ has enjoined. At the same time, it is not a perfect faith or repentance that is required, as some, by urging beyond due bounds, a perfection that can nowhere be found, would shut out for ever from the Supper every individual of mankind. If, however, thou aspirest after the righteousness of God with the earnest desire of thy mind, and, humbled under a view of thy misery, dost wholly lean upon Christ's grace, and rest upon it, know that thou art a worthy guest to approach that table — *worthy* I mean in this respect, that the Lord does not exclude thee, though in another point of view there is something in thee that is not as it ought to be. For faith, when it is but begun, makes those *worthy* who were *unworthy.*

Already in the Didachè ("The Teaching of the Twelve Apostles"), dated from the end of the first or the beginning of the second century, it is said that the people have to partake of the Lord's Supper after having examined whether they are reconciled with God and with their brothers, so that the celebration of the Lord's Supper may be pure and not be defiled (ch. 14).

Our fathers understood the meaning of this self-examination very well when they stated in the *Form for the Celebration of the Lord's Supper:*

In order that we may now celebrate this holy supper of the Lord to our comfort, we must first rightly examine ourselves.

True self-examination consists of the following three parts:

First, let everyone consider his sins and accursedness, so that he, detesting himself, may humble himself before God. For the wrath of God against sin is so great that He could not leave it unpunished, but has punished it in His beloved Son Jesus Christ by the bitter and shameful death on the cross.

Second, let everyone search his heart whether he also believes the sure promise of God that all his sins are forgiven him only for the sake of the suffering and death of Jesus Christ and that the perfect righteousness of Christ is freely given him as his own, as if he himself had fulfilled all righteousness.

Third, let everyone examine his conscience whether it is his sincere desire to show true thankfulness to God with his entire life and, laying aside all enmity, hatred and envy, to live with his neighbour in true love and unity.

That is a good description and elaboration of what was already said in the days right after the apostles. It is to be summarized in one sentence: true self-examination means to know and to profess your sin and misery, your deliverance in Christ, and your thankfulness.

Is it not remarkable that these three words are exactly the three parts of the Heidelberg Catechism? So, to be able to examine ourselves we must know the Heidelberg Catechism, we have to be instructed in the doctrine of the church, just as had been promised by the parents of the children of the covenant at the baptismal font.

If we compare the explanation of our self-examination with the contents of the Heidelberg Catechism, we can understand the better the answer to Q. 81: "Who are to come to the table of the Lord?" (in the old Latin version of the Heidelberg Catechism the formulation is: "Who are *allowed* to go to the Lord's table?"): "Those who are truly displeased with themselves because of their sins and yet trust that these are forgiven them and that their remaining weakness is covered by the suffering and death of Christ, and who also desire more and more to strengthen their faith and amend their life." What else is this than: those who know and profess their sin and misery, their deliverance and their thankfulness?

That means very clearly: instruction in true faith has to precede the access to the Lord's Supper!

Discernment

So the Apostle Paul wrote to the Corinthians concerning *proclamation* and *examination* in connection with the Lord's Supper and both words have to do with *faith*. But that is also the case with the third word used by the apostle in this respect, in the same passage; he writes in verse 29: "For any one who eats and drinks without *discerning* the body eats and drinks judgment upon himself."

There are commentaries which say that "the body" is just the body of the church. For instance, James B. Jordan writes (Jordan, 1982, th. 17): "Discerning the body for the child may be translated as 'obey your parents.' " But that is wrong. The apostle uses here a strong word that actually means "to make a decisive distinction." The word is often used in connection with "to be able to discern good and evil," and that is to be applied to mature people.

I quote again the majority report for the Christian Reformed Synod 1986:

> This means, first of all, that those who come to the table will need to discern that *this meal is not just a Sunday morning snack* but is, in fact, a participation *in the body and blood of Christ* given for the life of his people (1 Cor. 11:25-26). Anything other than a recognition of the giver of the heavenly food and drink will bring destruction rather than life through the eating (1 Cor. 11:30), the same destruction that fell on the Israelites who failed to discern God's gift in the heaven-sent quail (Num. 11:33; Ps. 78:30).
>
> As indicated earlier, this discernment of the body will include recognizing that *being part of the body of Christ means being part of the body of believers.* Participants in the supper will receive true nourishment when they recognize the unity they share with others in the covenant community as a result of partaking of the one loaf (1 Cor. 10:17), the one Lord Jesus Christ. Partaking meaningfully will require a true discernment by each participant that in holy communion Christ himself is feeding his people — and that of those fed people, I am one (cf. Heidelberg Catechism, Q. & A. 54).

So also the third word used by the Apostle Paul has to do with *faith*, and also with *instruction* in faith.

Now some reason that a child can believe in a childlike manner and that this must be enough to admit it to the Lord's Supper. That is not the way of thinking of the Apostle Paul, for he used strong expressions which are only to be applied to what is promised by the parents of the children of God's covenant: "to instruct their child in the doctrine of the church, as soon as he or she is able to understand, and to have him or her instructed to the utmost of their power!"

History

Finally I would like to show something from history, especially from Calvin and I will end with some conclusions. Defending the admittance of children, one often reasons: during many ages children were allowed to partake of the Lord's Supper, but then, suddenly, it stopped. What are we to say about that?

Indeed, infants and small children participated in the Lord's Supper, especially in the Eastern church, but also in the Western church, and especially with the growth of a superstitious view of the sacrament, people feared to spill so much as a single drop of the transsubstantiated blood of Christ.

But we have to bear in mind two things.

In the first place: not all the texts to which one appeals show indeed that very young children partook of the Lord's Supper. For instance in the *Constitutiones Apostolicae* (a writing from the end of the fourth century) it is said after the dismissal of the non-baptized: "Mothers, take your little children with you." But it is absolutely not sure that these little children (sometimes even babies) did indeed receive the elements of the Lord's Supper. I am of the opinion that here is only said that the mothers were not to leave the children alone in the back of the church when they came forward to receive for themselves the bread and wine.

There is also an indication that in the early church children were instructed by their parents and were led to the minister in order to show their faith. Both lines are mentioned by Calvin.

In his *Institutes* he writes first that some people say (I give here the whole quotation of Inst. IV, 16, 30).

. . . that there is not greater reason for admitting infants to baptism than to the Lord's Supper, to which, however, they are never admitted: as if Scripture did not in every way draw a wide distinction between them. In the early Church, indeed, the Lord's Supper was frequently given to infants, as appears from Cyprian and Augustine (August, ad Bonif. Lib. i.); but the practice justly became obsolete. For if we attend to the peculiar nature of baptism, it is a kind of entrance, and as it were initiation into the Church, by which we are ranked among the people of God, a sign of our spiritual regeneration, by which we are again born to be children of God; whereas, on the contrary, the supper is intended for those of riper years, who, having passed the tender period of infancy, are fit to bear solid food. This distinction is very clearly pointed out in Scripture. For there, as far as regards baptism, the Lord makes no selection of age, whereas he does not admit all to partake of the Supper, but confines it to those who are fit to discern the body and blood of the Lord, to examine their own conscience, to show forth the Lord's death, and understand its power. Can we wish anything clearer than what the apostle says, when he thus exhorts, "Let a man examine himself, and so let him eat of that bread, and drink of that cup?" (1 Cor. xi. 28.) Examination, therefore, must precede, and this it were vain to expect from infants. Again, "He that eateth and drinketh unworthily, eateth and drinketh damnation to himself, not discerning the Lord's body." If they cannot partake worthily without being able duly to discern the sanctity of the

119

Lord's body, why should we stretch out poison to our young children instead of vivifying food? Then what is our Lord's injunction? "Do this in remembrance of me." And what is the inference which the apostle draws from this? "As often as ye eat this bread, and drink this cup, ye do show the Lord's death till he come." How, pray, can we require infants to commemorate any event of which they have no understanding; how require them "to show forth the Lord's death," of the nature and benefit of which they have no idea? Nothing of the kind is prescribed by baptism. Wherefore, there is the greatest difference between the two signs.

So far the quotation of Calvin's *Institutes*. Calvin never denied that there is a strong connection between Baptism and the Lord's Supper, but he stressed also very much that there is a strong connection between Baptism and Profession of Faith.

Delayed response

In this respect Calvin often uses the expression "delayed response."

At the time of our baptism the LORD God, by means of His servant, sealed His promise to us. At the time we were not yet able to see or hear this, for we were not yet conscious of things. But nevertheless, God *did* speak to us at that time. Before we could utter one word the LORD had already spoken to us. And He kept on speaking to us, He kept impressing that baptism on our hearts. At one time the LORD said: "You are Mine, My child!" He told us so in baptism. And He kept calling us like that, as we grew up and matured. That is the reason why there is such a close connection between baptism and confession. At our baptism we were unable to answer for ourselves. Our parents had to do that for us. Otherwise we would have to respond to God's address then already.

Saying that confession is really a delayed response to baptism is not claiming too much. Calvin taught this already in one of his early writings, not long after the first edition of his *Institutes*. The Reformer was only twenty-seven years old at that time. He writes: "Covenant children must be instructed so that they may give a testimony of their faith in the end, which they were unable to do when they were baptized."

In his *Institutes* he relates that in the early church it was also customary for the children of Christians, after they were grown up, to be brought before the minister "in order that they might fulfill the duty required of adults; presenting themselves for baptism." For, according to Calvin, when they were baptized as small children, they could not yet make their profession.

The Reformer put it like this: a small child cannot speak yet and has not yet come to his/her senses. Therefore, for covenant children, making profession of faith is the discharge of an obligation, required of them at their baptism, but temporarily delayed.

Calvin wrote: Only one valid reason can be given to the Lord as to why covenant children would not yet be able to make confession of faith. And that one reason is that the children of the covenant lack sufficient knowledge as yet to partake in the Lord's Supper. You must be able to examine yourself, says Paul to the Corinthians, before being able to celebrate the Lord's Supper (1 Cor. 11:28). This requires knowledge, also self-knowledge which toddlers and very young children do not have yet.

According to Calvin, there is no other possible reason that can stand up before the LORD. Certainly not this one: "I am not quite ready, I am not sure that I really believe in Christ." God has sealed His promise in baptism. Then what right does anyone have to doubt? Who may disregard these promises? Then Calvin addresses the young people and says: "You should have made profession of your faith at the hour of your baptism. Then already the LORD gave you this obligation. Only because of your weakness has this confession been postponed!"

Baptism may not be postponed, for the LORD has a claim on the child that is born into His covenant. Baptism should be administered as soon as feasible to the children of believers. "The consistory should ensure that the covenant of God is sealed by baptism to the children of believers as soon as feasible" (Article 17 of the Church Order of the Canadian Reformed Churches). We should not keep the LORD waiting! But this is also the way it is with confession. That too should take place as soon as possible for the children of the covenant. Calvin then refers to a custom in the old church, and says: this took place at the end of childhood, or at the beginning of adolescence. He writes somewhere that to him it seems best if "a child at the age of ten years would present himself to the congregation to make profession of faith." In the Dutch refugee Church of London, the cradle of the church of the Reformation in the Netherlands, the age was set at fourteen — still very young by our standard. We should keep in mind that instruction in the doctrine of the church was started at an earlier age than now. But one thing is certain: from the hour of baptism the demand for confessions calls to be fulfilled. Therefore any unnecessary delay is wrong.

Not a part of us

Once we have discovered the close connection between baptism and confession, we are more and more brought to worship God's good pleasure. It is not just "normal" that we are born covenant children. It is not just a matter of course that the LORD gave us parents who presented us for baptism. Behind this is God's gracious election, His good pleasure. It is written about the Saviour Himself that His Father in heaven spoke at His baptism: "This is my beloved Son, with whom I am well pleased," (Matthew 3:17). The LORD addressed us likewise in baptism. He has called us by name and joined us to His Name. In doing so God has shown His good pleasure in our lives. His good pleasure goes out to us; His goodwill. The LORD *honours* Himself in this way. And what an honour this is for us!

This too is what we are about to discover when we make profession of faith. Then we look back to our baptism and worship God's good pleasure in our life. So this confession is not a part of us, a kind of diploma we present ourselves with. No, it is a certificate of God's grace in our lives. This is included in that address "Beloved in our Lord Jesus Christ."

When Peter made his good confession before the Lord: "You are the Christ, the Son of the living God" he was not complimented for having done something good. No, rather, Christ said: "Peter, this did not come from yourself." He was blessed, but not because of his own merit. The reaction of the Saviour was: "Blessed are you, Simon Bar-Jona! For flesh and blood has not revealed this to you, but my Father who is in heaven," (Matthew 16:17). Others hadn't talked Peter into this. It was not his own idea either. The Father revealed this to him. It is God's good pleasure in his life. The LORD made him able to make this confession. It is indeed Peter who expresses himself, and he also speaks from the heart. But he expresses what God Himself has put into that heart: the worship of God's good pleasure.

Some conclusions

There is much more to say about this topic, but I do not wish to make this series of articles too long.

I have two main conclusions.

In the first place: children may not partake of the Lord's Supper, but according to the promise of their parents at the baptismal font, they have to be instructed in the doctrine of the church and they have to make profession of faith, in order to be able to proclaim Christ's death, to examine themselves and to discern the body.

In the second place: this profession of faith is actually a delayed response to their baptism and it must be given as soon as possible; that means: when a child has grown up and when he or she is able to make important decisions in life. That time will vary for the one matures sooner than the other. If a child of the covenant is instructed for several years, and he or she wants to make profession of faith at the age of — let us say — sixteen or seventeen, there is nothing against it. But it is wrong to postpone profession of faith one year after another. Under the influence of pietism, young people were taught that they had to tell their "story of conversion," and that this was not possible when they were young. Thus many young people waited then until they were twenty-five or even thirty years old, and also many of them never dared to make profession of faith, because they could not say that they were really born again.

Let us stress to our children that it is a great privilege to be born as a child of God's covenant, to be baptized, and also to be instructed in the doctrine of the church, in order to be and to remain a living member of Christ's Church! So that they seek to pass through the door of the public profession of their faith in order to proclaim Christ's death and resurrection at His table as part of His congregation.

CURRENT STREAMS IN MODERN LITURGY

The First Centuries

In the first centuries, the church remained faithful to the sobriety of the worship services which dated from the time of the apostles.

Several documents which date from the post-apostolic period of the church, provide us with some material about the course of the liturgy.

Justin Martyr, in his *Apology* (ca. 153 A.D.) tells us something about the weekly gatherings of the congregations: "And on the day called Sunday there is a gathering in one place of all who dwell in the cities or in the country places, and the memoirs of the apostles or the writing of the prophets are read as long as time allows. Then when the reader was finished, he who presides gives oral admonition and exhortation to imitate these excellent examples.

Then we all rise together, and offer prayers; and as stated before, when we have ended our praying, bread, wine and water are brought. And he who presides similarly offers up prayers and thanksgiving, as far as lies in his power, and the people express their approval by saying: "amen." And each receives a share and partakes of the gifts for which thanks has been given, and through the deacons some is sent to those not present.

"According to Justin the gatherings consist of two parts": the Word-part and the sacrament-part. After the preaching, those who have not been baptized leave the church.

The sacramental part begins with a kiss (of peace) after which the bread and chalice are brought in. *Hippolytus of Rome* (170? - 235 A.D.), in his *Apostolic Tradition* written around the beginning of the third century, wanted to follow the tradition of the apostles in the celebration of the Lord's Supper. After greeting each other with a kiss of peace, the "sacrifice" is brought by a deacon to the one who presided, after which the thanksgiving was expressed and then the one who presided exhorted the congregation: "Let us raise our hearts" (*sursum corda*). The congregation then answers and then follows a prayer in which God is thanked for the sending of His Son.

Also in the fourth century, an important place is still reserved for the preaching, such as is shown in the sermons of Chrysostom (345?-407) in the East and Augustine (354-430) in the West.

Change and Degeneration

The fourth century, however, also saw a change in the liturgy. In the liturgy of Jerusalem which dates from the second half of the fourth century, which came into existence under the leadership of Bishop Cyril (412-444 A.D.), the Lord's Supper occupies a central place, and then an emphasis is put on the acts being dramatized by the bishop, who represented Christ.

The Lord's Supper liturgy of Cyril is also very elaborate. After the washing of the hands and the kiss of peace, the 'sursum corda' followed. After this there was a prayer of thanksgiving and then the congregation sang the "Sanctus." A special prayer (*epiklese*) for the coming of the Holy Spirit, clearly shows that a change has taken place in the Lord's Supper: "We plead the good God to send the Holy Spirit down upon the sacrificial gifts, so that He can change the bread into the Body of Christ and the wine into the Blood of Christ. In addition to this sacrifice of atonement, says Cyril, we offer our litanies, first for the living then for the dead. Afterward: the Lord's prayer is prayed and then the invitation comes from the cantor, who in a song encourages everyone to participate in the "holy mysteries." Everyone is then supposed to approach "not with extended hands, nor with spread out fingers." But with your left hand make a throne for your right hand which is going to receive the King. Receive then the Body of Christ in the hollow of your right hand and then say, "Amen." When you have sanctified your eyes through the contact with this Holy Body, carefully eat it and make sure that you do not lose any." Then the 'participation in the blood of Christ' follows, and then finally the liturgy is closed with a prayer of thanksgiving (Cross 1966:67ff.).

From Jerusalem, this liturgy, dating from the second half of the fourth century, was spread throughout the East and the West. Slowly but surely the changes crept in. Not only did these changes over-evaluate the office-bearers (all the liturgical acts of the bishop receive great attention), but the Lord's Supper becomes the heart of the liturgy and in the place of the thankoffering they substituted the offering of atonement.

More and more in the times that follow, the essential aspect of the worship service, the meeting of the speaking God and the responding congregation, is lost. God speaks less and less. The pulpit is moved to the side. In a secret manner, more or less substantially, God is almost exclusively present in the sacraments. More and more, the congregational participation is eliminated. The two who meet each other, are God and the priest, God and the clergy, and the congregation may watch and follow this spectacle from afar. At the beginning of the Middle Ages, when the dogma of 'transsubstantiation' has been officially established and the altar has become completely dominant, they have become miles separated from the worship service of the New Testament and the ancient church of the first centuries. And that's the way it still is in the Roman Church. For: has contemporary Rome changed anything at all?

Rome Today

Then we must state that, despite all the elasticity characteristic to Rome — I could also say: regardless of all the diplomacy which Rome regularly uses —, essentially nothing has changed. Yes, indeed, Rome herself is ostensibly busy with reformation of the liturgy. In more than one document, Roman theologians have given assurances that much has changed through Vaticanum II. Have they not put great emphasis on the use of the vernacular languages in the worship services? But the foundation of the Romish worship service, the core of the issue, has been left untouched.

The Constitution of the second Vatican council clearly says: "By means of the last supper, our Saviour, in the night He was betrayed, instituted the eucharistic Sacrifice of His Body and Blood, so that the sacrifice on the cross could be continued throughout the ages until He returns." And soon after this, the "Christian believers" are encouraged to dedicate the "unblemished sacrifice" (Mulders/Kahmann, 1967:29).

It is then noteworthy that the Latin text of the Constitution continually uses the word "Sacrificium" and then time and again writes this word with a capital letter. As far as Rome herself is concerned, it is here that the emphasis is made. And then we have arrived precisely at the same characterization which Luther already gave concerning the popish mass. Luther says: the mass of Rome can be represented by the one word: sacrificium. And with this we touch the heart of the Romish worship service. It is by means of the sacrifice cult, that they want to appease God. But, Luther continues: the mass which our Saviour instituted is not a sacrificium, but a *beneficium*, God's *gift* to us, His goodness. In reference to this, the Swedish Lutheran theologain, *Vilmos Vajta,* has correctly shown that behind this whole Romish concept of the mass, there is an incorrect understanding of God and His image. He says: Luther sees a merciful God approach us, who comes with the ministry of atonement, but the Romish mass recognizes a God, whom *we* must reconcile (Vajta, 1954:55). After Vaticanum II, the Romish theologians wrote beautiful things concerning the importance of the participation of the faithful in the liturgy of the church. Controversially, they emphasize the idea that the liturgy is not the concern of the individual, but a communical act of the Body of the church, which must always be considered present in the liturgy.

But with this it is simply maintained that redemptive history has been continued in the liturgy, that the bloody sacrifice on the cross on Golgotha must be bloodlessly repeated in the mass, and that the salvation-giving reality (heilschenkende werkelijkheid) "comes to existence *ex opere operato* in the sacramental signs and in particular in the eucharistic sacrifice, in which the measure of effect (uitwerking) depends on the disposition of the administrator and the one who receives it." (According to E.J. Lengeling in the R.C. standard work 'Liturgisch Woordenboek,' wherein as concerns the "ex opere operato," he especially points to the Encyclical of Pope Pius XII 'Mediator Die et hominum' (1947), and also continually quotes from the constitution concerning the liturgy of Vaticanum II (Lengeling, 1965/68:1573-1595). All of the R.C. liturgy continues to be directed by this Sacrificium, and also when the Constitution dedicates a paragraph to the *'sacrae Liturgiae instauratione'* this renewal must be read in the light of the chapter *"De sacrosancto Eucharistiae mysterio"* which completely maintains the basic thoughts of the Romish liturgy.

High Church (in the Netherlands state church).

Concerning the liturgical movement in the "reformation" integrated in the RCC: this movement tends to lean in the Romish direction. A few points:

1. Coming out from behind the Reformation and its decisions, they want to return to the liturgical style of the first centuries and strive to infuse a contribution from the Eastern Orthodox churches, which is coloured by dramatization;

2. They want to restore the sacramental acts in their liturgy to their full honour especially with respect to the celebration of the Lord's Supper, in which the actualization of the salvation and the representation of Christ are established;

3. The (worship) service must be increasingly seen as a service of Scripture and

124

Table, in which the word is *spoken* and *broken* and in which salvation is proclaimed and demonstrated;

4. The preaching must be taken out of its exceptional position and be *reduced* to only *one* of the many elements, and they want: the sacraments in the church service, but preaching must not have a dominant position anymore;

5. A roster of Bible readings, order of events throughout the year and the calendar must be carefully dictated, as well as services for special hours (cf. Romish breviary, pht), special prayers and responsories.

In short: the Reformed acquisitions must be scrapped, the mystery of the sacrament must be central and there should be a multitude of liturgical elements according to the dictates of the high church.

Many of these matters have already been established in the "Dienstboek voor de Nederlandse Hervormde Kerk." In this book you can find more than 30 "orders of service." For all possible events, a great number of prayers, following the sequence of the ecclesiastic (liturgical) year, for the house congregations, for the dedication of a church-building, etc., etc.

And then in addition to this they have the "Liedboek voor de Kerken" (a very comprehensive hymnal) with an inexhaustible supply of songs. There is even a "Dagboek bij het Liedboek" (a daybook) with a complete "kalendarium" which provides an ecclesiastical calendar covering ten years.

Liberal

For many years there have also been liberal thinkers who have given themselves lots of latitude in the liturgical sense. Was it not in the previous century in the sombre province of North Holland that a preacher made the announcement to his congregation: "Today I'm not going to preach from the Bible, but instead I will preach to you about the flowers?" And were there not also liturgics who refused to use the trinitarian form at the baptism, and then instead baptized in the name of "faith, hope and love" or even in the name of "freedom, equality and fraternity?" In the *liberally inclined* left wing of the liturgics we can also place a person such as *S. Krikke*, who did research into the causes of the increased secularization. The church gets the blame.

He writes: "Concerning the most important causes of the extensive development of the 'fringe-church' and the rejection of the ecclesiastical liturgy, it's my theory that the causes must be principally sought in the many changes present in the life-view of those in the fringe-church, changes which have far-reaching consequences for religious life" (Krikke 1976:5).

"Their experiences as they relate to life are no longer found in the doctrine of the church, and for their religious needs they find no satisfaction in the ecclesiastical liturgy. The worship services such as they are conducted today have no meaning for them."

The question then arises: what are these experiences and needs? In his search for an answer to this question, S. Kirkke, points to the totality of religious doubt of modern man. One is in a position to believe much less. Only the form and the attitude still remain, but this form and attitude are empty. For that reason Krikke talks about a "Christian lack of faith" ("Christelijke geloofsloosheid"). The Holy Scriptures are time-bound books, which concern wars fought in God's Name or about a resurrection after death, etc., but one must interpret all of this extremely critically. The greatness of "God" must be swept out of the way. That's a minimum demand. Man regulates life himself. What he formerly ascribed to God or the gods, depending on whether he was

Jew or Christian or heathen, must now be attributed to man. Therefore: not the non-church (secular) people of today, but the church itself must be placed in the defendant's chair. Krikke analyzes the purpose and the aims of the books, the orders, the forms which are presently used in the liturgy. Everything is at fault.

In his criticism he finds fault with the Prayerbook, the Hymnal, etc. The final conclusion is: the churches are ignoring the changes in the structures, they are not receptive to the disappearance of the ancient sense of religion. They have continued almost completely on the old religious track which is based on an antiquated image of God, image of the world, image of man, and in this way they are at work to alienate even more people from the church.

Mystery without Myth

Of course, now the question inevitably arises: what content must the liturgy then have? According to Krikke, the liturgy must fit into the situation of modern man and must accommodate modern thought. Vulnerable man of today, must be brought into contact with the Mystery of life and history by means of an up-to-date service. This mystery could be given the name "god", but then it should be emphasized that this name should not be used in a traditional sense, in which God is seen as a person or spirit. It is to be a mystery without a myth. That is to say: without a personal God, without Christ as both God and man, without the testimony of the resurrection of the dead and a faith in God with all that it embraces. In this Nothing, in this emptiness there *does* seem to be a need for fellowship and allowance must be created for support, comfort and reception. You must be able to tell others about your restlessness, and fear, your joy and your suffering. There must be an empty space which breathes rest. "In all her parts and facets," Krikke writes, "the liturgy shall have to breathe this spiritual companionship and christian friendship, usually only verbalized indirectly but felt in everything and living in the consciousness of every participant. As core according to content and form, the liturgy of such a fellowship must incorporate the realization that we people, via the undercurrents of life are committed to each other and that we belong together" (Krikke, 1976:134).

So it concerns a liturgy of warmth, empty space, a liturgy of the mystery of the fellowship of friends.

Does Scripture have a function in this liturgy? No way. Krikke says: "The sanctification of one book has had its time. The only place where that could still be maintained would be within the walls of a solid fortress of orthodoxy. For the defenders of those walls it is painful, however, that such old bulwarks have absolutely no use anymore in modern war" (Krikke, 1976:160ff.). The question arises: is the preaching still necessary? Krikke says that we should rather speak about meditation. "The word meditation gives us a fairly accurate rendition of what is possible and desirable in this liturgy: gathering thoughts about all the possible aspects of the Mystery, process them, pass them on, and make them the subject of a communal reflection."

Krikke would like to begin a service as follows, for example — and that is then his formulation of the "Votum": "Let us dedicate this service (gathering) to the deepest and best things, which we may know, let us reflect on those things together so that we can live as humans" (Krikke, 1976:145).

It is unnecessary to mention here that we are confronted here with a modernistic mysticism, which has rejected the Word of God and that is completely humanistic and horizontalistic in its structure. This cult has nothing to do with worship service — a service to the glory of the LORD, the God of the Scriptures. Krikke has submitted himself to the teachings of a Bultmann and a Tillich, and has left behind the myths,

126

and the image of the God of the Scriptures. In fact, he has left the whole Bible behind, and he is left with an empty husk, indeed: an empty space, which has absolutely no filling or content.

Worship Service as Action

Those who started off as liberalists, raising the slogans of the French Revolution, should not be surprised that at a certain point in time they have arrived at *communism*. That progression is also noticeable in the development of modern theology. In the last decades those theologians travelled via liberal theology to the *"Entmythologisierung"* (= the de-mythologizing of the Bible, pht) of Bultmann and afterwards, via the 'God-is-dead theology' of Robinson, via the theology of evolution, of the revolution and liberation to what is essentially nothing other than a politicized neo-Marxist philosophy, critical of society. In liturgical respect, this development has led to the *"Gottesdienst als Aktion"* (= Worship service as Action).

The renewed theology (that's what they still call it), had to lead to new liturgy, namely, a liturgy of political action. In 1968 they started with this in Cologne. From there this so-called "worship service" blew over to other areas of Germany, and soon afterwards also arrived in the Netherlands, under the leadership of *Dorothee Sölle,* (presently a professor at Union Seminary, New York), and *Fulbert Steffensky.*

The point of departure for this new liturgy was the sad state of the official liturgy in which there was so little time for daily concerns, problems and needs, and in which there was hardly any place for a plea of solidarity with those who have been lost, those who suffer discrimination, the oppressed, the poor, the exploited and those suffering privation. But in this *Aktion-Gottesdienst* this would all be changed. Central to this liturgy they would have an analysis of the real state of this society: information about the deeper backgrounds of what ails this society; protest against the existing relationships; planning and action to thoroughly change those relationships, the present structures of this society. *"Aktion-Gottesdienst,"* according to one of their spokesmen means: *"Die Tagersordnung der Welt behandeln-sachgemäsz und unreligiös"* (= deal with the daily order of the world — orderly, to the point and non-religiously).

That is why in 1968, they arrived at the "politisches Nachtgebet," in Cologne, which consisted of 3 parts: information, meditation and action. After the reading of Matt. 25:42-44, they say: "Today the words of Jesus sound as follows: I was hungry; you chemically destroyed the harvest of my land! I was hungry for self-determination; you colonized my country! I was a stranger in my own country; you bombarded my country!" and it ends with: "I bled to death; you simply watched it happen on television" (Seidel/Zils, 1970:278ff.).

They do not close the Bible then, but by this means they have to "translate" the Bible for today.

Of course, the number of texts for this *Aktion-Gottesdienst* remains quite restricted. That does not matter, for they only use what they can profitably employ for their goals. They even admit that they make a *"selective"* use of the prophetic tradition in the O.T., a selection which is critical of cult and society, and in this way they, *"die spätkapitalistische Bürgergemeinde aufrüteln"* (= want to shake up the late capitalistic society.) As fruit of this movement, the Netherlands received an organization called "Christians for Socialism." According to their own admission, the church services have received a double task for them:

1. To pass on the perception that reality in society is marked by class struggle, for which the (neo) marxist analyses and criticism of society can provide all the necessary help;

2. To activate Christians to become involved in the liberation movements for the oppressed. In other words to activate Christians to become involved in making the necessary changes in society for which the Bible reveals previously unkown possibilities.

The Aktion-Gottesdienst has its own confession, developed by Dorothee Sölle. This credo is as follows:

> "I believe in God
> who did not make the world into a finished product
> as something which had to remain the same
> who does not govern according to eternal laws
> which are unchangeably fixed
> and not according to natural ordinances
> wherein there are rich and poor present
> people who know everything and
> people who don't know anything
> people who rule and others who
> have been subjected to rulers.
> I believe in God
> who wants the opposition of the living
> and the change of all situations
> by means of our politics. . . .
> I believe in Jesus Christ
> who is resurrected in our lives
> to make us free
> of prejudice and high-handedness
> of fear and hatred
> so that we will continue his revolution
> on the road to his kingdom."

Dorothy Sölle has simply discarded the 'God of the Christians.' Jesus chose to side with the outsiders, atheists, the rejects of society and the victims of exploitation. Therefore, those who want to meet Christ, will meet him in the suffering neighbour of today. For they will meet him exclusively in *this* says Solle.

World Council of Churches

It is remarkable how the development of Aktion-Gottesdienst parallels the development of the World Council of Churches, the W.C.C.

While the theology of Karl Barth dominated the assembly at Amsterdam in 1948, in the following meeting in Evanston, racism was the point of order. In New Dehli in 1961, the Russian church was admitted, who had declared that they supported and blessed the politics of the communists on "exclusively religious motives," because these were supposedly to rely on the principles of humanity and justice. This church was accepted as a full-fledged member. In Uppsala, in 1968, the theology of revolution was victorious, with the motto, "Everything will become new." Uppsala undeniably showed clear signs of marxism, and it was precisely that same year that the liturgy of political action was initiated in Germany. Also at Uppsala Bible texts were used for revolutionary purposes. Had the Lord Jesus Himself not given the example of revolutionary action over against the established structures, by turning the tables of the moneychangers upside down? Uppsala was followed by Nairobi in 1975. There the theology of liberation established a strong presence. But when they refer to "liberation," they do not mean a liberation from sin and guilt, but the liberation — with force if necessary — from oppressive structures. In Vancouver 1983 Dorothee Sölle was applauded strongly.

The whole so-called worship service of Aktion-Gottesdienst has become nothing more than a political meeting, and the word 'liturgy' is misused for the purposes of political indoctrination and provocation.

One wonders in the meantine, what is worse: to deny the Bible and leave it closed, as in the case of modernistic liberalism, or to annex the Bible for self-prescribed purposes and then select texts, which are torn out of context, to serve the purpose of political activities, as that is done in the case of Aktion-Gottesdienst.

The Apostolate

Elements of both of the last mentioned "theologies" (though they are not so consistently expressed) are to be found in the *"apostolate-theology"* of J.C. Hoekendijk (1912-1975). He was born in Indonesia, and died in the United States, held professorships in New York and Utrecht and before that he was associated with the W.C.C. in Geneva. He could justly boast of a varied experience in the area of mission and the ecumenical movement. Hoekendijk wants to reach what he calls, the "fourth person."

The first person is the heathen who has established his first contacts with the gospel.

The second person is the Christian who has accepted the gospel.

The third person is the Christian who maintains that he has enriched himself in the European personality culture (which, according to Hoekendijk is actually an impoverishment).

The fourth person is the one who has become totally estranged from the Bible through the new world view of modern learning. He is post-Christian, post-ecclesiastical, post-civilian, and post-personal. The gospel has no message anymore for this fourth person. The worship service in its present form has even less appeal. He is becoming more and more alienated.

One can see parallels with a liberalist such as Krikke. Also Hoekendijk maintains that this estrangement is as a result of the form and method in which Christians have delivered this to the people of our times.

But Hoekendijk does not end up in an empty space, as the new form of liturgy. But he does come to the conclusion that there must be a radical break-through in the structure of the congregation. All the rigidity and inflexibility must disappear. A mobile church must be developed, which concretely exercises solidarity with the neighbour by divesting itself completely of this sacral style, language and place.

The ideal is that in this way the church may overwin her civility, liberate evangelism from suspicion of expansionism of its own culture milieu and force a break-through in the direction of the afore-mentioned fourth person. Hoekendijk summarizes all of this under the term, the apostolate.

Just as the apostle once fought against Judaism, which had established a demand of circumcision of the heathens, similarly we must not reject the demand which the church exercises in her proselytizing zeal to those who come to her, namely, that these people must submit and accustomize themselves to codes, forms and mannerisms of the group. According to Hoekendijk, the church is only a vehicle by means of which the gospel propels itself through the world. The church is simply a function of the apostolate. The one and the other have important consequences for the worship service. The church should divest itself of the "monument-complex" (syndrome) and build churches which look as much as possible like tents, because the mobile society also demands a mobile church. Therefore, in the place of the one cathedral of the large congregation, there should be small gatherings of *house-congregations* of students, for example, or nurses, inhabitants of one apartment, pensioners, military, and so forth: every possible forgotten group. Then, for all intents and purposes, the offices in the church may be dropped — the congregation is mature, is it not? — and after all, basically they were levers of conservatism, protectionism ("bevoogding") and hierarchy. The mature world demands the activity of the "lay-person." They are all mobile units, and then, this is the way the liturgy should function too. No preaching of the minister, no guardianship of the elders, but rather, the mutual edification in house congregations, and activities directed to the outside. The church can no longer be a separate building, no Divine habitation of the Spirit, but a mobile unit for a mobile God, who constantly breaks up camp. And what presently takes place in the congregation building (the present church), every Sunday, according to Hoekendijk, that can take place every day in the house congregation. With this difference, that here it will take place in an overseeable context: in a group where everyone knows the other, and therefore where they can also correct each other. If the need for office-bearers is called for — Hoekendijk thinks that they are actually a blockade to the Spirit — then everyone can pitch in and give a hand to lend assistance wherever necessary, strengthening the weaknesses and then also guarding the preservation of the congregation or its restoration. Furthermore, the congregation is mature and must help itself, also in the worship service of the house congregation.

The Mobile Unit

But Hoekendijk's house congregation — he speaks about a para-parish (=parochie) which rises above the normal one — is not the house congregation of the Scriptures. When the apostle speaks about this form of gathering, it concerns the small congregation which could meet in a house. And when Scripture speaks about a parish, the *par-oikia,* then it does not picture the image such as seen by Hoekendijk in the later corruption of the parish of the Middle Ages, but instead, it is simply a normal denotation of each local church.

Moreover: with his house congregation, Hoekendijk wrenches the richly varied life of the congregation to pieces. It is part of election that the LORD brings together great and small, rich and poor, learned and unlearned, and makes them into a pluriform congregation. But Hoekendijk has dissolved God's one congregation into a number of sociologically pre-determined groups. And then: is the congregation not mature? And does she not have the Spirit? Indeed, but God has given the ministry of reconciliation and He has given the ministry of the offices to work the perfection of the saints, and through His Word and Spirit He wants to gather a congregation for Himself.

Can the world save herself without "God" in the old sense of the word? Must the "church-guardianship (=kerk-voogdij), such as Hoekendijk calls it be abandoned? But this abandonment will lead irrevocably to lawlessness on the one side and to the autonomy of modern man on the other side, while the "liturgy of the mobile unit" will be conducive to spiritualism, causes neglect of the ministry of the Word and splits the church up into a number of groups which are like-minded and directed to similar ends (cf. Trimp, 1971:90ff; cf. also Van Gurp, 1989:335, where he points to the fact that Hoekendijk advocates a liberation of the "world which is enacted without atonement through the blood of Christ").

130

Seeing and hearing

In the meantime, the ecumenical movement has continued on. In the early days of the W.C.C., between the first and second assemblies, the conference for liturgy, convened by the section "Faith and Order," still attempted to find the *greatest-common-denominator-subject* for the liturgy. The preparatory committee, chaired by G. v. d. Leeuw, who died before the conference in Lund in 1952, came with an extensive report, embodied in the work, "Ways of Worship" (Edwall, 1951). Theologians of various feathers worked together: people of the liturgical movement, Lutheran, Romish, Anglicans, Baptists, Quakers, etc.

They looked especially at the Anglicans and Lutherans who are situated somewhere in between the "liturgy of seeing" and the "liturgy of hearing." For that reason they felt that they should not distinguish too much between the "churches of the sacrament" and the "churches of the Word." The fulness lies in the unity of both. There will have to be a *compromise*. At the conference in Lund, one of the Anglicans said: Word and sacrament are inseparable anyway. Sacrament without the Word could add to superstition, but conversely the Word without sacrament could soon degenerate to a Word without power.

But: they could not find a conclusive formula, regardless of the six points on which they did agree. Lund's achievement was that the liturgical movement was led into ecclesiastical lines. For the rest they did not achieve more.

Pluriform

The thread was finally and seriously taken up again in Uppsala, the assembly of the W.C.C. in 1968. But also here the matter stagnated. At the plenary session of the section dealing with *liturgy and a secularized world,* a noteworthy incident took place. A French interpreter, whose task was nothing more than to translate the speeches of the delegates into the official languages spoken at the conference, involved himself in the discussion and informed the leaders of the section that he was of the opinion that any attempt to come to a compromise would be useless. Whatever other churches were planning was their business, but what really concerned him was that the European churches would radically change their liturgy so that they could take up contact with the non-believers, because the latter are in the majority almost everywhere. The debate that was taking place was useless, according to him, because the non-believers were not present at the conference.

Uppsala stranded. Where it concerned the worship service, they chose a representative from the Eastern Orthodox church. Even though the topic was supposed to deal with the liturgy in a secularized world. The Eastern Orthodox concept of the church soon became an issue. Liturgy there is primarily an act of withdrawal from the world. It's something holy and heavenly. For the chairman, the issue of secularization was then also: the secularization of the worship service itself. Consequently, the matter became deadlocked before it even began. Several things were still said about the unity and diversity in the worship services in various churches, and new research projects were commissioned. No longer was there any talk of a compromise or a greatest-common-denominator. The *diversity,* the pluriformity variety of the different church liturgies came to the foreground.

The whole issue of the secularized world and the adaptation of the liturgy to that situation, did not even get off the ground. What they did establish at Uppsala was that we as Christians should refuse to take part in any form of division of races or classes in our worship services and also that our fellowship with Christ must demonstrate that we share our bread with the hungry brothers in the world.

In the worship service, are we not engaged in a battle with God against the demonic powers of the world?

The dialogue must be continued. But the complaint is: specifically in liturgical respect the dialogue does not "work."

In subsequent assemblies of the W.C.C. they did not get much further. At the meeting in Nairobi, the whole issue of liturgy was not even made a point of order on the agenda. But they do perceive that there is a tendency to allow the existence of the diversity or pluriformity in the matter of liturgy.

V
"PREACH THE WORD" (2 Timothy 4:2)

REFORMED PREACHING AND MODERN EXEMPLARISM

Introduction

About half a century ago there was a survival of Reformed preaching in the Netherlands. More attention was paid then to the history of redemption and Christological preaching.

It came to attention as a Scripturally-based protest against a method of explaining the Bible and preaching which hindered a good understanding and use of Scripture.

The redemptive-historical method, which is required by Scripture itself, stands opposed to the so-called *exemplary method*. What exactly was the exemplary method? Briefly, it was a method of considering the meaning of all kinds of moments in biblical history in such a way that we as believers receive an *example* of how we are or are not to act. Especially persons in Biblical History were considered as examples for later generations.

In the early 1930s already, K. Schilder stimulated an approach to Scripture quite different from the exemplary approach. He wrote, for example, *Here and there we still encounter Lenten sermons in which the figures around Christ receive the primary attention. There is the talk of Judas, Peter, Pilate, Herod, the Sanhedrin, Mary, etc... (their inner conflict, their comfort, their hardening hearts), while the first and foremost question is forgotten, namely what Christ has done, what God has let his Son experience, what the Son has experienced in and through the actions of those figures around him (Schilder, 1930: 204).* In a speech of 1942, the late Prof. B. Holwerda also mentioned several illustrations of the exemplary method. For instance, Abraham's temptation of Genesis 22, the offering of Isaac, is an example for our struggle of faith. The purpose of Elijah's prayer is that we have to learn to pray in the same way. A sermon on John 20:24-29 concerning Thomas must be a sermon on doubt, and so on (Holwerda, 1983:12; Van 't Veer, 1983:5).

While Schilder and Holwerda protested the exemplary method they did not deny that this method could make true remarks: pointing to certain texts can lead to an explanation of affirmation of what Scripture teaches us in other texts. But the question was and still is whether the exemplary method did full justice to a text by demonstrating the place, significance, the function of that specific text within the complete revelation of salvation in Jesus Christ? Clearly it did not. Too often, not God's work of redemption in Jesus Christ was the focal point, but *men,* pious men, doubting men, Christian men, with all their problems and troubles were in the centre. The Lord Jesus Christ was not being preached as Saviour and Redeemer, but persons in the Bible were being portrayed as examples for us.

Many sermons and meditations of the past half century underline the weakness and impoverished nature of the exemplary method. Look at the following two examples. Jesus Christ's attendance at the wedding feast at Cana was often used for wedding ceremonies in this way: young couples today ought to invite Jesus to their wedding party. He ought to be present at our marriage feasts. His presence ought to influence our behaviour at a convocation of family and friends. Another example is that of the two men on the road to Emmaus after the resurrection of Jesus Christ (Luke 24:13-25). An exemplary sermon would go something along these lines: our heart must be burning in the same way as the hearts of the men of Emmaus. That is possible when Christ accompanies us on our way. Sometimes two of you may be walking along just like these men. If Jesus came, would you be ashamed of your conversation? For that matter, when you are alone, are you thinking about Jesus? The problem with such an exemplary approach is that the specific moment in the history of salvation and redemption is neglected. The result is a loss of depth and a generalization of the very special and specific point with which the Holy Spirit wants to touch and to move us. Therefore there was actually a plea for the *redemptive-historical* method in the time of Schilder and Holwerda, over against the exemplary approach (Arnold, 1984:82ff.).

Two forms

The old exemplary method actually had two different forms. We can speak of '*mere exemplarism*' and '*synthetic exemplarism*.' The first method totally neglects the history of salvation and redemption because each story is treated as an independent story. The second method acknowledges, at least theoretically, the significance of the redemptive-historical moment, but when it comes to the practical application of the relevant passage of Scripture, it turns again to delivering general examples. It tries to combine two contradictory methods, which is impossible.

An example of mere exemplarism can be taken from a sermon on Mark 6:46b, *He went up on the mountain to pray.* The sermon does not speak about what Christ is doing for us, but what we have to do and how well behaved our life ought to be. The theme of the sermon is 'solitude' and the three heads are: 1. The fact that solitude must be sought; 2. The place where solitude must be sought; 3. The reason why solitude must be sought.

An example of synthetic exemplarism can be taken from a sermon on Daniel 5:25-28, *Mene, mene, tekel, parsin.* First this sermon speaks about the struggle between God and Satan, between Christ and the devil. However, after the preacher has said some good things from the text, he jumps suddenly to a statement such as, "The highest God is our Judge as well. He will judge us." Then comes another jump, "He will judge us as Reformed Churches; let us not be careless and self-sufficient!" Then follows yet another jump, "What about us, if God's judgment comes to us personally? You may see it or not, my hearer, but the fingers of a man's hand appeared in your life and wrote on the plaster of the wall of your home. Who would not be alarmed? Those in whom God works renewal of life! They say by themselves: numbered and brought to an end!" (Arnold, 1984:82ff.).

Synthetic exemplarism is still very much alive. We discover it in all kinds of Biblicism today, especially in *fundamentalism,* originating in the U.S.A. Of course we cheer on the struggle of the fundamentalists against liberalism, but unfortunately so many fundamentalists have no eye for the progress of God's revelation, and do not see the development of redemptive history. A fundamentalist may preach on a certain text, try to understand that text in its historical framework and background, but then suddenly jump to the situation of the present time.

The present time

Careful attention ought to be directed to the fact that there is a new type of exemplarism, born in recent years and taking off in a different direction from former exemplarism. This new type of exemplarism uses the Bible for all kinds of *revolution,* and leads to the theology of revolution. This was evident already twenty years ago in the reports of Uppsala, 1966 of the W.C.C. Young people who wanted to disturb the established order and structures of society said: "We follow Jesus the great revolutionary: he overturned the tables of the money-changers and pigeon-sellers (Matthew 21:12) and he spoke so sharply against the highly esteemed Jewish leaders!" This Jesus is their great example for subversive actions and impertinent demonstrations! They point also to the *prophets*. Did not the prophet Amos condemn very sharply the capitalistic man of Samariah? Did not Isaiah and Zephaniah put into the pillory esteemed men and women who filled their houses with blood and fraud? Furthermore, do not the Psalms complain of the oppression of the underdog? Do not the imprecatory Psalms receive renewed impetus, fighting against the oppression of minorities, against colonialists and against rich industrialists? (Schilder, 1974:41).

Of course the interpretations of the new breed of exemplarism are easily refuted. Jesus Christ purified the temple in order to restore it to what it had to be: a house of prayer — a house of God. Christ's actions were not revolution but reformation. Similarly, the prophets of the Old Testament did not lead a class-struggle and did not plead for a policy of division of incomes, but warned the people of all levels, high and low, against apostasy within God's covenant: in social, cultural and political life. As for the Psalms, their references to the poor must be seen in the light of those who are 'miserable' and 'humble' before God, while the arrogant oppressors and persecutors are those who neglect and misjudge the covenant of the LORD. Everything in Scripture must be placed within the framework of God's covenant with his people. There is no mention of this in the mouths of the revolutionary youths who quote the above texts. So clear is all of this to those who follow the redemptive-historical method that this new breed of exemplarism is not taken very seriously.

However the matter is more important and serious than it appears. Today's exemplarism may be superficial but it is in a certain way penetrating. It pays attention to the often neglected Old Testament and causes the modern man to improve, protect and secure life for the future. Therefore this approach to interpreting Scripture which has its roots in an older form of exemplarism and which has become very popular today, ought not to be taken lightly. It has no appreciation for what should be first and foremost in Biblical preaching: the place, significance and function of Biblical persons in the redemptive-history of God's salvation in Christ.

Differences

It can be asked: is there a great difference between modern exemplarism and that which has been delivered in sermons for a long time? Did revolutionary young people derive their method from preaching which they heard as they were growing up? Just think of the *negro spirituals* which are not readily connected with contemporary revolutionary doctrine and practice. Negro spirituals often articulated the black understanding of Jahweh, Moses, Jesus Christ and many other persons of the Bible. They sang about the Jordan River, Elijah's ascension, Daniel's rescue from the lion's den, the rescue of Daniel's friends from the fire, the rescue of Paul and Silas from prison, and many other similar stories of the Bible. Such songs were entitled, "Go Down, Moses," "Deep River," "O Freedom, Freedom Over Me," "Mary Had a Baby," "Were You There?" and "Nobody Knows the Trouble I've Seen." They have been sung already for decades. These spirituals were often applied to situations of slavery and redemption from slavery. This was not the only point in these songs. There was an eye for the redemptive-historical place which certain events have in the Bible. Many negro songs speak also of redemption of sinners by the blood of Jesus Christ.

However exemplarism was clearly manifest in negro spirituals. This was due to the influence of white preachers. Paul Breman writes in his book, *Spirituals* (p. 31): *It must be the most directly appealing passages of the Scripture, which were related to their own situation, which had been picked up and worked out. The slavery of the Israelites, the promised land, the difficulties in the desert were also to the white people of the frontier areas seizing and understandable subjects, which found expression in countless songs* (Breman, 1959: 31). Keep in mind that this author speaks about white people. But this is connected with the intricate investigation of the origin of negro spirituals. Most of the white preachers were Methodists. That means their influence on the negroes was of a strongly pietistic and Arminian nature, where *men*, with their doubts and struggles, received an unscriptural place. Consequently the negro spirituals were saturated with an exemplaric use of the Scriptures. In fact, often a direct equation was made between the bondage of Israel and the miseries of negro slavery in America. For further study on this point read the book of H.R. Rookmaaker, *Jazz, Blues, Spirituals,* in which he teaches that negro spirituals originate from the newer methodist hymns of John Wesley (Rookmaaker, 1960, passim).

In recent years there has been a marked revival of interest in the negro spirituals by those who use Scripture for revolutionary purposes. So there is definitely a connection between modern exemplarism and what young revolutionaries have been hearing from the pulpits. The connection between the two is quite clear. The struggle against racism often has a revolutionary character. In this struggle the Bible plays an important role. Think of the familiar prophetic text of Isaiah 40 verses 4 and 5: *Every valley shall be lifted up, and every mountain and hill be made low; the uneven ground shall become level, and the rough places plain. And the glory of the LORD shall be revealed, and all flesh shall see it together, for the mouth of the LORD has spoken.* These and similar passages receive an important place in the demonstrations of black people. Think of a famous speech of Martin Luther King who interpreted these words of Isaiah as his "dream," his perspective of peace between black and white people and complete equality between them. Here the passage of Isaiah is treated in an exemplaric fashion as the element of liberation is lifted out. In fact, the liberation and redemption of sinners and their gathering as the people of the Lord is taken as an example of the liberation of black people. It is totally disregarded that Isaiah speaks of a liberation from God's judgement; Instead it is made into a liberation from oppression of other peoples. The redemptive-historical salvation of the Church is transformed into a liberation of groups of men at different points in history. (Van Dam, 1984:10ff.).

Theology of Revolution

The theology of revolution is a very large and broad field of study. This theology wishes to speak about more than the examples of Jesus, Amos and Isaiah. It wishes to comprehend the whole Bible and the whole development of culture and the whole history of all ages in one single group. One could object: this is no longer exemplarism, for exemplarism isolates one fact from its historical Biblical context. Yet it is exemplarism (Schilder, 1974:81). Because now it involves more than just pious men as examples: it is a comparison of the *changes in history,* in which we live together as citizens of the world with social and structural revolution and historical, stimulating powers. The present world is changing very quickly, a world in which everything is going to be unsettled and must be unsettled, as the one condition for a better world. This is accompanied by *spiritual crises* which are obviously very hard on the older generation which is used to familiar patterns. However it is also very hard on the younger generation, which sees itself standing before a chaos with no way out. In such a situation of despair young and old alike are looking for help.

Therefore just as in earlier days when people tried to struggle with certain problems in their life by finding examples in Scripture of people who were confronted with similar struggles, so today, especially the youth use exactly the same method when confronted by the great emptiness and despair all around them. Today's problems are numerous and they are universal. Therefore in the chaos of transition to a new and unknown world, people appeal to the Bible for help in a way that is similar to previous generations. A modern theologian might say: "Let the people of Israel be our example. According to the Scriptures, Israel was always enroute to something new and better. Israel was called to go out, towards an unknown future, without the familiarity of trustworthy patterns, leaving behind the familiar religious, social and political structures. Israel travelled on to an unknown country." Thus people are urged to believe in a God who is not bound to one place but is mobile and teaches one to be mobile (cf. Wielenga, 1971:163).

Harvey Cox

Harvey Cox is typical of the radical new American theologians. He wrote *The Secular City, Secularization and Urbanization in Theological Perspective*, 1965. Four years later he wrote *The Feast of Fools: A Theological Essay on Festivity and Fantasy.* Harvey Cox called the first book more Apollonian and the second more Dionysian. In the first book he wrote: *The starting point for any theology of the church today must be a theology of social change. . . The Symbol of the secular city provides the starting point. . . Secularization denotes the removal of juvenile dependence from every level of a society; urbanization designates the fashioning of new patterns of human reciprocity* (Cox, 1969:91ff.). In the second book Harvey Cox does not revoke his earlier work: *This book is intended as a companion piece to the earlier work, not as a recantation. Politically, for example, I have become considerably more radical. . .* (Cox 1970 VII). It is remarkable that Cox often quoted Martin Luther King in his books; there is certainly a relationship between Cox and Negro spirituals. He writes that God liberates captured people from economic and political slavery. He did not liberate them into a certain form of inward tolerance or spiritual liberation. It is not enough to say: "Inward, in my soul, I am free." Instead liberation opens for them the way to a new political and economic existence in the world. For instance, the exodus of Moses' day when the Israelites were freed from their slavery to Pharaoh and led out of Egypt is a *blue print*, an *example*, for every kind of exodus thereafter. The whole treatise of Biblical data must be substructured by the vision of the mobile God who demands mobility of his people, to break off by revolution the old strucutres, and to realize a new society in a world made by man — the secular city.

It has been said that Harvey Cox professed a form of conversion during the 1980s in his book, *Religion in the Secular City.* Now he says that the technopolis is the hope of the future failed. Now he denounces modern theology. It appears to be a conversion but that is not really so. His new religion is called 'post-modernist.' He draws attention to the cultural dimensions of theology and how man's beliefs are to translate into *action.* But in spite of his talk of post-modernism, he is still a modernist, only the emphasis is on action. The theology of Harvey Cox is really an extension of liberation theology (cf. Marsden, 1984:3ff.).

Dorothée Sölle

There has been a remarkable development in modern theology over the last few decades. Those who started off as liberals, raising the slogans of the French Revolution, not so surprisingly arrived at *communism*. Many theologians such as Harvey Cox travelled via liberal theology to the "Entmythologisierung" of Rudolf Bultmann who said *God presents himself in the encounter with our neighbour.* They travelled via the 'God is dead' theology of *J.A.T. Robinson* who said, *God is the predicate of love, he is to be known in the neighbour and the neighbour is to be known in God.* They travelled via the ideas of *Paul van Buren* who said, *Only those pronouncements of the Bible are credible, which could be verified in the practice of co-humanity.* They travelled via the theology of revolution and liberation to what is essentially nothing other than a politicized neo-Marxist philosophy, critical of society. When Harvey Cox now says that only action counts, his intention is to base his post-modern theology not on the Scriptures but on the poor, and thus, not the poor of the church but the poor of the world. The poor must be at the centre of attention and the theology which focuses on them will be characterized by sacralism and radicalism (cf. Deddens/Drost, 1989:44ff.).

It is remarkable that the expression of Harvey Cox, *Only action counts,* was also used by revolutionary *Dorothée Sölle,* in her 1968 book, *Gottesdienst als Aktion.* She dared to say things like, *God is not dead, but God is red,* and *we meet God in our neighbour.* As for preaching Dorothée Sölle is of the opinion that ministers must not preach to people but inform them. Information must be given as to the deeper background of what ails this society. There must be an analysis of the real state of this society. There must be a protest against existing relationships, and a plan of action to change those relationships thoroughly, to change the present structures of society.

As far as her confession is concerned, I point to chapter IV of this book concerning *Current streams in modern liturgy.*

Feminism

Obviously it does not come as a big surprise that *feminism* should pick up on exemplary meditations. In a meditation about the song of Mary, Dorothée Sölle shows how this is an example for the modern woman. Mary herself is an example in these women:

It has been written that Mary said: He has shown strength with his arm,
He has scattered the proud in the imagination of their hearts,
He has put down the mighty from their thrones, and exalted those of low degree.
We say it now in this way:
We shall expropriate our owners and laugh at those who claim to know the female being.
The leadership of male over female will come to an end!
It has been written that Mary said: He has filled the hungry with good
things, and the rich he has sent empty away.
He has remembered his servant Israel,
In remembrance of his mercy.
We say it now in this way:
Women will travel to the moon and will make decisions in parliament,
Their desire of self-determination will be satisfied,
The hunger for power will be nourished,

Every ground of their anxiety will disappear,
They will not be exploited any longer!

This is an example of how feminism uses Scripture in an exemplary fashion. Feminists insist that critical women are to read the books of Exodus and those that follow with their own eyes. Then they will be conscious of the disobedience of women to authorities and that Moses liberated his people from Egypt. Moses' sister exhorted Pharoah's daughter to adopt Moses as her own child. Pharoah's daughter was disobedient to him. Mirjam went in front of the revolution according to Numbers 12. These creative and disobedient women are stimulating examples, as well as Deborah, Hulda and many other women of the Old and New Testament (cf. Arnold, 1984:84).

Christian Rock

Sometimes, instead of using special persons in the Bible as examples, certain expressions or images are extrapolated in an exemplaric fashion. This is done for instance by young rock and roll performers who call themselves Christian.

One example is the group U2, formed in the late seventies in Dublin, Ireland. They pretend to have a Christian message in their songs. The main song of their latest album is:

I believe in the Kingdom Come
Then all the colours will bleed into one
But yes I'm still running
You broke the bonds
You loosed the chains
You carried the cross
And my shame
You know I believe it
But I still haven't found what I'm looking for.

One member of the group said, "To me truth is between there and there. So I look for images, not lines." Another one added, "God forbid if we ever found what we were looking for. What a horrible experience that would be!"

This is not Biblical Christianity, but the false modern concept (promoted by liberal theologians that truth is always evolving and never constant. It sounds humble, but is in reality a very haughty stand over against God who 'has spoken to us by a Son' (Hebrews 1:2) and completed His revelation to His people. If we cannot find it today, we never will indeed! Despite all its Biblical imagery and poignant appeals, U2 does not bring the joyous message of salvation in Jesus Christ as it has been revealed in the Scriptures. True faith is a sure knowledge and a firm confidence that the Word of God is trustworthy and that Christ has indeed died for us on the cross. This jubilant certainty which must characterize Christian music is not found with U2 (Stam, 1987:22).

New and Old

The new breed of exemplarism is gaining popularity all over the world. It is often defiant and revolutionary: God and men marching together; God is in movement and man is in movement and the Church is in movement; here is the meaning of "God with us." There is an inflammatory and an even poetic-prophetic element to this exemplarism. It may seem to be completely different from the exemplarism of half a century ago, but that is not so. Indeed, they are totally different with respect to acknowledging the Scriptures as the Word of God, nevertheless in their methodology they are similar. Biblical persons and events are only examples. They are separated from their redemptive-historical context and isolated from the continuing revelation of God's covenant. Just look at the consequences. Those who are faithful to the Scriptures and those who are very critical can both reject infant baptism with the same fragmented appeal to Mark 16:16. Both can appeal to Matthew 25:40,45 the one to help men in need and the other to help rebels. On both sides there is an arbitrary and improper use of the Scriptures.

Proof or Appeal?

Both kinds of exemplarism occur not only in Europe and America, but also in South Africa. One finds there the pietistic-methodistic exemplarism, but also the exemplarism of the theology of liberation in order to justify a revolutionary movement.

Both kinds of exemplarism appeal in very arbitrary and selective fashion to Scripture. Apartheid is allegedly proven by Genesis 9:25 *Cursed be Canaan; a slave of slaves shall he be held to his brothers,* and by Joshua 9:27: *But Joshua made the inhabitants of Gideon that day hewers of wood and drawers of water for the congregation and for the altar of the LORD.* But on the other hand the advocates of the theology of liberation will use the Exodus story to teach that God is at the side of the oppressed people and he punishes the oppressor with military violence. Both kinds of exemplarism arbitrarily take a passage from Scripture, removing it completely from its context and using it as an example to make their point (Deist, 1982 A; cf. Arnold, 1984:85).

But what is now the proper response to both forms of exemplarism? Deist replies that one has to discern between *proof* of Scripture and *appeal* on Scripture. Proof of Scripture points to the Bible as being the truth. To support dogma one delivers some verses of the Bible as proof texts. This kind of use of the Bible can be found in the Heidelberg Catechism according to Deist. But an appeal on Scripture is totally different. An appeal does not look to Scripture for authoritative proof, but as a reference point: one makes a declaration on his own responsibility, and in doing so, looks to Scripture to find those who came to the same conclusion in former days in their own circumstances. The proof of Scripture points to an imperfect faith, a faith which does not stand on what one believes. It needs authority from outside. But an appeal on Scripture has its starting point based on one's own responsibility. One makes up his own mind in his circumstances, and then points afterwards to Jesus, Paul, Peter, or whoever wrestled in their circumstances and in their culture to do God's will (Deist, 1982:286).

Now Deist himself also comes to a selection of the Bible with an appeal on Scripture. He claims to make up his mind on his own responsibility and goes back to a Biblical testimony in order to explain *why one witness of the Bible is here more relevant than another, according to my opinion.* But that is also an arbitrary use of the Bible. By rejecting both forms of exemplarism, Deist introduced a new form. It is an exemplarism also found in the Netherlands and used by someone such as H.M. Kuitert who advocates that an appeal on Scripture is relevant in order to provide a certain point of view with the authority of Scriptures; that happens then not beforehand but afterwards; the theological considerations follow afterwards when positions have already been taken. Here is an exemplaric use of the Bible. It is not the exemplarism of the historical equation mark, such as the exemplarism of pietism-methodism or of the theology of revolution, but a new form. It can be labelled as the exemplarism of the *co-searcher* who intends to go in the line of former biblical searchers and afterward quote persons in the Bible in order to underline what he did on his own responsibility. But also in this method, the one history of salvation has been split into many stories, which have little or no connections with each other. They are only *models* and one model is more relevant than another (Arnold, 1984:86).

The one response

It should be clear that rejecting old and new examplarism by replacing them with a third kind is not suitable. There is only one suitable response to exemplarism and that is the response of the Reformed confession of the Scriptures as a unity, as the one revelation of redemption, given in a redemptive-historical way. Already half a century ago, men like K. Schilder, B. Holwerda, M.B. van't Veer, J. Kapteyn and others demonstrated this in their preaching and in their writings.

It was indeed a reformation in preaching. In his dissertation Sidney Greidanus criticized especially the examplaric method but he also made some remarks on the redemptive-historical method. He had at least four points: generally speaking this method would fall short in application; especially K. Schilder's sermons were objective, schematic and logical treatises; there is a speculative element in these sermons; finally, Holwerda wrongly identified *fact* and *text* (Greidanus, 1970:174 ff.). In the same year of the publication of this dissertation C. Trimp disproved these objections extensively (Trimp, 1970:345 ff.).

Two remarks of H.J. Schilder should be added. In the first place the living redemptive-historical preaching, that is for the congregation. The bread that does not pass away, but that nourishes, unto eternal life, suffers a loss by the emphatic and expressive 'drawing of lines.' Not that the redemptive historical line (or lines) is (are) unimportant. On the contrary, the preacher must try to recognize these carefully and show the congregation the special moment of the history of the event. Of course it can happen that he sometimes uses the term 'line,' but it may not become a 'shibboleth' in order to characterize solid redemptive-historical preaching. It is actually (although in itself an 'image') more a working term than one in the sermon, more a *terminus technicus,* a term of methodology of the subject. The congregation does not live from 'lines' of whatever methodical data, but from the gospel which shows her place on the way of salvation throughout the ages. Therefore she must know where she stands, how far she has pursued her way, how the way of salvation was guided by her LORD from then to now and into the future. But she will scarcely or needlessly or painfully learn that, if she is going to be nourished by drawing of lines and such.

In the second place, closely connected with this: The congregation must see before her eyes *her riches* in the incarnated and now exalted and returning *Saviour;* besides that also her 'poverty' in comparison with the salvation which no eye has seen yet (cf. Lords' Day 22, Heidelberg Catechism, answer 58). The congregation must also become conscious of her present riches in relation with the still preliminary revelation to the fathers and to the people of Israel in the old dispensation. In connection with this the sermon has to point to what the people of God did not have at that time, but now do have. A text like 1 Peter 1:10ff. demands this teaching and also a comprehensive answer like Lord's Day (answer 19) delivers no less than that one text. At the same time the matter of 'not yet' can receive its own necessary accent and working out. But a term like that — such as, for instance, the contrast 'poor — rich' — must not become a *passe partout* and the data not a ruling motive. For this would happen at the cost of the salvation in Christ, which was already present in the Old Testament in the promise of the gospel. So it was there already revealed, given and enjoyed. The text from Peter speaks about that and the later answer of the Catechism points clearly to that as well. This does not even mention yet the emphasis of the apostle Paul on the revelation of and the living from the gospel of the justification by faith, already from the very beginning (especially Romans 4 and Galatians 3). Besides that, in the Old Testament has been stressed the prefiguration; but prefiguration already presents Messianic wealth so that an over-accentuation of the 'not yet' motive would come in conflict with the clear language of Scriptures. So both of these one-sided emphases must be prevented (Schilder, 1976:170 ff.).

Response

It must be said: true and careful redemptive-historical preaching is the only response to all kinds of exemplaric preaching. It is necessary to preach Jesus Christ as Saviour, as chief Prophet and Teacher, as High Priest and Eternal King, and then the congregation will learn about their service as a living member of Christ. This will lead to truly Christological preaching. Sometimes it may be difficult to discover how Christ would be centred in the preaching, and yet, preaching must be *Theocentric,* not *Anthropocentric:* not man, not even a pious or faithful man may be at the centre, but God with his virutes and mighty deeds.

If we consider things in this way, we do not see any contrast between Theocentric and Christocentric (or Christological) preaching. *He who is reading Scriptures on his best, rejects the dilemma Christocentric or Theocentric as a wrong dilemma, because Christocentric is at the same time also Theocentric* (Kapteyn, n.d.:244).

Furthermore, if Christological preaching is considered in the right way, then it is also clearly *Pneumatological* preaching, for the work of God the Holy Spirit is very closely connected with the redemptive work of Jesus Christ.

Criticism

We have already heard the reproach that redemptive-historical preaching would lead to schematism, speculation and objectivism. C. Trimp rejected that criticism completely. But recently he said that by stressing the history of salvation, the order of salvation *(ordo salutis)* is neglected. He said that partially in connection with Holwerda's speech of 1942 (Holwerda 1983:passim), which is considered more or less as the program of redemptive historical preaching (Trimp, 1986:93ff).

I think Trimp is right when he relativates Holwerda's speech as just a new beginning. However when reading Holwerda we come to the conclusion that he pointed precisely to the fact that in Philo's *allegorical* way of exegesis, he had already shifted very easily from the history of salvation to 'the order of salvation.' And that is exactly the danger of exemplaric preaching, for exemplarism isolates one fact from its historical Biblical context. Yet it is salvation, so that the principal lesson of history became moral instruction; in his way he lost view of the history of redemption. He read into each story that which God did in every individual soul and then he drew a parallel with what God does for our soul. Holwerda warned against this method and showed the danger of old and modern exemplarism! However it was especially in the published sermons of Holwerda that it became clear that his preaching was not only Christological, but also Theological, and last but not least, also Pneumatological. He paid full attention to the work of the Triune God, stressing the fact that the Holy Spirit works in our hearts with the Word of God. Reading these sermons, as well as those of K. Schilder and M.B. van't Veer, demonstrates that neither the trinitarian aspect nor the order of salvation is neglected. Therefore true trinitarian preaching is the only response to exemplaric preaching.

But the reproach is repeated. H. Krabbendam quotes the applications of two redemptive-historical sermons (without mentioning where they are published) and comes then to the conclusion that this method is to be rejected: *The text functions somewhat as a 'window' through which the phases and facts of Christ's march through history are witnessed. It is hardly surprising that the text as text, therefore, is frequently curtailed in its scope, ignored in its purpose, or even violated in its nature, as it is ultimately made to serve the cause of what may be described as 'aesthetic contemplation.' Indeed, preaching in the redemptive historical tradition is often comparable to a ride in a Boeing 747 high above the landscape with its hot deserts, its snowpeaked mountains, its dense forests, its open prairies, its craggy hills and its deep lakes. The view is panoramic, majestic, impressive, breathtaking, and always comfortable. But there is one problem. The Christian is not 'above' things. He is in the middle of things* (Krabbendam, 1986:235).

He pleads then for a so-called *covenantal-historical methodology, which honors God not only in His trinitarian self-disclosure, but also in His threefold objective of regeneration, justification and sanctification* (Krabbendam, 1986:234).

How does one respond to this? In the first place, it is not fair to jump from (possible) wrong application to the method as such. In the second place, it is not true that the redemptive-historical method places men above things on earth. God's people today are addressed by the messages of God's Word. They are encouraged, comforted, but also admonished and warned by the great deeds of God in redemptive-history.

It is therefore, not true that redemptive-historical preaching as such does not respond to the many needs and problems of people today. When exemplarism was attacked in the 1930s it was said that without such preaching the preacher does not go into the real sorrows and needs of the wrestling believer. In the same way one could say today that without such exemplaric preaching modern man is left all alone with his despairs.

The answer is consistent. The Christian in all his troubles of faith is only really helped when he is addressed by the redemptive-historical revelation of the Scriptures. Modern man can only be addressed in the midst of chaos when the minister preaches to him with the command to repent and believe (Canons of Dort, II 5) which is given in the infallible Word of God and unfolded in the course of the revealed history of salvation. Thus ministers have the rich task to preach the only Mediator Jesus Christ who redeems his people from their sins and places his people as a blessing for the world. He is known only from the Holy Gospel.

As far as Krabbendam's 'solution' is concerned he does not do justice to history. For history is then actually limited to the history of individual examples of regeneration, justification and sanctification. But that is no history any more, let alone redemptive history. In this way the *ordo salutis* takes the place of redemptive history. Although Krabbendam rejects the exemplaric method, he actually works it into his 'methodology,' which goes in a *soteriological* way, instead of a way in which the LORD is centred.

Krabbendam's essay has the title *Hermeneutics and preaching*. This title indeed raises an important matter. For hermeneutics is essential to this discussion. We may even say, the cardinal question is indeed a *hermeneutic* one: is there a recognition of the unity of the Scriptures and history of salvation? Sadly in today's theological world this idea of hermeneutics is clearly lacking. The notion of God's one, redemptive history as a whole is disappearing more and more. In connection with this, the confession that the Word of God is inspired by the Holy Spirit is virtually obsolete. Eugene A. Nida writes: *Exegesis may be described as the process of reconstructing the communication event by determining its meaning (or meanings) for the participants in the communication. Hermeneutics, on the other hand, may be described as pointing out*

143

parallels between the biblical message and present day events and determining the extent of relevance and the appropriate response for the believer (Nida, 1981:30). So on the basis of the proper type of hermeneutics, preachers must note parallels in modern life. Not one word is said about redemptive-history. Not one word is said about the inspiration of Holy Scripture by the Holy Spirit. The preacher's task is to lead the congregation in finding relevant *parallels* in modern life. In spite of the variety in modern exemplarism, there is an obvious unity among them.

Conclusion

May we say that the whole matter of *examples* in the Bible is excluded? N.H. Gootjes pointed to the fact that indeed examples are used in Scriptures, but always in connection with the great deeds of the LORD. There is sometimes an example in God's way of acting, or in the acting of the Redeemer. However these examples place God, not men, in the centre. We have not the task to imitate God (in the sense of to try to do what He did), but to obey Him in the office to which we are called (Gootjes, 1987:3; cf. Schilder, 1981:139ff.).

The fact that the Biblical events can be used as examples does not follow from the work of the Holy Spirit in the intercourse with God's people, but from the work of the Holy Spirit in the description of those events (Gootjes, 1987:23).

I started with the importance of preaching the Word of God. Now at the end I will stress the great responsibility regarding the way of preaching. I maintain the term redemptive-historical preaching. We have to administer the Word of God *Who goes a way in history with His people and Who reveals His wonderful Name on the way in words and works before the eyes of small and weak human beings* (Trimp, 1986:112).

Unfortunately, the isolation of Reformed preaching is a fact. Reformed ministers must be faithful, holding to the true preaching and be continually aware of all kinds of deformation in preaching.

THE SIFTING EFFECT OF PREACHING

Important matter

If we reflect for a moment on the sifting or the separating effect of the preaching of God's Word, we have to realize that the preaching as such is an enormous event. We have to do with a very important matter, which can only fill us with awe and wonder if we consider that God is coming to men in the form of speech. God's kingdom comes to us in, with, and through the preaching of God's Word. The kingdom of God and especially He in whom this kingdom is represented and realized, our Lord Jesus Christ, is the contents of preaching. But also special *aspects* of God's kingdom are called the contents of preaching. The New Testament speaks more than once about a preaching of *conversion*. God's coming kingdom is realized in the way of conversion in those to whom the preaching of the kingdom comes.

Moreover preaching is also a preaching of conversion *for the forgiveness of sins.* If the kingdom comes in the preaching, it brings with it forgiveness of sins, and not only that, but also the complete, full salvation in Christ. Therefore we can also speak of the preaching of the *gospel.*

It is very important to see in the first place this positive function of preaching.

But we have to be aware also of the negative side. "By the preaching is also realized the *judgment* of God." This happens in a twofold manner: First in those who believe.

144

They are and have been condemned and damned in Christ. The preaching of Jesus Christ is the most imaginable crushing sentence. For in Him the *forgiveness* of sins, *grace* is proclaimed. But there is only talk of forgiveness and grace for ungodly people! Forgiveness and grace *can* not be granted and *are* not to be granted except to those who are struck by God's condemning judgment. Therefore there is nothing in the world so totally destructive for man than the preaching of forgiveness and grace. For this preaching is the absolute and permanent condemnation of everything that is man himself, what he has and what he is doing. Added to this, however, the preaching brings about judgment to those to whom the proclamation of the kingdom proceeded but who did not believe it. Paul declared to the Corinthians, ". . . we preached Christ crucified, a stumbling block to Jews and folly to Gentiles, but to those who are called, both Jews and Greeks, Christ the power of God and the wisdom of God" (1 Cor. 1:23,24) (Veenhof, 1959:227; cf. also De Klerk, 1987:106).

Element of judgment

It is clear from the preaching of our Saviour Himself, especially from His preaching in parables, that the preaching of the kingdom contains not only God's blessing but also an element of judgment. Christ causes sifting, exactly by this way of preaching. The parable of the Sower shows that the seed brings to the light the condition of the soil. When the disciples ask the Saviour what this parable means, the answer is, "To you it has been given to know the secrets of the kingdom of God; but for others they are (preached) in parables, so that seeing they may not see, and hearing they may not understand" (Luke 8:9, 10). After this parable Christ declares, "For nothing is hid that shall not be made manifest, nor anything secret that shall not be known and come to light. Take heed then how you hear; for to him who has will more be given, and from him who has not, even what he thinks that he has will be taken away" (vs. 17, 18). The light (about which also vs. 16 speaks) means undoubtedly the gospel itself, which is preached by the Saviour. What is hid but what has to come to light is the unbelief and sin, which the hearers of the gospel bear in their hearts, but which have to become manifest by the preaching which reveals the hearts. So there is a great responsibility in hearing: Christ impresses upon His people both the blessing and the curse of the covenant, grace as well as judgment (Geertsema, 1987:52ff.)

Blessing and curse

The Holy Scriptures are full of the two sanctions of the covenant, the twofold effect of blessing and curse.

Extensively in Leviticus 26, God's blessing is promised to the people of Israel if this people listens to the LORD. But, ". . . if in spite of this you will not hearken to Me, but walk contrary to Me, then I will walk contrary to you in fury . . ." (vs. 27). I think also of Moses' preaching of the sanctions of God's covenant when the people were standing upon the Ebal and the Gerizim (Deut. 27: 11-26, and also chapter 28). The notes on the old Dutch translation speak in this connection typically of "the register of the blessings" and "the register of the curse."

The prophets further develop the theme of covenant blessing and covenant wrath (Van der Waal, 1978:33).

The preaching of God's Word is given in order to be accepted, not only in the course of time, when it suits, but right away, "today," Psalm 95 says. The hearkening to God's *voice* is the listening to God's *Word*. Otherwise, hardening can appear, as was the case in the desert (vs. 9ff.). Later on, this Psalm is quoted, not only in Romans 10 (where Paul deals especially with the preaching of God's Word), but also in Hebrews 4, in the context of the proclamation of the gospel.

To take offence at the Word

Scripture tells us that one can also take offence at the Word. In the preaching of Isaiah, it is said of the LORD Himself, ". . . He will become a sanctuary, and a stone of offence, and a rock of stumbling to both houses of Israel, a trap and a snare to the inhabitants of Jerusalem. And many shall stumble thereon; they shall fall and be broken; they shall be snared and taken" (Is. 8:14,15). See also Isaiah 28:16, where it is said that God is laying in Zion a stone, a tested stone. Psalm 118 deals with the stone which the builders rejected, which however has become the head of the corner. The Saviour applied these words to Himself as the Messiah (Matt. 21:42 and 44) and the apostle Paul applied "the stumbling block" to the Jews, that the gospel went to the gentiles. The same is done by the apostle Peter before the Sanhedrin when he was defending himself (Acts 4:11), and in his first letter he made a contrast between "you who believe" and "those who do not believe" (1 Peter 2:7). The first category is building faith on the cornerstone Jesus Christ, while the second category "stumble because they disobey the Word" (vs. 8). That Word, Peter just argued at the end of the first chapter, "is the good news which was preached to you" (1:25). The unbelievers are stumbling. But they were destined to do so (2:8). The Word itself hardens them so that they stumble and fall.

To death and to life

The idea of a twofold function of the preaching is also found in another form in the second letter of the apostle Paul to the Corinthians. In the framework of the progress of the preaching of the gospel it is said that God "spreads the fragrance of the knowledge of Him everywhere. For we are the aroma of Christ to God among those who are being saved and among those who are perishing, to one a fragrance from death to death, to the other a fragrance from life to life" (2 Cor. 2:14-16).

It is remarkable that the apostle calls *himself* "the aroma of Christ." What is first said of the proclamation of the gospel is now applied to Paul himself. The apostle says, I myself, in my work, in my travelling, in my struggle for the church, in my prayer and care for the flock, I am the aroma of Christ. In other words: he identifies himself actually with the service of the gospel as such. This is possible indeed because this service demands total commitment. The fragrance of the knowledge of God is at the same time the aroma of Christ. For in Christ the knowledge of God comes to its fulness and depth. If this service of the gospel is executed by the whole person, the apostle says it will have a double effect. That double effect is totally different. The same gospel will work life to the one and death to the other.

This is a very remarkable idea!

The same Word, the same gospel has two effects which stand diametrically over against each other. The same Word works for the one death and for the other one life. But it is the one, indivisible Word. So there is not a twofold Word, a twofold preaching and a twofold proclamation. No, exactly the same Word has a twofold effect. It brings to the unbelievers God's judgment of death and it causes destruction. But in those who believe precisely the same word works life by the power of God's grace. While it causes in the one an action from death to death, an action that leads inevitably and irresistibly to death, that same Word causes in the other an action that leads unquestionably to life. That means: it is indeed wonderful, to hear the Word of

God and to obey it. Then more light will be received, more glory, a going on from strength to strength, from the beginning of eternal joy to fulness of joy. But it is also terrible to be touched by the same Word, to hear it, but then to lay it aside. Then it means to go back from death to death, from death to eternal judgment, from condemnation to even heavier punishment. But always there is happening something, the one or the other (Douma/Deddens, 1965:20ff.).

Resistance against the Holy Spirit

It is clear from the Scriptures that one can resist the Word of God. One resists then at the same time the Holy Spirit who is working with the Word. Stephen reproaches in his redemptive-historical sermon the Jewish leaders of his days, "You stiff-necked people, uncircumcised in heart and ears, you always resist the Holy Spirit. As your fathers did, so do you" (Acts 7:51). The fathers have persecuted the prophets who brought the good Word of God. These prophets announced beforehand the coming of the Righteous One. But the Jews of his own days have betrayed and murdered Him. They have received the law — God's own Word — as delivered by angels. But they did not keep it. They rejected the Word of God (vs. 52,53).

This resistance against the Holy Spirit is also clear from the last book of the Bible. The exalted Christ writes in Revelation 2 and 3 His letters to the seven churches in Asia. Seven times the Saviour ends these letters with the admonition, "He who has an ear, let him hear what the Spirit says to the churches." For His Word comes with grace and with judgment, with advantage and with disadvantage. He who resists that Word, undergoes the hardening effect of the Holy Spirit with that Word. It must be brought to the light, according to the Word of the Saviour in the gospel, in which direction it goes with the hearers. The antithesis will increase to its climax, and there are only two possibilities: "Let the evildoer still do evil, and the filthy still be filthy, and the righteous still do right, and the holy still be holy" (Rev. 22:11). Meditating upon this text, K. Schilder called it "the two-edged sword, driven into the flesh of the *church* by the Bishop of the souls Himself" (Schilder, 1958:223).

John wrote these words precisely in the context of the mandate that the words of the prophecy of his book must not be sealed (vs.10). The prophetic Word must be passed on and the preaching of the antithetical Word has to go on until the very end of history.

Always efficacious

Especially the letter to the Hebrews stresses extensively that God's Word is efficacious. Always a strong, powerful effect of God's Word is present, also regarding those who outraged the Spirit of grace, although they had become partakers of the Holy Spirit, had tasted the goodness of the Word of God and had once been enlightened (Hebr. 6:4ff., cf. also 10:29ff.).

"A powerful effect is ascribed to the goodness of God's Word — so the gospel or the promise — also in the unbelieving members of the church. Without a doubt it is not saving. It is not the beginning and the guarantee of the ultimate fulfilment of God's Word in the new world. But it is indeed very real and very far-reaching. One must also be aware that it is even said of these apostates that it is impossible to restore them again to repentance — here considered as a change of insight. So there came about in these men indeed by the word such a repentance, which is now annulled in and through their apostasy and will never be renewed any more. But it was there once!

Moreover it is significant that it is said of those apostate members of the church that they crucify the Son of God on their own account and hold Him up to contempt.

One wonders how this is possible *stricto sensu*. However, this expression is completely transparent for him who understands the nature of the Word, drawn by this letter. The crucified and resurrected Saviour is presented in the goodness of God's Word with all the gifts which He obtained and distributes. In that Word He comes to the people and He gives Himself to them. Therefore the rejection and the contempt of that Word is in the full sense to assault Christ Himself and to hold Him up to contempt. In this way the letter to the Hebrews is preaching the mighty truth that the Word of God is always efficacious, although not always in the same measure, in the same direction, and with the same effect. The Word of God is like the rain, which descends from heaven always as the same rain. But land which has drunk the rain that often falls upon it, and brings forth vegetation useful to those for whose sake it it cultivated, receives a blessing from God. But if it bears thorns and thistles, it is worthless and near to being cursed; its end is to be burned (Hebr. 6:7,8). In this way the letter to the Hebrews teaches and illustrates the saying of Paul that the Word of God is always a penetrating fragrance, for many certainly to life, alas for most people to death" (Veenhof, 1946:22ff.).

The Word of the Spirit

The Word of God is the Word of the Holy Spirit. Christ said to His disciples before He left, "When the Spirit of truth comes, He will guide you into all the truth; for He will not speak on His own authority, but whatever He hears He will speak, and He will declare to you the things that are to come. He will glorify Me, for He will take what is mine and declare it to you" (John 16:13,14). This is worked out in the letter to the Hebrews. "For the Word of God is living and active, sharper than any two-edged sword, piercing to the division of soul and spirit, of joints and marrow, and discerning the thoughts and intentions of the heart" (Hebr. 4:12). C. Veenhof wrote in connection with this, "He who hears the Word of God has to do with the Holy Spirit, who is pushing the work of God in this world to its completion. He will come inevitably in the grasp of the Spirit. Wherever the Word of the Scriptures is raised, there is the working place of the Holy Spirit. He who is listening to the Word, lets the Holy Spirit work in him. This Word may never be separated from the Spirit. He never lets it go. It is even wrong to say that the Word is an instrument of the Spirit. For He IS always His Word. He is always Himself addressing the people in His Word. He is seizing them and He is achieving in them the Father's good pleasure. Therefore to speak about the Word 'as such' is a folly and a blasphemy. As the Word of the Spirit it calls the dead to life and it drills through the hardest walls of hearts. But as the Word of the Spirit it also hardens the hearts of all who resist against God and makes them at last inaccessible to each and every working of grace. In short, as the Word of the Spirit it is the seed of regeneration and the food of the soul, but also the hammer, which is mercilessly smashing everything that rises against God (. . .) The Word is pushing through to what is deeply hidden and is growing together in the dark shafts of human life. It tears asunder everything and it draws what was first tucked-away into the blinding light of God's holiness. Everything that comes up in the heart of man such as desires, endeavours and thoughts are sifted and judged by the Word according to the holy right of God. That is — according to the letter to the Hebrews — the majesty and the power, the salvation and the terror of God's Word which is preached among us" (Veenhof, 1946:42 ff.).

Old Testament

We see this double effect of God's Word and the preaching of God's Word already in the Old Testament. Time and again there is the preaching of God's promise, but at the same time also the preaching of the threat of God's covenant. Noah was an instrument in God's hand for God's judgment, according to Genesis 6 and 7. But beforehand he warned the people. Therefore he is called "a herald of righteousness" (2 Peter 2:5) and it is also said, "by faith Noah, being warned by God concerning events as yet unseen, took heed and constructed the ark for the saving of his household; by this he condemned the world and became an heir of the righteousness which comes by faith" (Hebr. 11:7).

When God later gives His promise to Abraham, the LORD says about his descendants, "they shall come back here in the fourth generations; for the iniquity of the Amorites is not yet complete" (Gen. 15:16). First they were warned, but when the iniquity is complete they will be destroyed completely.

Not only in the historical books of the Old Testament is this double effect of God's Word shown, but also in the prophetic books. Isaiah writes in his prophecy, ". . . as the rain and the snow come down from heaven, and return not thither but water the earth, making it bring forth and sprout, giving seed to the sower and bread to the eater, so shall My Word be that goes forth from My mouth; it shall not return to Me empty, but it shall accomplish that which I purpose, and prosper in the thing for which I sent it" (Is. 55:10,11). God's Word and its preaching is not empty, so that nothing will happen when it is brought to the people, but it is the living Word of God, which always has effect.

The LORD says to His prophet Jeremiah, "I am watching over My Word to perform it" (Jer. 1:12). The prophet has to proclaim that Word to the people and because of the iniquity it is even called first the *destructive* Word, and after that the *constructive* Word: "Behold, I have put My Words in your mouth. See, I have set you this day over nations and over kingdoms, to pluck up and to break down, to destroy and to overthrow, to build and to plant" (1:9,10). There is a separating effect of the preaching of God's Word, and that effect is shown in both the Old and New Testament of the Bible.

Calvin

This sifting effect of preaching is clearly understood by the Reformers and especially by John Calvin. In his *Institutes* he quotes with respect to this the calling of Jeremiah and the mandate to preach the breaking and building Word. Then he continues, "But the prophecy of Isaiah presses it even farther home, for the Lord sends him out thus: 'Go and say to the children of Israel, Hear and hear but do not understand; see and see but do not perceive. Make the heart of this people stubborn, and their ears heavy, and shut their eyes; lest they perchance see with their eyes, and hear with their ears, and understand with their hearts, and turn and be healed' (Is. 6:9,10; cf. Matt. 13:14,15; Mark 4:12; Luke 8:10; John 12:40; Acts 28:26,27; Rom. 11:8). Observe that he directs his voice to them but in order that they may become even more deaf; he kindles a light but that they may be made even more blind; he sets forth doctrine but that they grow even more stupid; he employs a remedy but so that they may not be healed. And John, applying this prophecy, states that the Jews could not believe Christ's teaching (John 12:39), for this curse of God hung over them" (Calvin, Institutes III, 24, 13).

Calvin stressed very much that the first function of the preaching is the power of God for salvation, according to Romans 1:16. It is the *gospel,* good tidings. But preaching of the Word of God can also have a condemning, a deadly effect. With respect to this C. Veenhof wrote, "In an intensive way Calvin deals with the fact that the preaching of the gospel can have this twofold effect. However, and with that we touch immediately the kernel of his expositions in this respect, Calvin does not think one moment to place this double effect on the same line. On the contrary, he states with emphasis that the relation between the preaching and the salvation worked by it, is totally different from the relation between the preaching and death, worked by it. Or, to say it in another way, Calvin teaches that, from the point of view of preaching there is a discongruity on principle between the working of the gospel with an effect of salvation and the other one in which it functions as a power of perdition. That the preaching of the gospel is working salvation is namely its specific nature, its genuine character, its proper office. If the preaching becomes a reason of condemnation and death for those who reject it, that is concerning this preaching something accidental, something occasional, even something that is clashing with its real nature. If the preaching of the gospel in contrast with its nature changes in a deadly, condemning power, that has to be ascribed to the malice, the sin, the guilt of men. The deadly and condemning effect of the preaching of the gospel is indeed regarding the godless people something proper, something genuine, but concerning the gospel this effect is always something accidental, something occasional, something that goes directly against its nature" (Veenhof, 1965:98ff.).

I purposely gave this extensive quotation of Calvin by C. Veenhof. In his reproduction of Calvin concerning the so-called occasional, accidental matter of preaching he went a little bit too far, according to my opinion. The condemning working of preaching is indeed not the first function of preaching according to Calvin. But at the same time the Reformer warned more than once against onesidedness and exaggeration with regard to this. J. Kamphuis pointed already to the fact that Calvin used more than once the softening expression "in a manner of speaking," or "so to say" with relation to the deadly effect of preaching (Kamphuis, 1968:162ff.). Calvin did not promote complete inequality in the matter of the quickening and mortifying effect of preaching. L. Goumaz elaborated on that in his summary of Calvin's commentaries on the New Testament concerning the office in the church, namely in a chapter about "The twofold authority of the office."

I quote, "Christ has assured on the one hand those who are His of the grace which is promised to them in the gospel in such a way 'that they expect this with an equally great certainty as if He had come down from heaven in order to testify it personally'; on the other hand the LORD has frightened the hardened sinners, by assuring them that their contempt of the ministers of the Word and the proclamation of forgiveness will receive its sanction. The ministers are but human beings, 'earthly vessels'; this weakness causes that they see their preaching constantly questioned. But Christ assures that in reality this weak human word proclaims the forgiveness of sins for those who receive it with confidence, but also the judgment of God to the wicked who refuse to accept the promise of grace" (Goumaz, 1964:114).

Calvin was very pessimistic concerning the number of unbelievers and hypocrites in the church. He wrote, "If the same sermon is preached, say, to a hundred people, twenty receive it with the ready obedience of faith, while the rest hold it valueless, or laugh, or hiss, or loathe it" (Calvin, Institutes III, 24, 12).

A. Kuyper

Later on also A. Kuyper stressed the first function of the preaching, namely the proclamation of the kingdom of heaven. "But also the other way around," he wrote in *E Voto*: "From week to week has to be announced in the name of God the judgment of condemnation to everyone who resists faith and who does not convert to God wholeheartedly. Like a hammer that smashes the rock, this terrible Word of our God has to come down on the souls of those who are hardening their hearts. As a two-edged sword that horrible word of judgment and eternal condemnation has to penetrate between the separation of soul and spirit and between the separation of joints and marrow. It has to be made impossible to you more and more to resist your God, so that you are doing finally one of the two: to give in over against God, or: to go out and to say: no, I do not come back under such a preaching. But in that way the key-power is executed" (Kuyper, 1892:310).

K. Schilder

When the Holy Spirit is hardening the hearts of those who hear the Word of God but refuse to accept it, He abandons at the same time these unbelievers to Satan. Meditating on the text about Judas "after the morsel (or the sop), Satan entered into him" (John 13:27), K. Schilder wrote, "The sop which Jesus gives has the same effectiveness and the same effect as the Word which God gives. That Word, also, never returns void; it achieves whatever pleases God and quickly effects the purpose for which God sent it. That Word forces choices upon men. It converts men, or it hardens them. It makes men bow, or it stiffens their necks in haughty obstinacy. Both, the sop and the Word, send out the Spirit unto repentance, or Satan unto a hardening of the heart. Take the sop; listen to the Word. Afterwards men can say of you: Then entered the Spirit into him; or they can say: Then entered Satan into him. The one or the other effect will follow" (Schilder, 1938:176ff.).

I quote also something of what K. Schilder wrote in *Christ in His Suffering* about the text "Simon, Simon, behold, Satan demanded to have you, that he might sift you like wheat, but I have prayed for you that your faith may not fail" (Luke 22: 31,32): "Christ knows that Satan is but the second, that God is the first cause of the sifting. Therefore He turns to God asking that faith may not abate — May they remain in Thy hands, Father! Thou dost sift; and Satan sifts. But Thy method is not his! — Satan wants to keep the chaff and blow the wheat away. Christ would retain the wheat and take the chaff out of it. By sifting, Satan wants to suppress the good by the evil; Christ, also by sifting, would overcome evil with good" (Schilder, 1938:263).

Opened and closed

Many texts from the Holy Scriptures are still to be mentioned, in which the sifting work of God the Holy Spirit is shown, as He is working with God's Word. For the Word of God is the sword of the Spirit, which cuts from two sides, as is said in the Notes of the Old Dutch translation on Hebr. 4:12. They point then also to Revelation 19:15, where is said of the exalted Christ that He is called the Word of God and that from His mouth issues a sharp sword with which to smite the nations, and He will rule them with a rod of iron. When He smites with the sword of the Word, nobody can stop Him. In Revelation 3 He is called "the holy One, the true One, who has the key of David, who opens and no one shall shut, who shuts and no one opens" (vs.7). He gives indeed an open door in Philadelphia (vs.8), but it is also possible that one closes his ears to what the Spirit says to the church, and that one does not want to open the door, although the knock at the door is clearly to be heard." (3:20).

That brings us to what we confess in Lord's Day 31 of the Heidelberg Catechism about the keys of the kingdom, to which A. Kuyper already pointed. First the kingdom is opened by the preaching of the gospel. But in the case of hardening of hearts follows the closing of the kingdom. That is the double effect of preaching. In this way the Word of God comes to all the hearers, without distinction, with command of faith and conversion. I quote with regard to this Prof. B. Holwerda: "They all have to hear without distinction the promise. Then this promise itself will achieve separation: the one believes, the other one hardens his heart. They all have to hear without distinction the admonition. The one is converting, the other one refuses conversion. In this way the kingdom of God is opened for the one and closed for the other one by this comforting sermon. But also the one is brought to conversion and the other one to hardening by this chastising sermon. But always something happens, the one thing or the other. Nobody remains the same under the sermon. That is the enormous seriousness of each and every sermon . . ." (Holwerda, 1955:82). Elsewhere Holwerda wrote: "What about so-called distinctive preaching? Does the minister have to divide the congregation into groups, and does he have to address himself to every part separately and distinctively? Let him preach the gospel to all of them! Then he uses the axe of Christ for *all of them*. Only then! Woe to the preacher who assumes there to be separations and brings the word of the text only to the one part. He has to bring it to *all of them*; in this way Christ will *make* separations! This makes the sermon a thousand times more dangerous" (Holwerda, 1957:77).

Conclusion

I come to a conclusion. Besides the blessing effect of preaching there is also the condemning effect of it and this effect is not something accidental or occasional, but the reverse of the first effect. This twofold effect may never be neglected in preaching. Often the word of the apostle Paul is quoted that we can eat and drink at the Lord's Supper judgment upon ourselves (1 Cor. 11:29). But what about to *hear* judgment upon ourselves? Precisely in connection with the fact that we can spurn the Son of God and profane the blood of the covenant by which we were sanctified, and outrage the Spirit of grace, the letter to the Hebrews mentions the "fearful prospect of judgment, and a fury of fire which will consume the adversaries" (Hebr. 10:27). Then the Spirit hardens the hearts, He abandons to Satan. He abandons the unbelievers to themselves, to their own sins.

Let us maintain our confession in the Canons of Dort, "It is not the fault of the gospel, nor of the Christ offered by the gospel, nor of God, who calls through the gospel and who even confers various gifts upon them, that many who are called through the ministry of the gospel do not come and are not converted. The fault lies in themselves" (III/IV,9). Indeed, "the fault lies in those who are called, in *their* culpable carelessness or slackness or worldly-mindedness" (Meijerink, 1971:44).

Take heed then how you *hear*!

But also: take heed then how you *preach*!

VI
"YOU SHALL BE MY WITNESSES" (Acts 1:8)

REFORMATION AND MISSION

"Minus the apostles?"

More than once it has been said by historians (and not only by adversaries of the Reformation but also by some who belong to Reformation circles) that it would be possible to write a complete history of Reformation times without even using the word *mission*. The Reformers, they say, did lot of good things in all respects, but they did not do anything concerning mission. The whole matter of mission was something done in Reformation times by the Roman Catholics, and the churches of the Reformation discovered the importance of mission no earlier than about a century later.

It is also said that actually *Pietism* awakened the call for the great commission to go out and to bring the gospel to the gentiles.

In Germany they used for that so-called lack of mission the word "Missionslauheit" (lukewarmness regarding mission) and they applied that word to Luther and to Calvin as well.

Many of those writing concerning this matter have stated that the Reformers (and they apply that especially to Luther and Calvin) wrongly believed that the missionary mandate of Matthew was limited to and fulfilled in the apostolic era. J. Verkuyl writes for instance, "It is incomprehensible that the Reformers and their contemporaries did not relate Jesus' promise in Matthew 28 to be present even to the end of the age to the fulfillment of their missionary task, but it is undeniably true" (Verkuyl, 1978:19). In the circles of the ecumenical movement is even said, "Calvin made the most amazing mistake for an able man when he tried to reform the church by reconstructing it after the pattern of the apostolic age *minus* the apostles. The Spirit that has directed the history of the primitive church was wiser than Calvin" (E.J. Palmer on the Conference on "Faith and Order," at Lausanne, 1927).

The conclusion is that the Reformers themselves did not encourage the sending out of missionaries or contribute to the theological study of our missionary task. The missionary consciousness had to wait until a later time and was initiated only with the coming of the so-called further Reformation and Pietism. "Then actual Protestant participation in world mission and the theoretical reflection upon this activity really began" (Verkuyl, *ibid.*). But as far as the Reformers themselves are concerned, there is not to be found even a *latent* missionary zeal: there is a complete *vacuum* in this respect.

Complete vacuum?

What to say about these reproaches?

In the first place, it is unfair as well as scientifically inadmissible to summon the Reformers before the tribunal of a modern missiological concept, which has itself its historical limitations and its theological defects. In his dissertation, J. van den Berg points to this answer of especially some Lutheran authors, and he adds, "Too often indeed, missions have been identified with the 'business of missions,' with the organizational aspect of modern missionary life" (van den Berg, 1956:5). In the second place, when the Reformers give sometimes the impression that it was the special task of the apostles to proclaim the gospel to the gentiles, we have to consider that they said that over against the "apostolic succession," as if the Pope of Rome were the direct successor of the Apostle Peter. I give two quotations of Calvin's Commentary on *Matthew 28:19 and 20* in this respect: "So we learn that the Apostolate is not an empty title of honour, but a responsible office; and that there is nothing more absurd nor more intolerable than that false men should usurp the honour to themselves, live at ease as kings, and do away with their responsibility to teach." And concerning the last verse of the gospel according to Matthew, "We must note that this is said not only to the apostles, for the Lord promises His aid not to one age alone, but to the end of the world. It is precisely as if He said that, whenever the ministers of the gospel are weak, and labour under the lack of everything, He would be the Guardian, so that they may come out victorious over all the world's conflicts. Thus today clear experience teaches that Christ works in a hidden way, marvellously, and the gospel prevails over numerous obstacles. All the more intolerable is the sin of the papal clergy, who make this a pretext for their sacrilegious tyranny. They claim that the church cannot err, being ruled by Christ, as if Christ, like a common soldier, hired Himself as mercenary to different leaders, and did not keep His authority firmly to Himself and declared that He would defend His doctrine, so that His ministers might confidently expect to be victorious over the whole world."

So this is to be said in the first place: that the Reformers stressed the unique place and task of the apostles and that they denied the claim of the Pope to be the successor of the apostles.

But there is more. He who reasons that there was a complete lack, a vacuum in respect of the idea of mission in the mind of the Reformers, is absolutely wrong. Let us start with the main Reformers, Luther and Calvin.

Luther over against Turks and Jews

We start with Luther, the first in chronological order. It is an evident fact that Luther placed himself also in missionary respect over against the Roman Catholics of his days. When Luther discovered the accent on *human* activities in Roman Catholic mission work, he stressed that mission work is in the first place the work of God Himself. Christ is the Head of the church, He leads her, He saves her, He sanctifies her, He purifies her, but He also increases her. He edifies and preserves His church and He uses for that purpose each and every member of the church. Luther says, "Jeder einzelne Christ ist dazu bestellt, dem anderen ein Christus zu werden." That means that all Christians have to be involved in the spreading of the good news of the gospel. Actually Luther here said important things in respect of what is called later on *home mission,* but this also has to do with mission as such.

Speaking about Acts 8 where it is described that the eunuch, a minister of Candace the queen of the Ethiopians, was converted and being baptized, Luther said he could not imagine that the eunuch would not have *propagated* the gospel of Jesus Christ in his native land.

As far as the Turks are concerned, it is well-known that Luther was very sharp over against them. But is it also known that Luther reproached the Pope in Rome that he had undertaken crusades against the Turks (or the Moslems) but that he did not bring the gospel of Jesus Christ to them? That would be the first mandate for the Pope, according to Luther: to let the Moslems hear the Gospel of our only Saviour Jesus Christ! Another example concerning the Turks: In Luther's time there were Christians made captives by the Turks in Eastern Europe. Then Luther said: these captive Christians have the important task to bring these Turks who are Moslems in contact with

Luther's Catechism. I ask, what else would that be if not mission work?

As far as the Jews are concerned, Luther mentions them often in one breath with the Turks, not as alien races, but as peoples who consciously deny Jesus Christ, who trust in their own human power and who expect everything from their own merits. In the first years after the Reformation of the church, Luther had a benevolent attitude over against the Jews. He had the firm expectation that they would be converted to Jesus Christ, now that the gospel had been brought to light again. He regarded it as an evident fact that the Jews had not found the glory of the New Dispensation during the dominion of the Pope: "The papists behaved themselves in such a way that, being a Christian, one should rather become a Jew than the other way around. If I had been a Jew, I would have preferred to become a *pig* rather than a *Christian!*"

Luther was the first one who understood that the gospel had to be brought to the Jews, because this people in the first place has rights to Christ. In this way came into existence what is called Luther's mission book *That Christ is a born Jew.* He cooperated with Jewish scholars and used their knowledge of the Hebrew language in order to understand the Jewish background the better. Luther discovered also that the Jews had come to their trade in money, to their practice of usury especially as a result of the attitude of many Christians who did not leave to them any possibility of life. But that, he hoped, would be changed: "All Israel will be saved." It was a bitter experience for Luther when he saw that things developed in a totally different way. He took offence at the Jewish mockery of the Messiah of the Christians, and when he heard that in Bohemia a number of Christians had become Jews, he wrote some very extreme statements against the Jews. "Ultimately it was a kind of 'harsh mercy' and it was an attempt to save those who would be willing to be converted." These severe statements were regrettable and they caused much evil. But let us bear in mind that Luther was absolutely not an anti-Semite. From Luther is also the prayer: "Oh God, heavenly Father, please turn aside and let Thy wrath be satisfied over them for the sake of Thy beloved Son Jesus Christ. Amen" (Kooiman, 1959:171).

Eschatology

More than once it has been said that Luther was so strongly convinced that Christ would come back very soon that there was no room in his theology for missiology. It has also been said that Luther had the idea that it was not worthwhile any more to go out with the Gospel because of his eschatological ideas.

Indeed, Luther had the conviction that Christ's return on the clouds of heaven was not very far off. But it is absolutely wrong to derive from that fact that Luther had objections against mission work. Precisely in the tension of Christ's coming back, we have to fulfil our task. Luther often called the day of Christ's return the "sweet last day." But he said at the same time, "If I knew that Christ would come back tomorrow, I would still plant a tree today."

Conclusion concerning Luther

When we take account of the circumstances of Luther's times, of the struggle over against the papal clergy, also of the fact that there was a close connection between church and state and that it was almost impossible to go abroad with the gospel, our conclusion must be that it is totally wrong to say that Luther did not see anything of the mission task of the church.

Calvin

In my first article about Reformation and Mission I paid special attention to Luther and I said that it is absolutely wrong to say, as many authors do, that Luther did not say anything concerning the Scriptural calling with regard to mission work. Some point in this respect especially to the Reformers' exegesis of *Matthew 28:19*, as if Luther and Calvin were of the opinion that the apostles had already done all the mission work, so that actually nothing was left for later times. But I stressed that we have to read Luther and Calvin in the context of their writings and, as far as this text is concerned, that over against Rome they very sharply rejected the idea of the *apostolic succession.*

At the same time it can be said that there are several places in Calvin's *Commentaries on the Bible* and also in his *Institutes* where we can see that Calvin did indeed have the idea that mission work had to be done and that it was not finished at all.

Let me mention first some texts of the Old Testament. In his Commentary on *Isaiah 12:4 and 5,* the Reformer writes, "He [the prophet Isaiah] means that the work of this deliverance will be so excellent, that it ought to be proclaimed, not in a corner only, but throughout the whole world. He wished, indeed, that it should first be *made known* to the Jews, but that it should afterwards be spread abroad to all men. This exhortation, by which the Jews testified their gratitude, might be regarded as a forerunner of the preaching of the gospel, which afterwards followed in the proper order . . . We ought especially to be inflamed with this desire, after having been delivered from some alarming danger, and most of all after having been delivered from the tyranny of the devil and from everlasting death." He continues his exhortation by showing what is the feeling from which this thanksgiving ought to precede; for he shows that it is our duty to proclaim the goodness of God to every nation." While we exhort and encourage others, we must not at the same time sit down in indolence, but it is proper that we set an example before others; for nothing can be more absurd than to see lazy and slothful men who are exciting other men to praise God."

This is nothing else than the fervour of Calvin in seeing the duty of mission works as "proclamation to every nation."

Also in his Commentary on the last book of the Old Testament, the prophecies of *Malachi,* Calvin stresses more than once that God's Kingdom is not complete yet but that it is growing and increasing also in our times and that we also are involved in that continuation of God's Kingdom.

New Testament

In his commentary of the Gospels, Calvin mentions in respect of *Matthew 24:14,* "And this gospel of the Kingdom will be preached throughout the whole world, as a testimony to all nations; and then the end will come," that there are *"antipodes"* and other far removed peoples, whom even the last fame of Christ has not reached. So the gospel of the Kingdom must be preached to all nations!

In a similar way we can read Calvin's opinion concerning the spreading of the gospel in his commentary on the letters to Timothy. In connection with *1 Timothy 2:4* he writes: "The Apostle simply means, that there is no people and no rank in the world that is excluded from salvation; because God wishes that the gospel should be proclaimed to *all* without exception."

Also Calvin's similar comments on the second letter to *Timothy* and the letter to *Titus* are to be mentioned, let alone what he said more than once in sermons on texts of the New Testament.

156

Institutes

It is repeated many times in all kinds of books that Calvin said in his *Institutes* that the whole matter of mission had been finished at the end of the apostles' times. I said already that Calvin was of the opinion that there are no direct successors to the apostles, over against the ideas of the popes that they esteemed themselves as such, Calvin denied the "apostolic succession" and stressed that the office of the apostles was a very special and extraordinary office. But in the same context of his *Institutes* in which Calvin stressed this, he also added: "Although I deny not, that afterwards God occasionally raised up Apostles, or at least evangelists, in their stead, as has been done in our time" (*Inst. IV, 3, 4*).

Time and again it is to be read in Calvin's *Institutes* that it is our duty to proclaim God's goodness all over the world, and there are many places in the *Institutes* in which Calvin points to the fact that the heathen nations may be involved in the whole matter of salvation. It is also repeated time and again that especially in his *Institutes* Calvin put so much emphasis on the doctrine of election that this doctrine is not to be combined with the idea of mission. This would then be a kind of "theological excuse": because of the accent on election and reprobation, the Reformed would have locked the door to mission work. But he who carefully reads the whole part on the divine election and reprobation in Calvin's Institutes (*III, 21-24*) sees immediately that this argument misses any foundation. Quoting Augustine, Calvin assures us, "Because we know not who belongs to the number of the predestinated, or does not belong, our desire ought to be that all may be saved; and hence every person we meet, we will desire to be with us a partaker of peace" (*Inst. III, 23, 24*). It is true that Calvin discerns between general and special calling. The general calling has to do with the outward preaching of God's Word, and the special calling is the work of God the Holy Spirit through which the preached Word of God is attached in the hearts of men. But nowhere the conclusion is to be found in Calvin's *Institutes* that the Word of God is not to be proclaimed and to be preached to all nations.

Prayers

Not only many sermons (more than 2000) of Calvin have been preserved, but also many prayers at the end of the sermons. Often these are prayers which have to do with the further propagation of the gospel. Then Calvin prays that the Word just preached may not only reach its goal in the hearts of the hearers, so that the congregation may bear many fruits, but also that the Word of God may be preached elsewhere and that it may also reach the hearts of the ignorant and those who have gone astray. In no way can one conclude from Calvin's prayers that the Reformer had no insight into the work of mission. On the contrary: many times he prayed that the gospel might be spread throughout the world.

Geneva

When we have a look at the immense amount of work Calvin did in Geneva, we may even conclude that Geneva was a kind of *mission centre*. From all parts of Europe the students came to Calvin's city in order to be instructed in what he called the "pura doctrina," the pure doctrine of the gospel. And after having studied there, they spread the gospel over Europe, in many countries.

Some have objected more than once that this was only the preaching of the Word in countries which were already more or less Christianized. But when we take into account how terrible the ignorance of the people was, we may say that it was indeed mission work, namely to bring the gospel of Jesus Christ to the people that did not know its most elementary principles.

Besides, from Geneva Calvin wrote hundreds and hundreds of letters to many people in Europe, also to encourage the propagation of the gospel.

No attempts?

Some have said, All right, but are there indeed attempts by the Reformers to go out with the Gospel and to proclaim the good tidings to the gentiles?

Now first of all I can point to what Luther said about the Jews and the Turks and how the people had to contact them.

In the second place I can repeat that Calvin had much influence in the whole of Europe and that there were many contacts in many countries. In the third place it must be said that in Reformation times the trade routes were especially in the hands of Spain and Portugal, Roman Catholic nations, so that it was almost impossible for the German, French, and Swiss people to go outside of Europe. But last but not least, in the fourth place: there was indeed a very important attempt at mission work in Calvin's times, namely in *Brazil*.

I will tell more about that in the next article, the Lord willing.

The mission venture in Brazil

The French nobleman Gaspard de Coligny, who would become later on, in 1572, a martyr in the terrible massacre of Bartholomew's day, conceived the project of planning to send ministers to a French colony in Brazil. The goal was not only to support the colonists in spiritual respect, but also to bring the gospel to the Indians in order to convert them to faith in Jesus Christ. De Coligny was in contact with a certain De Villegaignon and he influenced the French King to allow De Villegaignon to sail out with two vessels to the new world. It was principally Protestants who accompanied him. De Villegaignon was also in contact with Calvin. In November, 1555, the expedition arrived at Rio de Janeiro. In the beginning they had a very hard time. There were dangers from two sides. The Portuguese, who claimed to have authority over that area, were very hostile, and the natives were also very dangerous. Disappointed and discouraged, some of the colonists returned to France. With those who remained, De Villegaignon took up his residence close to the coast on a small island which he gave the name "Coligny" (cf. VanderLinde, 1937:376ff.).

Request for ministers

Already after a short time, De Villegaignon sent letters to De Coligny and to Calvin in which he asked them to send some preachers and also more colonists "in order to come to a firmer establishment of the colony and to a further expansion of the Kingdom of Jesus Christ." Then two preachers were delegated from Geneva, the first one was Peter Richer, a doctor of theology, and the second one was William Chartier. These ministers departed from Geneva on September 8, 1556. Several people accompanied them. Altogether there were thirteen who were willing "to bring the Kingdom of Christ to the new world." In France they find many Huguenots who dared to undertake the venture with them. In this way a group of three hundred people was gathered at Honfleur and they departed with three ships on November 19, 1556. On the tenth of March 1557 they arrived in the colony.

Great expectations

There is a double report concerning the first three weeks after their arrival: a letter of Richer to an unknown person and also a letter of Richer and Chartier together to Calvin. Especially the last letter gives us an insight into the relation in which Calvin stood to these men and their work. It appeared that they were very closely connected with the Reformer. They wrote to Calvin, "Our fellowship in which we are connected by the Holy Spirit to the body of Christ, unites us together so strongly that the enormous distance which separates us, cannot hinder that we are with you in the Spirit, in the certainty that you also bear us in your heart."

In order to strengthen this fellowship, they want to let Calvin participate in their sorrows and joys. They are very happy with the way they were received by De Villegaignon. They call him their father and brother and they expect much from him and from his work. They have hope that rather soon a big congregation can be instituted to proclaim God's praise and extend Christ's Kingdom. At the end of their letter they ask Calvin's intercession for their work of mission, "in order that God may complete this building of Christ at this end of the earth." The church of Geneva gave thanks to God on these favourable messages from Brazil, "for the extension of Christ's Kingdom in a country so far away, on a piece of the earth so strange and among a nation which seems to be totally ignorant of the true God."

In Richer's letter we find more data about the religious life of the natives in and around the colony. He portrays the life of the natives in very dark colours. The summing up of the sins and misdeeds reminds us of what the apostle Paul writes in Romans 1. How can the preachers of God's Word get access to such people? Besides, they stand before an almost insuperable language barrier. Yet they do not despair. "Because the highest God Himself entrusted this office to us, we hope that one day this country of Edomites will become Christ's dominion."

Treason

But the great expectations of these missionaries proved false. It appeared that De Villegaignon was not the man he was supposed to be. After the first celebration of the Lord's Supper, quarrels broke out in circles of the colonists. Some of them were in favour of bringing more Roman Catholic elements into the celebration. Their spokesman was a certain Cointa, who had studied at the Sorbonne University in Paris. De Villegaignon sided with him, after having first sent Chartier to Geneva in order to ask Calvin for advice. Especially a letter from the cardinal of Lorraine caused him to conduct himself harshly over against the Protestants. Finally, their worship services had to be held in secret, just as in their fatherland. In this way the original attempt to build a Protestant colony as a centre of mission work among the heathen originals was frustrated. In this situation a group of them wanted to go back to France. De Villegaignon expelled them from the island. They fled to the continent of Brazil, where they tried to contact the aboriginals. They also attempted to bring the Gospel to them. One of them had already progressed so far in their language that he could give them a small dictionary of the language of the "*Topinambu*," as they called them.

Return

But the refugees could not hold out for a long time. All kinds of hardships finally caused their return to France. Some of them preferred to go back to the colony. But De Villegaignon condemned them as heretics. One of them escaped, four others testified to their faith in a courageous way. The result was that De Villegaignon had them thrown from a rock into the ocean. The names of these first martyrs of Reformed mission deserve to be mentioned: Pierre du Bordel, Matthieu Vermiel, and Pierre Bourdon. It is a bitter thought that these martyrs did not fall as a consequence of the resistance of the Gentiles, but by the perfidious treason of a fellow Christian. De Villegaignon spared the life of the fourth one, because he could serve the colony with his handicraft, according to his opinion. Those who stayed on the ship safely reached the French coast. Richer became a minister of the church at La Rochelle.

The colony was deprived of its best men, so it could not hold out either. De Villegaignon returned to France and remained an enemy of the Reformation for the rest of his life. He died just before the year of the martyrdom of Gaspard de Coligny. However, he did not die as a martyr, but in the greatest misery. . . .

One of the fellow travellers, Jean de Lery, described the whole journey extensively and when later on his book was reprinted, he dedicated it to Louise de Coligny, the daughter of Gaspard de Coligny.

Louise de Coligny was the fourth wife of William of Orange, who survived her husband. De Lery mentioned in this dedication "the reverent remembrance of the Prince of Orange." In 1569 he had met the Prince, being delegated to thank him for the defense of the French Reformed churches, which he had undertaken with great sacrifices. On that occasion Prince William had answered that he wished he could do more for the service of the Lord and of the churches on behalf of which the delegates had spoken. So also the name of Prince William I of Orange is mentioned in the report concerning the first Reformed mission venture!

Calvin to Farel

Calvin was closely connected with this attempt at mission work. In his letter to his friend Farel, he wrote on Feb. 24, 1558, about De Villegaignon as someone "who was sent by us to America ('a nobis *missus* fuerat'), where he has treated the good matter in a bad way because of his immeasurable hot-headedness." Calvin wrote this letter about six years before his death. He deplored it very much that this first attempt at Reformed mission work in Brazil was not a success. But the failure was definitely not due to the Reformer himself. He encouraged the planning of De Coligny. He sent missionaries to the colony. He functioned as their spiritual father and gave his advice. They brought before him all their troubles and sorrows, and Calvin's encouragement gave guidance to their work.

Our conclusion is that also in practical respects Calvin very much promoted mission work, although prospects were not favourable.

Propagation of the gospel

We discovered that — in spite of all kinds of criticism — Calvin strongly promoted the work of mission, also in practical respects. He also encouraged others to propagate the gospel, and he was very grateful when he discovered that the propagation of the gospel met with success.

He wrote his dedicatory epistle to the first edition of the second part of his commentary on the *Acts of the Apostles* "to the most serene King-elect of Denmark and Norway, Frederick" and said at the end of it, "I shall touch on one thing which is appropriate for a royal personage. When the power of the whole world was in opposition, and all the men who had control of affairs then, were in arms to crush the gospel, a few men, obscure, unarmed and contemptible, relying on the support of the truth and the Spirit alone, laboured so strenuously in spreading the faith of Christ, avoided no toil of dangers, remained unbroken against all attacks, until at last they emerged victors. Accordingly, for Christian princes, distinguished as they are by a certain authority, since God has provided them with the sword for the defence of the Kingdom of His Son, there is no excuse for not being at least just as spirited and faithful in the discharge of such an honourable task." Under the pressure of the Lutherans, Frederick refused this dedication of the 1554 edition. So Calvin dedicated the second edition of 1560 to Nicolas Radzivil, "duke in Olika, palatine of Vilna." But that does not diminish the well-meant words of the first edition with regard to the propagation and defense of the gospel.

It is also known that Calvin called *Luther* "an apostle," elected by God Himself.

In 1549 Calvin wrote a letter to King Sigismund of Poland wherein he expresses his joy about the progress of the gospel in Poland.

In the same letter he mentioned the name of *Johannes à Lasco*, a Polish noble-man, who later on played an important role in London and also in Germany. Calvin said, "I foresee that he will transfer the torch of the gospel also to other nations."

In 1561 Calvin wrote in a letter to the Scottish Reformer *John Knox,* "I rejoice exceedingly, as you may easily suppose, that the gospel has made such rapid and happy progress among you."

Finally, in the same year, Calvin wrote a letter to *Bullinger* about the progress of the gospel and the request for more preachers of God's Word: "It is incredible with what fervent zeal our brethren are urging forward greater progress. Pastors are everywhere asked for from among us with as much eagerness as the priestly functions are made the object of ambition among the Papists. Those who are in quest of them besiege my doors, and pay their court to me as if I held a levee. They vie with one another in pious rivalry, as if the condition of Christ's Kingdom were in a state of undisturbed tranquility. On our part, we desire as much as it lies in our power to comply with their wishes, but our stock of preachers is almost exhausted. We have even been obliged to sweep the workshops of the working classes to find individuals with some tincture of letters and pious doctrine to supply this necessity."

Calvin wrote this letter just three years before his death. One can say, this has to do with the ministry in the congregations, but we may also say: this has to do with the propagation and the progress of the gospel. Calvin was very concerned about that. It is, therefore, absolutely wrong to state that Calvin lacked the idea of apostolate!

Martin Bucer

Calvin was closely connected with *Martin Bucer,* especially in his Strasbourg years, in 1538-1541. It is interesting to know Bucer's ideas about mission. We may say that he expressed himself very clearly about the task of mission. More than Luther and Calvin, Bucer stressed very much that the apostles only made a beginning of the work of mission in their times. He stated that the apostles had indeed received a special calling for the propagation of the gospel in the whole world. But speaking about the apostle Paul, Bucer said that "the apostolic fire was present in him in great measure as an example also for the times to come." He also stressed that the apostles had received extraordinary gifts: prophecy, healing, tongues. But therein, Bucer said, is an indication that "just as the beginning, also later on all the power would be delivered to the church to gather the church of God out of the whole human race." For although these extraordinary gifts were limited to the apostolic era, yet the church would also later on be able to fulfil the calling of Jesus Christ without the miracles of the beginning of the Christian church. Already in his book, dated from 1523 *Instruction of Christian Love,"* Bucer said, "The believer, like a perpetual spring, must pour out the goodness which God imparts to him through Christ by furthering the welfare of all men" (Bucer, 1980:49).

Starting with these ideas, Bucer reproached the rulers that they neglected mission. He said, it is true that desire for expansion drove them into the world, but at the same time they had no desire to win the people for the church and for Christ. The Spaniards hurt the native population in a terrible way and tortured them. "Is that, then, what they call the propagation of Christianity?" he asked. Bucer also paid special attention to the Jews. He wrote, "Exactly through the sinful neglect of mission work among the Jews, now the Jews became usurers in the midst of Christianity." In this respect Bucer also made a comparison with the Turks. He said, "In the same way we can say that the Turkish became violent oppressors of the Christians, and also that newly discovered islands and nations have become a source of much misery for the Christian peoples."

As we saw before, Luther stressed that mission work is the work of God Himself. Bucer agreed with that, but he stressed at the same time that this does not exclude that we as God's people have also a task. As he put it, "There is also a human element in the proclamation of the gospel."

Very important is this statement of Bucer: *"Omnis ecclesia Christi debet esse evangelisatrix"*: each and every church of Christ has to be a mission church, a church that evangelizes.

Conclusion

There is more to be said about Reformation and Mission (cf. Joosse, 1988:passim). But I think it is very clear now that it is impossible to describe the Reformation times while leaving out the word *mission*. On the contrary: we may discover great powers which were already present in Reformation times in the hearts of men like Martin Luther, John Calvin, and Martin Bucer. Later generations took these powers over and would develop them in obedience to the great commission, given by the King of the church to the church of all ages!

IN THE WORLD, BUT NOT OF THE WORLD

Introduction

We all know that our Belgic Confession in Article 29 speaks of the *hypocrites*, who are mixed in the church along with the good and yet are not *part* of the church. Actually they are *in* the church, but not *of* the Church. They are in fact people of the *world*, although they call themselves members of the Church.

We can also say it the other way around: the true believers are *in* the world, but they are not *of* the world. And if we say that, we have to remember the words of our Lord Jesus Christ in His well-known High-Priestly intercession of *John 17*: "Father, I have given them Thy Word; and the world has hated them because *they* are not of the world, even as *I* am not of the world. I do not pray that Thou shouldst take them out of the world, but that Thou shouldst keep them from the evil one. They are not of the world, even as I am not of the world. As Thou didst send me into the world, so I have sent them into the world" (vs. 14-16,18).

That is what John wrote in his gospel concerning the fact that the true believers are *in* the world, but not *of* the world. And in his first letter, the same apostle wrote:

"Little children, you are of God, and have overcome them (namely the spirits who are not of God); for He who is in you is greater then he who is in the world. They are of the world, therefore what they say is of the world, and the world listens to them. We are of God." And in the same chapter John wrote, "as He (that is Christ) is so are we in this world" (1 John 4:4,5,17). So, if we are *in* the world, but not *of* the world, we have a great task over against this world, the task to proclaim that Jesus Christ is the only Redeemer and Saviour, the task to bring the good tidings of the gospel to the people of the world.

Alien or alienated

It belongs to the nature of the Church of our Lord Jesus Christ to seek *outsiders*. The Church has to do that with the gospel, the infallible Word of God, which has been entrusted to her.

Who are 'outsiders'? They can be people who are entirely alien to God and His service, who live without God in this world. They can also be people who have been *alienated* from the Lord God and who still have a vague (although usually a wrong) idea of who God is.

"First of all," Paul wrote to Timothy, "then I urge that supplications, prayers, intercessions, and thanskgivings be made for all men, for kings and all who are in high positions, that we may lead a quiet and peaceable life, godly and respectful in every way. This is good, and it is acceptable in the sight of God our Saviour, who desires all men to be saved and to come to the knowledge of the truth." The last sentence of this passage is very remarkable: God desires *all men* to be saved and to come to the knowledge of the truth. In the background of this apostolic command we must see the promise of the gospel that whoever believes in Jesus Christ crucified shall not perish but have eternal life. This promise of John 3:16 is quoted by the Canons of Dort in ch. II, art. 5 concerning "the universal proclamation of the gospel." This article continues: "This promise ought to be announced and proclaimed universally and without discrimination to all peoples and to all men to whom God in His good pleasure sends the gospel, together with the command to repent and believe."

That means: the Church has a very responsible task! If the Church is a true Church, then she desires to reach all these men who are alien to or have been alienated from God and His service with God's Word and to call them or to call them *back* to the communion with God and His people.

Office-bearers

But one says: all right, the Church has to fulfil this task, and it is a very responsible task indeed. But the *Church*, that means: the *office-bearers*, ministers, elders and deacons. So let *them* do everything concerning evangelism. And one even quotes for instance *Eph. 4:11-13*, where Paul mentions the office-bearers and their task. The office-bearers, we learn from that passage, are gifts of the exalted Christ Himself. Paul writes: "And His gifts were that some should be apostles, some prophets, some evangelists, some pastors and teachers, to equip the saints for the work of ministry, for building up the body of Christ, until we all attain to the unity of the faith and of the knowledge of the Son of God, to mature manhood, to the measure of the stature of the fulness of Christ." G. VanDooren, however, pointed to the fact that in this quotation from the Revised Standard Version translation one *comma* too much is used. We read: "Christ's gifts were that some should be apostles (and so on), for the equipment of the saints, (comma!) for the work of ministry." I quote now VanDooren: "The com-

163

ma after 'the saints' shouldn't be there! You see how putting one comma too much after that word, changes the whole sentence, the whole picture even of the Church of Jesus Christ. *With* that misplaced comma you see before your eyes ministers and elders and deacons running around, doing all the work. Theirs (according to that evil comma) is a *threefold* office. They must equip the saints (but do not ask me what for . . .). Then they must do (all) the work of ministry. And finally they must build up the body of Christ. You haven't heard a word about what that body, the whole congregation, has to do. No, everything has to be done by the 'special' office. Paul mentions here the 'preacher and teacher.' That would then mean that ministers have to do all the running (which easily becomes a running around in circles). But Paul would not object against adding the elders, even the deacons. *But that comma should not be there!*" (VanDooren, 1979:47).

That is according to the manner S. Greijdanus explains this text. He says: "Here is not pointed to a special office, but here is spoken of the office or service of all believers. Each elected one and every believer has his office: the one this, the other that. For the fulfilment of this task they must be completely equipped. And for that equipment of the believers to their service the Lord granted the several special offices and office-bearers" (Greijdanus, 1925:91).

We ask then: is there a task for the office-bearers? The answer is: sure, there is a great task. The office-bearers shall especially by preaching, catechesis and home visits point the members of the congregation to this calling and shall equip them unto the fulfilment of this calling.

So we can understand that Paul continues in verse 15 and 16: "We are to grow up in every way into Him who is the head, into Christ, from whom the whole body, joined and knit together by every joint with which it is supplied, when each part is working properly, makes bodily growth and upbuilds itself in love."

Consistory

Sometimes indeed the impression had been given that the whole matter of evangelism was a responsibility of the consistory of the Church, as for instance in the Netherlands at the synod of 1923, which stressed the task of the consistory concerning evangelism. But synod of Kampen 1975 decided that the decisions of 1923 should no longer be considered as a good expression of the evangelistic task of the Church. Synod of 1975 quoted first 1 Tim. 2:1-4, Eph. 4:11-16 and C.D. II, 5, and stressed then the task of the *members* of the congregation.

It is not to be denied that there is a task for the office-bearers; in the sermon, in catechism class, in home visits. But what about the task of the consistory as a whole? Well, the consistory must be on guard that things do not grow out of hand. So "the consistory shall continuously accompany this task of the members of the congregation by means of supervision and instruction," synod said. There can be a *guidance* from the side of the consistory, according to what the apostle Paul said to the consistory of Ephesus, saying farewell to them on the beach of Melitus: "Take heed to yourselves and to all the flock, in which the Holy Spirit has made you overseers, to care for the Church of God which He obtained with the blood of His own Son. I know that after my departure fierce wolves will come in among you, not sparing the flock; and from among your own selves will arise men speaking perverse things, to draw away the disciples after them. Therefore, be alert."

The task of the consistory is therefore, to accompany the activities of the members of the congregation in all regards, in evangelism as well. But the work itself is to be done by the believers.

Salt and light

It appears from Scriptures and from the practice of the early Christian Church that the propagation of the gospel is a matter of the whole congregation. The apostles act as *ambassadors* of Jesus Christ with special authority, but the congregation *bears* from her side the apostolic mission work with her *gifts and talents.*

The Church is placed *in* the world, but she may not one moment be *of* the world. Neither can she go *out of* the world, but she has to fulfil her task in the *midst of* the world. And then, in the midst of the world, among the gentiles, the Church must show herself and prove herself as the holy Christian Church. So the apostle Peter says: "As He who called you is holy, be holy yourselves in all your conduct; since it is written: 'you shall be holy, for I am holy.' " And *holy* does not mean *sinless* or *pure*, but it means: to be separated, to be *sacred,* to be prepared to the service of the only true God.

The apostle Paul often appeals to a holy conduct in connection with *baptism.* The members of the congregation are baptized. They are set apart by God Himself. Hence the calling: "Cleanse yourselves and make holiness perfect in the fear of God" (2 Cor. 7:1).

Holiness — that is the new and for Christians the characteristic attitude of life, which is to be manifested in daily life and which comes forth from the communion with their God and Saviour in faith and gratitude. *Negatively* this holiness means a total break with sinful conduct of life. *Positively* it means a life in accord with the will of God, in order to show that Christians are totally different from the people of the world.

Being the salt of the earth, they have to penetrate the world and let their lights shine before men, Christ said in His sermon on the mount, "that they may see your good works and give glory to your Father who is in heaven." In the same way the apostle Peter will later write to the exiles of the Dispersion, chosen and destined by God the Father and sanctified by the Spirit for obedience to Jesus Christ and for sprinkling with His blood: "You are a chosen race, a royal priesthood, a holy nation, God's own people, that you may declare the wonderful deeds of Him who called you out of darkness into His marvellous light: (1 Pet. 2:9).

Godly walk

In the same chapter, Peter admonishes the exiles of the Dispersion: "Maintain good conduct among the Gentiles, so that in case they speak against you as wrongdoers, they may see your good deeds and glorify God in the day of visitation."

The Heidelberg Catechism refers to this text in Lord's Day 32 in answer to the question why we must do good works. One of the reasons to do good works is 'that by our godly walk of life we may win our neighbours for Christ.' We may *win* them if we walk godly. So our Christian behaviour in the world is very important with respect to those who are outside. Sometimes we can *win* the outsiders even without words, and that is the other text from the same letter of Peter, to which the Heidelberg Catechism refers: "Likewise you wives, be submissive to your husbands, so that some, though they do not obey the word, may be won without a word by the behaviour of their wives, when they see your reverent and chaste behaviour."

So there must be a right Christian behaviour. But what does that exactly mean? In the letters of the apostles we find three points which are especially important in order to understand this. These are the three elements which I will elucidate from the Scriptures, namely:

concord of the Church;
obedience to the commandments;
joy of faith.

Concord

In the first place the apostles stress the *concord of the Church*. When the apostle Paul writes to the Philippians that he might hear of them that they stand firm in one spirit (Phil. 1:27), then he points especially to the common contention for the faith of the gospel. In the same context he calls that concord the mark of a conduct, worthy of Christ's gospel. Not only does concord fortify the members of the congregation together in order to testify outside, but concord itself is a testimony as well. So we read in the following chapter (2:1ff.) the urgent summons (sometimes called *the most emotional appeal* of the apostle Paul): "So if there is any encouragement in Christ, any incentive of love, any participation in the Spirit, any affection and sympathy, complete my joy by being of the same mind, having the same love, being in *full accord and of one mind*. Do nothing from selfishness or conceit, but in humility count others better than yourselves. Let each of you look not only to his own interests, but also to the interests of others." In the same chapter the apostle admonishes: "Do all things without grumbling or questioning, that you may be blameless and innocent, children of God without blemish in the midst of a crooked and perverse generation, among whom you shine as light in the world." Actually Paul writes here that the Philipians must do everything without '*peevish discussions*', in the same way as he writes to his spiritual son Timothy as well.

But immediately he continues: "So that in the day of Christ I may be proud that I did not run in vain or labour in vain." That means also: that Paul's *mission work* will not be in vain. And that would be the case indeed if they should not hold fast the word of life, the word of preaching. Then they themselves would not be true *fruits* of Paul's diligence. But at the same time the apostle is thinking of a possible defeat of the continuation of his work towards *other people*. Paul is always afraid of that: the *discord* which lies everywhere in wait, and impedes time and again the progress of the gospel in this world. Wherever Judaists or other people contradicted the gospel, which Paul proclaimed, they withdrew men from Christ alone, and then the mission work suffered a loss. Then the powers were spent in competition and dispute. Paul calls that "to proclaim Christ out of partisanship" (Phil. 1:17). Besides that, the world would have reason to turn away from the preaching. Hence we can understand the great offense the apostles had to *discord*, also of *private quarrels*.

But one has not only to maintain concord on account of the progress of the work of God *inside* one's own congregation, no, one must radiate love also to the *outside*, in order to attract other people in this way. When the apostle Peter admonishes 'to have unity of spirit, sympathy (that means actually *compassion*), love of the brethren, a tender heart and a humble mind,' then he directly connects this with the admonition, not to return evil for evil or reviling for reviling, but on the contrary to *bless*. Surely Peter has in view here the outsiders. The mutual bond in the congregation does not mean at all a repelling attitude to those who are outside, but is connected with entirely similar feelings to fellow-men. Brotherly love cannot exist without the true Christian affection and humbleness.

Those two qualities are always connected with *self-denial*, even with the blessing of the oppressor.

In the same way the apostle Paul writes to the Romans in chapter 12. In this chapter Paul progresses even twice from brotherly love and concord of the church, to the blessing of the persecutors. It's of great concern to him that the members of the congregation have the right attitude to the outsiders. "If possible," he writes in verse 18, "so far as it depends upon you, live peaceably with all." And to Timothy he writes: "Shun youthful passions and aim at righteousness, faith, love and peace, along with those who call upon the Lord from a pure heart (2 Tim. 2:22). And to the Thessalonians he says: "Now may the Lord of peace Himself give you peace at all times in all ways" (2 Thess. 3:22). We may not be the reason of a quarrel. If it happens through no fault of ours, then we may not be revengeful. Time and again this is said in the New Testament letters and it is proven by the Old Testament. To outsiders the true Christianity must appear from that. All desire of *vengeance* must disappear for Christians. It *can* disappear for him who know that God will do justice. But the main thing is: desire of revenge must be strange to anybody who himself received *grace*. So this attitude is a *Christian preaching par excellence*.

Beautiful is what the apostle writes in verse 20 (still in Romans 12), that the benefits which the Christian delivers the enemies will at last be so *unbearable* (hence those 'burning coals upon their heads'!) that they will be shamed into giving up their hostile attitude. So here we find the shame of the slanderer by means of positive deeds of love.

Such an attitude of a Christian is not *passive* but the highest *activity*. On the same line we see the end of this chapter: Do not be overcome by evil, but overcome evil with good." (vs. 21)

Obedience

Besides this trait of concord and brotherly affection in which the holy Christian behaviour reveals itself, the apostles very much emphasize *obedience*. Most of the time people used to see this obedience in the light of the *law*, namely of the *fifth commandment*. But in the passage 1 Peter 2:13-3:6 the whole appeal of obedience is an aspect of the *new obedience*, rooted in the faith in Jesus Christ. That starts already in verse 12 of chapter two: you may never suffer as wrongdoers. The world slanders often. But if the world hates you, it may never be because of your bad behaviour!

We quoted already the beginning of chapter 3 that the husbands may be won without a word, by the behaviour of their wives. The situation was such that there were Christian women, who possessed heathen husbands. That is difficult and hard: an unbeliever in your own family! They had not been married as a mixed couple, mixed in the sense of a believer together with an unbeliever. No, rather through the conversion of the woman and the fact that the husband had not been converted, but remained a heathen, the marriage became mixed up. But what now? Did these women have to leave their husbands when they got troubles? No, Peter says, *be not inobedient*, but stay submissive day by day. Show in your behaviour what it means to be a true Christian. If the husband does not want to listen to words any more, maybe he will look at your conduct. In this way he could be attracted! And further on the apostle writes (vs. 15): "But in your hearts reverence Christ as Lord. Always be prepared to make a defense to any one who calls you to account for the hope that is in you, yet do it with gentleness and reverence; and keep your conscience clear, so that, when you are abused, those who revile your good behaviour in Christ may be put to shame. For it is better to suffer for doing right, if that should be God's will, than for doing wrong."

To make a defence — that does not mean: to allow yourself to be drawn by everybody, to speak with everybody at any time he wants to dispute. No, it is: if you are called to *defense,* especially in *trials,* then you have to make a defense. Then you have to profess the Lord, you have to speak freely and frankly, without diplomacy.

But yet: with gentleness and reverence, that means: with submission and meekness, with careful caution. Your attitude, for instance an attitude of challenge, may not become the reason of hatred and persecution. So the slanderers will be ashamed and otherwise they would not. A Christian is always a *priest*: if indignity and persecution appear for Christ's sake, the Christian has to bear that and to suffer that. Even then he has to pray for his enemies.

Joy

There is still another quality of Christian behaviour in the world and that is *joy.* The gospel is a good and joyful tiding. That must be seen! Christians have to show that. Joy is always communicative, attractive and contagious. That concerns especially the true Christian joy, that is joy-in-oppression. Hence the apostle Paul can write in his letter to the Philippians: "Rejoice in the Lord always; again I will say, Rejoice."

But too easily one can respond in this way: "All right, but a man does not always have the same mood. . . ." No, it must *radiate* from us, even in difficult circumstances, that we belong to our faithful Saviour Jesus Christ. When Paul wrote his letter to the Philippians, *they* were far from their native land and *he* was in prison. So there were difficult circumstances on both sides. But yet this letter is called: the letter of joy. The apostle himself is an exponent of this joy with his joy even in martyrdom. And he writes: "I am glad and rejoice with you all." But in one breath he continues: "Likewise you also should be glad and rejoice with me: (Phil. 2:17,18). It is this joy in circumstances otherwise so sad which contrasts with the frame of mind of the neighbourhood and which irresistibly attracts the outsiders.

So Paul can write to the *Thessalonians*: "You become imitators of us, and of the Lord, for you received the word in much affliction, with *joy* inspired by the Holy Spirit; so that you became an example to all the believers in Macedonia and Achaia" (1 Thess. 1:6,7).

Therefore the utterance of this joy, for instance in Christian singing, can be a preaching to outsiders as well. Paul is speaking about that to the Colossians: "Let the word of Christ dwell in you richly, teach and admonish one another in all wisdom, and sing psalms and hymns and spiritual songs with thankfulness in your hearts to God: (Col. 3:16).

The history of mission in Europe started with such joy-in-oppression, and especially with songs of praise in the night! "And the prisoners were *listening* to them" (Acts 16:25).

Word and deed

These three aspects, concord, obedience and joy are decisive for our Christian behaviour in the world. We have to present a pious *example* to the outsiders, and in this way we must attract them. But you can ask: what about *speaking* to outsiders? Do we not have to speak to them at all? The apostle often places deed and word on one line and mentions them close together.

We read for instance in 1 Thess. 4:11 and 12: "We exhort you, brethren, to do so more and more, to aspire to live quietly, to mind your own affairs and to work with your hands, as we charged you; so that you may command the respect of outsiders, and be dependent on nobody." When the apostle Paul wrote this letter to the Thessalonians, the congregation had been instituted not that long before. But yet they had been oppressed very soon after that start. Now the outsiders observed very closely the members of the congregation: how would they behave themselves? Now keep in mind, Paul says, especially three things:

1) *You must be quiet.* Do not be noisy fellows. No sensational behaviour! Do not cause scandals!
2) *You must mind your own affairs.* That means: be not meddlesome. Do not meddle in other people's affairs. Meddlesomeness leads to pride and quarrel and envy.
3) *You must work with your hands.* That means: stay at your own place, where you belong. There you serve God with diligence and exertion. You have to do that as a servant or as a free man, having a good job or a humble occupation. Everybody has to do what is put upon his shoulders. Be not dependent on others.

If the congregation lives in this way, she may command the respect of outsiders.

But then she has no doubt the task to *speak* to the outsiders! Pay attention to what the apostle Paul is writing to the *Colossians* in chapter 4, verse 5 and 6: "Conduct yourselves wisely towards outsiders, making the most of the time. Let your speech always be gracious, seasoned with salt, so that you may know how you ought to answer everyone."

The Church of Colosse, living among Jews and gentiles, had to conduct herself *wisely.* Wisdom is always connected with care and caution. That does not mean: to beat around the bush, to be dishonest. But it means: do not tackle everything at once, do not needlessly go into all kinds of subjects! We have to know the times and the opportunities. If the world hates us, then it must not happen because of our follies, shortcomings and imprudences.

And then: *we have to make the most of time,* like the wise dealings of a merchant. He does not buy everything, nor does he buy continuously, but he waits for the good opportunity, the best possibility. So we have to *speak* with the people of the world. We have to do that personally, but speaking together, for instance in groups, is not excluded from that.

But our speech must be *gracious,* the apostle says. That does not mean that we can flatter, that we can beat around the bush. No, it means: our speech must be *attractive.* We may not speak without *contents,* without any *context.* We may not be annoying to outsiders! Do not be *boring!*

And: not without *salt.* Salt makes food tasty and averts decay. So we have to avoid depraved words, any dirty and musty speech! "You may know how you ought to answer everyone," the apostle says. That means: if worldly people are *asking* something, if they have sincere questions, then we *have to answer.* But we cannot give the same answer to everybody. Sometimes we have to *warn,* if we have the opportunity to do, so just as Paul did over against the people and Peter did over against the Jews and the rulers.

Sometimes worldly people are quarrelsome. Then most of the time it will be better to keep *silent.*

The one desires *instruction.* Look for such an opportunity!

The other one is a *disobedient child* of God's covenant. Call him back to God's Church!

The one is a *mocker,* who wants to provoke. The other one is a totally *worldly* man. But we have to know — and that is a matter of much wisdom! — how we ought to answer everyone.

But we know what James writes: "If any of you lacks wisdom, let him ask God who gives to all men generously and without reproaching, and it will be given him. But let him ask in faith, with no doubting" (James 1:5,6).

Attractive and merciful

That must be — in short — our Christian behaviour in the world. We are set in this world and we cannot go out of the world. That is what Paul is writing in his first letter to the Church of Corinth (1 Cor. 5:9).

B. Holwerda said — and I will end with his remarks which are worthy of consideration "There we meet that famous expression: we cannot go out of the world. But if you want to use this word, take it exactly as it is written. It does not mean: if you contact the world, then you can palter with the truth, you do not need to be too precise. No, Paul had just said in 1 Corinthians 5: you are redeemed by Christ's cross and now you have to celebrate the feast of pureness and truth. You cannot live a double life, and vacillate between two opinions. Your Christianity may not be a varnish, a jacket that you put off when you join another society. If you refuse encounter with the world, then you go out of the world. Then you would judge the world. But that is not your task. You can judge only as office-bearers judge sinful people in the Church. God Himself will judge those who are outside. God judges the world.

So it is exactly contrary to what we think about it. We say, if we are going to walk on the brink, does the Bible not say that we cannot go out of the world? And we reassure ourselves. We are aware that we receive our part of the rejoicing of the world. Otherwise we would wrong ourselves. But Paul says it just the other way around. *Not*: you would wrong *yourselves*, but: you would wrong the *world*! Encounter with the world? Yes, but provided that we know ourselves always as *missionaries*, who seek the salvation of all of them whom God wants to save. Provided that you do not make an excursion of the *service journey* to which God calls you. So: attract the outsiders. Be moved with mercy toward the people of the world.

He who reforms his encounter according to God's Law, he has to *say* something. He also knows what it means: not *of* the world, but yet always *in* the world. He has found his lifestyle for good" (Holwerda, 1947:15f.).

I want to finish with the following *conclusions*:

1. It belongs to the nature of Christ's Church to seek with the gospel which has been entrusted to her also those who are alien to or have become alienated from God and His service. According to the apostolic command the Church makes intercession to God her Saviour. For He desires all men to be saved and to come to the knowledge of the truth. The Church desires to reach all these men with God's Word and to call them to the communion with God and His people (1 Tim. 2:1-4; C.D. II, 5).

2. The office-bearers will, especially by preaching, catechesis and home visits, point out this calling to the members of the congregation and will equip them for the fulfilment of this calling (Eph. 4:11-16).

3. The consistories will continually accompany this task of the members of the congregation by means of supervision and instruction (Acts 20:28-30).

4. The members of the congregation, being the salt of the earth, have to penetrate the world and to let their light shine before men (Matt. 5:13-16, 1 Pet. 1:15, 2:9).

5. It is very important that by our godly walk of life we may win our neighbours for Christ (1 Pet. 3:1,2; H.C., answ. 86).

6. Characteristic for a godly walk are in the first place: concord and love of the brethren (Phil. 1:27-2:10; 1 Pet. 3:8-12; Rom. 12:9-21).

7. Furthermore an important requirement is: obedience, especially to the civil government and to the husband (1 Pet. 2:13-3:6).

8. In Christian behaviour toward those who are outside, joy must radiate from God's children (Phil. 2:18, 4:4; Col. 3:16; 1 Thess. 1:6).

9. Speaking to the outsiders is also important, but there must be a harmonious coherence of deed and word (1 Thess. 4:1-12; Col. 4:1-6).

10. When approaching those who are outside, one has to keep in mind the need to attract them, and to be moved with mercy toward them (1 Cor. 5:9, 10, 13).

QUESTION CONCERNING THE JEWS

Introduction

Once again Israel is in the centre of attention. Various problems have arisen regarding the people of the old covenant people — problems which cannot be easily solved. Millennialists have all kinds of ideas and theories concerning the Jews, giving us an excess of subject material relating to many Scripture passages and providing quite a number of exegetical problems. Moreover, the present state of Israel has given rise to many questions in connection with this. These questions are not so much related to the present status of Israel as to the future of the country and its people. And it is of great importance what the Jews themselves think of the fulfillment of God's promises. In other words, what kind of Messiah expectations are prevalent in Israel? If I am not mistaken, there are essentially three questions demanding an answer:

1. What is the Scriptural information about Israel's future as a nation?
2. How should we regard the present-day development of the state of Israel?
3. Which thoughts do the Jews themselves entertain concerning the Messiah?

We have very briefly formulated the questions, and it will become evident that they will overlap here and there, but at least we will have a guide to assist us in the maze of the numerous problems that have arisen.

Scriptural information

In the first place we shall deal with the information provided by the Scriptures concerning the future of Israel as a nation. Some have expressed as their opinion that with the coming of the Lord Jesus, Israel as nation has completely lost its special position. According to them "Israel" is today the New Testament church, nothing else. All the promises which the LORD gave to Abraham and his seed have been totally reflected to this New Testament church. According to them, there is absolutely no more hope for a national Israel. G.Ch. Aalders offers as his opinion that after the coming and death of the Messiah, Israel's national existence as a people was ended completely and forever. He speaks this way absolutely and without any reservations. The Old Testament, according to Aalders in this pre-war book, knows nothing about an awaited earthly future for Israel: "The earthly future of Israel, which was foretold in the Old Testament *has* already arrived according to the word of prophecy, and has already been annulled" (Aalders, n.d.:257f.).

Many years have passed since this book by Aalders made its appearance. There has been a war since then which seemed to have made an end of the Jews. Hitler, Eichmann and their satellites managed to destroy no fewer than six million Jews, a slaughter which has no equal in history. However, a miraculous event took place: not only did a remnant of the Jews survive (even though in Europe, for instance, only 28% of the pre-war population), but a large number of them managed to unite together and settled in the new state of Israel. On May 15, 1948, the State of Israel was established as an independent state in Palestine. And then arose the question: What about the earthly future of Israel, which according to men such as Aalders could no longer

171

be expected? Many people immediately came to the conclusion that this indicated a national rebirth, a complete return, even a total conversion to God. Above all, however, and that is our concern at the moment, many saw in the occurrences of 1948 the confirmation of the prophecy which they interpreted in a millennialistic sense. We cannot circumvent millennialistic theories with regard to the future of the people of Israel when we consider the problem of the Jews.

The thousand years

For that reason we will briefly summarize the essential beliefs of millennialism. Millennialists believe in a first and a second return of Christ, and between these two events lies His thousand-year reign with a restored Jerusalem at the centre. Long before there was any question of the return of the Jews to Palestine, these people already voiced a strong expectation of the return of the Jews to the Holy Land, based on Old Testament prophecies, and also on some information in the New Testament, to which they give their own interpretation. They believe that Israel's national task was temporarily given to the gentiles, and that this task will last only until the times of the gentiles have been fulfilled (Luke 21:24). Israel's spiritual task was temporarily assigned to the New Testament church, from the time of the outpouring of the Holy Spirit, to the first return of Christ. Then, according to 1 Thessalonians 4:17, the church will be taken up into the air, and that moment will signify the marriage of the Lamb, although it is not yet the end of the world. The taking-up of the church designates the final period of time. Then God will return to Israel and this people will again take over its task from the church. God will renew the ties with Israel through the 144,000 of Revelation 7, who will be missionaries on earth during the great persecution, the final period of the times of the gentiles, which commenced at the lifting up of the church. However, the conversion of Israel will be accompanied by heavy persecution and distress, for Israel will be gathered to the arms of Jesus only through the great persecution of the anti-christ. Jerusalem will prove more and more to be a rock of offense, until all the nations will gather together against her. That signals the great Armageddon, and in her distress Israel will learn to seek the Lord Jesus. Then the moment will have arrived that God will pour out His Spirit over them. Christ shall again place His feet on the Mount of Olives and return with all His holy ones who had been lifted up to Him earlier. By divine intervention all the armies gathered in the valley of Armageddon against Jerusalem shall be defeated. The Beast and the false prophet shall be cast into the pool of fire. God shall again establish the throne of David and the millennium of Christ shall dawn in full glory. At that time Satan will be bound so that he can no longer tempt the nations. People will gather from all the ends of the earth to Jerusalem to worship the King who is seated on the throne of David. The church will share in the glory of Christ and sit as kings and priests with Him on His throne. Also, the temple will be rebuilt and the priestly service will be restored according to the prophecy of Jeremiah 33:18. The new temple at Jerusalem will be the spiritual centre of the whole world. Many people and mighty gentiles will come to worship God in Jerusalem. This will be the great mission dispensation of history. In this present day there are only individuals who come to believe, but then "all the gentiles will come to Him and fall down before His face." At the end of Christ's reign of peace follows a short time when Satan's bonds will be untied, and he will once again cause a rebellion. These are his final movements, however, for this rebellion will seal his own doom. After a cleansing process by fire, whereby the elements will melt, and God Himself will use atomic energy, the last stains — reminders of sin — will be removed. Then will dawn the new heavens and the new earth, where righteousness dwells.

Texts

It is impossible to discuss all the texts which are put forward by the millennialists to promote their ideas. Their main argument is their opinion that everything that is written in the prophecies must be taken *literally*. Let us take their interpretation of Isaiah 11:15 and 16 as an example: "And the LORD will utterly destroy the tongue of the sea of Egypt; and will wave His hand over the River with His scorching wind, and smite it into seven channels that men may cross dryshod. And there will be a highway from Assyria for the remnant which is left of His people, as there was for Israel when they came up from the land of Egypt." Their argument is as follows: the crossing of the Red Sea actually happened, so it must be the same for this prophecy. And since it has not yet taken place, there is only one conclusion, namely, that it must still happen! Moreover, they say, the prophecies speak of Israel's being gathered out of all nations (cf. Jeremiah 32:37 and Ezekiel 36:24), whereas the exile involved only Assyria and Babylon. In addition there is the prophecy that Israel will once again be planted in its country and will never again be plucked out of it (Isaiah 11:11, Isaiah 14:1, Amos 9:15), whereas it certainly was plucked out again after the return from exile. Special references are made to the prophecies of Zechariah, since he prophesied after the exile. A favourite quotation is Zechariah 14, which calls Jerusalem the divine worship centre for the entire world.

As for the New Testament, they find support for their position in Acts 15:14-17, where James points out that "God has first visited the gentiles and after that will return and rebuild the dwelling of David which has fallen so that the rest of men may seek the Lord, and all the gentiles who are called by My Name." A final proof to them is the parable of the barren fig tree. For three years Christ sought in vain for fruit from the people of Israel (Luke 13:7). His personal presence could not bring a change in that barrenness, and although he found leaves, there was no fruit. Hence His curse: "May no fruit ever come from you again" (Matthew 21:19). This *seems* to be evidence that Israel has totally lost its special importance, but (according to them) these words refer only to this dispensation. And so they say that in this dispensation Israel as a nation has never brought forth fruit and will not do so. However in the next dipensation of Messianic salvation, Israel *will* bring forth fruit. The time of the end will bring the summer near when the fig tree will again bud forth (Matthew 24:32). That budding of the fig tree will occur when Israel returns to Palestine.

How should we evaluate this viewpoint? In the first place, we can never be satisfied with a literal fulfillment of prophecy in itself. When millennialists apply the texts which refer to Jerusalem's restoration and future only to the earthly Jerusalem, then they come into thorough conflict with the Scriptures themselves. The name "Jerusalem" in the Bible does not apply to the Jerusalem in Palestine only. I merely refer to what Paul writes in Galatians 4:24-26 about the distinction between the Jerusalem of his day and the Jerusalem that is above. Think also of what John says in the book of Revelation about "the holy city, the new Jerusalem coming down out of heaven from God" (Revelation 21). There is also Hebrews 12:22: "But you have come to Mount Zion, and to the city of the living God, the heavenly Jerusalem." So the Scriptures clearly forbid us to dwell only on the earthly Jerusalem whenever the city is mentioned. Also in this aspect the Old Testament is explained via the New! It is obvious that a literal interpretation of prophecy can lead astray when we see the millennialistic belief (based on Jeremiah 33:18) in the restoration of the Levitical priesthood with burnt offerings, cereal offerings, and sacrifices. This, however, is in direct conflict with the continuing witness of the letter to the Hebrews, especially the chapters 7 to 10. "Now if perfection had been attainable through the Levitical priesthood . . . what further need would there have been for another priest to arise after the order of Melchizedek?" (Hebrews 7:11). "For if that first covenant had been faultless there would have been no occasion for a second" (Hebrews 8:7). "Consequently, when Christ came into the world, He said, 'Sacrifices and offerings thou hast not desired, but a body hast thou prepared for me; in burnt offerings and sin offerings thou hast taken no pleasure.' Then I said, 'Lo, I have come to do Thy will O God,' as it is written in the roll of the book" (Hebrews 10:5-7). And especially 10:9: "He abolished the first in order to establish the second."

So we are also not to anticipate a literal fulfillment of Isaiah 11:15,16, that a highway will be made through the Red Sea and the River (Euphrates), for where today there is no longer mention made of the Philistines, Edom, Moab, Ammon, etc., why should the same not apply to the former?

An interesting proof text is Acts 15:14-17. If the context had been closely kept in mind, it would have been obvious that James was not at all discussing the *future* restoration of Israel and the fallen dwelling of David. On the contrary, he argues that at that particular time the fallen dwelling of David *was* restored. The kingship of Christ has now come, and it may be expected that the gentiles who turn to God will now no longer be asked to keep all kinds of Jewish laws and statutes.

The interpretation of the withered fig tree is also incorrect. The expression "(not) ever again" is used more often in the Bible to indicate a permanent situation. Moreover, one may not automatically identify the fig tree with the Israel in Palestine. Matthew 24 deals with the signs of Christ's return and it is natural that Christ uses the symbol of the fig tree: in Palestine the fig tree gets its leaves in the spring, in contrast with many other trees that are green all year long.

Now a comment about Israel's being gathered out of all nations, from the four corners of the earth. The millennialists feel that Israel was exiled only to Babylon and Assyria and so the "gathering" cannot refer to the return from exile. They forget, however, that Israel was indeed scattered throughout many places. Jeremiah 43 describes how Johanan took the remnant to Egypt. Also their theory concerning the two returns of Christ: the contrast between 1 Thessalonians 4 (return on the clouds) and Zechariah 14 (standing on the Mount of Olives) is untenable. For in the first place, Paul does not speak about Christ's remaining in the air, but about the believers' being brought up to meet Him. Moreover, he connects to this return the destruction of those who do not await the Lord's coming. In the next chapter he mentions the people who say: here is peace and security, and *those* are the ones who will be caught by the destruction. There will be no escape, says Paul; in other words, repentance is no longer possible, for the end has come. Therefore it is the same return as mentioned in Zechariah 14, even though it is seen from a different perspective. But it is one and the same return, when everything in Judah and Jerusalem will be holy to the LORD.

Positive

Although we reject all these millennialist views and interpretations that does not mean that there are no positive references concerning the future of Israel. I think of Christ's discourse on the last days as Luke renders it in ch. 21:23,24: "For great distress shall be upon the earth and wrath upon this people, they will fall by the edge of the sword and be led captive among all nations, and Jerusalem will be trodden down by the gentiles, until the times of the gentiles are fulfilled." This, then, refers to a dispersion of Israel, which at the time of its prediction was still totally in the future and would be extremely severe. Jerusalem would be trampled by the gentiles, nations different from God's covenant people. This prophecy was very literally fulfilled during and after the destruction of Jerusalem in A.D. 70. At that time and also later in history the Jews were persecuted, hunted and scattered all over the earth. Who does not know the history of the crusades, when the Christians rose up to rescue the "holy places" out of the hands of the Saracens? The Turks dominated Palestine until 1917, after which the Arabs virtually became rulers. However, when speaking about the signs of the times, Christ emphatically used the word "until." The dispersion would not last forever, but until the times of the gentiles would be fulfilled. We do not know exactly what is meant by the times of the gentiles. Perhaps it means that they were to rule over Israel and Jerusalem and thus to execute God's judgment. It may also mean that Israel was to receive an opportunity to return to God. Perhaps it is both, for the one does not exclude the other. One thing is sure, however: God has set a time limit also to the trampling of Jerusalem by the gentiles, a beginning and an ending. Added to this is the fact that the end of the trampling of Jerusalem does not immediately indicate the end of the world.

Romans 11

Some promises for Israel remain yet unfulfilled; think especially of what Paul writes in Romans 11. Here the apostle begins by asking: "Has God, then, rejected His people?" It is obvious that "His people" in this case means the seed of Abraham, of the tribe of Benjamin." Then the apostle refers back to the time of Elijah. *At that time* the LORD established His faithfulness to His promises by keeping for Himself 7000 men who did not bow the knee to Baal. "So, too, at this present time there is a remnant chosen by grace." The faithfulness of the LORD is not bound to a number. Did not the New Testament church totally and completely have its origins in Israel? Did not the LORD start with them when He instituted His church in Jerusalem, first gathering them from Judea, and after that sending His apostles to the gentiles? If is because the LORD maintained the old line, the line of election through grace, that salvation by-passed the greater part of Israel. For the majority in Israel sought their salvation by means of works and were therefore hardened (vs. 6-10). But Paul emphasizes that their rejection of Christ, their stumbling over this rock, does not mean their permanent rejection. "Have they stumbled so as to fall? By no means" (vs. 11). The LORD executed His complete counsel of salvation through their trespass, so that by this means salvation might come to the gentiles. Not to the exclusion of Israel, however, but in order to make Israel jealous. For as long as Israel has not come to repentance, there is a great deficiency. Therefore, because of his love for his own people, Paul feels all the more compelled to journey all over to bring the gentiles to repentance of Israel. In the first place he argues that God is able again to accept Israel, to bring it to repentance, to graft in again the broken-off branches. If God is able to graft in the branches of a wild olive tree, that is, if God is powerful enough to bring the gentiles to faith, how much more the natural branches, that is the Jews. And the LORD not only *can* do this, He also *will* do it. Paul warns in vs. 25: "Lest you be wise in your own conceits, I want you to understand this mystery, brethren: a hardening has come upon part of Israel, until the full number of the Gentiles come in, and so all Israel will be saved." If one has followed the discourse of Paul closely, he will understand that it would be completely illogical for Paul to switch suddenly to *spiritual* Israel at this point. Doekes in his commentary on Romans 9-11, writes: "In these three chapters Israel is mentioned no less than eleven times. The ten previous references unquestionably point to the Jews in contrast to the gentiles. What specific reason would force us now to a different conclusion? Surely not the context, for the distinction between Jews and gentiles does not stop at vs. 25 but continues in the next verses. Nor is it the prophecy which Paul advances as proof of the truth he has stated and which testifies to it with the expressly used names of Zion and Jacob. Everything pleads for letting "all Israel" be understood to mean the Jewish people. Obviously a contrast exists between "all" and "the remnant chosen by grace" (vs. 5). As long as "all" is not understood to mean the total number of individuals, a mass conversion. This must not be interpreted to refer to the *number* of the Jews which will be saved, but to Israel as a *people" (Doekes, 1915:298). S. Greijdanus also remarks in his commentary on Romans 11 that it is not the number as such that is at stake here, but the people as a whole (Greijdanus, 1933:516). Is this such a strange thought? Paul himself refers to the Old Testament prophecy that the LORD will banish ungodliness from Jacob. The very sad fact of today is: the Jews are enemies of the gospel. They have rejected the glad tidings of Christ's coming. Yet they do remain the beloved of the LORD! Not because of themselves but according to God's election, for the father's sake.* And so one line is drawn through the history of salvation. At first the nations were all disobedient; therefore they were rejected, and the Lord then chose Abraham, Israel, out of grace, to be His people. But that was not because the LORD cut off those nations. No, when the LORD called Abraham and chose Israel, He had in mind the deliverance of those people. That salvation of the nations was realized when God sent His Son, Jesus Christ. However, that salvation was also realized through the disobedience of Israel, because they nailed the Lord Jesus to the cross and rejected Him. So the LORD was merciful to Abraham and Israel in their calling and election, so that we in turn might gain mercy, and the salvation from the Jews might come to us. In this way *we* have received mercy, so that through *us, they* might again obtain mercy. And as Paul the Jew, led us to Christ, we must now lead the seed of Abraham to Christ. Therefore there is, for Jews and gentiles both, only one road to salvation throughout the ages, to the end of time: the way of God's mercy.

The state of Israel

Now that we have discovered that the history of the Jews is not concluded after all and that God did not close off the road for His old covenant people, we must answer the following question: How should we view present developments in the state of Israel? For as D. Holwerda states in his outlines on Romans, we do not face an ethnological problem but rather an eschatological event (Holwerda, 1949:66). The constitution of the state of Israel in 1948 is not a coincidence or an interesting geographical phenomenon! No, it is a sign of the times, a fact which is very closely related to the prophecy of the Scriptures. For even when we strongly reject the millennialist theories, do we not face the prophecy of the Scriptures with regard to the developments in present-day Israel, and should all these events not be regarded in the light of prophecy, especially in the light of Christ's prophetic speech concerning the future and Paul's hymn of praise to God's mercies in Romans 11?

G.Ch. Aalders, who in his pre-war commentary came to the conclusion that there is no future for Israel, still maintains in his post-war brochure (published in 1949, a year after Israel became a state) that what has happened in Israel, and whatever still may happen, has no connection with divine prophecy (Aalders, 1949:31). Also the book *Israel*, published in 1955 by G.Ch. Aalders and H.N. Ridderbos, expressly emphasizes: Israel is rejected as a nation — and that is that (Aalders, 1955:19). Yet after reading the many books available on Israel today, we strongly feel that this is an eschatological question. All events proceed to the fulfillment of the prophecy, to the fullness of times. However, and that is the other side of the coin, let us not rejoice prematurely. For example, when we recall the attitude of the Dutch Reformed (Hervormde) Synod in the Netherlands regarding the so-called "dialogue" with Israel, we might conclude that now already a large-scale, massive and even national return of the Jews is in effect.

They expressed agreement with Karl Barth's statement: "The glory of the risen Lord is reflected in the church, but His suffering is reflected in Israel." They even go so far as to say that Israel has been set among the nations as a mirror in which we see our inability to live by God's grace and power, and also as a mirror which shows the judgment of God. Israel judges itself to be the Messiah of the nations and for that reason the church and Israel are not two independent entities which exist beside or over against each other. No, the church and Israel are one in Christ. For that reason there is to be no more mission work *in* Israel but dialogue *with* Israel.

Special function?

We will not dwell on this except to remark that in this way the accent has been shifted completely. They have taken as their basis that the Jewish people has to fulfill a special function in history and believe that now the era of complete brotherhood and spiritual unity has arrived. Such a conclusion is premature, to say the least. The facts give us a different picture. Since the people of Israel after the defeat of the Bar-Kochba uprising in the years A.D. 132-135 were permanently sent away from Palestine, the prayer for the peace of Jerusalem has never ceased. The wish expressed after every Passover, "next year in Jerusalem," originated many centuries ago. Originally this desire was strongly religious in character without any political overtones. Jerusalem became the city of pilgrimage. Many Jews travelled there to visit the holy city. A portion remaining of the old temple wall was used especially on Fridays to mourn and to pray (the so-called wailing wall). Great was the desire to be buried on the Mount of Olives in order to be among the first to greet the Messiah when He returned to raise the dead. In the 14th century there was again a Jewish congregation in Jerusalem which maintained itself there and became the centre for studying the Mosaic laws. The congregation concerned themselves with nothing else and existed from the gifts and donations sent by other Jews outside Palestine.

Beside this religious Zionism, the previous centuries saw the origin of a political Zionism which arose mainly because of anti-semitism. As long as the Jewish people lived in segregated areas (ghettos) they were not too badly off. But in the French Revolution, when the rights of man were proclaimed, the situation changed. The Jews also liberated themselves from old custom and ties. Then followed the disillusionment. Many people felt that a Jew always remains a Jew, and of course the latter experienced the results of this belief. This state of always being isolated promoted nationalistic feelings and created a desire for a national home of their own, a native country. In 1897, a Zionistic organization was established with the aim to establish a home in Palestine. Through the blazing hatred against the Jews and the terrorism of the Nazis, the Jews all the more considered a national existence of their own as the only solution. This resulted in the great Exodus; a stream of Jews travelled from their dwelling-places to the old homeland. Although in 1932 there were only 180,000 Jews in Palestine among a general population of one million, this number quickly increased after the war to one million Jews. The hatred, the enmity and the attempts to wipe them out completely, became the strongest motives to seek an independent existence in Palestine.

No conversion

Originally there were great contrasts within the Jewish people, especially with regard to the Zionistic aspirations. The orthodox Jews kept themselves aloof from Zionism, especially because it has a political background. Radical elements were not satisfied with a national homeland but wanted a complete Jewish state. Others supported the idea of co-existence with the Arabs who lived there already. Most of the differences have gradually disappeared because of the need to present a united front to the world outside. There are still important differences between religious and political Zionism, and whereas the latter is liberal, the former is typically Jewish and conservative in the Jewish sense. In no way therefore do the events of today indicate a total conversion of the Jews. That is still out of the question. We will return to that point when discussing the third question. As far as political developments were concerned, when the English decided on May 15, 1948, to give up their mandate, the Jews proclaimed the state of Israel in the area designated by the U.N. The Arabs, however, who had long felt threatened by the massive invasion of the Jews, had also not been idle. The Arab countries had formed a coalition with Egypt, and on the same day that England gave up its mandate, Arab troops entered Jewish territory. After a fierce conflict, in which the Jews suffered severe losses but to everyone's amazement stood firm and even gained territory, the armistice was concluded at the end of 1948 and the Jewish state could consolidate itself. Practically all the Arabs had fled Jewish territory. It continues to be an uneasy peace with an explosion every so often.

Aside from that, in the years following 1948 steady progress has been apparent, especially in the economic sector. The accomplishments of Israel during these years are almost unbelievable. A tremendous amount of Jewish capital has entered the country. Modern cities have been built, electrical generators, oil refineries, and all kinds of other industries were established. An enormous amount of work is still being done and the energy of the Jewish people demands our admiration.

Blood and soil

And yet, and that is the last point, does the return to the *country* of the fathers also a mean a return to the *God* of the fathers? We have already expressed our doubts about such a conclusion and now at the end we want to justify our doubts. We have previously mentioned the war between Israel and the Arabs. The war is considered a holy war by the Zionists, which fact unites the Zionists in Palestine together today. It is the conflict of yore between Ishmael and Isreal, about which Israel already sang in the Middle Ages when they feared the threat of the Arabs. Today, however, it is no longer the fearful cry of those days, but now it is a cry for self-assertion. It is the same contours of hatred and enmity against the Arab world, the enemy of ancient times, which control the Israel of today. Present-day Israel does not praise God's mercy as Paul did in Romans 11 but praises itself, in total contrast with the praise of Romans 11. Today Israel sings of blood and soil. While the destroyers of this people, the Nazis of Germany, gloried in German blood and German soil, the Jews now glory in Jewish blood and Jewish soil. They sing of self-vindication and of salvation by their own efforts. For now I touch upon an essential point in the present Jewish development: they are full of . . . themselves, of national values and national pride. And they even go so far that they imagine themselves as nation, as people, to be the messiah who was to come. This Israel does not differ from the Christian faith in that it places in the future what for us has already happened. No, they see the messiah incorporated in the people, the nation, "blood and soil." That is why their fighting is so fanatic. Today Israel sings:

A generation that wants to be saved;
Only then do you rise to your task and are delivered,
Only then do you rise to your task and deliver!

Please note: what is said *passively* in the second line, has become *active* in the third. They are delivered, yes indeed, but because they save themselves. The nation is its own saviour, its own messiah. And when does this happen? When they *want* it themselves. The will power of a people is the actual power of salvation.

Conclusion

I could underline this thought with more examples, but we should come to an end.

Today's Israel has a messianic theory which flatly contradicts the Scriptures. It does not follow the way of the covenant and the grounds for pleading which the covenant provides. By saying this we do not wish to imply that this is the last word from Israel, and even less that this is our last word *about* Israel. The dismissive formula — "once rejected as covenant people, always rejected" — does not fit within the framework of the Scriptures. However, we do say: let us beware of premature conclusions regarding the return of the Jews to Palestine. The last word concerning the Jews, also about the future of this people, has not yet been spoken. Who knows what the future may bring, also for this chosen people of old. As long as *we* now speak up. With the return of so many Jews to the old homeland perhaps possibilities for a true conversion may be given — possibilities which cannot as yet be imagined. For let us not forget one thing: conversion must always come through prayer and work. Yes indeed, it is God's doings from A to Z, but the LORD uses people in His kingdom and those people may not be idle. They must approach God in prayer, also for this nation. Do we still remember this old covenant people in our prayers?

However, they and we must also come together through action. That does not mean a dialogue in which two parties simply some together to supplement each other. No, in this age of levelling off and of syncretism we are again called to confess the antithesis. We must confess the antithetical word that our only salvation lies in the Christ of the Scriptures. Therefore our work among this people must be done from a missionary viewpoint. In the Netherlands a new initiative is being undertaken in that direction, and I believe that there indeed lies a task, no matter how difficult. C. Van Dam, in his article, "Mission work among the Jews?" in *Clarion*, September 19, 1986, has also pointed to this task. May the LORD, the God of His people who propels the history of the nations, also of the old Jewish people, to the end of times, still give us the time, the power, and the desire, so that this nation may again as people of God find in Jesus Christ the promised Messiah who has come and will return. Then they will no more sing of blood and soil, not even the song of Moses only, but together with all the saved ones sing the song of Moses *and* of the Lamb, the song of His blood:

Thee, holy Lamb of God, we bless;

Thou'st through Thy cross redemption sent us.

VII
"THE WORD OF GOD IS NOT FETTERED"
(2 Timothy 2:9)

HOW DO WE READ THE CHURCH ORDER?

Reopening of debate

In 1988 there was a debate in *Clarion* about the first part of Art. 31 of the Church Order, *"If anyone complains that he has been wronged by the decision of a minor assembly, he shall have the right to appeal to the major ecclesiastical assembly. . . ."* To summarize the debate: W.W.J. VanOene was of the opinion that an appeal is only to be made if one is personally wronged, while J.D. Wielenga defended the view that the right of appeal is given with the responsibility of all the members of the churches to see to it that the churches are governed by the pure Word of God. The debate was stopped after counterplea and rejoinder in the *Clarion* issue of September 11, 1987.

However, I asked for reopening of the debate. I did that for two reasons. In the first place, I noticed that several people still had questions about the matter. (One of them already wrote an article about it, but knowing that the debate was stopped, he did not ask for publication.) The second reason is that, in my opinion, this topic is so important that we have to discuss it again. It was decided at that meeting that the discussion be reopened.

No principles?

W.W.J. VanOene (1987:221) said concerning the first part of Art. 31 C.O.: "I would certainly not say that 'a general principle was applied,' namely, 'the general principle that wrong decisions of minor assemblies can be appealed.' Our Church Order does not lay down or contain principles. Our Church Order shows how the 'principles' laid down in the Word of our God and repeated in our confessions are to be applied in the life of the churches."

Now it is so that many principles are to be applied in the life of the churches. Not all of them are written down in the Church order. Therefore I want to underline what, already a hundred years ago, was said by the professor of Reformed church polity in the time that the churches returned to the Church Order of Dordt, F.L. Rutgers: "The church order pronounces only principles. Their elaboration and explication are left to ecclesiastical assemblies." In the following passage F.L. Rutgers stresses this again: "The church order only gives general principles." Elsewhere he says that the Church Order has actually two pillars. The first one is the former Art. 1 (in the C.O. of the Canadian Reformed Churches now Art. 74), namely, "No Church shall in any way lord it over other Churches, no office-bearer over other office-bearers." The second is Art. 31 in which it is guaranteed that God's Word has the final say in the church. Rutgers calls them the two pillars of the Church Order, or the two main principles (*College-dictaten* 1892/'93).

Especially regarding Art. 31 C.O. Rutgers wrote: "The principle is here that God's Word has more authority than all the authority of ecclesiastical assemblies" *(Ibidem)*. I expect that the Rev. VanOene will reply, "but that is only the opinion of one man, and I am not bound to human opinions." We should bear in mind that this was said precisely after the return to the Church Order of Dordt in a time (the time of the Doleantie) that hierarchy and human wisdom had the upperhand in the church. In that same time it was said that there are three principles of Reformed church polity: 1) absolute binding to Scriptures, and therefore also 2) absolute authority of Christ Himself in the church and 3) exclusion of every human dominion in the church. I may again refer to the church polity expert of the Doleantie time, Rutgers, who said that this former Art. 1 (now 74) is a very important principle which, at the first Dutch synod after the Reformation, even preceded the article about unity in doctrine (Art. 2 of the Synod of Emden, 1571). Then Rutgers continued, "Not that this former Art. 1 is *the* fundamental principle, as if in this one point everything is already said. It is certainly true that belonging to the confederation of churches also brings along certain obligations. Nevertheless, with the acknowledgment of this principle expressed in Art. 1 of the Synod at Emden 1571 the whole Reformation is at stake." (Rutgers, 1918:156).

No *via media*

I agree with W.W.J. VanOene that the Church Order is not taking the "golden mean," the *via media*, in order to avoid the two cliffs of hierarchy and independentism. It indeed does not do so. But we add immediately: the Church Order goes the good Reformed way, following the Scriptures and the confession. This means that *principles* are laid down in the Church Order. One of the principles is that no church, no office-bearer, may lord it over other churches or office-bearers. This principle goes back to what our Saviour commanded His disciples, "The kings of the Gentiles exercise lordship over them; and those in authority over them are called benefactors. But not so with you; rather let the greatest among you become as the youngest, and the leader as one who serves" (Luke 22:25, 26, cf. also Matthew 20:25-27). We may say that the Church Order has a scriptural and confessional character. This does not mean that the Church Order has a value or authority equal to that of Scripture. But it means that the Church Order is built upon the basis of Scripture and confessions.

In our book *Decently and in Good Order*, G. Van Rongen and I came to the conclusion that the Church Order is a further exposition of what our churches confess on the ground of God's Word. I quote, "It is true, a number of clauses included in the Church Order are nothing more than agreements between the churches to handle certain matters in an identical fashion, where in fact different paths could be chosen. Also contained in our Church Order are several stipulations which cannot be traced back to any commandment of Christ or His apostles, yet they were laid down as being beneficial to the churches in showing unity and presenting a common front. We may refer here e.g. to Articles 32, 43, and 44c. Apart from that, it is not a kind of code, containing all kinds of detailed rules and regulations. However, generally speaking our Church Order is based on the 'Spiritual order' which we are taught in the Scriptures. It is therefore an important element in maintaining the unity of faith among the churches and in each local congregation. This does not mean that our Church Order is a perfect document. It goes without saying that neither creeds, confessions, nor church orders ever attain equal level with Holy Scripture; if ever anything in them is recognized as being incorrect or wrong, it must be amended. The late Professor P. Deddens of the Kampen Theological Seminary used to say: 'To have a Church Order is a good thing, but only together with an open Bible!' " (p. 13ff.)

This means also (and my father stressed that in is inaugural speech of 1946, just after the "Liberation"), that all human decisions in the church need examination. I translate from another speech of my father the following words: "Church polity, as it is summarized and expressed in the Church Order, is a matter of confession. The contents of the Church Order is nothing else but a specified explanation of what the Belgic Confession says e.g. in the articles 7, 27, 28, 29, 30, 31, and 32. Basis and all-important factor of it is that Jesus Christ is the only King of the church. He rules the church by His Word and Spirit by means of the consistory, the *only* body which received from Him authority for leadership and rule in the local church" (Deddens, 1950:17).

Open Bible!

I want to stress especially the matter of the "open Bible" when discussing the Church Order. This year a book was published in the Netherlands with the title *"De kerkorde, regel voor vrede in de kerk"* (The Church Order, rule for peace in the church). The author is H. Bouma and it is published in the series *Woord en Wereld* (no. 8), Ermelo. It is remarkable that Bouma shows from page to page that the Church Order is based on the Scriptures. Time and again he quotes texts from the Bible in order to demonstrate that not only a confederation of churches is based on the Bible, but also that all kinds of articles of the Church Order are to be considered in the framework of texts, c.q., passages from the Scriptures.

We read in this book, "As for the matter of an appeal to broader assemblies, this matter is not something trifling or to carry one's point. Article 31 C.O. discusses a wrong due to a pronouncement ('uitspraak'), not a decision ('besluit') but a sentence, a judgment." Bouma continues, "Imagine that a consistory came to a decision on a certain point. But somebody in the congregation is of the opinion that this decision would harm the church and its Lord. Then one shall bring this before the consistory with good grounds. Then the consistory has to examine that decision and it has to come to a decision about its first decision: was it a good decision or was it not? So, an appeal about a decision is not mentioned here, but an appeal about a pronounce-ment, a judgement. One must not appeal to a broader assembly too rashly, but first of all call the consistory involved to further reflection" (Bouma, 1989:43).

I agree with the Rev. Bouma in this respect. But what is now the scriptural background of the right of appeal? Of course, that no injury, no injustice, no wrong is to be tolerated in the church. Therefore there must be the possibility of an appeal.

Inadmissible?

Now the question is, is an appeal to a broader assembly inadmissible when it comes from someone who is not personally wronged? Not really! If there is injury, injustice, wrong in the church, everybody must have the right of appeal with regard to that evil. Why? Because injustice must be taken away, as soon as possible. Imagine that the person who is wronged by a minor assembly will become seriously ill after the decision. Imagine that he passes away before he can do anything. Or imagine that he was so upset that he withdrew from the church. Of course, such action would be wrong. But the question is, what about that wrong decision? Is then injustice to re-main because there is no possibility of an appeal? May nobody else appeal? Is everything then blocked and will the injury be maintained? Here we have a ground which shows the need of an open Bible when we read our Church Order. The Bible says, "How long will you judge unjustly and show partiality to the wicked? Give justice to the weak and the fatherless, maintain the right of the afflicted and the destitute" (Psalm 83:2, 3). The late Prof. Dr. S. Greijdanus quoted this text in connection with the bad decisions of the General Synod of 1944 in the Netherlands.

Now this is just one text. There are many more texts in the Bible which point to the necessity that injury and injustice must be taken out of the church, without delay.

The freedom of God's children must be honoured in the church, including the freedom that they have the right to point to injustice and injury, and to appeal unjust decisions also when injury is done to others. It could be that consistories and also other ecclesiastical assemblies are blinded, so that they do not see that there is something wrong.

Confession and Church Order

We need an open Bible when we read the Church Order. But there is also a close connection between the Church Order and the Confession. I quote with respect to this Prof. J. Hovius of Apeldoorn, "Already in Wezel 1568 the *principles* are indicated according to which ecclesiastical life had to be developed." (Hovius, 1962:15). Of course, in the Church Order some practical rules are given, but the main purpose of the Church Order is to *preserve* the churches by the Scriptures as summarized in the Confessions. Hence Hovius did not say: the Church Order is only an application of the Confession, but he stated that "there is an essential and very close relation between our Confession and our Church Order. Both are structurally as well as essentially correlated."

We may even say — and this has been taught for many years in "Kampen" — with the words of W. Niesel in his book about Reformed Confessions and Church Orders: "According to Reformed doctrine, also the order of the church has a confessional character" (Niesel, 1938:V).

Only if personally wronged?

This brings me again to Article 31 of the Church Order. I read in Joh. Jansen, *Korte Verklaring van de Kerkenordening,* (Kok, Kampen, p. 143), that this article implies that decisions of ecclesiastical assemblies are not infallible but fallible. Jansen said this in the first edition of his book, in 1923, in which he adhered to the Church Polity of the Doleantie, as this was taught by F.L. Rutgers. The same was taught in Kampen for many years by Dr. H. Bouwman. I quote from his second volume of *Gereformeerd Kerkrecht:* "Now this article could be read in this way that the right of appeal is only given when someone is personally wronged by the pronouncement of a major assembly. *Undoubtedly this has not been the intention* (italics, added, K.D.), as appears from the general formulation of the synod of Emden (1571, in fact the first synod, K.D.), that anyone may appeal from the classical assembly to the provincial synod. *Anyway, the right of appeal is never limited to those cases in which one's own personal rights are violated or one is personally wronged"* (italics added, K.D.). H. Bouwman then gives several examples, also from the beginning of the federation of the churches in the Netherlands, and he concludes: "The legal ground upon which an appeal can be based, is broader than the case that someone is personally wronged. This legal ground is also there when someone is of the opinion that a decision made by the consistory is in conflict with the Word of God and dangerous for the congregation. It is in the nature of the case that there must be the possibility to receive justice in a higher instance (Bouwman, 1934:41ff.).

Self-evident

Why was H. Bouwman so certain in his writing about this matter? Did he not know that history is not normative? I think he considered it as self-evident that an appeal must be possible, not only if someone is personally wronged, but also if injury or violation of justice is at stake. This has to do with the *principle* that no injury, in whatever form, is to be tolerated in the church, and that it is merciful to point to that injury or violation of one's rights, so that injustice can be taken away.

Around the Reunion of 1892

Not only in the 16th century was this practice regarding the right of appeal for each and every member of the church maintained, but also later on. I take as an example what happened at the first synod after the reunion of the churches of Secession and Doleantie, namely the synod of Dordrecht 1893. This synod had to finish a matter with which the last synod of the churches of the secession dealt which, namely the synod of Amsterdam 1892. There was an appeal of a brother from Dedemsvaart on the decision of the maintenance of excommunication by the particular synod of Drenthe. This synod had maintained the decision of the consistory of Dedemsvaart. There was a discussion at the synod of Amsterdam 1892 whether or not the appeal was admissible. What was the case? Not the man involved, but his brother appealed. But the synod decided to deal with the appeal. Synod pronounced that *a member of the church may appeal on a major assembly when he or she is of the opinion that the consistory has wronged another member of the congregation* (italics added, K.D.).

Finally the whole matter was solved by the decision of the first synod after the reunion in 1893. I think this was an important matter, because the new federation of Reformed Churches had just started and also the brothers of the Doleantie agreed with the decision. (See the *Acts* of the Synod of 1892, Amsterdam 1892, p. 34, article 56, also p. 76, article 99. See also *De Reformatie* 31, no. 19, p. 151).

After the liberation of 1944

In the liberated churches after 1944 this principle was maintained. Immediately after the liberation a brief explantion of the Church Order was published in Enschede, written by the three local ministers, H. Meulink, H. Vogel, and I. de Wolff. (Enschede, n.d., 17.) In this booklet they say: "This article deals with the right of appeal. He who is of the opinion that he is wronged has the right to appeal to a major assembly. *This is in force for assemblies as well as persons* (italics added, K.D.). Then there follows in Article 31 that most important part, in which a guarantee is given against hierarchy which wants to impose on the churches and the consciences of men human ordinances which are in conflict with truth and justice." As far as I know, "Kampen" taught the students in the same way after the liberation, even until nowadays.

On guard

History is not normative. But history is very instructive. We can learn much from it. The reformer Bucer wrote once, "God's Church did not just today fall down out of heaven" (cf. Van't Spijker, 1972:40). This must make us modest.

I quote again J. Hovius: "The Church must be diligent that the Church Order does not degenerate to a petrified law that kills life in an atmosphere of formalism and legalism" (l.c., p. 25). This is not a sledgehammer argument, as VO says. It is a warning to read the Church Order always in the light of Scripture and Confession, taking into account their totality, comparing Scripture with Scripture, so that the articles of the Church Order are not read as an iron law, but in a *pastoral* way, because the church is the gathering of *living* members who, in the church, expect their salvation from Jesus Christ, the only Head of the church, who must always have the final word!

Now I come back to the question asked in the beginning. How do we read the Church Order? Do we read the Church Order in a formal, or even a formalistic way?

Do we say, when something is not literally mentioned in the Church Order, that the matter is out of order, and that we have nothing to do with it? It is an easy way to say: "inadmissible!" But is this correct? My answer is: no! We have to read the Church Order with an open Bible and we have to apply the admonitions of the Bible to the concrete situation in the church. This means as far as Art. 31 C.O. is concerned — the expression is again from my father — that we have to stand on *guard*. We have to examine whether decisions in the church are in conformity with God's Word, the confessions, and the Church Order or not. It is important that we keep in mind not only the literal text of the Church Order, but also the "spirit" of the Church Order. This is not something vague, something hanging in the air, but it is a matter of what I called "principles, derived from Scripture and confessions." A Church Order should never be in conflict with these principles, but must reflect them! I hope that the Rev. VanOene will reconsider his views in this respect. I also hope that the Canadian Reformed Churches will stand on guard concerning the scriptural principle of Art. 31 of the Church Order, so that no freedom and no right of any of God's children is contradicted or counteracted!

CHURCH POLITY AND CIVIL LAW

Spiritual body

When we speak about Church Polity, we should always bear in mind that the church of Jesus Christ is a *spiritual body*. This is especially important when we discuss the connection between Church Polity and Civil Law. In the Netherlands a debate was held about this topic. Last year J.R. Krol, Ll.M., who studied law and who is a crown prosecutor, published an essay entitled "A Reconnaissance around the Church Order" (Krol, 1988:227ff.). In that essay he regretted the fact that the General Synod of Kampen, 1975, did not appoint one or more lawyers to the committee for the revision of the Church Order. Says J.R. Krol, "The Reformed Churches need a thoroughly revised Church Order. For that purpose a committee of lawyers and theologians who are interested in matters of Church Polity must be established within our churches. In this committee there is then the possibility for both to discuss this revision together" (Krol, 1988:227).

A response to this essay came from W.G. de Vries in a few articles entitled "Church Order and Jurisprudence." He first reminded his readers of the fact that the most recent revision of the Church Order dated from the General Synod of Groningen-Zuid, 1978, about ten years ago, and then dealt extensively with the difference which exists between Church Polity and Civil Law. He especially pointed to the fact that in many countries Civil Law is based on the pagan Roman law. Also the Roman Catholic Church bases its Canon Law on this Roman law of nature. In this respect, the Canons of Dort, III/IV, Article 4 can be quoted: "To be sure, there is left in man after the fall, some light of nature, whereby he retains some notions about God, about natural things, and about the difference between what is honourable and shameful, and shows some regard for virtue and outward order. But he is so far from arriving at the saving knowledge of God and true conversion through this light of nature that he does not even use it properly in natural and civil matters."

W.G. de Vries continued by referring to lectures of the late F.M. ten Hoor, who was professor of Theology in Grand Rapids for many years after 1900. Ten Hoor said, "The naturalistic view of life denies the divine origin of law. It is derived from man, but not from a single man, because that should lead to individualism and should make law impossible. No, it is derived from society or the community. The state is here the source of law, also of ecclesiastical law" (De Vries, 1989:426).

I read practically the same in Ten Hoor's *Theological Encyclopedia,* his introduction on theology, dating from the year 1918. In this work Ten Hoor wrote about the theology of ecclesiology, "The Church has the right to make regulations. But these regulations must always proceed from the Scriptures, and no elements may be brought in which are in conflict with the principles which are embodied in Reformed Church Polity." In other words, there is a great difference between Church and State in this respect. "The true status of the Church is only to be known from the Scripture, and that status is in agreement with the spiritual body of Christ" (Ten Hoor, 1918:13). "It belongs to the task of Church Polity to give an exposition about the relation between Church and State. Emphasis must be put on the Church's independence from the State, and also upon the fact that the civil government has to recognize the Church and her right of property. In this respect it may not be forgotten to point out from history that whenever the government exercised its power in and over the Church, this caused incalculable damage to the Church" (Ten Hoor, 1918:14).

Luther and Calvin

In the law of nature, as followed by the Roman Catholic Canon Law, the Church is treading in the footsteps of the State. However, the Reformers of the 16th century rejected this idea completely. As for Luther, on December 10, 1520, Luther burned not only the papal bull with which the Pope had condemned and excommunicated him, but also the whole papal law, as stated in the *Corpus Juris Canonici,* the whole collection of Roman ecclesiastical laws. It is no wonder that lawyers of that time opposed Luther's act. Unfortunately, after Luther the lawyers won the battle, and the result was that the churches again became dependent on the State in several countries, especially in Germany.

As for Calvin, it is well-known that the Reformer of Geneva had a lifelong struggle with the State regarding the rights of the church. Calvin stressed very much the *spiritual* character of Church Polity. He often used the term *disciplina,* not only for what we call church discipline, but also for the care for the souls. In this matter not only the office-bearers are involved, but also all the members of the congregation. Calvin never argued in a formal, let alone, a formalistic way, so that, for instance, because of faults in the procedure a whole matter of "disciplina" could be blocked. He always stressed the matter of the care for the souls. The specific nature of Church Polity is then that discipline is to be executed. "It is something else than the law of nature, civil law, law of societies or whatever."

It is interesting to quote Calvin's introduction on church discipline:
Necessity and nature of church discipline
        The discipline of the church, the discussion of which we have deferred to this place, must be treated briefly, that we may thereafter pass to the remaining topics. Discipline depends for the most part upon the power of the keys and upon *spiritual jurisdiction.* To understand it better, let us divide the church into two chief orders: clergy and people. I call by the usual name "clergy" those who perform the public ministry in the church. We shall first speak of common discipline, to which all ought to submit; then we shall come to the clergy, who, besides the common discipline, have their own.
        But because some persons, in their hatred of discipline, recoil from its very name, let them understand this: if no society, indeed, no house which has even a small family can be kept in proper condition without discipline, it is much more

necessary in the church, whose condition should be as ordered as possible. Accordingly, *as the saving doctrine of Christ is the soul of the church, so does discipline serve as its sinews, through which the members of the body hold together, each in its own place.* Therefore, all who desire to remove discipline or to hinder its restoration — whether they do this deliberately or out of ignorance — are surely contributing to the ultimate dissolution of the church. For what will happen if each is allowed to do what he pleases? Yet that would happen, if to the preaching of doctrine there were not added private admonitions, corrections, and other aids of the sort that sustain doctrine and do not let it remain idle. Therefore, discipline is like a bridle to restrain and tame those who rage against the doctrine of Christ; or like a spur to arouse those of little inclination; and also sometimes like a father's rod to chastise mildly and with the gentleness of Christ's Spirit those who have more seriously lapsed. When, therefore, we discern frightful devastation beginning to threaten the church because there is no concern and no means of restraining the people, necessity itself cries out that a remedy is needed. Now, this is the sole remedy that Christ has enjoined and the one that has always been used among the godly [Italics added, K.D.] (Calvin, *Institutes*, IV, 12, 1).

Calvin speaks about a *spiritual* jurisdiction. For him the ecclesiastical law has its own nature. That has to do with the "Spiritual order which our Lord has taught us in His Word," according to what we confess in Article 30 of the Belgic Confession. The French text gives, "selon la *police spirituelle*," and the Latin text: "*spirituali illa politia*."

Service

In this way Reformed Church Polity was set up as a spiritual order. It was stated already in Emden, 1571, and confirmed at Dort, 1618/19, in the presbyterial Church Order. "The church is the subordinate of its Personal Head, the living and present Jesus Christ. The presbyterial church government is then, according to the principles of the Church Order of Dort, the ministration of the *one* supremacy of the *one* Head, Jesus Christ, in His church as *one* body" (Van der Walt, 1976:170ff.).

There is one keyword in the whole matter of church government, namely, *service*. The office-bearers, and also the members of the church have to serve Jesus Christ, the only King of the church, and they have to serve each other. This is what Christ Himself taught His disciples and also the church of all ages: "The kings of the Gentiles exercise lordship over them; and those in authority over them are called benefactors. But not so with you; rather let the greatest among you become as the youngest, and the leader as one who serves (Luke 22:24 ff.). Christ Himself gave the great example: ". . . I am among you as one who serves" (verse 27).

No Church Polity?

So Church Polity (and also the Church Order) has a *spiritual* character, because the church of God is a spiritual body. Not the light of nature, but the light of God's Word must guide the church, also in this respect.

But there are people who say that actually church and law form an impossible combination and that the church must therefore get rid of the whole idea of Church Polity.

A representative of this idea was Rudolph Sohm, who was a Lutheran professor of law in several places, but by the end of the 19th and the beginning of the 20th century taught at Leipzig in Germany. He said: If then the church has a spiritual character, why was Church Polity introduced? The term is actually contradictory. The date that it was introduced was the date the church fell into sin. Sohm had three arguments in support of this view:

1. Law as such is formal, but in Christ's church the matter upon which everything depends is whether or not there is agreement with God's Word and will.
2. Law as such implies the obligation that everyone has to bow before it. It also compels those who are unwilling; but in Christ's church free obedience, which arises from love and which does not even have the slightest idea of compulsion, alone is important.
3. Law as such belongs to the world, to what is destined for earthly life; but the church of Christ is spiritual and the complete structure of the church is in accordance with it (cf. Oldenhuis, 1977:10ff.).

Already in 1894, at the occasion of the transfer of his rectorate at the Free University of Amsterdam, the "father" of the Church Polity of the Doleantie, F.L. Rutgers, disproved these arguments.

Rutgers' response can be summarized by saying that he argued in the first place that law in its original quality is not in conflict with the nature of the church. In the beginning there was a perfect harmony between church and law. The visible church on earth consists of believers who want to live on the basis of the Word of God alone. These believers are not perfect, but afflicted with many failures, just like all mankind. The brokenness of life made Church Polity indispensable for the well-being of the earthly church. The peculiarity of Church Polity is that it is explicitly subordinate to the nature of the church. Although Church Polity as such is not in conflict with the nature of the church, and it is even impossible for the church to exist without it, nevertheless Sohm's criticism on several hierarchical and collegial systems of Church Polity are of value. *If Church Polity loses its serving function, it becomes a disturbing factor which deforms and disorders the church* [italics added, K.D.] (Rutgers, 1894:37).

Principles of the Scriptures for Church Polity

Later, in the struggle of the church around the "vrijmaking" S. Greijdanus also argued in the line of F.L. Rutgers. Church Polity is possible, indeed, but we have to bear in mind that Christ alone is the Head of the church. The church is the Lord's particular possession. We have to regulate all our ecclesiastical actions according to the revealed will of God. Christ is the chief Shepherd. Men can only be shepherds if they remain in Him. But, all ecclesiastical action of office-bearers or assemblies should be tested by the Word of God. The church is a *spiritual* unity under Christ the Head. Apart from the apostles, the Lord did not give general, regional, provincial, national or ecumenical office-bearers. The local church has received office-bearers from God Himself, not by common consent. They are servants of the Lord, and they may serve also God's people.

S. Greijdanus elaborated on some principles, especially with respect to the relation between consistories and major assemblies, and he wrote at the end, "The Lord knows the desire for hierarchy and for tyranny, also among those who are His, also under religious attire, also among the guides of the Church, even among His apostles. But He condemned it and He forbade His disciples to yield to it. 'But you are not to be called rabbi, for you have one teacher, and you are all brethren' (Matt. 23:8)" (Greijdanus, n.d.:41).

No legalism

To stress the spiritual character of Church Polity also means that we may not go the way of *legalism*. W.G. de Vries pointed especially to that danger in a second article in *De Reformatie* about "Church Order and Jurisprudence." I quote, ". . . when we would receive in our Church Order all kinds of water-tight formulations, with exact description of rights and competences and exceptions, then the danger of legalism comes up, according to my opinion." In connection with this, he quotes F.L. Rutgers again, who wrote in another brochure about the federation of the churches in the beginning of the 17th century in the struggle with the Arminians: "The federation of Churches was upheld by maintaining the common confession of the Churches; but it was thrown out of action, where it was necessary to preserve the pure confession; it was broken, where deviation from the confession had already undone it" (De Vries, 1989:447).

Juridical view?

In a third article in *De Reformatie*, W.G. de Vries paid special attention to what he called a *juridical view* on the Church Order. He points to a danger in this respect. He wrote that the Church Order is there "in order to protect the confession. Therefore, the Church Order does not need to deliver all kinds of water-tight descriptions. After all, also the Reformed confession does not know juridical systematics. . . ." (De Vries, 1989:470).

De Vries added that it is precisely an advantage that neither the confession nor the Church Order delivers juridical views. He gave the example of question and answer 74 of the Heidelberg Catechism. "Lord's Day 27 says that the infants are grafted into the Christian church 'by baptism.' One who reasons in a juridical way would say:'so, before baptism they were not members of the church.' However, the baptismal questions to the parents demands from them the confession that our children are sanctified in Christ and *thus* as members of His Church ought to be baptized. So, baptism seals that what was present already. Besides, Lord's Day 27 starts with the statement that 'infants as well as adults belong to God's covenant and congregation' and that therefore they should be baptized too. No juridical systematics, but warm words of the covenant concerning membership of the Church."

I would like to add to that that the same happens in connection with the membership of adults who are baptized. The third question which is to be answered by the adult is in the second part: "Believing in Him, do you confess that you receive the remission of sins in His blood and that by the power of the Holy Spirit you have become a member of Jesus Christ and His Church?" He who reasons in a juridical way would say: apparently the person concerned *was* already a member of the church; hence the church must in this case be the invisible church. That is a reasoning just the other way around than in the case of baptism of infants. I even once heard someone build upon this matter a whole theory about the church. But again, we hear here warm words of God's covenant about the whole matter of membership of the church. The brother or sister who is to be baptized as an adult is not considered in a formal, legalistic way, but is considered as belonging to Christ's church. The consistory had contact with the brother or sister concerned and allowed him or her to make profession of faith and to be baptized.

Our conclusion is that we must not read the Church Order or the liturgical forms in a juridical, but in a pastoral way, and that we must not mix up Church Polity and Civil Law. If we would do that, it would become a very dangerous situation for the church.

Church before the court

Last time I warned against mixing Church Polity and Civil Law. I promised to point to a concrete case in which these two were indeed mixed up. It happened in the Netherlands this year. *Nederlands Dagblad (ND)* of Feb. 11, 1989, reported that a 27-year-old man took the consistory of the "Christelijke Gereformeerde Kerk" at Ede to court in Arnhem. In his accusation he complained that he had been wronged by the consistory. He was a baptized member of the church and he had wanted to withdraw from the church. His reproach was that the consistory had not struck out his name from the membership rolls, immediately when he had requested that. After that he had asked the consistory to give him his attestation. The consistory did not comply with this request, but acted according to the rules of the Church Order. Afterwards the consistory let him know that the man could receive a declaration in which it could be mentioned that his name had been removed as a baptized member of the congregation. Indeed, this declaration was provided. The following Sunday the withdrawal was announced to the congregation and the matter was also mentioned in prayer. Shortly after that the man threatened to bring the matter before the court. He enlisted a lawyer's services and demanded corrections in the prayer and in the letter written by the consistory to him personally in connection with his choice. As far as that letter is concerned, he especially took offence at the passage which said that withdrawal was not only a matter of administration, but that it involves contempt of baptism as a sign of God's covenant. Actually three parties were summoned before the court: the congregation, the consistory, and the minister of the church.

Encroachment?

The *ND* of Feb. 17, 1989, reported on the court session held at Arnhem the day before. The plantiff's lawyer was of the opinion that no condition could be made in the case of withdrawal. He also stated that the prayer of the minister in which the man had been committed to God, was an encroachment on the personal sphere of life and on the right of privacy. The church's lawyer, however, claimed that this was not a civil dispute and that therefore the civil judge was not allowed to pass judgment. In this case, the internal ecclesiastical law is applicable. The defendant's lawyer also said that actually the plantiff wanted to silence the church. He wanted to forbid the church to say that withdrawal from the church is to be put on a par with disparaging baptism. As far as the prayer in the church is concerned, a civil judge may not pass sentence on that. It is a different matter to have an opinion about it. But prayer has its own place. It is spoken to God. The church may never be forbidden to pray for someone's conversion, repentance, and return to the church.

Sentence

The *ND* of Feb. 25, 1989, published the sentence of the court of Arnhem. The day before, the judge had condemned the "Christelijke Gereformeerde Kerk" at Ede and had ordered the church to place a correction in the church bulletin, because the interests of the baptized member who withdrew himself were not adequately taken into account. The judge did not deem it necessary that the correction of the prayer be announced in a public worship service because of the disturbing effect this would have on the whole of the worship service. But the prayer had to be corrected in the church bulletin. According to the judge, a misleading picture was given by the minister in his prayer. The consistory should have mentioned besides its own point of view also the point of view of the baptized member. This correction in the bulletin had to be made because it was practically impossible for this man to put forward his opinion. If the church did not place the correction, a penalty of 10,000 guilders was to be paid. The defendent also had to pay a sum of 1.500 guilders to the plaintiff as compensation for "immaterially" suffered damage, and finally, both parties had to pay their own costs.

Freedom of religion

What are we to say about this? In the first place: the relation between the church and its members is regulated by ecclesiastical laws, of which the matter of church discipline is a part. Church polity is beyond civil law. That is the consequence of freedom of religion. Those who are not members of the church have nothing to do with church polity. Over against them the church has to stick to the rules of civil law. A withdrawal from the church is a matter of transition from the one situation to the other. But the judge has to acknowledge that in that situation the matter of freedom of religion has still a strong impact.

But the judge came to a different conclusion. He based himself with respect to this on the letter, written at the moment that the man was still a member of the church. The consistory, however, rightly said that the service of God is not to be separated from membership of the church. Therefore the minister could pray for his conversion in connection with the announcement of withdrawal. This minister did not go too far. His office of supervision and discipline implies also his coming to his own conclusion on the basis of someone's confession and conduct. Neither that conclusion of the minister nor the consistory, nor the declaration of the member about himself lends itself to examination by an outsider, in this case the secular judge. In a comment entitled "Pulpit-prayer" the editor of *ND*, Dr. J.P. de Vries wrote: "The opinion of the consistory about someone's confession and conduct is usually not mentioned in public. The only firm exception is the execution of church discipline in the last phases. He who withdraws himself from the church, himself commits a public deed, about which the church may give its opinion, also in public. The fact that for such a person concrete intercession is made, belongs to the calling of the church. If a judge is going to judge that prayer on the point whether or not justice is done to the person mentioned in it, then he steps into affairs which do not belong to his competence. The question whether a misleading image was given of the motives of the former baptized member, is a confessional matter and the judge may not judge that. If somebody is of the opinion that he is wronged in a pulpit prayer, then the federation of churches has its own ways of appeal. As long as they are still open, the wordly judge should declare himself incompetent. Only if the federation would declare the complaint inadmissible because he is not a member of the church any more, he can go to the civil judge. But that possibility was not even investigated in this case" (ND, Feb. 25, 1989).

Appeal

What was the consistory of the Christelijke Gereformeerde Kerk at Ede to do now? Did it have to give in and place a correction in the bulletin of the church? Or did it have to appeal? A very important matter is here at stake. The court presumed to give an opinion in an ecclesiastical case, a matter of Church Polity. I am of the opinion that the court's judgment was very arrogant and overbearing. It involved itself with prayers, addressed to God Himself. This would create a precedent, and in this way the church could be hindered by the state in all kinds of affairs. This is what the consistory at Ede also considered. It took several hours before the consistory made a decision.

The minister of the church declared to *ND*: "It was not easy to make a decision. What would best serve the honour of the LORD and the coming of His kingdom? We had to consider that question time and again" (ND, March 11, 1989). The care for the souls, for the whole congregation stood in the forefront. The consistory considered this a primary responsibility. It may be that a consistory suffers injustice because of it. This consideration was completely in agreement with the attitude of the consistory over against the baptized member and the pulpit prayer. On the other hand, the consistory understood very well that the acceptance of this sentence could have consequences for the future. The whole matter of a precedent is very important. So finally the consistory decided to appeal. It will take some time before this appeal to the higher court of Arnhem leads to a sentence.

Very dangerous

I hoped wholeheartedly that the sentence of Arnhem's court will be nullified. Imagine what can happen if this sentence functions as a precedent for other cases. A very dangerous situation could come up. Imagine that a member of the church committed abortion or euthanasia, and that the consistory of the church censures such a person. Then that person would be able to bring the consistory before the court and complain that he or she was wronged and discriminated against. The church still says: this was against the law of the LORD, you shall not kill. But it was allowed by the civil law! Now the church could be condemned and could be forced to stop church discipline and even be compelled to give corrections, because of the supposed discrimination. But unfortunately, the *Nederlands Dagblad* of June 17, 1989, reported that the appeal of both parties in the case of a former non-communicant member of the "Christelijke Gereformeerde Kerk" of Ede was cancelled. Pending the appeal the consistory did not have to correct the pulpit prayer in which was said that the non-communicant member had turned his back to the church. Now both parties reached an understanding of compromise. According to a special *Act,* however, both parties maintain in an unabridged way their points of view and their convictions. The agreement means that no correction will be made from the side of the consistory. But judicially the requirement for correction is maintained, although the former non-communicant member no longer demands the execution of the sentence. In a letter to the members of the congregation the consistory hopes and prays that this agreement may lead to peace and unity in the congregation. In the decision the interests of the congregation had been given priority by the consistory.

I think this decision is unsatisfactory. The sentence of the judge is still maintained. Although it is just one sentence of a judge of a lower court, nevertheless it can have consequences. Especially this question is at stake: can secular judges pass sentence on matters concerning the worship services of the church? Now a precedent is not excluded and the whole matter as such is not solved. We have to maintain: Church Polity and Civil Law are two different matters, not to be mixed up!

TRUE ECUMENICITY

Ecumene

The word *ecumene* is used about fifteen times in the New Testament and means "the whole world." Some examples are ". . . *all the world* should be enrolled" (Luke 2:1); the devil showed Jesus Christ "all the kingdoms of the *world*" (Luke 4:5), according to the Acts of the Apostles, Artemis was worshiped by "all Asia and the *world*" (Acts 19:27); in Revelation 12:9 Satan is called "the deceiver of the *whole world*." Striking are the examples of the connection between mission and ecumene, as Matthew 24:14, ". . . this gospel of the kingdom will be preached throughout the *whole world*," and Romans 10:18, "Their voice has gone out to all the earth, and their words to the end of the *world*." Again and again for "world" or "the whole world" the word *ecumene* is used. The root of this word is *oikos*, which means *house*. So *ecumene* actually means "the inhabited world, the world where people are living."

Thinking ecumenically should not be left to the world or to apostate communities, for it is a matter which no less concerns the true church. The church has a mandate which concerns the whole world, the whole inhabited world, for the whole world is the church's mission field. In fact, we speak this ecumenical language each and every Sunday in our public worship services. The late Prof. Dr. K. Schilder pointed to this fact in a speech addressed in 1951 to the League of Young Women's Societies in the Netherlands:

All of you speak "ecumenical language," every Sunday. Then you confess, with the church of all places: I believe a holy, catholic, Christian church. And "catholic" has the same meaning as "ecumenical." The "ecumene" means "the entire inhabited world"; therefore "ecumenical" means: "pertaining to the entire cultural world" or "concerning the entire human race." In your *Book of Praise* you can find an ecumenical heirloom, the Nicene Creed, which dates back to the so-called first Ecumenical Council of 325. There the Arians were condemned as well as the Cathari (or Novatians); who could, so it says, not join the ecumenical church if they did not agree with the dogmas — that's what it says — of the universal and catholic church. Stipulations were also made concerning the so-called baptism of heretics.

We, too, speak an ecumenical language. But that means also that we have to keep in mind "the entire inhabited world" as far as the church is concerned, and to strive for unity with those who have the same faith as we have.

Striving for unity

Is striving for unity good? It definitely is. Christ Himself prayed in His moving high-priestly prayer, "I do not pray for these only, but also for those who believe in Me through their word, that they may all be one; even as Thou, Father, art in Me, and I in Thee, that they also may be in Us, so that the world may believe that Thou hast sent Me" (John 17:20, 21). Paul, in his epistle to the Ephesians, which sometimes is called "the epistle of the church," exhorts his readers to be "eager to maintain the unity of the Spirit in the bond of peace. There is one body and one Spirit, just as you were called to the one hope that belongs to your call, one Lord, one faith, one baptism, one God and Father of us all, who is above all and through all and in all" (Ephesians 4:3-6).

Unity of faith

Whoever seeks the unity of the church and strives for unity among God's people, desires a good thing.

However, what character does this unity bear and what is meant by it?

When Christ spoke about unity in His high-priestly prayer He did not only mean an outward unity, but He founded that unity in the unity which exists between the Father and the Son: the closest and firmest communion that there is.

When Paul wrote to the Ephesians that they should be eager to maintain the unity of the Spirit in the bond of peace, he also pointed to the one Lord and the one faith that bound them together. When the Heidelberg Catechism speaks about the one holy catholic church, we read that the Son of God gathers for Himself a church in the unity of the true faith, and that bond is expressed in the creeds, which are also called the "ecumenical symbols," and in the Reformed confessions.

Reality and caricature

So the point is to clearly and plainly separate reality from caricature. Like the true ecumene in essence has nothing to do with today's ecumenical movement, the true unity is equally far remote from the false striving for unity that is pursued today.

The present-day ecumenical movement wants to force a unity which is not founded in the unity of faith, but which shows, with a minimum of foundation, a maximum of joining hands. But sooner or later such a building must fall. He who pays hardly any attention to the foundation, but who wants to let a colossal skyscraper arise, should not be astonished when it appears after a short time that such a building cannot possibly last.

Then one does not get the reality, but a caricature. And a caricature is an exaggeration or magnification of some most characteristic forms, traits or qualities. But these characteristics of ecumenism are exactly its weaknesses. Whoever reads the last book of the Bible sees Satan, in the figure of anti-Christ, busy in creating the anti-church, through which the great mass is fascinated, says Revelation chapter 13. Does not Paul say that Christ will slay the man of sin with the breath of His mouth? (2 Thessalonians 2:8)

In this light we should therefore look at present-day ecumenism. We should judge this striving and this movement by the Scriptures. That also means: we should not become introverted and strange. But we should propagate antithetically the true ecumene and the true unity, and in this distinguish clearly between reality and caricature.

Antithesis

It is very important, therefore, to maintain the scriptural idea of *antithesis* when we are thinking about the ecumene. I quote again the speech of Dr. K. Schilder:

No wonder that the Bible is full of the ecumenical proclamation of the Great Ecumenical drama. Ecumenical is not a new term but a very old one. The Jews already had transcribed the Greek word "oikoumene" in their rabbinical scriptures untranslated, in Hebrew letters. Luke starts the Christmas message with the ecumene: Caesar Augustus wants the ecumene registered for the Roman Empire, the Beast of Daniel, and of Revelation; but from a stable in Bethlehem, at that very moment the Great Son of David starts to "register" the ecumene for himself, and for the God-of-David.

Ecumene is then the inhabited world, viewed as the operative area of world politics. The Beast grasps at the latter: but the Spirit has been ahead of him for centuries, when He had David anointed as king of the birthplace of theocracy, i.e., as king of Israel's ecumenically directed community, keeping the ecumenical seas of the world pure. Jesse's living-room, where David was anointed, and the stable of Bethlehem, from where the Son of David starts His world regiment, are the stages of God's ecumenical Movement, a movement as old as the world ruled by God's Covenant. Emperor Nero, who in the Revelation of John is an image of the ecumenical anti-Christ, is called Ecumenical Daemon in Greek emperor's titles, just as Emperor Claudius is called Ecumenical Benefactor, or Saviour.

"Ecumenical" here has become a matter of world politics and world culture. Therefore Scripture commands ecumenical preaching (Matt. 24:14). Over against the Satanical temptation of ecumenical world power, Christ places the "it is written"; He wants to become the Ecumenical Saviour-Judge only through obedience (Luke 4:5). Christ predicts an ecumenical temptation in the last days (Rev. 3:10), and catastrophe (Luke 21:26); and thus the prophet Agabus predicts an ecumenical famine (Acts 11:28). In that, he is an ally of John on Patmos who, at the opening of the third seal, sees the black horse of famine dash across the world (Rev. 8:5,6). All this is the beginning of the ecumenical judgement (Acts 17:31).

In short: the Bible continually, from Genesis to Revelation, speaks about the one great ecumenical Drama. On the one side is the ecumenical preaching (Rom. 10:18, Ps. 19:4); on the other side is the ecumenical error, the ecumenical temptation under leadership of the anti-Christ, God's great adversary, with his "catholic," i.e., universal, propaganda service, with his ecumenical contraspeech against the Speech of God and against all his sayings. . . .

That is why the church will find her first task forever in the proclaiming of that centuries-old antithesis. She does not tolerate a break-through with false slogans of unity between those parties who have believed the biblical antithesis, or at least have acknowledge it, but she wants a breakthrough, with the sharp weapon of that biblical antithesis, among all groups and all movements, also the ecumenical church movement without creeds, also the ecumenical youth movement, which have denied and ridiculed the biblical idea of antithesis, and cursed it as the greatest folly and fragmenting force.

God's Word is the norm

It is very clear that God's Word is the norm for our ecumenical thinking and acting. We agree completely with what was written by the Dutch Committee for Churches Abroad:

Speaking of ecumenical calling we are dealing with a calling which, as coming from God, is obeyed only in the way of paying close attention to the divine rules prescribed for its execution. It is this norm which shapes its course and defines the limits which must be observed in the pursuit of its goal. Any other way of dealing with this calling is self-willed and fraught with danger to the church of Christ.

So we are left with the question: what is this norm?

A significant indication with regard to the nature of true ecumenicity is to be found in the truth that ecumenicity deals with and aims at unity in Christ. It is this unity which is both its starting point and its goal. Ecumenical endeavour is not what it claims to be if it does not engage in making visible the relationship which exists in Christ between such as believe in Him. According to Scripture the unity in Christ is primarily a given unity. It is the gift of the exalted Saviour to the people which the Lord has made Himself to a peculiar treasure.

This unity is a spiritual unity, given with and in the calling with which they, who have been given to Christ by the Father, are called. However, they who have been brought together in Him must also obediently come together in Him. They should endeavour to keep the unity of the Spirit in the bond of peace, for there is one body and one Spirit. The fact that the unity in Christ is a given one does not exclude that there is a command to strive for it. The gift is at the same time an order.

Furthermore, the very fact, that the unity of the believers is a given unity, is an indication of the norm which must be observed in dealing with the ecumenical

195

calling. Christ is the life, but He is also the way and the truth. In being the life He is the source and power of the bond which links all believers to Him and at the same time interlinks them one to another. In Him, being the way, the true believers find the way to their unity in Him. In addition to all this the unity in Christ is a unity in Him as the truth. So it is quite evident from Scripture that the unity in Christ is made manifest in a unanimous and faithful confession of the truth.

Not all unity is scriptural

The conclusion is evident that not all unity of churches is scriptural. I quote again the brochure *For the Sake of True Ecumenicity.*

He, who in the name of unity wishes to maintain the teacher of error in the congregation, violates the unity in Christ. Likewise he, who exerts himself to reach unity with teachers of false doctrine, is making efforts for a unity which is not agreeable to the Lord, though he may do so claiming devotedness to ecumenical vocation. An unfaithful teacher proclaims another gospel, which is no gospel, and the apostle Paul writes concerning such a man: "let him be accursed" (Gal. 1:6-9; 5:10).

Essentially we find here the same as what is said with regard to the high priest Eli and the curse he brought upon his own house and upon Israel, when with words only he tried to correct his ungodly sons, Hophni and Phinehas, but did not take measures to purify the service of the tabernacle from what defiled it. Did not the Lord say then: "Wherefore honourest thou thy sons above Me?" And also: "Those that honour Me I will honour, and they that despise Me shall be lightly esteemed"! (1 Sam. 2:29, 30).

All Christians, however, who exert themselves to attain the binding of all to the truth of Christ, strive for the true unity in Him. They indeed build upon the foundation of the apostles and prophets, of which Christ Himself is the chief cornerstone. In the light of all this scriptural evidence the rule for complying with the ecumenical calling is the biblical mandate of unanimous and honest acceptance of the Lord's holy and infallible Word (Eph. 2:20).

Confessional standards

We have to say also that the confessions of the church are very important in connection with true ecumenicity. Prof. K. Schilder pointed already to the "ecumenical creeds." In the brochure of the Dutch Committee we read about the confessional standards:

In the continuing struggle to keep their congregations in the unity of Christ the Reformed churches of various countries have obtained their confessional standards. They have received these standards as a gift from the hand of God, for it was He, who enlightened them through the working of the Holy Spirit to recapitulate in thankfulness and obedience what they first had found in Scripture. Subsequently these standards served them as an agreement of fellowship in the Lord and Saviour.

These Reformed churches continued to accept and defend their standards as being fully in conformity with the truth revealed unto us by God in His word.

This attitude toward their confessional writings will strongly influence the manner in which Reformed churches meet the ecumenical calling. They are not permitted to forget their allegiance to their standards when contacts are made with churches abroad. If, more or less, they would forget, then not only no justice is done to what in their own congregations is maintained as divine truth, but also, sooner or later within these churches the loyalty to their standards will be endangered.

Any confessional standard, which is no longer always and everywhere dealt with in all seriousness, is by that very fact undermined and drained of its vitality and power of being a binding consensus.

It is for this reason that ecumenical fellowship is possible only when cooperating churches can honestly declare with regard to each other's confessional standards, that they are in conformity with the Word of God. In no other way can form be given to the obedience to the first rule of true ecumenicity, that it shall serve unity in truth.

There is, however, more to be said here. The churches, cooperating in ecumenical fellowship, must also have the mutual confidence that they all sincerely maintain their standards and live up to them. In all these churches there must be an unreserved and reliable subscription to the standards. They have to make sure that in all these churches there is faithful doctrinal discipline, in order that the unity of faith be maintained against error and also that the flock of Christ be protected.

From all these considerations it follows that if any of the cooperating churches might become deficient with regard to doctrine or doctrinal discipline the other churches shall give attention to their first obligation: to induce this church to return immediately to the first love and the first works. No partiality shall be shown in doing so. It is not important whether or not the church concerned has a large membership or a glorious and impressive past. The only thing that matters is that the unfaithful church stands in the need of correction and reformation.

If such a destitute church then does not return to sound doctrine and the use of doctrinal discipline, the other churches shall see to it that is done what they are bound to do. They shall not yield but remove that church from their fellowship. Sound doctrine is always incompatible with a lying tongue. Where falsehood in doctrine is tolerated the Lord of all truth is dishonoured and the congregation is destroyed. What communion has light with darkness? (2 Cor. 6:14).

"Let the church be one"

Not only in the Scriptures and in the confessions of the church is true ecumenicity apparent, but it is also stressed in the course of the history of the church.

In the *Didachè* or "The teaching of the Lord through the twelve apostles to the gentiles," a very old document already known to the church fathers and at least going back to the second century, this prayer is found in connection with the Lord's Supper: "As this piece (of bread) was scattered over the hills and then was brought together and made one, so let your Church be brought together from the ends of the earth into your Kingdom. For yours is the glory and the power through Jesus Christ forever."

We have a rhymed version of this part of the *Didachè* in our *Book of Praise*, namely, in Hymn 46:

> "As grain, once scattered on the hillsides,
> Was in the broken bread made one,
> So from all lands Thy church be gathered
> Into Thy kingdom by Thy Son."

Reformation times

From the very beginning the Reformers of the 16th century emphasized the unity of the church. Already in 1518 Luther spoke in favour of a general council of the church, with the one principle that the Holy Scriptures would be the decisive norm. He asked for such a "free, general, Christian council." By "free" he meant independent of papal control, and by "Christian" he understood that judgments were to be based on the principle of the Scriptures alone and that laymen were to be enfranchised. In 1520, after the ban of the pope, he renewed his appeal for a general council. But when finally a general council was held, starting in 1545 at Trent, it was only a papal council. . . .

Also Calvin was in favour of a general council, but he strongly stressed the difference between true and false councils. The condition for a true general council is that Christ would be presiding it:

Now it is Christ's right to preside over all councils and to have no man share His dignity. But I say that He presides only when the whole assembly is governed by His Word and Spirit.

In the following paragraph Calvin continues:

Christ will be in the midst of a council only if it is gathered together in His name. As a consequence, it will benefit our adversaries but little to mention councils of bishops a thousand times over; nor will they persuade us to believe what they contend — that councils are governed by the Holy Spirit — before they convince us that these have been gathered in Christ's name. Ungodly and evil bishops can just as much conspire against Christ as good and honest ones can come together in His name. We have clear proof of this fact in a great many decrees that have come forth from such councils. . . .

I now reply with but one word: Christ promises nothing except to those who are gathered in His name. Let us therefore define what that means. I deny that they are gathered in His name who, casting aside God's commandment that forbids anything to be added or taken away from His Word (Deut. 4:2; cf. Deut. 12:32; Prov. 30:6; Rev. 22:18-19), ordain anything according to their own decision; who, not content with the oracles of Scripture, that is, the sole rule of perfect wisdom, concoct some novelty out of their own heads. Surely, since Christ promised that He would be present not in all councils whatsoever but laid down a special mark by which a true and lawful one might be distinguished from the rest, it behooves us never to neglect this distinction. This is the covenant which God of old made with the Levitical priests, that they should teach from His own lips (Mal. 2:7). He required this always of the prophets; we see that this rule was also imposed upon the apostles. Those who violate this covenant God deems worthy neither of the honor of the priesthood nor of any authority.

Calvin strived for the unity of the church with all his power. In a letter to Thomas Cranmer he wrote in 1552:

. . . would that it were attainable to bring together into some place, from various Churches, men eminent for their learning, and that after having carefully discussed the main points of belief one by one, they should, from their united judgments, hand down to posterity the true doctrine of Scripture. This other thing also is to be ranked among the chief evils of our time, viz., that the Churches are so divided, that human fellowship is scarcely now in any repute amongst us, far less that Christian intercourse which all make a profession of, but few sincerely practise. If men of learning conduct themselves with more reserve than is seemly, the very heaviest blame attaches to the leaders themselves, who, either engrossed in their own sinful pursuits, are indifferent to the safety and entire piety of the church, or who, individually satisfied with their own private peace, have no regard for others. Thus it is that the members of the Church being severed, the body lies bleeding.

So much does this concern me, that, could I be of any service, I would not grudge to cross even ten seas, if need were, on account of it.

More than once Calvin wrote movingly about the divisions of the church. He called them the "horrible mutilations of Christ's body," and the Geneva Catechism made it quite plain that this body ought to be "one."

In 1560 the well-known Catharina de Medici undertook the initiative towards a kind of national council in France. It was called "The Colloquy of Poissy" and Theodore de Bèze delivered an excellent defense of the Reformed faith, but the result was disappointing and not long afterwards the Romish caused a massacre among the Reformed.

Besides the attempt of Thomas Cranmer in the same year that Calvin wrote his letter to him (1552), three other attempts for an international, ecumenical synod were made. H.H. Kuyper pointed to these attempts in his farewell lecture in 1937, entitled *De Katholiciteit der Gereformeerde Kerken (the Catholicity of the Reformed Churches)*. There was in the first place the attempts of Queen Elisabeth in 1577, and, in connection with it, the Convention of Frankfurt with as its fruit the *Harmonia Confessionum* (mainly the work of de Bèze). In the second place H.H. Kuyper mentioned the design of Pierre du Moulin, who raised the matter at the Synod of Tonneins in 1614 and who visited England with a view to promoting the unity of the churches. He was appointed as one of the delegates of the French Reformed churches to the Synod of Dort 1618/'19. However, the delegates from France could not attend this synod in Holland, because the French king prohibited them to leave France. Nevertheless, the Synod of Alais, 1620, accepted the Canons of Dort.

Ecumenical Synod of Dort 1618/'19

This brings us to the Synod of Dort 1618/'19. This synod is called a national synod, but the actual work of drawing up and finishing the Canons of Dort bore an international character. There were twenty-six delegates from abroad: delegates from England (among them even a bishop) and from Germany and Switzerland; from the Palatinate, Hessen, Basel, Bern, Emden, Nassau, Bremen, Schaffhausen, Zürich, and Geneva. These foreign delegates did not function as ornaments, but had a great influence in the deliberations and upon the formulation of the decisions. They participated in the synod no less than the delegates from the Netherlands. Therefore, in this respect the Synod of Dort can be called international and ecumenical. The background of these delegates was not the same; they did not all have the same confessions, although they were of a Reformed-Presbyterian character. Nevertheless, they all worked together in the formulation of our third form of unity!

Presbyterian Scotland

After the Synod of Dort 1618/'19 a period of silence followed; no national synods were held in the Netherlands, let alone international synods. However, the Presbyterian churches of Scotland, England, and Ireland paid attention to the matter of international and ecumenical synods or councils. This had already been done in the *Scots Confession of Faith of 1560*. In Article 20 this confession says that "generall counsalles" are to be revered and embraced, unless they "pretend to forge unto us new artickles of our faith, . . . or to make constitutionis repugning to the worde of God." This was also done in the *Second Book of Discipline*, drawn up by Andrew Melville, in which an ecumenical synod was mentioned in so many words. Also the Westminster Assembly paid attention to it in the *Form of Presbyterial Church Government* of 1645.

In the nineteenth century it was again Scotland which took up the matter. The

Presbyterians hoped to present an alliance of *churches* in the *Evangelical Alliance* of 1846. But that alliance had a different, more personal character. Besides, they were much involved in the *Alliance of Reformed and Presbyterian Churches* which met also with the approval of the Secedued Churches of the Netherlands. So, in the 19th century as well the Free Church of Scotland had a worldwide view!

Secession churches

Scotland saw the Disruption of 1843 (the beginning of the Free Church of Scotland), while nine years earlier the Secession started in the Netherlands.

The churches of the Secession of 1834 had the same worldwide view. The act of Secession of 1834 showed the true ecumenical intention by saying that "the undersigned want to unite themselves with any assembly based on God's infallible Word in whatever place God has established it." The people of the Secession were not narrow-minded; they had good insight into true ecumenicity. I quote what J. Faber said in his speech *The Significance of the Secession of 1834 in the light of our confession of the Holy Catholic Church:*

In the beginning period before the establishing of the school in Kampen they sent young men to Geneva to attend lectures of Merel d'Aubigné and Malan, men of the Swiss Reveil. The Synod of Leiden, 1857, sought ecclesiastical fellowship with the Free Church of Scotland and with the Reformed confessors in the Republic of Transvaal. And who does not know that in 1858 the Rev. Dirk Postma was sent to South Africa to be instrumental in the reformation of the church in that part of the world? The existence and the life of the so-called Dopper churches in South Africa, the Dutch Reformed Church, is connected with the Secession of 1834. Deputies of the United Presbyterian Church of Scotland visited Kampen, and Brummelkamp and Van Velzen were delegated to Scotland. Already at the Synod of Hoogeveen in 1860 the churches of the Secession received official delegates of the United Presbyterian Church of Scotland. Brummelkamp Jr. writes that the seceded church of the Netherlands then and later owed much to its correspondence with the Scottish brethren who already possessed a rich experience.

In 1868 three Christelijke Gereformeerde ministers attended the International Theological Conference in Wezel. In 1877 Brummelkamp and Van Velzen participated in the Pan Presbyterian Council. This Council intended to establish a communion or fellowship between Presbyterial churches.

In 1875 Lucas Lindeboom wrote a brochure entitled *The Christian Reformed Church: something about its situation, calling and future.* Lindeboom, later professor in Kampen, was still minister in Zaandam. He wrote about contact with other churches. The Synod of Groningen had expressed sympathy with the Reformed Church in France. Lindeboom now urged that more fellowship should be entertained with the churches in Scotland, South Africa and America (cf. Faber, 1986:14ff.).

It is remarkable that especially in the circles of the Secession which stressed the sharp distinction between true and false church, true ecumenicity was discovered and experienced!

World Council of Churches (W.C.C.)

In 1948 the World Council of Churches (W.C.C.) started. The character of the W.C.C. is described in its Constitution as follows: "The World Council is a fellowship of churches, which accept Jesus Christ our Lord as God and Saviour." In an official declaration the W.C.C. added to this Constitution the clause that it "does not concern itself with the manner in which the Churches will interpret the foundation." In other words, when becoming a member of the W.C.C. a "denomination" must agree with the foundation, at least officially, but how it reads and explains that foundation is up to that "denomination" itself. The W.C.C. does not want to concern itself with the "interpretation." Not many words need to be wasted on the completely ambiguous, and therefore unbiblical character of this foundation, which, because of the arbitrariness of its interpretation, can be subscribed to by even the most liberal and sectarian group. This, in fact is done. It would be difficult to be more unbiblical for an organization which claims to be a community of faith. It can hardly be more misleading. In the course of time the W.C.C. continued in its liberal direction of modern theology in which Jesus Christ is no more than a good example of solidarity.

International Council of Christian Churches (I.C.C.C.)

In the same year 1948 the "opponent" of the W.C.C. was born, the International Council of Christian Churches (I.C.C.C.). The foundation seems to appeal to us very much: the plenary Divine inspiration of the Scriptures in the original languages, their consequent inerrancy and infallibility, and, as the Word of God, the supreme and final authority in faith and life; the holiness and love of the one and Triune sovereign God, Father, Son, and Holy Spirit; the essential, absolute, eternal Deity and the real and proper but sinless humanity of our Lord Jesus Christ; corruption of man; salvation of the redeemed and the everlasting suffering of the lost; those are just some doctrinal points from the Constitution of the I.C.C.C.

But however solid the foundation seems to be: concerning the criteria of being a church, it is silent in three languages. The whole church problem is obviated. They think in terms of a spiritual unity across the church walls: the Baptist can remain Baptist, the Methodist can remain Methodist, etc. So that means that neither the sacraments nor church discipline is mentioned.

Not only the Baptists were admitted, which reject God's covenant with us and our children, but they also admitted member churches, which, Arminian in creed, deny election.

In this I.C.C.C. they speak about the acceptance of the "fundamental truths of Scripture" and in fact they reduce that foundation to the Apostles' Creed. As if infant baptism, the covenant of grace, election, the conversion of man who is powerless in himself, the three marks of the true church, all would be peripheral. As if these matters should not belong to the fundamental doctrine of Scripture. To the I.C.C.C. the church seems to have one enemy only, namely communism. As if liberalism and other forms of humanism are not equally mortal enemies to the church of Christ.

Reformed Ecumenical Synod (R.E.S.)

After World War II also the "Reformed Ecumenical Synod" (R.E.S.) started.

In 1949 its first meeting was convened in Amsterdam at the initiative of the synodical churches. These churches did not participate in the W.C.C. Delegates from several Reformed and Presbyterian churches from all over the world were present. Already in 1946 a constitutional meeting of this "synod" was held in Grand Rapids, Michigan, prepared by the Christian Reformed Church in the U.S.A. The churches accepted as basis "the Holy Scripture, as interpreted in the Forms of Unity of the respective Churches who participate in this assembly." The goal was

to seek what is most subservient to the general building up of the participating churches and to give a common testimony of the faith, which was once for all delivered to the saints, and to assist each other in the maintenance of the purity of the doctrine and the reformation of life.

The synod of the (Liberated) Reformed Churches in the Netherlands of Amersfoort 1948 decided to decline the invitation to participation. Participation was considered unacceptable, because the synod had objections against the basis: the several confessions, mentioned in the basis were contradictory, according to the judgment of the synod (Art. 75, 3,A).

Another reason to decline the invitation had to do with the goal of the R.E.S. . . . The Synod of Amersfoort considered that reaching the goal of the R.E.S., "namely, 'maintaining the purity and the reformation of doctrine and life', depends first of all on the obedient and faithful proclamation of God's Word in the local churches, wherever in the world they are," but that "the churches which invited us have deviated from this obedient and faithful proclamation" (Art. 75,3,E).

The committee which delivered a report to the Synod of Groningen-South 1978 concerning contact with churches abroad added a consideration regarding basis and goal of the R.E.S. This committee pointed to the fact that the synodical churches had publicly deviated from the Reformed confessions, and were now also a member of the W.C.C. (the synodical churches had decided at the Synod of Sneek 1969/'70 to ask for membership of the W.C.C.). These W.C.C. churches contribute to funds supporting revolutionary movements. It is therefore impossible to sit at one international "synod" table together with churches which involve themselves in revolutionary activities.

At the Synod of the Reformed Churches held in Groningen-South in 1978 it was also pointed out how bad the influence could be of churches who tolerate modernism: "This evil influence by means of papers of the R.E.S. in the Christian Reformed Church is extensively shown by the deputies of the Canadian sister churches in their last appeal to the Christian Reformed Church regarding the doctrine of the Scripture" (published in 1977; see Synod of Coaldale, *Acts,* p. 102ff. [Appendix VII]).

Not only by the Reformed Churches in the Netherlands, but also by churches participating in the R.E.S., objections were raised against developments in the synodical churches. The Kosin Presbyterian Churches of Korea left the R.E.S. In 1981 the Free Church of Scotland broke with it. Objections were voiced not only against a liberal view regarding Scripture, but also against the fact that in the synodical churches homosexuals were admitted to the Lord's Table. A number of member churches of the R.E.S. asked that the membership of the synodical churches be rejected. Finally it came to a crisis at the meeting of R.E.S. in 1988 at Harare. There it was decided to maintain the membership of the synodical churches. The consequence of it was that four groups of churches suspended or cancelled their membership: the Orthodox Presbyterian Church, the Reformed Churches of New Zealand, the Christelijke Gereformeerde Kerk (the Netherlands), and the Gereformeerde Kerken (South Africa). The conclusion must be that the R.E.S. is not the solution as the way to counter the ecumenism of the W.C.C.

International Conference of Reformed Churches (I.C.R.C.)

But is there, then, no possibility for true Reformed ecumenical activity? There is! The initiative came from the deputies of the Free Reformed Churches of Australia. They asked for

an ecumenical synod, or a session of a general synod, at which all the churches could be represented: from Africa, Australia, Canada, the Netherlands and Korea. We are of the opinion that it is of great importance to have a conference together and to have oral contact as churches who stand on the same basis.

This proposal was submitted to the Synod of Groningen-South 1978. The deputies for churches abroad were of the opinion that here a matter was broached which had to be considered seriously. They were convinced of its great importance and gave some reasons for that. In this way a penetrating testimony could be given of the unity of the Reformed Churches in all five continents, over against contemporary religious leagues of churches. Besides, it could be an encouragement for the small and/or young churches abroad, who live very much isolated: to know and to recognize each other could promote the bond between the churches. There could also be cooperation in matters which the member churches have in common, such as the development of a Reformed strategy of mission over against modern liberal mission theories and practices.

The Synod of Groningen-South decided to give a mandate to new deputies for churches abroad, namely, to deliberate with the sister churches and prepare an international meeting of churches. The Synod of Arnhem 1981 made the decision that the sister churches abroad and also the churches with which contact was practised, would be invited to a constitutional meeting for the convocation of a Reformed international conference. This constitutional meeting was held in Groningen-South in 1982. The meeting adopted the name *International Conference of Reformed Churches* (I.C.R.C.). The following basis was accepted: "the Holy Scripture of the Old and New Testament, as confessed in the Three Forms of Unity and in the Westminster Standards." The I.C.R.C. will meet every four years. The Synod of Cloverdale 1983 decided that the Canadian Reformed Churches would join the I.C.R.C. The first conference was in Edinburgh 1985.

The first meeting of the International Conference of Reformed Churches took place in Edinburgh 3-10 September, 1985, and brought together *ten member* churches and observers from nine other churches. The participants came from many different countries, representative of all continents.

This being a first meeting, the discussions were largely of a theological nature, homing in on the concept of the church and the covenant in the Reformed Confessions.

While there was evident agreement on the bases of Reformed Confessions of the 16th and 17th centuries, underpinning unanimous affirmation with regard, e.g. to the Bible as the inspired and infallible Word of God and the only rule of faith and life; the Lord Jesus Christ as God and King of this world to whom all people and governments must give account: there was also recognition of difference of perspective on matters of less importance.

Conference recognized the Christian duty of securing the closest possible unity of Reformed Churches on the practical level. With this in mind, and having regard to the fact that Christ gathers His one catholic church out of all tribes, nations and peoples, there was set up a committee on Missions with a directive to investigate areas of mutual helpfulness in missions and in the training of those called to leadership in missions. Conference also appointed a committee to study the text of the three ecumenical creeds, in order to come to a common text that can be recommended to the member churches."

At the I.C.R.C. conference at Langley, British Columbia, 1989, reports concerning mission work and the text of the three ecumenical creeds were discussed. Papers were presented on the following topics: *Contextualization in Mission, Apartheid, Hermeneutics and the Gift of the Spirit, The Elder as Preserver of Life in the Covenant, Christology,* and *Nehemiah the Reformer.* In the I.C.R.C. we have a truly Reformed ecumenical organization over against its caricatures in other larger bodies. The I.C.R.C.

is not aiming for competition. It seeks to be a group of churches which want to be and to remain Reformed, churches which want to maintain the infallibility of the Word of God and to be faithful to the Reformed confessions, based upon that Word.

Are there differences between the member churches? Certainly there are. The confessions are not exactly the same. Let us not neglect that fact. There is a different historical background which is not to be denied. But let us not over-state the differences as if the one member is Reformed and the other one is not. Exaggeration is wrong. However, the differences in confession and also in church polity are to remain a matter of discussion. If there is the strong will to be and to remain Reformed churches, over against all kinds of false ecumenicity, and if we together have the strong desire to bow before the infallible Word of God, the blessing of the LORD can be expected.

Finally

True ecumenicity — is it possible? In many ecumenical organizations the antithesis is forgotten and humanism (in a new form) has taken its place. Criticism of the Bible and falsification of the Scripture mark much of today's ecumenism in an alarming way. In antithesis with the Babylon of false ecumenism, the appeal is still there: "Come out of her, My people, lest you take part in her sins, lest you share in her plagues" (Rev. 18:4). Churches who want to stand for the unabridged maintenance of God's Word and the confessions based upon it, see it as their remaining calling to be church of the living God, "the pillar and bulwark of the truth" (1 Tim. 3:15). They also see it as their calling to help and support each other in the fulfillment of this calling.

In dependence on and with confidence in the mighty Kurios, who bought His people with His precious blood, we are able indeed to fulfil this ecumenical calling. We can do so if guided by Word and Spirit, in the unity of the true faith, looking forward to the great multitude which no man can number, "singing the song of Moses and the song of the Lamb, saying, 'Great and wonderful are Thy deeds, O Lord God the Almighty!' " (Rev. 7:9, 15:3).

VIII
A WOUNDING ENEMY OR A HEALING PHYSICIAN?

(SOME REMARKS ABOUT
CHURCH DISCIPLINE AND ATTESTATIONS)

Maintenance?

Church discipline is a very important topic. It is called the third mark of the true church according to Article 29 of the Belgic Confession: "It exercises church discipline for correcting and punishing sins." Yet nowadays church discipline seems to be neglected everywhere. Already a century ago A. Kuyper complained that church discipline was going out of practice, "We do not exaggerate if we state that in the circles of the modern, the ethical, and irenical wing, church discipline is simply abolished and does not exist any more."[1]

Now, a hundred years later, we have even more reason to complain. In some so-called Reformed circles it is said that the church may give a *iudicium* (disciplinary judgment) but the church must be very careful in connecting consequences to it. The consequences of a *iudicium* are always sentences, which lead to the execution of a judgment, and so would be the maintenance of church discipline.[2]

Former ages

As far as the period before Kuyper's time is concerned, was church discipline not for several ages the poor cousin of the Reformed Churches? Within a century after the Reformation of the 16th century, Rev. Otto Belcampius of Amsterdam complained that the whole country was full of idolatry and atheism. He wrote, "one considers heaven a fairy tale and a decorated fable. They consider hell as an idle dream."[3] Then he asked the question, "Was there ever an age before in which the lofty and Almighty name of God was used so shamefully and frivolously? Cursing and swearing falsely is so common that it is not only heard from profane, worldly people, but also from members of the church. Was there ever before a time when the day of the LORD, the day of holy rest, was so despised, so profaned by all people in all places, as it is done now in this century?[4] Then Belcampius arrives at the question, "If it is so terrible, why does the consistory not oppose this at all?"

The well-known Rev. Jacobus Koelman asked the same question. Quoting Calvin, he starts by saying that doctrine is the soul of the church and discipline is its strings. But what about church discipline in Amsterdam? Koelman formulates the following accusation, "The consistory is only concerned and active with the great sins, which are also punished by the government. But for the rest, the consistory does nothing. In the large congregation of Amsterdam nobody has been censured for 18 years, let alone excommunicated. Is that not a shame?"[5]

What Koelman said was indeed true. It appears that the last case of church discipline — in a long time — was in the year 1659. There was only a "blacklist" of those who were kept from the Lord's Supper, but there was no progress in church discipline. The list was only made for a reference in case someone asked for an attestation. For the rest, nothing was done. Besides, many people were quite unconcerned if the consistory denied them the Lord's Supper.

The notary Rosa had a child by his maid, but he did not at all mind the interdiction of the Lord's Supper. He reacted that the whole matter of church discipline was nothing else but hypocrisy and foolish grandeur. When visited at home he declared his intention to ignore the decision of the consistory and to participate in the Lord's Supper, "even if the executioner would stand behind him." Finally the consistory gave in after Rosa promised he was willing to abstain from the Lord's Supper three times.

It is remarkable that the consistory was actually only active in those cases in which the government also punished. A certain Styntje was placed by the consistory in the so-called spinning house — actually a prison for women. That was done for drunkenness and theft. Sophia Broeckman, who committed adultery when her husband was in Brazil, kept her company. Grietje Everts was scourged and banished for a period of six years because of theft. Another sister of the congregation was branded, being a whore. Also banished but without first being scourged was Geertrui Willingh who had stolen the basin from the Lord's Supper table. Another woman was placed on the scaffold with a plate on her breast, inscribed with the message, "This woman has falsely deceived the deacons of the Reformed Church."

Sometimes the ladies were locked in the spinning house on the request of the family, for no other reason that they were of "bad behaviour." In some cases more details were delivered. For example, Barbar Stroobach was imprisoned on the request of her mother because of drunkenness, and Catherina Daniels on the request of the deacons because she was said to be undisciplined and a slanderer.

Men were also punished by the consistory. Albert Hermans was placed on the scaffold because he kept a brothel. Hidde Tjerckx was taken in custody in the act of visiting a brothel. He apologized, saying that he did not know that it was a whorehouse. But he and the whore herself were put in chains.

It was also possible to escape going into custody. A member of the church who was a lawyer had apparently committed the same sin as Hidde Tjerckx, but he could buy his way out. He had to pay 300 guilders to the deaconry and promise that he would not practice law for one year. Joost Janszoon Cock, former keeper of the spinning house, on the other hand, was unable to pay the required sum and he was imprisoned.

Sometimes the consistory punished in a strange and cruel way. A man who had committed corpse robbery in 1677 was put into the pillory, clothed in a shroud with one foot in a coffin. The plate on his breast had the inscription, "Robber of dead."

In connection with all these cases there is a special case which I must tell you. That is the story of Jan Klaassen and Katryn. I think everybody knows the names, but do you also know that they really existed? Although church discipline was almost abolished in that time, Jan Klaassen and Katryn were censured in Amsterdam in 1686. In several places in the capital of Holland Jan Klaassen presented his puppet show. He amused many people with what was actually the representation of his own marriage life, which was far from ideal. He was not the only one who was guilty. His wife Katryn was a real Xanthippe and she was also a drunkard. The result was a complete breakdown in their relationship and Katryn left her husband. Then we read in the minutes of the consistory, "Katryn Pieters, seedy-looking, in drunkenness and living in a separate household, will be summoned. Her husband Jan Klaassen will also be summoned." But Katryn did not appear because the caretaker could not find her at her address. She had already moved. Jan did appear at the consistory meeting. He explained that his wife had left him and, as for himself, he was not willing to be reconciled with her. However, the following week both of them did appear before the consistory. Several evil doings were then mentioned. Jan had meanwhile committed adultery and his wife continued to live as a drunkard. The consistory decided to place them under church discipline. After they were notified Jan and Katryn disappear from the minutes of the consistory for good. But they did not disappear from history. They never dreamt that they would become one of the most popular and well-known couples in Amsterdam![5]

A Scriptural matter

Why do we tell all these stories? To stress that not only outside the Reformed Churches, but also in the circles of the Reformed Churches themselves, church discipline was either neglected or misunderstood. Deformation of the church meant time and again also deformation of church discipline. We have to rediscover that church discipline is really a Scriptural matter, which should not be lacking in the church of Jesus Christ.

It is not for nothing that it is confessed in Article 29 of the Belgic Confession as one of the marks of the true church, because it is based on God's Holy Word. In our edition of the *Book of Praise* no prooftexts are given, but in the Dutch edition of the "Gereformeerd Kerkboek" some texts from the New Testament are mentioned. I will come back to that but I first want to say that also texts from the Old Testament can be quoted to prove the necessity of church discipline.

Of course we have to bear in mind that during the old dispensation church discipline worked in a somewhat different way, especially with regard to what we confess in Article 25 of the Belgic Confession, where we read, "We believe that the ceremonies and symbols of the law have ceased with the coming of Christ, and that all shadows have been fulfilled." But in the same article we also confess that their truth and substance remain for us in Christ and that we still use the testimonies taken from the law to confirm us in the doctrine of the gospel.

There was not a sharp distinction between civil law and church polity in the old dispensation, so I will not refer to texts which deal with sins that are to be punished by the government. However, there are also other texts. I will start with Exodus 22:20, "Whoever sacrices to any god, save to the LORD only, shall be utterly destroyed." That means, the sinner must be excommunicated, but in Old Testament terms it meant he had to die." Capital punishment was also involved when someone in Israel blasphemed the Name of the LORD, according to Leviticus 24:10-16. We can also point to Deuteronomy 13:6, 22:24 (in the case of violation of one's neighbour's wife) and 24:7 (concerning theft by one of the brethren). In all these cases discipline is to be transferred in New Testament terms as *excommunication*.

There are even more rules, however, concerning church discipline in the Old Testament. For instance what is written in Deuteronomy 19:15, "A single witness shall not prevail against a man for any crime or for any wrong in connection with any offence that he has committed; only on the evidence of two witnesses, or of three witnesses, shall a charge be sustained." It is remarkable that in this text the word "any" is used three times: any crime, any wrong, any offence. In other words: there are no exceptions! Also in the Old Testament the aim of church discipline is "to put the evil away from among you," that is, from among the congregation. In this respect see also Deuteronomy 17:7 and 19:19. Church discipline then, is limited to the congregation.

It is also important that "evil" inside the church is not something impersonal. "It manifests itself in those who 'let themselves be governed by sin'." Thus the apostle Paul can quote the verse from Deuteronomy by mentioning a *person:* "Put away from among yourselves that wicked *person*," 1 Corinthians 5:13, see also 5:2.[5] The late Prof. B. Holwerda writing about the Old Testament expression "an abomination in Israel," pointed out that the phrase does not just mean that the sin took place on Jewish territory; it refers to unrighteousness "that severs the antithesis between Israel and Canaan. . . . These therefore are sins that radically abolish any difference between Israel and Canaan; sins which, since Jahweh did not accept them from the Gentiles, are all the more unbearable in Israel, and therefore are punished by death."[6]

Much more could be said about church discipline in the Old Testament, but I will restrict myself to these examples. I pointed already to the fact that in 1 Corinthians the book of Deuteronomy is quoted. It is very clear from this passage in Corinthians that church discipline is necessary according to the apostle Paul. It is actually the *Church* of Corinth that is addressed by the apostle Paul saying, "Drive out the wicked person from among you." It is remarkable that the expression "among you" or "from among you" is used three times in this chapter (verse 1, 2, and 13).

That the congregation must be involved in the whole matter of church discipline is also clear from Matthew 18:17. After having quoted the rule of the Old Testament concerning two or three witnesses, our Saviour Jesus Christ says in verse 17, "If he (the sinner) refuses to listen to them, tell it to the church; and if he refuses to listen even to the church, let him be to you as a Gentile and a tax collector." So there is active cooperation by the congregation itself. I think Prof. J. Kamphuis is right, saying: "This cooperation is not confined to the approbation of decisive acts taken by the church session; it also consists of activities that concentrate themselves, in faith, on the 'sinner' within the church."[7]

There are also more passages in the New Testament which directly or indirectly enjoin church discipline. In Matthew 16:16-19 Christ gives Peter the power to bind and to loose. "Doubtless Christ here speaks to Peter as representative of all the apostles, for in John 20:23, this same power is attributed to all the apostles. However, the apostles are but the representatives of the New Testament church, and so we may conclude that in Matthew 16:16-19 and John 20:23 Christ charges the church to exercise discipline."[8] In other passages God's Word tells us not to have fellowship with heretics and those who have forsaken the Lord (see for instance Titus 3:10 and 11; 2 John 10; and Revelation 2:14-16).

There are also passages which condemn intermingling of believers and unbelievers, the holy and unholy. For example, 2 Corinthians 6:14. "As will be understood, the necessity for ecclesiastical discipline is found particularly in the New Testament injunctions which demand its exercise. In other words, discipline must be maintained in the church because God commanded it. Besides the passages indicated the following may be cited: Romans 16:17; 1 Thessalonians 5:14; 2 Thessalonians 3:6, 14; 1 Timothy 5:1, 2."[9]

How is discipline to be practised?

How is church discipline to be practised? First, the general rule must be maintained that he who examines another person must first examine himself. With respect to this we are reminded of the clear words of the Form for the Celebration of the Lord's Supper, "True self-examination consists of the following three parts: First, let everyone consider his sins and accursedness, so that he, detesting himself, may humble himself before God. . . . Second, let everyone search his heart whether he also believes the sure promise of God that all his sins are forgiven him only for the sake of the suffering and death of Jesus Christ. . . . Third, let everyone examine his conscience whether it is his sincere desire to show true thankfulness to God with his entire life and, laying aside all enmity, hatred and envy, to live with his neighbour in true love and unity."[10] We must not overlook the third part. If any accusation is brought forward against a brother, it may never be done because of enmity, hatred or envy. The background must always be: true love and unity with him.

208

In the second place church discipline is to be practised by mutual discipline. The members of the church have to admonish each other.[11] Many passages in the Bible *prescribe* mutual discipline. For example, 1 Thessalonians 5:11, "Therefore encourage one another and build one another up, just as you are doing"; Hebrews 3:12 and 13, "Take care, brethren, lest there be in any of you an evil, unbelieving heart, leading you to fall away from the living God. But exhort one another every day, as long as it is called 'today,' that none of you may be hardened by the deceitfulness of sin"; Romans 15:14, "I myself am satisfied about you, my brethren, that you yourselves are full of goodness, filled with all knowledge, and able to instruct one another."

This mutual exhortation, urged upon us by Holy Writ, becomes mutual discipline when there is a specific transgression. For example, Galatians 6:1, "Brethren, if a man is overtaken in any trespass, you who are spiritual should restore him in a spirit of gentleness. Look to yourself, lest you too be tempted"; James 5:19, 20, "My brethren, if any one among you wanders from the truth and someone brings him back, let him know that whoever brings back a sinner from the error of his way will save his soul from death and will cover a multitude of sins."

Furthermore, it may be remarked that Scripture enjoins mutual discipline since all believers are anointed with the Holy Spirit, sharing the anointing of Christ, to be prophets, priests, and kings under Him.[12] Here we have the matter of "the office of all believers." So it is to be stressed that "New Testament believers should not be treated as minors who have no voice in matters (Roman Catholicism), but as having come to maturity, having definite rights and duties."[13]

Official discipline

We can say that "official, ecclesiastical admonition and discipline is but the continuation of mutual, believer's discipline. When the latter fails the former begins to function. . . . And when church members refuse to do their Christian duty toward each other and no longer admonish each other, but desire to leave it all to the consistory, then the backbone of church discipline is severely injured."[14] The father of Doleantie church polity, F.L. Rutgers, said rightly, "The decay of discipline, which began already in the beginning of the 17th century, should certainly be attributed to a large extent to the fact that in the convictions of the church members this principle of our Church Order had been weakened."[15]

It is clearly said in Article 66 of the Church Order that the whole matter of Christian discipline "can be done only when the rule given by our Lord in Matthew 18:15-17 is followed in obedience."[16] The article begins by saying that church discipline has a *spiritual* nature. We do not start out by taking all kinds of "measures," but with spiritual admonition. Hence our Belgic Confession states in Article 32: "We accept only what is proper to preserve and promote harmony and unity and to keep all in *obedience to God*. To that end, discipline and excommunication ought to be exercised in agreement with the Word of God."[17] Both the confession and the Church Order stress that the church has to bow obediently before the Lord of the Scriptures and and to handle the matter of church discipline in a spiritual way. The Heidelberg Catechism agrees with an obedient and spiritual way of admonition and discipline in question and answer 85 where it reads that those who "show themselves to be unchristian in doctrine or life are first *repeatedly admonished in a brotherly manner*."[18]

Threefold purpose

According to what we find in the Scriptures and what we confesss in the church, we say that church discipline has a threefold purpose: "1. to promote God's glory to the church and to those who are outside; 2. to protect the church against all association with satan and his destructive power; and 3. to save the sinner from eternal perdition."[19] Often the emphasis is placed on the sanctity of God and the sanctity of the church. That is indeed an important element. In this way also the Westminster Confession professes in chapter 30: "Church censures are necessary . . . for purging out that leaven which might infect the whole lump; for vindicating the honour of Christ and the holy profession of the gospel, and for preventing the wrath of God. . . ."[20] The element of the sanctity, the holiness of God, of the holy profession of the church, may not be forgotten. But there is also — and even connected with it — the element of *sanity* of the church.

Already the church father, Augustine, stressed this element, especially overagainst the heresy of the Donatists, who declared the validity of the sacraments to be dependent on the personal holiness of the officebearers. They also declared themselves to be the only pure and holy church, over against the Roman Catholic Church.

In opposition to the Donatists, Augustine stressed the therapeutic element of church discipline. In a letter to Petilian, the Donatist, Augustine wrote that ecclesiastical discipline should not be disregarded and that nobody should be allowed to do exactly as he pleased, without limits, without a kind of healing chastisement. Augustine then quotes 1 Thessalonians 5:14 and 15 and he goes on to say, "when the apostle added the words, 'See that none render evil for evil unto any man,' he showed with sufficient clearness that there is no rendering of evil for evil when one chastises those that are unruly, even though for the fault of unruliness be administered the punishment of chastising. The punishment of chastising therefore is not an evil, though the *fault* be an evil. *For indeed it is the steel, not of an enemy inflicting a wound, but of a surgeon performing an operation.*"[21]

Often Augustine referred to church discipline as medicine. The believers need the medicine of the Holy Spirit. When church discipline is executed in love, gentleness may not recede from the heart. For what is more pious than a physician, bearing his iron tool? Without love, discipline is harmful. But the sinner is to be corrected in compassion and not killed by a murderer if church discipline is executed. The office-bearers are doctors, the words of Scripture are medicine and even severe discipline is a heavenly medicine.[21]

After Augustine, many dark ages followed, but it was especially the Reformer John Calvin who again understood so well the importance of church discipline. Calvin called church discipline "a delicate weapon."[23] Often Calvin quoted Augustine with respect to church discipline, especially in connection with Augustine's struggle against the Donatists. Calvin considered the Anabaptists of his days the Donatists of Augustine's time. "The Donatists . . . in an impious schism separated themselves from Christ's flock. The Anabaptists act in the same way today."[24]

Calvin stressed that the church must maintain church discipline in obedience, and that the office-bearers have to be severe in that maintenance, "but we ought not to pass over the fact that such severity as is joined with a 'spirit of gentleness' befits the church. This gentleness is required in the whole body of the church, that it should deal mildly with the lapsed and should not punish with extreme rigor, but rather, according to Paul's injunction, confirm its love toward them (2 Cor. 2:8)."[25] Even excommunication is corrective. "Although excommunication also punishes the man, it does so in such a way that, by forewarning him of his future condemnation, it may call him back to salvation." Then Calvin quotes 2 Thessalonians 3:15: "Do not look on him as an enemy, but warn him as a brother" and he ends this section with the words, "Unless this gentleness is maintained in both private and public censures, there is danger lest we soon slide down from discipline to butchery."[26]

Definition

Having discovered the various elements of church discipline in Scripture, in the confessions and in some writings, we can answer the question what church discipline really is. In his extensive work *Politica Ecclesiastica,* G. Voetius gives the following definition of church discipline: "The Ecclesiastical discipline is the personal and judicial application of the will of God in order to awaken and raise up the consciousness of the sinner and to prevent and to take away the offences in the church."[27]

H. Bouwman, in his treatment of church discipline, correctly remarks, "that we should not pay too much attention to the derivatives of terms such as 'discipline' (both *'tucht'* and 'discipline' in Dutch) because over time words receive a certain (interpretive) character." He defines discipline as "the maintenance of the rules given by Christ." Bouwman's definition has the advantage of conciseness and shows more clearly than Voetius that "God's Word stands central in the matter of discipline."[28]

Yet, Kamphuis has objections. In his opinion, Bouwman's definition is too general as well as too superficial. "To be sure, the church has the task of maintaining the rule of God's Word in the church. She, however, also has that calling outside ecclesiastical discipline, for instance through the teaching and admonitions in the preaching, in catechism classes and on family visits. We could also say that it is too superficial, for very little is said about the essence of discipline. At least an effort (attempt) should have been made to indicate clearly what God's Word says concerning discipline."[29] So Kamphuis comes to the following definition. Church discipline is "The judicial maintenance of the holiness of God's congregation over against the destructive power in the lives of those in the congregation who are dominated by sin."[30]

In spite of several good elements in this definition, I also have criticism regarding this definition. Instead of the term *judicial* (which reminds me too much of civil law) I prefer the term, used in Article 32 of the Belgic Confession, and Article 66 of the Church Order, namely *obedient* maintenance. Obedient is a comprehensive word, namely obedient to the mandate, given in the Holy Scriptures by the LORD Himself. Moreover, I like to add to the holiness of the church also the *soundness* of the church, especially over against ideas of the Donatists, the Anabaptists, and the like. Finally, I miss something about the manner and the purpose of church discipline. Church discipline has to be executed in a spiritual and pastoral manner, and not without the congregation, just we we saw before. As for the purpose: the goal is in the first place not to destroy the sinner, but to save him. So I came to the following definition: *Church discipline is the obedient maintenance, in a spiritual and pastoral manner, in coopera-tion with the congregation, of the sanctity and sanity of God's Church, over against the satanic power in the lives of those in the congregation who are dominated by sin, so making an effort to save them.*

What are the steps?

In this definition I like to emphasize the fact that church discipline is to be executed to those who are dominated by sin. That means, not to sinners as such. We ar all sinners and only when we harden our hearts must one step after the other be undertaken. In Article 67 of the Church Order, consistory involvement is mentioned. This may only occur when the rule of Matthew 18 has indeed been executed, or when the sin committed is of a public character. The last case can differ, of course, in a small or big congregation. Article 68 outlines the steps involved in church discipline. The first disciplinary step is suspension from the Lord's Supper. The last step of the procedure (and hopefully not the final step) is excommunication.

There is a "non-disciplinary" denial of admission to the Lord's Supper, namely, when a certain case — e.g. a quarrel between two church members — was not solved in time.

However, this article deals with disciplinary denial only.

It is a matter of course that those who have been denied admission to the Lord's Supper are not entitled to answer the questions asked at the administration of the sacrament of holy baptism; neither are they allowed to participate in the election of office-bearers.

All this means that whereas one's rights within the covenant community has not yet been denied him by excommunication, their execution is suspended. Here there is a parallel with the suspension of an office-bearer, (who is still an office-bearer) but is not permitted to execute the duties of his office.

It is a matter of the consistory's being aware of its calling to keep the congregation of the Lord pure and holy and at the same time being long-suffering towards the sinner. There must be room for "numerous subsequent admontions."

This first disciplinary action is an initial step indeed. For the consistory has to watch the sinner's reaction: Will he repent? Is it clear to him from this "provisional excommunication" — as the denial of admission to the Lord's Supper is also called — what will happen if he continues in his sin?

The accepted form extensively shows us the seriousness of the excommunication: The sinner is in the Name and authority of Jesus Christ our Lord declared to be

excluded from the fellowship of Christ and from His Kingdom. He (she) may no longer use the sacraments. He (she) has no part any more in the spiritual blessings and benefits which Christ bestows upon His Church. As long as he (she) persists in sin, let him (her) be to you as a Gentile and an outcast.[31]

This shall happen only with the advice of classis.

This ecclesiastical assembly acts in a supervising capacity. Its judgment regarding the necessity to continue the procedure of church discipline has to be the same as that of the consistory.

To state that such advice of classis may be neglected if only it has been obtained, would be a perfect illustration of formalistic reasoning. By "advice" is meant: "the concurring advice," as in Article 71. Latin has: *ex classis iudicio*. An eventual revision of the Church Order could easily clarify the text at this point.

This supervision is voluntarily accepted by he consistory because of the serious character of church discipline: It is a matter of life or death! The consistory, entrusted with the authority by the King of the church, has to be absolutely sure that they are on the right track.

Excommunication is often called "an ultimate remedy" (see under Article 66). Surely, it is executed for the well-being of the congregation, but first of all for that of a sinner, who — because of it — may recognize that it is his own obstinacy which keeps him from partaking of Christ and all His benefits, and may — as yet — repent.

This article also deals with what must be done between the first and the "last" disciplinary action.

First of all it presupposes that the admonitions are continued, as may be apparent from the words, "If he continues to harden himself in sin."

Next, the three public announcements to the congregation are mentioned.

The form our churches have adopted for this purpose covers in its respective parts all the stipulations made here, whereby information is given about the above-mentioned attempts, the denial of admission to the Table of the Lord, and the many admonitions.

Three announcements are to be made:

1. the first one does not include the name of the sinner, in order to spare him. The element of patience and long-suffering and the desire that the sinner may repent as yet may be apparent.
2. the second announcement includes the name. But it shall be made after consent has been given by classis (see under Article 73).
3. the third announcement informs the congregation about the imminent excommunication.

From the first announcement on, the congregation is urged to pray for the sinner. From the second on, they are asked to admonish him.

And all this "if he does not repent!"

By making these announcements — the time lapses between them is determined by the consistory — the silent consent (= again: consensus) of the congregation is obtained: Excommunication is a matter of the whole congregation, for her own holiness is at stake![32]

Non-communicant members

The second part of Article 68 is about the way church discipline regarding non-communicant members should proceed.

The sins of these members are not specified. They may consist of indifference and aversion to the covenant or even hostility to the service of the LORD.

The procedure is as follows:

The consistory has to admonish such persons. This is at the background of the words "In case a non-communicant member hardens himself in sin." When these admonitions reach the point that the person concerned does indeed harden his heart, a public announcement is made in which the name of the sinner is not mentioned. This, too, is intended to have the congregation pray for him or her.

A second such announcement is made after the advice of the classis has been obtained. It includes the name and the address of the person concerned, and the date at which the excommunication shall take place if there is no repentance.

The Church Order does not make any mention of a certain age. Not every younster reaches the age of adulthood at a fixed time!

This means that the "good-Reformed" rule must be obeyed which says: Every case must be judged on its own merits. However, sometimes the sin of "scandalous godlessness" has led to excommunication at the age of 21, and indifference to the service of the LORD at the age of 30.

The terms "communicant" and "non-communicant members" on the one side and "excommunication" on the other, have only their sound in common. In order to prevent confusion it may be advisable to try to find other terms. "Baptized members" is not suitable either, because also the "confessing or communicant members" were once baptized!

The final sentence of the article regards the procedures concerning both communicant and non-communicant members.

The above-mentioned rule that every case shall be judged on its own merits means that no fixed time-limit between the various announcements can be set, and that this must be left to the discretion of the consistory.

Article 68 does not make mention of any forms for excommunication. However, they have been included in the *Book of Praise*.[33]

"Again received. . ."

Previously I said that excommunication was hopefully not the final step in the procedure of church discipline. In Lord's Day 31 the Heidelberg Catechism says, those who are excommunicated "are again received as members of Christ and of the church when they promise and show real amendment." There is still the possibility of repentance and therefore also the possibility of readmission. Lord's Day 31 is in the section of the catechism which deals with deliverance! The Church Order, too, discusses readmission in Articles 69 and 70. Repentance will create joy in heaven and on earth. In heaven among God's angels, and on earth, within the congregation of the Lord Jesus Christ!

On all sides it is clear that church discipline is not a matter of revenge. I even like to avoid the term *punishment* because that directs us too much to civil law. The term discipline is clear enough. It involves spiritual and pastoral care. The different steps show that patience is involved and also that the purpose is to save the sinner, not to let him perish.

We can see the same in the Articles 71 and 72 of the Church Order. The church has to be very careful in the whole matter of suspension and deposition of office-bearers. However, when they are engaged in a serious sin, the church may not hesitate to suspend them, and also, in the case of hardening of heart to depose them. But again, the confederation of churches in involved. The office-bearers are protected as much as possible and every effort is to be made to prevent mistakes or an injustice from being done. Above all, the sanctity and the sanity of the church must be beyond discussion!

Attestations

Pastoral care is also involved in the matter of attestations. What is an attestation? Let's begin by saying what an attestation is *not*. "It is not a membership statement or card which is on file with the church to which one belongs, and which can be claimed when the member sees fit, and then transferred to the church with which he desires to affiliate."[34] Many people are under the false impression that an attestation is a kind of membership card.

When a person moves from one place to another, it is normally expected that he will join the congregation of the confederation of churches (or in case he is leaving for abroad — one of the sister churches), in that area. Then the individual asks for an attestation, namely a testimony from the church that he is leaving. In normal cases this testimony is a letter of endorsement, declaring that he is sound (here we have again the sanity of the church!) as to doctrine and life, and deserves to be received into the membership of the church he desires to join.[35]

Actually the whole matter of attestations is very old. We read in the Acts of the apostles, when Apollos left for Achaia, he received a letter from the church at Ephesus. "The brethren encouraged him, and wrote to the disciples to receive him" (Acts 18:27). The apostle Paul actually wrote an attestation for Phoebe to the church at Rome: "I commend to you our sister Phoebe, that you may receive her in the Lord as befits the saints" (Rom. 16:1, 2). From 2 Corinthians 3:1 we learn that already in the times of the apostles, "letters of recommendation" played an important role.[36] In the beginning of the Reformation it was often dangerous to pass these letters along because of the inquisition, but already at the first Synod at Emden four articles dealt with the matter of "attestations or testimonies."[37]

In connection with the nature, the function and the value of attestations in church life I will try to answer seven questions.

Questions

1. *Is a person allowed to request an attestation if he does not move?*

   Answer: F.L. Rutgers says, "No." The consistory of a sister church may not have members *beyond the boundaries* of its local circles. No consistory may do that, because in that case proper supervision would be impossible.[38] H. Bouwman says the same, and he adds to that: "If an attestation is passed to somebody, it must always have a certain purpose. If it is as a testimony in the case of an office or occupation, or with a view to an exam, there is no reason to refuse. But in that case the attestation is a testimony with a certain purpose, and that must be mentioned on the attestation. In these cases it does not need to be announced to the congregation.[39]

2. *Is the attestation always to be handed over to the member who is moving, or is it to be sent directly to the church concerned?*

   Answer: See Article 62, Church Order. According to Reformed church polity the local church is a complete church, and not just a portion of a whole. A member of the church is, therefore, only a member of a local church. If he moves he will receive on his request the testimony from the consistory and he has to pass this on to the consistory of the church to which he moved. The attestation is not to be sent to the "new" consistory. But it is very desirable that a letter be sent from the first consistory to the second, in order to inform them that someone is coming and also what his address will be. In case the member concerned is slow in passing on his attestation, the "new" consistory can visit him and ask him why they have not yet received his attestation.[40]

3. *What should be done if a censured member requests an attestation?*

   Answer: Also the censured member must receive an attestation, but a true testimony must be given. Already in the 16th century, regional and national synods stated that no violence might be done to the truth. For example, the Regional Synod of Alkmaar 1599 reiterated the decision of the Synod of Dort 1578 regarding the distinction between people without blemish and those who are blemished. Then, this synod continued, "testimony will be given according to the truth and according to the occasion."[41] It is also good to inform the new consistory in more detail about the specific situation, because sometimes it is not possible to write everything on the attestation.[42]

4. *Are attestations of non-communicant members always to be sent to the consistory, also in the case of mature non-communicant members?*

   Answer: See again Article 62 of the Church Order. We already mentioned that attestations involving communicant members are to be handed over to the applicants, while in the meantime it is proper that the consistory to where he is moving is informed. The attestations of non-communicant members shall be sent directly to that consistory. "The difference between these two ways of issuing attestations lies in the fact that in the case of a non-communicant member the "new" consistory is requested to take this member under its supervision and discipline."[43] The non-communicant member is in ecclesiastical terms "under age," even if he is an adult. In Dutch there is a distinction between *attestatie* and *attest* (in English that difference also exists but in ecclesiastical terms it does not work). An *attest* is a kind of certificate or statement, while an *attestatie* is a testimony or a confirmation of truth. So in the case of non-communicant members the attestation is called *doop-attest* in Dutch. This is not to say that they do not yet belong to the congregation. It is rightly said in the "Form for the baptism of infants" that they must be baptized as heirs of the kingdom of God and of His covenant.[44] But it is right that their attestation is always sent to the consistory involved even when they are adults. It can also be stated, then, why they did not yet make profession of faith.[45]

5. *How long is an attestation valid?*

Answer: Of course the period of validity cannot be indefinite. Already the Regional Synod of Alkmaar 1587 (and also that of Delft of the same year) decided that attestations should not be valid for more than three months, "unless there were sufficient reasons to act differently."[46] The churches of the Secession decided in 1877 that the period should not be longer than one year and six months.[47] This was confirmed by the Synod of Rotterdam 1885.[48] In other words the length of validity can vary. It is true that after some months the attestation can have lost its significance. Since the date of issue many things can have happened. Bouwman suggests that some questions should be asked if someone waited quite long before he passed the attestation to the consistory. What was the reason for the delay? In such a case the person may be requested to declare that he agrees with the confession of the church. Alternately he may be admitted to the Lord's Supper after a period of probation.[49]

6. *Is every church obliged to accept all attestations?*

Answer: According to Reformed church polity each and every local church is an independent body. Therefore each and every consistory is free to criticize an ecclesiastical testimony. This happened especially in the period of conflict with the Arminians in the time of the Synod of Dort 1618/1619. Attestations of Remonstrants were not automatically accepted, until further investigation.[50] It can happen, therefore, that the consistory has reasons for further investigation before the person is admitted to the Lord's Supper.

7. *Why are attestations to be announced to the congregation?*

Answer: On behalf of the office of all believers, the congregation must be involved in the whole matter of attestations. It is possible that there are objections against the doctrine or conduct of the member concerned. Members should request an attestation at least a couple of weeks before they move in order to give the congregation the opportunity to bring forward objections. It is a general rule that the request for an attestation is announced once to the congregation.[51]

But let the congregation be involved! Just as in church discipline, cooperation with the congregation is very important. The consistory must never become a kind of government or board that is separated completely from the members of the church. That is not a matter of mistaken democracy, but it concerns our behaviour in the church of Christ, in which all hierarchy is from the devil!

Notes

[1]Kuyper, A., *E Voto Dordraceno 3*, III, Kampen: Kok, n.d., p. 265.
[2]Cf. Kamphuis, J., *Om de heiligheid van de gemeente*, Kampen: Van den Berg, 1982, p. 24ff. (English trans. in: *Lux Mundi* Vol. 5, No. 4, Dec. 1986, p. 10ff.; also in: *Diakonia*, Vol. 2, No. 5, June 1989, p. 70ff.).

3Evenhuis, R.B., *Ook dat was Amsterdam* III, Amsterdam: Ten Have, 1971, p. 26.

4Evenhuis, op. cit., p. 27ff.

5*Ibid*, op. cit., p. 31ff.

6Holwerda, B., *Oudtestamentische voordrachten III. Exegese Oude Testament (Deuteronomium)*, Kampen: Van den Berg, 1957, p. 451; cf. ook J. Kamphuis, op. cit., p. 22, 31.

7Kamphuis, op. cit., p. 35.

8Monsma, M. and I. van Dellen, *The Revised Church Order Commentary, 3* Grand Rapids, MI: Zondervan, p. 289; cf. also J. De Jong, *Verklaring van de Kerkenordening van de Nationale Synode van Dordrecht van 1618-1619: college-voordrachten van F.L. Rutgers over gereformeerd kerkrecht*, Rotterdam: Libertas, 1918, p. 10ff.

9Monsma/Van Dellen, op. cit., p. 289ff.; Rutgers (De Jong) op. cit., p. 14ff.

10*Book of Praise*, Winnipeg: Premier Printing, 1984, p. 595.

11Van Rongen, G. and K. Deddens, *Decently and in Good Order*, Winnipeg: Premier Publishing, 1986, p. 91.

12Monsma/Van Dellen, op. cit. 290; cf. broader on the pastoral task of all believers: K. Deddens, *Een voortreffelijke taak*, Goes: Oosterbaan & Le Cointre, 1989, p. 79ff.

13Monsma/Van Dellen, op. cit., l.c.

14*Ibid.*

15Rutgers (De Jong), op. cit., p. 37.

16*Book of Praise*, p. 668.

17*Ibid.*, p. 465.

18*Ibid.*, p. 570.

19Jansen, Joh., *De Kerkelijke Tucht*, Arnhem: Tamminga, 1913, p. 183; cf. also: H. Bouwman, *De Kerkelijke Tucht naar het gereformeerd Kerkrecht*, Kampen: Kok, 1912, p. 172ff.

20Clark, Gordon H., *What do Presbyterians Believe? The Westminster Confession: Yesterday and Today*, Philadelphia, PA, 1965, p. 252ff.

21Schaff, Ph., *A Select Library of the Nicene and Post-Nicene Fathers of the Christian Church*, Vol. IV, Grand Rapids, MI: Eerdmans, 1956, p. 598ff.

22Weijland, H.B., *Augustinus en de kerkelijke tucht*, Kampen: Kok, 1965, p. 132ff.

23Goumaz, L., *Het ambt bij Calvijn* (Trans. and intro. K. Deddens), Franeker: Wever, 1964, p. 129ff.

24Calvin, J., *Institutes IV,* 12, 12, ed. John T. McNeill, *The Library of Christian Classics*, Vol. XXI, Philadelphia: Westminster Press, 1967, p. 1239.

25Plomp. J., *De kerkelijke tucht bij Calvijn*, Kampen: Kok, 1969, p. 76. Cf. J. Calvin, *Institutes IV,* 12, 8 and 9.

26Calvin, *Institutes IV,* 10, 12.

27Voetius, G., *Politica Ecclesiastica IV*, Amsterdam, 1676, p. 844, cf. J. Kamphuis, op. cit., p. 27.

28Bouwman, H. *De Kerkelijke Tucht*, p. 18ff.; cf. J. Kamphuis, op. cit., p. 27ff.

29Kamphuis, op. cit., p. 28ff.

30*Ibid.*, p. 29.

31*Book of Praise*, p. 612.

32Cf. Van Rongen/Deddens, op. cit., p. 95.

33*Book of Praise*, p. 607ff.

34Monsma/Van Dellen, op. cit., p. 258.

35*Ibid.*

36Cf. Bouwman, H., *Gereformeerd Kerkrecht II*, Kampen: Kok, 1934, p. 450.

37*Ibid.*, op. cit., p. 451.

38Rutgers, F.L. *Kerkelijke Adviezen II*, Kampen: Kok, 1922, p. 333.

39Bouwman, op. cit., p. 453.

40*Ibid.*, op. cit., 454.

41Bos, F.L., *De Orde der Kerk*, 's Gravenhage: Guido de Bres, 1950, p. 316.

42Bouwman, op. cit., p. 454; cf. also Joh. Jansen, *Korte Verklaring van de Kerkenordening*, Kampen: Kok, 1923, p. 354.

43Van Rongen/Deddens, op. cit., p. 89.

44*Book of Praise*, p. 585.

[45]Bouwman, op. cit. p. 459, gives as his opinion that it is possible to pass an attestation to an adult non-communicant member, but at the same time the consistory has to write on that attestation that the person concerned was disobedient by not yet making confession of faith. In any case a letter is to be sent to the new consistory according to his opinion.

[46]Bos, op. cit., p. 321.

[47]Bouwman, op. cit., p. 459.

[48]Bos, op. cit., p. 321.

[49]Bouwman, op. cit., p. 460.

[50]*Ibid.*, op. cit., p. 461ff.

[51]*Ibid.*, op. cit., p. 463.

BIBLIOGRAPHY

Chapter II

Greijdanus, S. — 1925. *De brief van den apostel Paulus aan de Epheziërs*, Kampen: Kok.

Greijdanus, S. — 1937. *Kommentaar op het Nieuwe Testament* IX, 2. Amsterdam: Van Bottenburg.

Hendriks, A.N. — 1981. *Over de schriftuurlijke fundering van het ambt van de dienaar des Woords*. In: Dienst 29:6.

Kirch, C. — 1947. *Enchiridion Fontium Historiae Ecclesiasticae Antiquae*. Barcelona: Herder.

Lightfoot, J.B. — 1976. *The Apostolic Fathers*. Grand Rapids: Baker.

Richardson, C.C. — 1963. *Early Christian Fathers*. Philadelphia: Westminster.

Trimp, C. — 1978. *Inleiding in de ambtelijke vakken*. Kampen: Van den Berg.

Trimp, C. — 1988. *'Bediening' in de apostolische kerk*. In: De Reformatie LXIII: 39.

Van Bruggen, J. — 1984. *Ambten in de apostolische kerk*. Kampen: Kok.

Van Rongen, G. — 1984. *Training in Godliness. Outlines on the Pastoral Epistles*. London, Ont.: ILPB.

Chapter III

Bakhuizen van den Brink, J.N. — 1976. *De Nederlandse Belijdenisgeschriften*, Amsterdam: Bolland.

Bouma, C. — 1942. *Kommentaar op het Nieuwe Testament* XI. Amsterdam: Van Bottenburg.

Braekman, E.M. — 1960. *Guy de Brès*, tome I. Bruxelles: Librairie des Eclaireurs Unionistes.

Calvin, J. — 1960. *Institutes of the Christian Religion*. Library of Christian Classics, vol. XXI. Philadelphia: Westminster.

Deddens, K./ Drost, M.K. — 1989. *Balance of Ecumenism*. Winnipeg: Premier Publishing.

De Pater, J.C.H. — 1950. *Guido de Brès en de Gereformeerde Geloofsbelijdenis*. 's Gravenhage: Willem de Zwijgerstichting.

Doekes, L. — 1975. *Credo*. Amsterdam: Bolland.

Drost, M.K. — 1982. *De waarheid boven alles*. Groningen: Vuurbaak.

Faber, J. — 1969. *Beknopte balans van het Concilie*. In: Almanak F.Q.I. Kampen: Van den Berg.

Faber, J. — 1982. *Schools and Creeds*. In: Reformed Perspective, I:2. Winnipeg: Premier Printing.

Holwerda, B. — 1958. *De betekenis van verbond en kerk voor huwelijk, gezin en jeugd*. Goes: Oosterbaan & Le Cointre.

Kamphuis, J. — 1977. *Van 'evangelisch' naar 'reformatorisch.'* In: De Reformatie LIII: 4.

Kamphuis, J. — 1980. *Algemeen*. In: De Reformatie LV: 49.

Kuitert, H.M. — 1970. *Verstaat gij wat gij leest?* Kampen: Kok.

Luther, M.   — 1962. *Luther's Works,* vol. XLV. Philadelphia: Muhlenberg Press.

Olevianus, C.   — 1778. *De vaste grond.* Amsterdam: Zeylmans van Selm.

Rothuizen, G. Th.et al. — 1965. *De Kogel door de kerk.* 's Gravenhage: Bert Bakker/Daamen.

Schaff, Ph./   — n.d. *The Nicene and Post-Nicene Fathers of the Christian*
Wace, H.   *Church,* Sec. Series (1952 ff.), vol. VII. Grand Rapids: Eerdmans.

Schilder, K.   — 1935. *Ons aller Moeder.* Kampen: Kok.

Taylor, E.K.   — 1964. *The Church.* In: *The Catholic Religion* vol. VII, London: Catholic Enquiry Centre.

Trimp, C.   — 1977. *Wat is 'Evangelisch'?* In: De Reformatie LIII: 2 ff.

Ursinus, Z.   — 1956. *The Commentary on the Heidelberg Catechism.* Grand Rapids: Eerdmans.

Van 't Veer, M.B.   — 1942. *Catechese en catechetische stof bij Calvijn.* Kampen: Kok.

Vonk, C.   — 1955. *De Voorzeide Leer* IIIA. Barendrecht: Barendrecht.

Chapter IV

Bavinck, H.   — 1930. *Gereformeerde Dogmatiek* IV. Kampen: Kok.

Bavinck, H.   — 1956. *Our Reasonable Faith,* transl. H. Zijlstra. Grand Rapids: Baker.

Biesterveld, P./   — 1905. *Kerkelijk Handboekje.* Kampen: Bos.
Kuyper, H.H.

Boon, R.   — 1973. *De joodse wortels van de christelijke eredienst.* Amsterdam: Van der Leeuwstichting.

Brienen, T.   — 1987. *De liturgie bij Johannes Calvijn.* Kampen: De Groot Goudriaan.

Brongers, H.A.   — 1954. *Schuldbelijdenis en genadeverkondiging in het Oude Testament.* In: Kerk en Eredienst IX.

Calvin, J.   — 1542. *La Forme des Prieres et Chantz Ecclesiastiques,* facs. 1959. Kassel/Basel: Bärenreiter.

Calvin, J.   — 1960. *Institutes of the Christian Religion. Library of Christian Classics* XXI. Philadelphia: Westminster.

Cross, F.L.   — 1966. *St. Cyril of Jerusalem's Lectures on the Christian Sacraments.* London: S.P.C.K.

Dankbaar, W.F.   — 1956. *Marten Micron, de Christlicke Ordinancien der Nederlantscher Ghemeinten te Londen (1554).* 's Gravenhage: Nijhoff.

Dankbaar, W.F.   — 1978. *Hervormers en Humanisten.* Amsterdam: Bolland

Davies, J.P.   — 1972. *The Westminster Dictionary of Worship.* Philadelphia: Westminster.

Deddens, K.   — 1975. *Annus Liturgicus?* Goes: Oosterbaan & Le Cointre.

Deddens, K.   — 1976. *Het begon in Jeruzalem.* Goes: Oosterbaan & Le Cointre.

Deddens, K.   — 1981. *Het liep uit op Trente.* Goes: Oosterbaan & Le Cointre.

Deddens, K.   — 1986. *Herstel kwam uit Straatsburg.* Goes: Oosterbaan & Le Cointre.

De Jong, F.   — 1957. *Bindinghe ende Ontbindinghe der Zonden.* In: Kerk en Eredienst XII.

Dekkers, E.   — 1947. *Tertullianus en de geschiedenis der liturgie.* Brussel/ Amsterdam: De Kinkhoren.

De Klerk, B.J.   — 1987. *Die Heilige Gees en die verhouding Skriflesing, Prediking en Gebed in die Erediens.* Potchefstroom: Universiteit.

Dix, G.   — 1954. *The Shape of the Liturgy.* Westminster: Dacre Press.

Dubois, R.   — 1965/68. *Lezingen in de mis.* In: Liturgisch Woordenboek II. Roermond: Romen.

Dugmore, C.W.   — 1964. *The Influence of the Synagogue upon the Divine Office.* Westminster: Faith Press.

Dijk, K.   — 1954. *Handboek voor de ouderling.* Delft: Meinema.

Edwall, P. et al.   — 1951. *Ways of Worship.* London: SCM Press.

Evenhuis, R.B.   — 1967. *Ook dat was Amsterdam* II. Amsterdam: Ten Have.

Franceschini, A./ Weber, R.   — 1958. *Itinerarium Egeriae.* Turnhout: Brepols.

Francke, J.   — 1973. *Van Sabbat naar Zondag.* Amsterdam: Bolland.

Goertz, H.   — 1977. *Deutsche Begriffe der Liturgie im Zeitalter der Reformation.* Berlin: Erich Schmidt.

Hasper, H.   — 1955. *Calvijns beginsel voor den zang in den eredienst* I. 's Gravenhage: Nijhoff.

Hendriks, A.N.   — 1970. *Datheens liturgie van 1566 en de besluiten der Nederlandse Nationale Synoden 1568-1581 met betrekking tot de orde van dienst voor de zondagmorgen.* In: Almanak F.Q.I.

Heyns, W.   — 1903. *Liturgiek.* Holland, Mich.: Holkeboer.

Koelman, J.   — 1694. *'t Ampt en Pligten van Ouderlingen en Diakenen.* Rotterdam: Reynier van Doesburg.

Koole, J.L.   — 1949. *Liturgie en Ambt in de apostolische kerk.* Kampen: Kok.

Koopmans, J.   — 1941. *Het kerkelijk jaar.* Wageningen: Veenman.

Krikke, S.   — 1976. *Veranderd levensbesef en liturgie.* Assen/Amsterdam: Van Gorcum.

Kroon, K.H.   — 1964. *Schriftlezing en kerkelijk jaar.* In: Jaarboek voor de Eredienst 1963/64.

Kruyf, E.F.   — 1901. *Liturgiek.* Groningen: Wolters.

Kunze, G.   — 1955. *Die Lesungen.* In: Leitourgia II. Kassel: Stauda Verlag.

Kuyper, A.   — 1911. *Onze Eeredienst.* Kampen: Kok.

Lekkerkerker, A.F.N.   — 1952. *Kanttekeningen bij het hervormde dienstboek* I. 's Gravenhage: Boekencentrum.

Lengeling, E.J.   — 1965/1968. *Liturgie.* In: Liturgisch Woordenboek. Roermond: Romen.

Lenselink, S.J.   — 1959. *De Nederlandse Psalmberijmingen van de Souterliedekens tot Datheen, met hun voorgangers in Duitsland en Frankrijk.* Assen: Van Gorcum.

Lenselink, E.J.   — 1969. *Les Psaumes de Clément Marot.* Assen/Kassel: Van Gorcum/Bärenreiter.

MacDonald, A.B.   — 1935. *Christian Worship in the Primitive Church.* Edinburgh: Clark.

Maxwell, W.D.   — 1931. *John Knox Genevan Service Book.* Edinburgh/London: Oliver & Boyd.

Maxwell, W.D.   — 1982. *A History of Christian Worship.* Grand Rapids: Baker.

Milo, D.W.L.   — 1946. *Zangers en Speellieden.* Goes: Oosterbaan & Le Cointre.

Moule, C.F.D.   — 1961. *Worship in the New Testament.* London: Lutterworth Press.

Mulders, M.H./   — 1967. *Sacrosanctum Concilium.* Hilversum: Gooi & Sticht.
Kahmann, J.

Nichols, J.H.   — 1968. *Corporate Worship in the Reformed Tradition.* Philadelphia: Westminster.

Oesterley, W.O.E.   — 1965. *The Jewish Background of the Christian Liturgy.* Gloucester: Peter Smith.

Old, H.O.   — 1975. *Patristic Roots of Reformed Worship.* Zürich: *Theologischer Verlag.*

Pidoux, P.   — 1962. *Le Psautier Huguenot* I & II. Basel: Bärenreiter.

Rayburn, R.G.   — 1980. *O Come, Let Us Worship.* Grand Rapids: Baker.

Reitsma, J./   — 1892-1899. *Acta der Provinciale en Particuliere Synoden,*
Van Veen, S.D.   *gehouden in de Noordelijke Nederlanden gedurende de jaren 1572-1620,* I - VIII. Groningen: Wolters.

Renoux, A.   — 1969. *Le Codex Arménien Jérusalem 121, Patrologia Orientalis,* tome XXXV. Turnhout: Brepols.

Renoux, A.   — 1971. *Le Codex Arménien Jérusalem 121, Patrologia Orientalis,* tome XXXVI. Turnhout: Brepols.

Roget, F.   — 1981. *Van Nicea tot Bonifatius,* transl. F. Boessenkool. Kampen: Kok.

Rordorf, W.   — 1972. *Sabbat und Sonntag in der Alten Kirche.* Zürich: *Theologischer Verlag.*

Schilder, K.   — 1937. *Jan Zwart* .In: De Reformatie XVII: 42.

Schilder, K.   — 1947. *In memoriam Jan Zwart.* In: De Reformatie XXII: 43.

Schilder, K.   — 1952. *Tolle Lege* I. Goes: Oosterbaan & Le Cointre.

Schotel, G.D.J.   — n.d. *De Openbare Eredienst der Nederl. Hervormde Kerk in de 16e, 17e en 18e eeuw.* Leiden: Sijthoff.

Seidel, U./   — 1970. *Aktion Gottendienst* II. Düsseldorf/Wuppertal:
Zils, D.   Jugenddienst & Haus Altenberg.

Snijders, A.   — 1956/68. *Kyrie Eleison.* In: Liturgisch Woordenboek II. Roermond: Romen.

Snijders, A.   — 1965/68A. *Lezingen in het Officie.* In: Liturgisch Woordenboek II. Roermond: Romen.

Trimp, C.   — 1971. *De dienst der mondige kerk.* Goes: Oosterbaan & Le Cointre.

Trimp, C.   — 1978. *Formulieren en gebeden.* Kampen: Van den Berg.

Trimp, C.   — 1983. *De gemeente en haar liturgie.* Kampen: Van den Berg.

Tuininga, J.   — 1986. *Children at the Lord's Supper.* In: Outlook, XXXVI: 6.

Vajta, V.   — 1954. *Die Theologie des Gottesdienstes bei Luther.* Göttingen: Vandenhoeck & Ruprecht.

Van der Leeuw, G.   — 1939. *Beknopte geschiedenis van het kerklied.* Groningen/Batavia: Wolters.

Van der Leeuw, G.   — 1940. *Liturgiek.* Nijkerk: Callenbach.

Van der Leeuw, G.   — 1949. *Sacramentstheologie.* Nijkerk: Callenbach.

Van der Meer, F.   — 1947. *Augustinus als Zielzorger.* Utrecht/Brussel: Spectrum.

Van Dooren, G.   — 1980. *The Beauty of Reformed Liturgy.* Winnipeg: Premier Publishing.

Van Gurp, P.   — 1989. *Kerk en zending in de theologie van Johannes Christiaan Hoekendijk (1912-1975). Een plaatsbepaling.* Haarlem: AcaMedia.

Van Rongen, G.   — 1956. *Zijn schone dienst.* Goes: Oosterbaan & Le Cointre.

Van Rongen, G.   — 1966. *Liturgy of God's Covenant.* Launceston: Inter-League Publication Board.

Van Rongen, G.   — 1987. *Reformed by Excellence!* In: Una Sancta XXXIV: 23.

Van Rongen, G.   — 1987A. *Historic Prayer.* In: Una Sancta XXXIV: 24.

Van Rongen, G.   — 1987B. *Public Confession of Sins.* In: Una Sancta XXXIV: 25.

Van Unnik, W.C.   — 1951. *De oorsprong van het Kerstfeest.* 's Gravenhage: Boekencentrum.

Van der Waal, C.   — 1979. *Het Pascha van onze verlossing.* Johannesburg/Franeker: De Jong/Wever.

Visee, G.   — 1986. *May — and Must — Our Children Participate in the Lord's Supper?* In: Christian Renewal, IV: 14-17.

Visser, S.   — 1947. *Schuldbelijdenissen.* In: Kerk en Eredienst II.

Wegman, H.A.J.   — 1976. *Geschiedenis van de christelijke eredienst in het Westen en in het Oosten.* Hilversum: Gooi & Sticht.

Zwart, A.   — 1947. *Heidensche en Christelijke Mysterien.* Brussel/Amsterdam: De Kinkhoren.

Chapter V

Arnold, J.J.   — 1984. *Nieuw — na oud-exemplarisme.* In: De Reformatie LX: 4.

Breman, Paul   — 1959. *Spirituals.* 's Gravenhage: Nijhoff.

Calvin, J.   — 1960. *Institutes of the Christian Religion. Library of Christian Classics,* vol. XXI. Philadelphia: Westminster.

Cox, Harvey   — 1969. *The Secular City.* New York: MacMillan Company.

Cox, Harvey   — 1970. *The Feast of Fools.* New York: Harper and Row.

Cox, Harvey   — 1983. *Religion in the Secular City.* New York: Simon and Schuster.

Deddens, K./   — 1989. *Balance of Ecumenism.* Winnipeg: Premier
Drost, M.K.   Publishing.

Deist, F.E.   — 1982. *Die Bybel leef.* Pretoria: Van Schaik.

Deist, F.E.   — 1982A. *Sè God so?* Kaapstad: Tafelberg.

De Klerk, B.J.   — 1987. *Die Heilige Gees en die verhouding Skriflesing, Prediking en Gebed in die Erediens.* Potchefstroom: Universiteit.

Douma, J./   — 1965. *Verkondiging en Triumf van het Evangelie.* Amers-
Deddens, K.   foort: Van Wijngen.

Geertsema, J.   — 1988. *The Gospel Brings to Light what in your Heart you Hide.* In: Clarion Year End Issue 1987, XXXVII: 1ff.

Gootjes, N.H.   — 1987. *Ons ten Voorbeeld Geschied.* In: De Reformatie LXII, nr. 48f, LXIII: 1ff.

Goumaz, L.   — 1964. *Het ambt bij Calvijn,* transl. and introd. K. Deddens. Franeker: Wever.

Greidanus, Sidney   — 1970. *Sola Scriptura. Problems and Principals in preaching historical texts.* Kampen: Kok.

Holwerda, B.   — 1955. *De dingen die ons van God geschonken zijn* III. Goes: Oosterbaan & Le Cointre.

Holwerda, B.	— 1957. *De wijsheid die behoudt*. Goes: Oosterbaan & Le Cointre.
Holwerda, B.	— 1983. *The History of Redemption in the Preaching of the Gospel*, transl. P. Y. de Jong. Iowa.
Kamphuis, J.	— 1968. *Onderweg aangesproken*. Groningen: Vuurbaak.
Kamphuis, J.	— 1987. *Heilsgeschiedenis en prediking*. In: De Reformatie LXII: 14.
Kapteyn, J.	— n.d. *Van Hem, die is, die was en die komt*. Goes: Oosterbaan & Le Cointre.
Krabbendam, H.	— 1986. *Hermeneutics and Preaching*. In: *The Preacher and Preaching*. Phillipsburg, N.J.: Presbyterian and Reformed Publishing.
Kuyper, A.	— 1892. *E Voto Dordraceno* III, Kampen: Kok.
Marsden, George	— 1984. *Harvey Cox' Conversion*. In: Reformed Journal XXXIV: 5.
Meijerink, H.J.	— 1971. *Canons of Dort, Third and Fourth Heads of Doctrine*. In: J. Faber et al., *To the Praise of His Glory*. Launceston, Tasm.: Publ. Organ. of the Free Ref. Churches of Australia.
Nida, E.A./ Reyburn, W.D.	— 1981. *Meaning Across Cultures*. Maryknol: Orbis Books.
Rookmaaker, H.R.	— 1960. *Jazz, Blues, Spirituals*. Wageningen: Zomer en Keuning.
Schilder, H.J.	— 1974. *Modern Exemplarisme*. In: De Reformatie L: 10ff.
Schilder, H.J.	— 1975. *Twee Oraties*. In: De Reformatie L: 49.
Schilder, H.J.	— 1976. *In Sion is het Woord nabij*. Groningen: Vuurbaak.
Schilder, H.J.	— 1981. *Het kerkschip biedt behouden vaart*. Kampen: Van den Berg.
Schilder, K.	— 1930. *Iets over het gereformeerd karakter der lijdensprediking*. In: De Reformatie X: 26ff.
Schilder, K.	— 1931. *Iets over de eenheid der 'Heilsgeschiedenis' in verband met de prediking*. In: De Reformatie XI: 50ff.
Schilder, K.	— 1938. *Christ in His Suffering*, transl. H. Zijlstra. Grand Rapids: Eerdmans.
Schilder, K.	— 1958. *Schriftoverdenkingen* III. Goes: Oosterbaan & Le Cointre.
Stam, Clarence	— 1987. *Christian Rock*. In: Reformed Perspective VII: 2.
Trimp, C.	— 1970. *'Exemplarische' of 'Heilshistorische' Prediking?* In: De Reformatie XLV: 42.
Trimp, C.	— 1971. *De dienst van de mondige kerk*. Goes: Oosterbaan & Le Cointre.
Trimp, C.	— 1973. *The Relevance of Preaching*. In: The *Westminster Theological Journal* XXXVI: 1.
Trimp, C.	— 1986. *Heilsgeschiedenis en prediking*. Kampen: Van den Berg.
Van Dam, C.	— 1976. *The Theology of Liberation*. In: Lux Mundi II:2, III:1, 1983/'84.
Veenhof, C.	— 1946. *Het Woord Gods in de brief aan de Hebreeën*. Terneuzen: Littooy.
Veenhof, C.	— 1959. *Prediking en Uitverkiezing*, Kampen: Kok.

Veenhof, C.	— 1965. *Calvijn en de prediking.* In: J. van Genderen et al., *Zicht op Calvijn.* Amsterdam: Buyten en Schipperheijn.
Van der Waal, C.	— 1978. *Search the Scriptures* II. St. Catharines, Ont.: Paideia.
Van 't Veer, M.B.	— 1983. *Christological Preaching on Historical Materials of the Old Testament,* transl. P. Y. de Jong. Iowa.
Wielenga, D.K.	— 1971. *Kanttekeningen bij de dusgenaamde theologie der revolutie.* In: *De akker is de wereld.* Amsterdam: Bolland.

Chapter VI

Aalders, G.Ch.	— n.d. *Het Herstel van Israel volgens het Oude Testament.* Kampen: Kok.
Aalders, G.Ch.	— 1949. *De oud-testamentische profetie en de staat Israel.* Kampen: Kok.
Aalders, G.Ch./ Ridderbos, H.N.	— 1955. *Israel.* 's Gravenhage: Van Keulen.
Bucer, M.	— 1980. *Instruction of Christian Love,* facs. ed. Michigan/London: Ann Arbor.
Calvin, J.	— 1960. *Institutes of the Christian Religion.* Library of Christian Classics, vol. XXI. Philadelphia: Westminster.
Dankbaar, W.F.	— 1949/'50. *Het Apostolaat bij Calvijn.* In: Nederlands Theologisch Tijdschrift IV, Wageningen: Veenman.
Dekker, D.	— 1975. *Reformatoren-kooplieden-predikanten.* In: De Civitate XXV: 5.
Doekes, G.	— 1915. *De beteekenis van Israels val.* Sneek: Boeijenga.
Greijdanus, S.	— 1925. *Korte Verklaring der Heilige Schrift, Epheze.* Kampen: Kok.
Greijdanus, S.	— 1933. *Kommentaar op het Nieuwe Testament,* VI, II. Amsterdam: Van Bottenburg.
Holwerda, B.	— 1947. *De reformatie van onzen 'omgang.'* Utrecht: Bondsbureau.
Holwerda, D.	— 1949. *O Diepte des Rijkdoms.* Utrecht: Bondsbureau.
Joosse, L.J.	— 1988. *Reformation and Missions.* Goes: Oosterbaan & Le Cointre.
Kooiman, W.J.	— 1959. *Luther — zijn weg en werk.* Amsterdam: ten Have.
Van Dam, C.	— 1986. *Mission Work Among the Jews?* In: Clarion XXXV: 19.
Van den Berg, J.	— 1956. *Constrained by Jesus' Love.* Kampen: Kok.
Van der Linde, J.	— 1937. *Calvijn en de Zending.* In: De Reformatie XVII: 46.
Van Dooren, G.	— 1979. *Get Out! and Get Rid of Dilemmas.* Winnipeg: Premier Publishing.
Van Swigchem, D.	— 1955. *Het Missionair karakter van de Christelijke gemeente.* Kampen: Kok.
Van 't Spijker, W.	— 1970. *De ambten bij Martin Bucer.* Kampen: Kok.
Verkuyl, J.	— 1978. Contemporary Missiology, transl. D. Cooper. Grand Rapids: Eerdmans.

Chapter VII

| Bouma, H. | — 1989. *De kerkorde, regel voor vrede in de kerk.* Ermelo, Woord en Wereld. |
| Bouwman, H. | — 1934. *Gereformeerd Kerkrecht* II. Kampen: Kok. |

Calvin, J.   — 1960. *Institutes of the Christian Religion.* Library of Chris-
                          tian Classics, vol. XXI. Philadelphia: Westminster.
De Vries, J.P.   — 1989. *Kanselgebed.* In: Nederlands Dagblad, Feb. 17, 1989.
De Vries, W.G.   — 1989. *Kerkorde en rechtswetenschap.* In: De Reformatie
                          LXIV: 20.
Deddens, P.   — 1946. *De ratificeering der besluiten van meerdere vergader-
                          ingen.* Groningen: De Jager.
Deddens, P.   — 1950. *Kerkrecht: veel kerk en weinig recht?* I. In: De Refor-
                          matie 26, nr. 1.
Faber, J.   — 1986. *The Significance of the Secession of 1834 in the light
                          of our confession of the Holy Catholic Church.* In: *Secession
                          and Liberation for Today.* London, Ont.: I.L.P.B.
Hovius, J.   — 1962. *Het verband tussen onze Belijdenis en onze Kerkorde.*
                          Sneek: Weissenbach.
Jansen, Joh.   — 1923. *Korte verklaring van de Kerkenordening.* Kampen:
                          Kok.
Krol, J.R.   — 1988. *Een verkenning rond de Kerkorde.* In: Radix XIV: 4.
Meulink, H. et al.   — n.d. *De Kerkenordening van de Gereformeerde Kerken in
                          Nederland.* Enschede: Te Sligte.
Niesel, W.   — 1938. *Bekenntnisschriften und Kirchenordnungen der nach
                          Gottes Wort reformierten Kirche.* Zürich: Zollikon.
Oldenhuis, F.T.   — 1977. *Rechtsvinding van de burgerlijke rechter in kerkelijke
                          conflicten.* Groningen: Vuurbaak.
Rutgers, F.L.   — 1894. *Het Kerkrecht in zoover het de kerk met het recht in
                          verband brengt.* Amsterdam: Van Schaik.
Rutgers, F.L.   — 1918. *Collegevoordrachten over Gereformeerd Kerkrecht,* ed.
                          J. de Jong. Rotterdam: Libertas.
Schilder, K.   — 1975. *Your Ecumenical Task.* Launceston, Tasm.: Launc.
                          Comm.
Schwarz, R.   — 1909. *Johannes Calvins Lebenswerk in seinen Briefen,* I
                          Tübingen: Mohr.
Ten Hoor, F.M.   — 1918. *Theologische Encyclopedie.* Grand Rapids: Calvin
                          College.
VanOene, W.W.J.   — 1987. *Reflections on synodical practices* III. In: Clarion
                          XXXVI: 5.
VanOene, W.W.J.   — 1987A. *Renewed reflections.* In: Clarion XXXVI: 10.
VanOene, W.W.J.   — 1987B. *Reflections continued.* In: Clarion XXXVI: 18.
Van Rongen, G./   — 1986. *Decently and in Good Order.* Winnipeg: Premier
Deddens, K.   Publishing.
Van 't Spijker, W.   — 1972. *Goddelijk recht en kerkelijke orde bij Bucer.* Kampen:
                          Kok.
Veenhof, C.   — 1956. *Over Synodale arbeid van Gereformeerde Kerken ten
                          aanzien van appèl-zaken.* In: De Reformatie XXXI: 19.
Wielenga, J.D.   — 1987. *Letter to the Editor.* In: Clarion, XXXVI: 10.
Wielenga, J.D.   — 1987A. *Letter to the Editor.* In: Clarion XXXVI: 18.

Chapter VIII

Book of Praise, Winnipeg: Premier Printing, 1984.
Bos, F.L.   — *De Orde der Kerk,* 's Gravenhage, Guido de Brès, 1950.
Bouwman, H.   — *De Kerkelijke Tucht naar het gereformeerd Kerkrecht,
                          Kampen: Kok, 1912.*

Bouwman, H.   — *Gereformeerd Kerkrecht II*, Kampen: Kok, 1934.

Calvin, J.   — *Institutes*, ed. John T. McNeill, *The Library of Christian Classics*, Vol. XXI, Philadelphia: Westminster Press, 1967.

Deddens, K.   — *Een voortreffelijke taak. Profielschets van de pastor.* In the Series: *Pastoraal Perspectief*, Goes: Oosterbaan & Le Cointre, Goes, 1989.

De Jong, J.   — *Verklaring van de Kerkenordening van de Nationale Synode van Dordrecht 1618-1619: college-voordrachten van F.L. Rutgers over gereformeerd kerkrecht*, Rotterdam: Libertas, 1918.

Evenhuis, R.B.   — *Ook dat was Amsterdam* III, Amsterdam: Ten Have, 1971.

Goumaz, L.   — *Het ambt bij Calvijn* (trans. and intro. K. Deddens), Franeker: Wever, 1964.

Holwerda, B.   — *Oudtestamentische voordrachten III. Exegese Oude Testament (Deuteronomium)*, Kampen: Van den Berg, 1957.

Jansen, Joh.   — *De Kerkelijke Tucht*, Arnhem: Tamminga, 1913.

Jansen, Joh.   — *Korte Verklaring van de Kerkenordening*, Kampen: Kok, 1923.

Kamphuis, J.   — *Om de heiligheid van de gemeente*, Kampen: Van den berg, 1982 (Engl. trans. in: *Lux Mundi* Vol. 5, no. 4, 1986, and *Diakonia*, Vol. 2, no. 5ff., 1989).

Kuyper, A.   — *E Voto Dordraceno 3*, III, Kampen, Kok, n.d.

Monsma, M. and
I. van Dellen   — *The Revised Church Order Commentary* 3, Grand Rapids, MI: Zondervan, 1969.

Plomp, J.   — *De kerkelijke tucht bij Calvijn*, Kampen: Kok, 1969.

Rutgers, F.L.   — *Kerkelijke Adviezen II*, Kampen: Kok, 1922.

Schaff, Ph.   — *A Select Library of the Nicene and Post-Nicene Fathers of the Christian Church*, Vol. IV, Grand Rapids, MI: Eerdmans, 1956.

Van Rongen, G./
K. Deddens   — *Decently and in Good Order*, Winnipeg: Premier Publishing, 1986.

Voetius, G.   — *Politica Ecclesiastica* IV, Amsterdam, 1676.

Weijland, H.B.   — *Augustinus en de kerkelijke tucht*, Kampen: Kok, 1965.